Bilingual Classics

双语经典

错箱记

〔英国〕罗伯特·路易斯·史蒂文森 〔美国〕劳埃德·奥斯本 著 吴钧陶 译

译林出版社

目 录

作者小序   1

第一章   莫里斯的疑窦   001
第二章   莫里斯的行动   018
第三章   演说家逍遥自在了   037
第四章   行李车里的司法官   050
第五章   吉迪恩·福西斯先生和庞大的箱子   056
第六章   莫里斯的折磨：第一期   068
第七章   威廉·登特·皮特曼向律师求计   086
第八章   迈克尔·芬斯伯里的假期   101
第九章   迈克尔·芬斯伯里假期的辉煌成就   125
第十章   吉迪恩·福西斯和布洛德伍德大钢琴   144
第十一章   音乐大师詹姆生   156
第十二章   布洛德伍德大钢琴的最后一瞥   176
第十三章   莫里斯的折磨：第二期   188
第十四章   威廉·本特·皮特曼的好消息   200
第十五章   "伟大的万斯"回家了   219
第十六章   皮革店最后的改组   228

译者后记   234

作者小序

"带点儿有分寸的轻率是再好不过的。"在正文里迈克尔·芬斯伯里说过这么一句话①；也只能以这句话来说明读者手中有着这本书的原因。作者要附带说明的只是，我们一个有了这把年纪，应该自知惭愧；另一个则太年轻，还得好好学习。②

R. L.史蒂文森

L.奥斯本

---

① 见第八十九页。
② 本书为史蒂文森与其养子奥斯本两人合著，写作于一八八八年，当时史蒂文森三十八岁，奥斯本十九岁。

第一章 莫里斯的疑窦

一个文学爱好者，舒舒服服地待在家里，他不会知道作者的艰难和辛苦。他拿着一本小说，笑盈盈地一页页翻过去，可不会想到那需要费多少钟点的工夫去查考典籍，在伯德雷恩图书馆①里从事研究，跟学识渊博而字迹难认的德国学者往返书信——总而言之，他不会想到，让他在火车上消磨一个钟头的东西，得有一个工程十分浩大的脚手架②先架起来，然后又拆掉！所以，我本来可以在这篇故事的开头先讲讲"通蒂"③的身世——他的出生地、家庭成分、可能从他母亲那儿遗传来的天分，以及能说明他聪慧早熟的显著事例等等——还可以写一篇文章，详尽叙述那个冠以他的名字的养老金法。这些材料都在我面前的

---

① 伯德雷恩图书馆（Bodleian）：英国牛津大学的一座图书馆，因重建该图书馆的 Sir Thomas Bodley（一五四五——一六一三）而得名。
② 脚手架（scaffolding）：建造房屋时搭的工作架。
③ 通蒂（Lorenzo Tonti）：十七世纪意大利那不勒斯银行家，首创一种联合养老金法，称为"通蒂氏养老金法"，规则是：由同年龄者联合积贮一定数目的金额，经过一定年限以后仍然生存者，分配其公积金。

分类架①里，但是我又不屑于这样卖弄。通蒂已经死了，我从没见过谁对他有一丝悼惜之意；至于"通蒂氏养老金法"哩，对于这篇不加渲染的故事来说，用一两句话也能够说明了。

有那么一群朝气勃勃的年轻人（人数越多越好），各人拿出一笔款子，汇总后委托受托人保管；过了一百年，出钱的死得只剩下一个人了，这笔款子连本带息就落在这个人手中，不过也只等于昙花一现；因为他这时可能耳朵已经聋了，你告诉他得了多大一笔财产，他都听不见——而且无疑他是行将就木，因此得到了等于没有得到。现在看来，这种办法显然富有异样的诗意和幽默感，因为这是一种没有一个当事人可能得到好处的办法；但是它的高尚的和公平合理的精神，使我们的祖父母一辈的人都乐于做此事。

当约瑟夫·芬斯伯里和他的哥哥马斯特曼还在穿着镶白绦边的裤子的孩提时代，他们的父亲——齐普赛街的一个富商——替他们加入了一个由三十七个人组成的资金充盈的小型"通蒂会"。入会费一千镑；约瑟夫·芬斯伯里到现在还记得当时到律师事务所去的情景，那个"通蒂会"的会员们——都是像他一样大的小孩子——聚集在一起，依次坐到办公室的那张大椅子上，在一位戴着眼镜、穿着长筒靴的和气的老绅士的帮助下，各人签上名字。他记得后来就跟这些孩子跑到律师屋后的草地上玩，他还跟一个

---

① 一种写字台上的鸽笼式的木格。原文为 pigeon-hole。

"通蒂会"中的兄弟大打了一场,那个孩子踢痛了他的胫骨。律师正在办公室里请聚会的那些父亲和母亲喝酒吃蛋糕,听到打斗的闹声就跑了出来,两个战斗员就被拆开,约瑟夫的战斗精神(因为他比另一个年纪小)获得穿长筒靴绅士的赞许,力言他像他这样大的时候,也是这样勇敢。约瑟夫心想,他小时候是不是穿着小长筒靴,秃着小光头呢?他晚上上床睡觉,自言自语地讲海战故事,讲倦了,是不是也穿起像这老绅士的衣服,拿出酒和蛋糕来款待另一些小男孩、小女孩呢?

一八四〇年,这三十七个人全活着;到一八五〇年,人数少了六个;在一八五六年和一八五七年,变化更大,克里米亚战争①和孟加拉兵变②带走了九个人。一八七〇年,原来的会员只剩下五个了,在我写这篇故事的时候③,连芬斯伯里兄弟两人在内,一共只剩三个人。

现在马斯特曼是七十三岁;他早已嗟叹年老力衰之苦,也早已退休,正住在他的儿子名律师迈克尔的家里,和外界绝无往来。约瑟夫呢,可不同了,他还是到处走动,还不过只是半老的样子,常在他爱去走走的街道上出现。这情形是令人遗憾的,因为马斯特曼过着(即使在细枝末节上)一种典型的英国式的生活。勤劳、有规律、庄重,并

---

① 一八五三至一八五六年俄、土之间的战争,战场在克里米亚半岛。当时英、法亦参战,派兵援土。
② 一八五七年印度德里附近印度土著军队发动的兵变,反抗当时的英帝国统治者,战争达两年之久。
③ 约在一八八八年。

且相信四厘公债,被公认为是一个精神矍铄的老人的基本条件。在这种种方面,马斯特曼都有着卓越的表现,现在到了七十三岁,他才 ab agendo①;可是比他小两岁的约瑟夫,虽然保养得极佳,但是一生怠惰,为人古怪,一直叫人看不起。他从事皮革事业,但早就厌弃了业务,别人也认为此道非他所长。他喜欢博闻周知,但没有及早节制自己的兴趣,于是他的壮年很快就开始耗费在这方面。没有比这种癖好更耗损精力的了,或许只有很自然地随之而来或因之而起的热衷于演讲的癖好,才会更厉害。约瑟夫却兼有这两点;这复合症十分凶猛,使得病人到处做义务演讲,几年之内,很快又发展到更严重的程度,甚至情愿跑三十英里的路,到小学校里去对幼童演讲。他不是一个学者;他读的东西只限于粗浅的教科书和报纸;他连百科全书都没有翻过;他说人生就是他的书。他声称自己的演讲不是讲给大学教授们听的;他的演讲是直接诉之于"人民的伟大的心",而人民的心,必然无疑,比人民的头脑更明事理,因为他的苦口婆心已经受到大家欢迎。譬如说,《如何靠一年四十镑的收入而愉快地生活》,这篇演讲就曾在失业群中轰动一时。《教育之宗旨、目标、意义与价值》,这个讲题就曾使他赢得浅见者的重视。至于他那篇有名的论说,《人寿保险与群众之关系》,在犬岛②的"工人协进会"里宣读,也曾受到盲目崇拜的男女听众的"满堂喝彩",

---

① 拉丁文,意思是什么都不做了。
② 犬岛(Isle of Dogs):伦敦泰晤士河中的一个岛。昔时为半岛,王族畋猎其间,猎犬驰骋,吠声闻于岛外,故名。

效果之大使他第二年就被推选为那个会的名誉会长,这职司非但没有酬劳,反而要居职者拿出钱来捐助,但是他的虚荣心却得到无上的满足。

约瑟夫在没有知识而比较开通的那一部分人中就这样赢得了声誉,就在这时候,他的家庭生活里忽然有了不少孤儿参加进来。他的弟弟雅各死了,就把莫里斯和约翰两个男孩子的负担加到他身上;同一年内,家里又增添了一个小女孩,她是约翰·亨利·海士尔坦先生的女儿,那位先生是一位钱少、朋友更少的绅士。他只在霍洛韦那儿的演讲厅里见过约瑟夫一次;但是那次经历却给了他以重大影响,他一回家就重新写了一份遗嘱,把女儿和她的前途都托付给那位演讲者。约瑟夫原是个好说话的人;然而承担这个新责任时,却不能说不带点儿勉强。他登报招请了一位保姆,买了一辆旧摇篮车。对于莫里斯和约翰他比较欢迎;这与其说是因为亲戚关系,还不如说是因为他的皮革店里(他已经忙不迭地把属于他们的三万镑投资到这家店里)近来生意莫名其妙地呈现出衰落的征象。他挑选了一个年轻能干的苏格兰人来经理事务,生意上的麻烦事,约瑟夫·芬斯伯里就再也不用操心了。他把受他监护的三个孩子也交托给这个能干的苏格兰人(他已结婚),自己动身到欧洲大陆和小亚细亚①去作长途旅行。

他一手拿着一本数国语言对照的《圣经》,一手拿着一本成语手册,就在欧洲十一个说着不同语言的地区中,

---

① 小亚细亚(Asia Minor):在亚洲西境,昔为东土耳其领土,第一次世界大战后,土领土仅限此一隅。

摸索行程。这两种向导,前一种不很符合这位哲学家和旅行家的要求,即使后一种也显然专为游客着想,而不敷人生问题的专家的应用。但是他却硬拉了一些翻译员——只要他能不付出任何代价而找得着他们的时候——为他做了工作,这样靠了种种办法他把调查的结果写满了好几本笔记簿。

他这样漫游了好几年,等到他所监护的孩子们已经长大,必须他亲自照顾的时候,才不得不回到英国来。那两个男孩子他已经送到一所良好且经济的学校里去读书,他们在那儿受到了优良的商业教育;这一来事情却有点尴尬,因为那爿皮革店可经不起法院查问。事情是这样的:约瑟夫为了准备交卸保管责任,查看了一下账目,却惊恐地发现他弟弟的财产交给他经管以后,别说没有增加,即使把自己全部财产分文不留地赔给他的两个被监护人,还仍然短少七千八百镑。这事情是当着一个律师的面通知了这两弟兄的,这时候,莫里斯·芬斯伯里就威胁他的二伯父,说要用严正的法律来解决,幸亏经过这位法律专家的劝告,他才没有走极端。

"石头里是榨不出油来的。"这位律师说。

莫里斯明白了这点,就跟他的二伯父和解了。约瑟夫这方放弃全部财产,并且把在"通蒂会"里可能得到的权益移让给侄儿,这权益已经大有希望了。莫里斯这方则答应留养二伯父和海士尔坦小姐(她也是遭难者之一),并且给他们每人每月一镑零用钱。这笔零用钱对于老头儿来说绰绰有余,至于海士尔坦小姐怎么能赖以添置衣着,可成了一个难题；但是她居然对付得了，而且从无怨言。她对她的不称职的监护人也真心敬爱。约瑟夫从来都是和善待人；他的年龄也帮他说了好些话，他那样全神贯注地追求知识，以及对于无论多么轻微的赞许都天真地感到愉快，也有着动人心弦的地方；因此种种，虽然律师郑重地对她说她做了牺牲，茱莉娅还是不愿给约瑟夫伯伯增加困难。

在布鲁姆斯伯里①的约翰街上一幢阴森森的大屋子里，这四个人就一同安住下来；表面上像是一个家庭，实际上只是一个财务上的结合体。当然，茱莉娅和约瑟夫伯伯两人等于奴隶，约翰呢，这位绅士喜好五弦琴、音乐厅、快乐酒吧间②，以及体育新闻，这样，无论在什么场合中都必然是一个次要人物；而这个帝国里的一切烦恼和乐趣就都由莫里斯来尝味了。圆滑的文人用以安慰无能和庸碌之辈的老生常谈之一，是说苦和乐总是难解难分地杂糅在一起，但是就莫里斯的情形说来，苦味一定远远多过甜味。他自己不怕麻烦，也不肯减少别人的麻烦；每天早晨他叫了仆役们来，亲手分发日常用品，测量白葡萄酒的深浅，数数吃剩的饼干，每星期账单送来，总要演出不快的话剧，厨师经常受到责难，做小买卖的直跑到后客厅里为了三个铜子儿跟他大吵大闹。浅见的人可能把他看作一个守财奴；但是在他自己看来，他却纯粹是一个被人诈骗的受害人，

---

① 布鲁姆斯伯里（Bloomsbury）：伦敦中区一地区，大英博物馆亦在此地区内。
② 快乐酒吧间（Gaiety Bar）：伦敦一座极华丽的快乐剧院内附设的酒吧间。

这个世界欠了他七千八百镑,他立意要这个世界偿还。

然而莫里斯的个性还是在对待约瑟夫的方法上才特别显露出来。他的二伯父好像是一宗股票,价格不稳定,但是他已经投入大量资金;因此他不惜任何代价来保护这个担保品。不管这老头儿有没有病,每月都由医师检查一次。他的饮食、衣着,以及时不时的旅行——这次到布莱顿,下次到伯恩茅斯①,就像婴儿吃奶面糊一样,完全由别人调配。天气不好的时候,他得耽在家里。天气好的时候,他得在九点半钟等在穿堂间里;莫里斯先要看看他可戴上了手表,可穿好了鞋子;然后两个人胳膊挽着胳膊,到皮革店里去。路上该是够索然无味的,因为他们之间根本没有好感;莫里斯总是不断责骂这个监护人盗用了款项,并且埋怨背了海士尔坦小姐这么个负担;约瑟夫呢,虽然性情够得上说是温和的,但对他这个侄儿多少带着点恨意。不过跟回来时路上的情形一比,这又算不上什么了;因为不管芬斯伯里家的哪一位,只要看一眼那爿店铺,或者店铺的业务情况,都足以使他不痛快一辈子。

店铺门上仍然有约瑟夫的名字;支票仍然由他签字;但这只是莫里斯的策略,为的是使"通蒂会"里其他会员都因而气馁。事实上,这爿店已经完全属于莫里斯了;他也发觉接到手的是一笔令人悲痛的遗产。他曾想卖掉它,但是人家出的价钱太可笑。他又试着扩充它,却反而把负债扩充起来;紧缩它呢,结果只紧缩了利润。除了那个能

---

① 布莱顿(Brighton)、伯恩茅斯(Bournemouth)均滨英国南海岸,为休养胜地。

干的苏格兰人以外,没有谁发过这爿店的财,苏格兰人(被撤职之后)用赚来的钱到邻近班芙的地方造了一幢房屋,闲居起来。每天,莫里斯坐在他的专用办公室里拆阅信件,想到这个喀里多尼亚①骗子,就要痛骂一顿。这时,老约瑟夫坐在另一张办公桌前,沉闷地等着命令,或者在他完全不明所以的东西上狠狠地签名。有一天,那个"石楠之乡"的人②竟然如此不近人情,把他二次结婚(跟亚历山大·麦克劳牧师的长女黛维达)的请柬寄来,大家都真担心莫里斯会发作起来。

皮革店里的工作时间已经减少到最低限度,即使像莫里斯,虽然责任感很强,可是面临着破产的阴影,也还是不肯在店里多待一会儿;于是经理和职员们就都嘘出一口气,打点打点,准备明天再来闲荡。我们的丁尼生勋爵③说过,"无事忙"是"延宕"的同父异母的姊妹,那么"营业习惯"自然是"延宕"的叔伯了。这时,那位皮革商人正在像牵着一只小狗似的,把他的活的投资对象押回约翰街;把他幽禁在穿堂间里,自己就尽一天所余的时间出外搜寻印章戒指,这是他生平唯一的癖好。约瑟夫不但有一般人所有的虚荣心,他还有演说家的虚荣心。他承认自己犯了过错,虽然别人(能干的苏格兰人)亏待他比他亏待

---

① 喀里多尼亚(Caledonia):苏格兰古时的拉丁名称。
② 苏格兰境内多石楠树,"石楠之乡"的人(the man of the heather)即指苏格兰人。
③ 丁尼生勋爵(Lord Alfred Tennyson,一八〇九——一八九二):英国桂冠诗人。

侄儿更甚；但是就算他双手浸透了血污，他觉得还是不应该给这样拖在一个年轻小子的游行马车车轮后面，不应该像个俘虏似的被罚坐在他自己的皮革店的厅堂里，不应该耳边只听见对他整个一生的恶毒的批评——不应该衣着被检查，衣领被翻上来，要查明他确实戴着无指手套，也不应该一直在别人的看管下被领出去、带回家，像个由保姆看管的婴孩一样。一想到这个，他就不免义愤填膺，忙不迭地挂起帽子、大衣和讨厌的无指手套，溜到楼上去找茱莉娅和笔记簿。至少那间休息室的不可侵犯性该得到莫里斯的尊重了；它该属于这老人和少女两人；她在那儿做自己的衣裳；他在那儿记下一鳞半爪的事情，统计鸡毛蒜皮的数字，把眼镜都沾上了墨水。

有时，他也在那儿慨叹"通蒂会"跟他的关系。"都是因为那个会，"一天下午他这样嚷着说，"不然他决不会留住我。那我就能做一个自由人了，茱莉娅。我可以很容易靠演讲来养活自己。"

"那是一定的，"她说，"他剥夺了你这种娱乐，我就觉得这也好算是他最缺德的一件事情。猫岛①（是这么叫的吧？）那儿许多好人那么看重你，写信来请你给他们做一次演讲。我还以为他总会让你到猫岛去哩。"

"他是一个傻瓜，"约瑟夫嚷道，"像他的处境，四周简直哪儿都是令人目眩神迷的生活奇观，然而看看他从中得到的好处哪，他最好还是困到棺材里去吧。你想他有多

---

① 并无这个地名，此处是海士尔坦小姐将犬岛记错了。

么好的机会呀！换了任何一个青年，得到这种机会，真要开心得跳起来啦。只要他愿意听，我能告诉他的见闻是说也说不尽的哩，茱莉娅。"

"亲爱的，不管你说什么，可千万不要太激动，"茱莉娅说，"因为你知道，倘若你有一点不舒服的样子，别人就会把医生请来了。"

"的确不错，"老人低声下气地答着，"我来做一点研究工作平平气吧。"他用拇指翻动着那一长排笔记簿。"我不知道，"他说，"我不知道（因为我看到你手头正忙着）你是否会有兴趣——"

"哦，我当然有兴趣，"茱莉娅嚷着说，"把你的精彩的故事念一篇给我听吧，那才对啦！"

他于是把一本簿子拿下来，急急忙忙把眼镜架上鼻梁，好像不让别人有打消原意的机会。"我打算念给你听的，"他一面说，一面一页页地翻阅，"是跟一个荷兰旅行向导的一段非常重要的谈话的札记，那人名叫大卫·阿巴斯，这字是'修道院长'一字的拉丁文[①]。所得结果证明我的钱花得很值得，花钱是因为阿巴斯起先显得有些不耐烦，我就受到感应（我知道这种说法很奇特），要负担他的饮酒费。札记大约只有二十五页长。对啦，就是这一段。"他清了清喉咙，念起来。

这段访问记，五百分之四百九十九是芬斯伯里先生（按照他自己的记载）的话，摘录自阿巴斯的简直一句也没有。

---

① "阿巴斯"的原文是 Abbas，"修道院长"的原文是 Abbot。

茉莉娅觉得毫无兴趣，她并不是非听不可；然而对于那个不得不答话的荷兰旅行向导说来，当时一定完全像在做噩梦一样。他似乎靠了频频向酒瓶求助才使自己安定下来；甚至（到末了）他终于不再依靠约瑟夫的小恩惠，宁愿自己出钱叫一壶。在这份记录里，一种陶然微醺的效果至少可以看得出：阿巴斯忽然心甘情愿地出来做证了；他开始自愿透露一些话了；在缝衣的茉莉娅带着一丝微笑刚抬起头来的时候，莫里斯冲进了家里，一个劲地喊着二伯父，一口气闯入休息室，高举的手摇着一份晚报。

他的确带来了重要新闻。陆军中将格拉斯哥·比格爵士，这位"印度星勋位司令官爵士"[①]，"迈克尔圣徒乔治圣徒勋位司令官爵士"[②]等等，他的逝世消息宣布出来了，那么"通蒂会"里那一大笔款子现在只是芬斯伯里兄弟两人之间的事了。莫里斯的机会到底来了。他们兄弟俩向来不和睦，这是事实。那时，马斯特曼听说约瑟夫到小亚细亚去了，深表不满。"我说这简直是胡闹，"他这么说，"你瞧吧——下次我们就要听到他到北极去了。"等旅行家回来，这种讥讽话又传到他耳中。那一次，马斯特曼纵然得到坐在讲坛上的邀请，都拒绝去听那篇《教育之宗旨、目标、意义与价值》的演说，是搞得最不痛快的一次。从这

---

① "印度星勋位司令官爵士"（KCSI）：指 Knight Commander of the (Most Exalted Order of the) Star of India，这是英国颁发给驻在印度官员的勋位。

② "迈克尔圣徒乔治圣徒勋位司令官爵士"（KCMG）：指 Knight Commander of the (Most Distinguished Order of) St. Michael and St. George，这是英国颁给军政人员的勋位。

以后,兄弟俩没有见过面。不过在另一方面,他们也从来没有公开吵过架,约瑟夫(遵照莫里斯的命令)总能放弃他做弟弟的特权;马斯特曼生平享有不贪和公正的好名声。这样一来,现在双方妥协的一切条件都具备了;莫里斯忽然看见自己收回了七千八百镑,并且摆脱了动荡不定的皮革生意,因此第二天一早就赶到堂兄迈克尔的事务所里来。

迈克尔是个在社会上有名气的人,年纪很轻的时候即已投身法律界,差不多不仗谁的支撑,就成了一个经手阴暗事务的贩子。大家知道他能承办没有胜诉希望的案子;大家知道他能从石头里挤出证据来,也能从金矿里挖出好处来;因而,在他的事务所里进进出出的形形色色的人,都是还只剩下一点名誉没有丧失而现在发觉这剩下的一点正岌岌可危的人;都是交友不慎,结识了歹人的人;或是体面攸关的信件落在别人手里的人;或是被自己的管家勒索的人。在私生活方面迈克尔是个注重享乐的人;但是他在事务所里见到的令人胆寒的事,大概很有力量使他头脑清醒,因为大家知道(在投资事务上)他宁愿殷实可靠,而不愿冒险逞强。尤其可以看出他这一点的,是他平生始终不渝地嘲笑的芬斯伯里的"通蒂会"。

所以莫里斯到他堂兄面前来的时候,一点都不担心事情的结果,他兴冲冲地把他的计划讲了出来。这位律师耐心听了将近一刻钟,让他滔滔不绝地谈完那些显而易见的好处。然后迈克尔站了起来,一边按铃叫书记,一边简简单单地说了一句话:

"不成,莫里斯。"

尽管这位皮革商说情说理，又天天跑来说情说理，都没有用。他提议拿出额外酬劳一千镑、二千镑、三千镑，也没有用；他以约瑟夫的名义提议只要总额的三分之一就算了，也没有用。回答依然是一样的："不成。"

"我不明白这究竟是怎么回事，"他最后说，"你对我提出的理由没有任何答辩，你没有一句话好说。照我看，我相信这是存心作对。"

律师对他莞尔一笑。"你至少可以相信一桩事，"他说，"我做什么都可以，可就是不打算满足你的好奇心。你看我今天已经多讲了几句话，因为对于这个问题，这是我们最后一次的会见。"

"我们最后一次的会见！"莫里斯喊起来。

"是马上离别前的一杯①，亲爱的孩子。"迈克尔回答。

"我不能让我的业务时间白白被糟蹋。就说你自己吧，你难道没有事情吗？你的皮革生意难道没有风波了吗？"

"我相信这是存心作对。"莫里斯固执地重复这句话。"你一直厌恨我，从小就看不起我。"

"不，不——没有厌恨过。"迈克尔用安慰的口吻回答。"说什么都不如说我喜欢你来得对；你有一种地方永远令人惊喜，你只要站开一点，看来就那么黑、那么动人了。你可知道，就那么对你瞧一眼，总觉得你很有浪漫的气息？——像所谓的一个历史不简单的人？真的，我耳朵里听见的，尽是说皮革生意的历史里充满故事哩。"

---

① 马上离别前的一杯（the stirrup-cup）：乘马临行前所饮的告别酒。

"好吧，"莫里斯说，不理会那些话，"到这儿来是没有用的了。我去看你的父亲去。"

"哦，不行，你不可以去，"迈克尔说，"谁也不许去看我的父亲。"

"我倒要听听这是什么道理。"他的堂弟嚷着。

"这并不是什么秘密，"律师回答。"他身体太坏。"

"要是他的身体真像你说的那么不行，"对方嚷着，"那更该接受我的提议了。我一定要去看他。"

"你一定要去？"迈克尔说，站了起来，按铃叫书记。

依照法拉第·邦德爵士，这位名字经常出现在病状报告书下端的准男爵医师的指示，现在已是时候，该把约瑟夫（这可怜的生金蛋的鹅）移到空气较好的伯恩茅斯去了；他们离开了嘈杂的布鲁姆斯伯里，首途赴那个有着许多别墅的茫茫一片的乡野：茱莉娅很高兴，因为她在伯恩茅斯有些旧友；约翰很失望，因为他爱好城市生活；约瑟夫不管在哪儿都无所谓，只要有笔、墨水和报纸就行，只要能够避免那办公室里的折磨就行。莫里斯本人能够省掉跑市中区的麻烦，能够有一个静下来想想的时间，也不见得会不乐意。他准备做任何牺牲；他什么都不想，只想把钱再要回来，自己从皮革堆中抽身；事情有点奇怪，因为总额已达十六万镑之多，他的要求又那么委曲求全——要是他想不出一个办法来说动迈克尔，可真有点奇怪了。"要是我能猜出他的原因来就好了。"他一再这样自言自语；不论白天走在布兰克森树林里的时候，晚上辗转床上的时候，饭桌前忘记进餐的时候,在更衣车①里忘记穿衣服的时候,这个问题总是萦绕在他脑际:迈克尔为什么拒绝呢?

终于在一天晚上,他冲进了弟弟的房间,唤醒了他。

"这是怎么着?"约翰问。

"明天就叫茱莉娅离开这儿,"莫里斯回答。"她一定得到城里去,弄好房子,找好仆人。我们全体也将在三天之内跟去。"

"哦,好极啦!"约翰叫着。"可是为什么呢?"

"我想出来了,约翰。"哥哥静静地回答。

"想出来什么了?"约翰问。

"就是迈克尔为什么不肯妥协的事,"莫里斯说,"这是因为他不能妥协。这是因为马斯特曼已经死了,他却隐瞒着。"

"天哪!"感情容易冲动的约翰叫着。"不过这有什么好处呢?他干吗要这样做呢?"

"为了骗取我们'通蒂会'里的钱。"哥哥说。

"他办不到;那样他一定要有一张医师签的证书。"约翰反驳道。

"你难道从来没有听说过有些医师可以用钱买通的吗?"莫里斯问。"他们就跟黑莓一样普遍;你只要花三镑十先令就可以买通他们的。"

"要是我是一个医师,那可非要五十镑以上不行。"约翰脱口而出。

---

① 更衣车(Bathing Machine):一种可以开至游泳场、海滨浴场等处,供人更衣的车子。

"而且！"莫里斯继续说，"迈克尔正非常需要这一大笔钱。他的当事人全都遭了难，他的业务是整个儿垮台了。要是竟然有谁能够应付这种事，那只有他自己；他准已把计划全部拟订好了；而且他这主意准是打得不坏，因为他聪明得很，这该死的东西！可是我也很聪明啊，而且势在必争。当我是个孤儿，还在学校里读书的时候，我就损失了七千八百镑。"

"哦，别啰唆了，"约翰打断他的话，"你为了把这笔钱要回来，所受的损失已经绝不止于此了。"

第二章 莫里斯的行动

于是在几天之后,应该有人(应该有 G. P. R. 詹姆士①的读者)看见,这无生气的家庭里的三个男人,在东车站上车离开了伯恩茅斯。这时天气阴寒多变,因此,约瑟夫被吩咐遵照法拉第·邦德爵士所规定的服装穿着起来;爵士(众所周知)对病人衣着的严格正不下于对于饮食。那些有教养的病人,在生活各方面,几乎没有谁不愿遵照这位苛细的医师的指示,至少也是遵照他的指示尽力地去做。"忌饮茶,太太,"读者一定听见他这样说过了,"忌茶、炸肝、含锑的酒和面包师傅做的面包。每晚十点三刻就寝;穿着方面最好穿全套合乎卫生的法兰绒。外边要穿一件貂皮的。还不要忘了买一双道尔·克伦比公司的卫生靴。"甚至在你已经付了诊费的时候,他还可能叫你回来,大声而郑重地加上一句:"我忘了一桩要紧的事。要像避开魔鬼一样,忌食熏鲟鱼!"不幸的约瑟夫像是衣服,连每

---

① G. P. R. 詹姆士(George Payne Rainsford James,一七九一——一八六〇):英国当时一位多产小说家,作品达一百部,多以史实为题材,有《黎塞留》(*Richelieu*)等。

一粒纽扣都要按照法拉第爵士的样本缝制；他脚上穿着卫生靴；身上一套衣服是用真正透气的料子裁制的；衬衫的料子是合乎卫生的法兰绒的，那是一种色彩稍嫌灰暗的针织品；外面包到膝部的是那件少不了的貂皮大衣。在伯恩茅斯车站（这位医师特别爱好的一站），那些搬运员就看出这位老绅士是法拉第爵士的作品。只有一样东西显出是他自己的本色，那是一顶盔兜式的步兵便帽；他曾经戴了这顶帽子，在以弗所①的平原上从一只垂死的豺狼口里逃生，在亚得里亚海上挨过一次大风暴②，自此以后无论什么东西都不能使它和我们的旅行家分离。

这三位芬斯伯里一上了车，进了车厢，就争吵起来，这回事本身就不体面，对莫里斯说来更是非常不幸。要是他在车窗前多徘徊一会儿，这篇故事就根本不必写了。因为要是那么着，他一定会看见（就好像搬运员们没有错过一样）另外也有一个穿着法拉第·邦德爵士的制服的旅客走来。然而他正有着别的事情哩，而且还认为这事情重要得多——其实天晓得，他这一错真是错尽错绝。

"我从没听见过有这种事，"他嚷着，继续他们整个早晨差不多没有停过的讨论，"这张汇票不是你的，是我的。"

"上面写明是付给我的，"老绅士回答，神情非常固执，"我自己的财产，我爱怎么办就怎么办。"

这张汇票款额八百镑，是在早餐时给他签背书③的，

---

① 以弗所（Ephesus）：小亚细亚的一座古城。
② 原文为 bora，指亚得里亚海北部的干冷凶猛的东北风。
③ 原文为 endorse，指由收款人在汇票或支票背面签名。

他干脆塞到口袋里。

"约翰，你听听看！"莫里斯喊着。"他的财产！他身上的衣服都是我的哩！"

"随他去吧。"约翰说，"我对你们两个都头痛了。"

"跟伯父说话可不该是这样的，先生，"约瑟夫叫着，"我决不能容忍这种不敬。你们是两个鲁莽、无礼而又无知到极点的年轻小伙子，我已经下了决心不让事情再这样下去了。"

"哦，胡说！"这位温文尔雅的约翰说。

但是莫里斯心里却不怎么安定了。那种反常的不服从的行动已经使他烦恼，而刚才这句有反叛意味的话他听来更觉不妙。他惴惴不安地看着这老先生。许多年前，有一次约瑟夫在做一次演讲的时候，听众满场起哄；他们觉得这位先生拿来款待大家的东西实在无味，于是把娱乐这个问题接过来自己解决了；这位演讲者（连同那位公立小学校长、浸礼会的牧师和一位暂时充任他的护卫的工人候补代表）结果就被撵出了会场。那糟糕的一天莫里斯不在场；要是他曾在场的话，那么他对现在看见的他二伯父眼睛里那种想要战斗的光芒，和嘴边那种咬牙切齿的动作，就一定会觉得眼熟。不过这些征兆即使让一个外行看来，也觉着有危险的气息。

"好吧，好吧，"莫里斯说，"等我们到了伦敦再跟你谈吧。"

约瑟夫不回答，连看都不看他一眼；他用发抖的双手拿出一份《英国机匠》杂志，装模作样地埋头阅读起来。

"我想知道什么东西使他这样嚣张。"这侄子思索着,"我实在不放心这种样子。"他狐疑地抓抓鼻子。

火车向前长驱而去,载着它经常载着的货物——那些早已湮没无闻的旅客,也载着老约瑟夫,他装作沉浸在刊物里的样子;约翰一边拿着一份《粉红报》①,一边打瞌睡;还有莫里斯,他心中辘轳般转着一桩桩旧恨新仇,还有疑团和惊心事。火车驶过了在海边的耶稣堂,在松树林中的赫恩,以及在蜿蜒的河旁的令伍特。迟了一些时候(但是对西南铁路②来说可不能算怎么长的时候),火车在一个车站的月台前停住,这是在新福里斯特的森林之中,它的真名(只怕铁路公司会对我"依法起诉")我不提,姑且把它化名为百朗亭吧。

许多旅客探头对窗外看着,其中一位老先生我想在这儿说几句,因为我现在快要把他结果掉了,而(在这整个故事里)我一点都不像还有机会遇见第二个这样正派的人。他的名字无关紧要,他的习惯却得说说。他穿了一身苏格兰呢制衣服在欧洲大陆漫游,消磨了一辈子;多年阅读《格里奈尼先驱报》,终于损伤了他的视力,他忽然想去看看亚述③的河流,于是到伦敦去找了一位眼科医师。通过眼科医师就找到牙科医师,再通过这两科医师找到内科医师,这种步骤好像是免不了的;不久就归在法拉第爵士的治下,

---

① 《粉红报》(*Pink Un*):当时在英国盛行的、用粉红色纸张刊印、登载赛马消息的报纸。
② 西南铁路(South-Western):一条从伦敦到英国西南部的铁路。
③ 亚述(Assyria):亚洲西部地区,位于阿拉伯之北,地中海之东。

穿上了透气的衣服,被送到伯恩茅斯去;现在他正要回去对那位作威作福的准男爵(他是他故乡中唯一的友人)做报告。那些穿着苏格兰呢制衣服的漫游者的情形是很有趣的。我们都会看见他们走进旅馆的公共餐厅(斯培西亚①的、格拉茨②的,或是威尼斯的),带着一种温和而忧郁的面貌,以及一种到过印度而未获成就的沮丧的神情。好几百个旅馆的账房里都晓得他们的名字;然而,如果明天这整个漫游大队不见了踪影,也不会引起别人丝毫的注意。所以假定只是其中一个人——譬如这位穿着透气衣服的先生吧——失踪了,当然更算不上一回事了!他在伯恩茅斯的账已经付清;他在人世间的全部财产都在行李车上的两个大皮箱里,而这些,过了相当一段时间之后,就会被当作无主的行李卖给犹太人,法拉第爵士的管家在年底可能少掉半克朗③的收入,而欧洲各个旅馆的业主相近这时候也会叹息在利润上有着虽小却是很显然的下降。可是影响也就是这么一点儿了。或许这位老先生对此亦有所感,因为当他把没戴帽子、鬓发灰白的头从车窗前缩进来的时候,带着一副够明显的愁容,这时,火车在那座桥下冒着烟,往前开着,愈开愈快,驰过那常青灌木和其他树木掺杂着生长的新福里斯特。

可是,在刚开过百朗亭几百码的时候,忽然起了一阵刹车的轧轹声,全车的人浑身打战,火车猛然停住了。莫

---

① 斯培西亚(Spezzia):意大利一城市。
② 格拉茨(Gräz):奥地利一城市。
③ 克朗(crown):英国旧货币名,值五先令,上面印有皇冠。

里斯·芬斯伯里听到腾起了乱糟糟的人声，跳到车窗边。妇女们在尖声大叫，男人们在从窗口翻到路轨边，路警们在嚷着，叫他们各守原位；与此同时，火车开始一点点增加速度，慢慢向百朗亭方向倒退；然而转瞬间，这种种声响都被一列猛扑过来的下行快车的催命似的汽笛声、雷鸣似的急驰声淹没了。

冲撞的那一刹那莫里斯没有听见声响。可能他已晕过去了。他做了一个怪梦，看见车厢从半中腰折断了，又碎成片片撒了一地，好像哑剧里的戏法；的确是的，他醒过来的时候，真的躺在露天的硬地上。他的头疼得要命；他把手举到额上一摸，看到手被鲜血染红了，倒也不觉得奇怪。他满耳只听见一种不堪忍受的、一阵阵的轰鸣声，他原以为恢复了知觉就会听不到了，可是不但不然，反而好像变得更响、更不留情地刺透他的耳鼓。那是惊天震地的雷鸣的声音，好像锅炉工厂在钉铆钉。

现在他的好奇心也开始活动，他坐起来，环顾四周。在这儿的路轨，绕着一座长着树木的小山丘，角度很小地兜过来；靠近他的这一方，整个儿都给伯恩茅斯火车的庞大残骸占了去；那列快车的残骸大部分都被树林遮蔽；就在转弯的地方，在一股股直冒的蒸汽，以及石冢似的堆散满地正在燃烧着的煤块中，可以看见横倒在那儿的两辆机车的残余部分，一个压着另一个。在这条轨道的那边，常青灌木林的边缘，许多人来来往往地奔跑，一面跑，一面喊，另外还有许多人一动也不动地躺在那儿，好像睡着了的流浪者。

莫里斯忽然得出了一个结论。"出了事儿啦!"他想着,对于自己这么明察秋毫得意非凡。差不多与此同时,他看见了约翰躺在近旁,脸色白得像纸一样。"可怜的老约翰啊!可怜的老家伙啊!"他想着,不知从什么忘了好久的地方涌出一种小学生似的感情,他以孩子气的相亲相爱的样子握住了弟弟的手。或许是手的接触碰醒了他吧;无论如何约翰是睁开了眼睛,一下子坐了起来,欲言又止地动了几次嘴唇,然后说:"什么事这样吵?"是恍恍惚惚的鬼似的声音。

那个魔鬼的锻冶场上的噪声,依然在他们耳朵里雷鸣般地震响。"让我们离开那东西吧。"莫里斯喊着,指指那边仍然从两个撞坏的机车里冒出来的蒸汽。他们互相搀扶,爬了起来,颤抖着,摇晃着,眼睛睁得大大的,看着这一片死亡的景象。

就在这时候有一队人朝他们走来,那些人已经组织了救护队。

"你有没有受伤?"其中一个大声问,那是一个年轻人,苍白的脸上挂着汗珠,从别人对待他的样子看来,他显然是个医师。

莫里斯摇摇头,年轻人冷酷地点点头,递给他一瓶酒。

"喝一点吧,"他说,"看样子你的朋友得赶快喝些酒才好哩。我们要每一个有活动能力的男人都参加,"他又说,"我们面前有极多的工作要做,没有谁可以逃避。要是你不能做别的,你可以去抬担架。"

医师刚离开不久,莫里斯借了酒力,神志完全清醒过来。

"我的天!"他喊起来,"二伯父约瑟夫呢!"

"是啊,"约翰说,"他在哪儿呢?他不会离这儿很远。我希望这老头儿没有摔坏才好。"

"来帮我去找。"莫里斯说,突然狠狠地下了一个决心,这跟他平常的态度迥然不同,于是片刻不稍待地迈开了脚步。"他可不能摔死了呀!"他喊着,向老天挥着拳头。

兄弟两个往来奔波,睁大着眼睛看着一个个受伤的人的脸,又把死去的翻过身来看看。他们这样验查了总有四十个人,可是仍然不见二伯父约瑟夫的影子。然后他们一路搜索过来,现在已走近了撞车的中心地点,这儿两只汽锅还是在喷出蒸汽,声音还是响得震耳欲聋。这儿是这块场地中尚未经救护队来收拾的一处地方,地面,特别是树林边上的地面,很不平坦——这儿一个坑,那儿一座顶着一丛金雀花的小丘。这种地方是可能隐匿好多尸体的,他们就像猎狗追踪猎物似的搜寻着。在前面领路的莫里斯突然停了下来,食指向前指着,一副悲痛的样子。约翰沿着他哥哥手指的方向看去。

在一个沙坑的坑底躺着一个曾经被称为"人"的东西。脸毁伤很严重,已经无法辨认;不过也无须辨认。那雪白的头发、貂皮的大衣、透气的衣料、合乎卫生的法兰绒——一切的一切,就连从道尔·克伦比公司买来的卫生靴,都足以证明这是二伯父约瑟夫的尸体。只有那顶步兵便帽一定是在那场激变中失落了,因为这死人光着头。

"可怜的老骨头啊!"约翰说,声音里有着真情流露的意味,"我真情愿拿出十镑来赎回我们刚才在车上对他不敬的罪愆!"

可是莫里斯只呆呆地看着这死人,脸上冷冷的,没有表情。他咬着手指甲,翻着眼睛,皱着的眉毛表现出一种悲痛的恼怒和悲痛的用心思索的样子,他静静站着,一声不响。到头来还是一桩不公平的事;他是一个孤儿,在学校里念书的时候被人盗用了钱,被人拖累在一爿没落的皮革店里,被人加了一个海士尔坦小姐的负担,被堂兄欺诈"通蒂会"里的钱,这一切我们差不多可以说,他已经以正人君子的风度忍受下来了,可是现在呢,他们竟然把他的二伯父弄死了!

"来!"他突然说,"抓住他的脚,我们必须把他弄到树林子里去。我决不能让任何人看见这尸体。"

"哦,胡说八道!"约翰说,"这又有什么用呢?"

"照我的话做就是,"莫里斯一面冲着他说,一面抬起这尸体的肩膀,"难道要我一个人背吗?"

他们把他抬到了树林的边缘,再走十几步就到了别人看不见的地方,再往后退一点,到了林中沙质的空地上,他们把这负荷放了下来,站着,厌恶地看着他。

"你打算怎么做?"约翰轻声问。

"当然是把他埋了!"莫里斯答复了,他打开一把小折刀,发狂似的掘起土来。

"用这劳什子你一辈子也掘不成。"另一个反对道。

"你要是不肯帮忙,你这个胆小鬼,"莫里斯尖声大叫,"你尽可以给我滚!"

"这是最最幼稚的蠢事,"约翰说,"但是我却不能让人称作胆小鬼。"于是勉强动手帮他的哥哥掘起土来。

这儿沙质的土很松,但是四周枞树的根纠结着,像一床席子垫在下面。金雀花刮破了他们的手;他们把坑里的沙土掏出来,常常弄得沙土上染着他们的血。在莫里斯不懈的努力和约翰的不热心的帮忙下这样过了一个钟点,可是壕沟还是只有九英寸深。尸体就被胡乱地扔到这里边;再盖上沙土,这之后还得掘一些沙土,并且割一些金雀花来堆在上面;然而在这肮脏的小土堆的一端,还是看得出凸着一双脚,而且那漆皮鞋的鞋尖在闪闪发亮。这时候他们两人都丧失了勇气,即使莫里斯也觉得这工作可怕得够受;他们于是像两头野兽似的偷偷摸摸地躲到近边最密的树丛中。

"我们最多只能做到这样子了。"莫里斯说着坐下来。

"那么,现在,"约翰说,"你或许可以客客气气地跟我谈谈,这究竟是怎么回事吧。"

"要是你自己还不明白,"莫里斯大声说,"毫无疑问,我对你说了也等于白说。"

"哦,这当然是关于那个'通蒂会'的什么鬼把戏啰,"对方回答,"但是这简直是胡闹。我们已经失去了它,这也就完了。"

"我跟你说说吧,"莫里斯说,"大伯父马斯特曼已经死啦。我知道这桩事,我听见一个声音这样说。"

"好吧,可是二伯父约瑟夫也死了哪。"约翰说。

"我要是说他没有死他就是没有死。"莫里斯回答。

"如果这样呢,"约翰大声说,"假如你的话是对的,大伯父马斯特曼是死了好久了,我们只要宣布真相,揭发迈克尔不就得了。"

"看来你是把迈克尔当作一个傻子了,"莫里斯嘲笑地说,"你难道还不明白这个骗局他已经准备了好几年啦?他什么都准备好了:护士、医师、殡仪馆,全都买通了,死亡证书上也样样齐备,只等填上日期!要是他一得到我们这里的事变的风声,你等着瞧吧,大伯父马斯特曼一定不出两天就死了,不出一个星期就埋掉了。可是你看着吧,约翰,迈克尔能做什么,我也能。他会玩一套空城计,我也会。他的爸爸要是永远活下去,我的二伯父也势必会活下去!"

"这是违法的,是不是?"约翰说。

"一个人多少得有点维护正义的勇气吧。"莫里斯大义凛然地回答。

"那么假使你猜错了呢?假使大伯父马斯特曼是活着而且手脚轻健呢?"

"嗯,就算是这样吧,"那阴谋家答复,"我们的情况可并不比从前坏;实际上反而更好。大伯父马斯特曼总有一天是要死的;而只要二伯父约瑟夫一直活着,他随便哪一天都可能死;可是我们现在却完全不用烦这个神了:我打算玩的把戏可以无限期地玩下去——一直玩到天国降临的时候。"

"我真不明白你打算怎样做!"约翰叹了口气,"可是你晓得,莫里斯,你从来都是一个粗坯,干不来细活的。"

"我倒要听听我到底把什么事情弄糟过,"莫里斯嚷着,"我搜集的一套印章戒指是全伦敦最好的哩。"

"嗯,你也知道那爿皮革店的情形,"对方提醒他,"那是被认为相当糟糕的。"

莫里斯倒是受得了这句话,不理睬,也不反诘,甚至心中也不怀恨,这是他有一种异常的自制力的表现。

"关于我们眼前的事情,"他说,"只要我们能把他弄到布鲁姆斯伯里就没有什么问题了。我们可以把他埋在地窖里,那地方好像是专为此而造的哩;然后我只要到外面去收买一个医师就行了。"

"为什么我们不能让他就埋在现在这个地方呢?"约翰问。

"因为我们对于这地段毫无所知,"莫里斯辩驳道,"这座树林可能经常有情侣来散步。你还是把脑筋转到真正困难的问题上来吧——我们怎么样把他弄到布鲁姆斯伯里去呢?"

种种办法都经讨论,都经否决。百朗亭火车站当然不行,因为这儿现在一定是爱打听之人和流言蜚语聚集之地,他们要想把一具尸首一下子运出去而不被人注意,那(比起任何事情来)是最最不可能的了。约翰有气无力地提议弄一只麦酒桶把尸首假作啤酒装出去,但是莫里斯认为这个办法不当之至,简直不屑作答。要是去买一只货箱,看来同样无望,因为既然这两位先生没有任何行李,那为什么需要一只货箱呢?他们要是需要干净的衣服才比较合理一点。

"我们尽朝这方面想可错了，"莫里斯终于这样嚷起来，"这事情必须从长计议。假定现在，"他又这样说下去，兴奋地、断断续续地，好像在自言自语，"假定我们租一幢租期按月计算的农舍。那么一个住户买一只货箱是不会引人注目的。再假定我们今天叫人让出了房子，今晚弄到了一只货箱，明天我就可以去租一辆客车——或者一辆我们自己可以赶马的货车——载着那只箱子，或者我们弄到的别的什么东西，到令伍特或者林德赫斯特或者别的地方去；我们可以在那上面弄个标签注明'标本'字样，你懂吧？约翰，我相信我毕竟摸准了路了。"

"嗯，这办法似乎比较行得通。"约翰承认。

"我们当然得用假名字，"莫里斯继续说，"用我们本来的绝对不成。你看就用'马斯特曼'这名字怎么样？它听起来既文静又庄重。"

"我才不愿意叫马斯特曼哩，"弟弟回答说，"你要是喜欢，你用好了。我要叫万斯——伟大的万斯，'最后六晚，决不延期'。像这样的名字才带点劲儿。"

"万斯！"莫里斯嚷着，"你难道以为我们是在演一出戏来玩玩吗？叫万斯的从来没有一个不是演艺馆里的歌唱家。"

"它好就好在这儿啊，"约翰回答，"它立刻让你有了个身份啊。你尽可自己叫自己福特斯库什么的，叫得震天价响，也不会有人来注意你；可是一叫万斯，他自然而然就高贵起来了。"

"不过带有戏剧性的名字还有很多哩，"莫里斯大声说，

"莱伯恩啊,欧文啊,布鲁啊,图尔啊——"

"我一个也不要!"他的弟弟回答,"我打算跟你一样,要在这事情里边找出一点个人的乐趣。"

"好吧,"莫里斯说,他看出约翰是决心固执到底了,"我就叫罗伯特·万斯吧。"

"我就叫乔治·万斯,"约翰喊着说,"如假包换的乔治·万斯!大家拥到我的周围来呀!"

他们把身上凌乱的衣服尽可能地整理好,这芬斯伯里兄弟就取一条迂回的道路回到百朗亭去找吃中饭的地方并去找一个适当的农舍。在一个偏僻的地方,要在短时期内找着一个备好家具的住所,并不很容易,但是幸运之神不一会儿就把我们的两个冒险家介绍给一个耳聋的木匠,他有着好多所备着家具的农舍,真心诚意地立刻供应给他们。他们拜访的第二个地方要一英里半以外才有旁的人家,对此,他们交换了一下满意的眼色。不过走近了一看,这地方不免有令人失望之处。这农舍坐落在遍长着常青石楠灌木的潮湿的洼地里;高大的树木遮在窗前,望不远;桷橼上的盖草看得出烂了,墙壁上又沾着斑斑点点有碍健康的绿霉。房间也小,天花板又低,家具只不过徒有其名;厨房里充满着一种怪异的寒气和一种潮湿的氤氲不散的气息;卧室里只有一张床。

莫里斯为了要使房钱减少,提出了这一缺点。

"很好,"那个人回答说,"要是你们不能两个人睡一张床,你们最好还是住别墅去吧。"

"其次哩,"莫里斯继续说,"又没有水。你们用的水是打哪儿弄来的呢?"

"我们从泉水那儿打水来把那个灌满。"木匠说,一面指着门旁一只大水桶。"说起来,泉水离这儿并不太远,而且用吊桶汲水也很容易。那儿就有一只吊桶。"

他们看着那只大水桶,莫里斯用胳膊肘儿捅捅他的弟弟。大水桶是新的,做得很结实。如果他们还缺少什么东西使他们拿定主意,那么那只特别实用的大水桶可起了决定性作用。交易很快做成了,一个月的租费当场付清,大约一小时之后就可以看见芬斯伯里兄弟回到这所糟透了的农舍里来,带着钥匙,这是他们租赁权的象征;一盏酒精灯,他们彼此打趣说这可以用来做饭;一个相当大的猪肉馅饼;还有一夸脱汉普郡①的最劣等的威士忌酒。他们已办妥的还不止这些事,而且已经(借口自己是风景画家)租好了一辆轻而坚固的两轮载货马车,预订明天一清早使用;所以当他们换了那种新身份的时候,他们大可以对自己说事情最棘手的部分已经迎刃而解了。

约翰着手烧茶;莫里斯在屋子里东找西找,一下子在厨房里的架子上发现了大水桶的盖子,开心得不得了。这样一来,可就是只完整的货箱了;既然没有稻草,这几床毯子(至少他自己没有一点儿意思要照这东西现有的用途用一用)正好作包装的代用品;困难一个一个地克服了,莫里斯几乎高兴得发狂。不过,还有一个问题尚待解决,这一个问题是他全部计划的关键所在。就是约翰肯不肯一

---

① 汉普郡(Hampshire):英国南部滨海之一郡,南安普敦在此郡内。

个人待在农舍里?他还不敢提出这个问题。

这哥俩儿兴致勃勃地在冷杉木桌旁坐下来,动手解决那个猪肉馅饼。莫里斯详述了他是怎样发现桶盖的,那位"伟大的万斯"兴奋得用地道的演艺馆的做法,拿叉子敲打桌子,表示赞美。

"这才对啦,"他喊着,"我一直说这种事必得要弄一只水桶才成。"

"当然啰,"莫里斯说,一面想,这正是让他弟弟做个准备的好机会,"你当然不得不待在这儿,等我通知你再离开这儿;我得对外宣称二伯父正在新福里斯特休养。我们两个都在伦敦露面是不成的,那样我们就怎么也解释不了那老头儿怎么不见的事了。"

约翰的下巴颏儿耷拉了下来。

"哦,不行!"他喊着,"你自己待在这间牢房里好了。我可不干。"

莫里斯涨红了脸。他看出无论如何要说服他的弟弟。

"请你想想,约翰,"他说,"'通蒂会'里的那笔钱。假如我成功了,我们各人就可以有五万镑存到银行里。是呀,差不多有六万镑。"

"但是假如你失败了,"约翰回答,"那怎么办呢?在那种情形之下我们银行里的账目又将怎样?"

"那由我来付一切费用好了,"莫里斯说,内心却在做斗争,"你什么也不用破费。"

"好吧,"约翰说,笑了一笑,"要是费用归你,一半利润归我,我倒不在乎在这儿待上这么一两天。"

"一两天！"莫里斯喊着，他发起脾气来了，好不容易才压制住，"哼，你就是想在赛马中赢五镑，也得比这多做点事吧！"

"也许是的，"那位"伟大的万斯"说，"那是由于天生爱好艺术之故。"

"简直荒谬绝伦！"莫里斯发作起来了，"我担着一切风险，我担负一切费用，我跟人平分利润，而你都不肯吃一点点小苦帮帮我。这是不合理的，这是不诚恳的，这甚至是不存好心的。"

"但是假定，"约翰提出异议，他哥哥的激烈的态度给了他相当深刻的印象，"假定大伯父马斯特曼根本还活着，而且还要活上十年，那么我就得烂在这儿十年不成？"

"当然不是，"莫里斯回应，声调变得温和起来，"我顶多只要你待一个月；要是那时候大伯父马斯特曼确实没有死，你就可以到国外去。"

"到国外去？"约翰急切地跟着说了一句，"那为什么不让我现在就去？对他们说约瑟夫和我到巴黎去见世面去了。"

"别胡闹。"莫里斯说。

"就算吧，可是你瞧瞧看，"约翰说，"这种房子，这种猪栏，又是这样寂寞和潮湿。你自己也说潮湿得很。"

"那只是对木匠这么说，"莫里斯分辩着，"为了压低房租。不过这是真的，你知道，我们现在住进了这幢房子，我觉得我见过比这儿更糟的。"

"那么叫我做什么好呢？"这牺牲者叫苦，"我若是要招待一个朋友怎么招待呢?"

"我亲爱的约翰,要是你认为不值得为'通蒂会'里这笔钱受这么点麻烦,就直说吧,我可以完全放弃。"

"你对这笔钱是绝对有把握的了,是不是?"约翰问。"好吧,"——他深深地叹了一口气——"把《粉红报》和所有的滑稽刊物按期寄来吧。我来挑这副担子吧。"

下午渐渐过去了,农舍里闻到的当地沼泽的气味,更觉刺鼻了;令人寒战的阴冷占据了各个房间;炉火冒着烟,一阵雨珠乘着顺风,从海峡飘来,打在窗户的玻璃上,沙沙作响。间或在沉闷的空气浓得死沉沉的时候,莫里斯就递过去一瓶威士忌,约翰起初欢迎这调剂品——可是维持不了多久。有人说这酒是汉普郡出产的最坏的一种;只有那些熟悉本郡的人才能领略出这"最坏"两字的味道来,所以到末了即使"伟大的万斯"(他不是识货的人)也对这苦汁挥手,不愿沾唇了。黄昏袭来,一支孤零零的兽脂蜡烛无力地抵抗着,使这儿染上了一种悲剧的色彩;约翰忽然停住他从指缝间吹出来的口哨——他已经被弄得只好练习练习这种技艺了——对刚才的让步深深慨叹起来。

"我不能在这儿待一个月,"他嚷着,"没有一个人待得下去。这事情是胡闹,莫里斯。就是下过巴士底监狱①的人也会起来反对这样一个地方的。"

莫里斯却很可钦佩地装出一副安之若素的样子,还提议玩玩掷钱游戏。这位外交家有什么事不肯迁就!约翰最

---

① 巴士底监狱(the Bastille):法国巴黎一座著名的要塞及监狱。始建于一三六九年,毁于一七八九年七月十四日开始的法国大革命。

喜欢玩这种游戏了,也实在是他唯一会玩的东西——他觉得其他一切游戏都太费脑筋——他玩起这个来技巧跟运气同样好。另一方面,对莫里斯自己来说,他对这玩意儿根本没有兴趣;他掷得不好,抛起来手气坏,输起来又要心痛。可是约翰的情绪已经危险,做哥哥的只得不惜任何牺牲。

到了七点钟,莫里斯已经输掉几个半克朗钱币,心痛得令人难以置信。即使有那一大笔"通蒂会"里的钱在他眼前闪烁,这也是他所能忍受的极限了;于是他说了句下次有机会再来报复的话,就提议吃点东西,喝点掺水的酒。

他们还没有用完这顿简餐,已经到了动手工作的时间。从大水桶里打出一吊桶的水,以应目前需要,然后大水桶被倒净了,滚到厨房的炉火前烤干;于是这两兄弟在不见星光的天空下,出发冒险去了。

第三章　演说家逍遥自在了

人类是否真正向往幸福,是一个疑问。没有一个月会平淡无事地过去,不是什么人家的被寄予厚望的儿子遁逃而投身到商界去,就是什么有身份的丈夫跟一个女助手私奔到得克萨斯①;或者牧师抛弃教区居民而出走,甚至法官退休也有所闻。照一个心胸宽大的人看来,那么,约瑟夫·芬斯伯里一心想要逃亡多半是不足为奇的了。他的命运(我想我们可以这样说)不能算是好的。我跟我的朋友莫里斯先生每星期有两三次从斯奈尔斯布鲁克公园同车进城,他实在是一个我所尊敬的人;但是作为一个侄儿却说不上够标准。至于约翰,他当然是一个好人;但是如果要他来单独担当起使某人跟某个家庭联结起来的任务,我想我们大多数人会投票赞成还是让他到国外旅行去的好。对于约瑟夫说来,约翰(假如他可算起着环节作用的话)并不是他唯一的环节;早就有旁的可爱的环节使这位老先生跟在布鲁姆斯伯里的家联结在一起了;而我说这句话并无丝毫意

---

① 得克萨斯(Texas):美国南部一州。

思指茱莉娅·海士尔坦（虽然他也相当欢喜她），我是指那一大沓他一生心血尽耗其中的笔记簿。他竟然得下决心，叫自己忍痛跟这些一鳞半爪的笔记分离，到世上东飘西荡，除了凭借记忆，再也无从追索，这事情本身实在有极深的悲凉况味，就是对他的两个侄儿说来，造成这局面也不是太聪明的事。

这个打算，或者至少可以说这种诱惑，已经有了好几个月的历史；现在一张付在他名下的票面金额八百镑的汇票，忽然到了他的手里，使得事情如箭在弦了。他珍藏着这张汇票，像他这样节俭的人，算是发了一笔横财了；他本来预备到了滑铁卢车站以后，混在人丛里逃走，或者（假如上述方法办不到）趁着夜色偷偷从家里溜出去，像梦幻似的融入伦敦几百万市民之中。然而老天来了一段离奇的穿插，铁路当局闯了祸，他无须久等了。

百朗亭惨案发生之后，他是最先苏醒的人中的一个，他爬起来，一看见两个侄子趴在地上，就想到机会来了，于是拔腿就走。一个七十多岁的人，方才遭遇火车失事，又要背着一身累赘的全套法拉第·邦德爵士的制服，是不大可能跑得很远的，可是树林近在咫尺，给了这逃亡者至少一个暂时的藏身的地方。这位老先生于是以一种异乎寻常的敏捷步子蹦到这里来，可是他很有点喘不过气来，又曾受到了相当厉害的震动，因此就近在一个树丛里躺下来，不久就陷入沉睡之中了。那时候如果有一个局外人在旁边看着，那命运的安排倒是非常有趣的：莫里斯和约翰正在沙地上掘坑预备把一个素昧平生的人的尸体藏起来的时候,他们的二伯父却正在树林里更深入几百码的地方甜睡得梦都不做,这情况自然好玩得很。

他是被近边大路上传来的热闹的喇叭声闹醒的,大路上正有一辆游览车载着一些迟归的游客赶过去。喇叭声使这老人兴奋起来,指使他的脚奔到那儿去,一转眼他已经站在大路上,眼睛在帽檐下东张西望,不知该怎么办了。远处响起了不疾不徐的车轮声,接着可以看见一辆货车赶了过来,车上载满了包裹,赶车的看来是一个好性情的人,他坐在双人车座上,一块木板上题着这样的字:"我江德勒,运送员。"在这位芬斯伯里先生的单调得令人耻笑的头脑里,还有那么一点儿诗意,并且仍然能发生作用;当他是个四十岁的轻浮的青年的时候,这点诗意曾使他远走到小亚细亚去,现在,在他恢复自由的最初几小时里,又使他想到搭了那位江德勒先生的马车,继续逃亡。这该是不花什么钱的;说得准确一点,可能是不费分文的,这点,加上戴了多少年的无指手套,穿了多少年的合乎卫生的法兰绒服装,现在想到可以见见天日了,他的心简直飞了出来。

江德勒先生看见这样一位老先生,穿着这样奇怪的服装,在这样偏僻的路边请求搭车,或许有一点诧异,然而他是一个好性情的人,乐于与人方便,因此就把这个陌生的人带上了车;对于礼貌,他有他的一套看法,因此什么话也没有问。大家静静的,在江德勒先生看来,实在够好了;但是,几乎车轮刚刚开始向前转动,他就发觉自己被困在一种片面的谈话之中。

"我晓得了,"芬斯伯里先生打开了话匣子,"看见这车子上混杂地堆着大包小盒,每样东西上面都有着不同的标签,又看见你赶着的是佛兰德斯的好母马①,我就晓得了你的职业,你是那伟大的英国运输系统里的一个运送员,那系统虽然有着它的种种缺点,仍不失为我国足以自豪的事业。"

"是的,先生,"江德勒先生含糊地回答,因为他实在不知道该说什么好,"这些邮包真叫我们运送员受累。"

"我这个人是不存偏见的,"约瑟夫·芬斯伯里继续说,"年轻时候我走了好些地方。不论是多么小、多么鲜为人知的事情我都要了解的。在海上,我学了航海术,学会了打海员们打的复杂的绳结,懂得了那些专门术语。在那不勒斯②,我研究做通心面的艺术;在尼斯③,则探求做蜜饯水果的原理。我在去看一出歌剧以前,从来都是先买了这歌剧的剧本,把主要的曲子用一只手指在钢琴上试弹,叫自己熟悉熟悉。"

"你一定见识很广,先生,"运送员说,一边轻轻鞭着马,"我真羡慕你。"

"你可知道这个'鞭'字在《圣经·旧约》里出现过几次?"那位老先生往下说,"一百(要是我记得不错的话)四十七次。"

"是真的吗,先生?"江德勒先生说,"我怎么也不会想

---

① 佛兰德斯的好母马,指佛兰德斯地区所产的母马。佛兰德斯原为欧洲古国,范围包括今荷兰南部、法国北部及比利时全境。
② 那不勒斯(Naples):意大利靠地中海的一个海港。
③ 尼斯(Nice):法国靠地中海的一个海港。

到这个。"

"《圣经》有三百五十万零一千二百四十九个字母。其中的诗歌我想总在一万八千首以上。《圣经》的版本很多;首先把它介绍到英国来的,是威克里夫①,那大约在一三〇〇年。所谓《分段圣经》,是一种著名的版本,之所以有这名称,是因为那是分段的。《布利却司圣经》也是一种著名的版本,之所以得此名称,或许是因为由布利却司刊印,不然就是因为刊印的地方叫布利却司。"

运送员虚应故事地说他觉得那当然不错,就把注意力转移到更合脾胃的事情上来——这时要从一辆载着稻草的货车旁经过;这事情不大容易,因为路窄,两旁又都有着沟渠。

"我看出来了,"车子安然地经过那辆货车之后,芬斯伯里先生开口说,"你用一只手抓住细绳,你应当用两只手。"

"啊,这我倒要听听高见了!"运送员鄙夷地大声说,"什么原因呢?"

"你明白不了,"芬斯伯里先生继续说,"我对你说的是一种有科学根据的事,基于杠杆的理论,属于机械学的范围。外间有几种一先令一本的入门小书很有趣,我相信干你们这行的一定会喜欢看看。可是我想你大概没有学会一种观察事物的艺术吧;至少在现在我们已经同车了好些

---

① 威克里夫(John Wycliff,一三二八?——三八四):英国宗教改革家,约在一三八二年(原文为一三〇〇年,疑为作者笔误)首先完成《圣经》英文全译本。

时候，而你还是连一桩事情也没有对我说过。这可犯了严重错误了，我的好先生。譬如说，我不知道你可曾观察到（你刚才经过那个赶稻草车的人的时候），你从左边走了？"

"我当然知道啦，"运送员叫起来，他现在已经进入敌对状态，"要是我不从左边走，他就可以请我吃官司。"

"不过，要是在法国，"老先生继续说，"我相信还有美国，你就一定会走右边了。"

"我一定不会，"江德勒先生着恼地嚷着，"我一定会走左边。"

"我观察到，"芬斯伯里先生还是只顾往下说，不理睬别人的话，"你只用线把马具绽开的地方缝好。我一向反对英国的穷人这样粗疏懒散。有一次我对一批有鉴赏力的听众宣读我的一篇论文——"

"我并没有用线缝，"运送员绷着脸说，"我用的是细绳子。"

"我一向反对，"老先生还在往下说，"我们国家里下层社会中的人，无论在私生活和家庭生活中，无论在劳动作业中，总是不会打算，不懂节约，奢侈浪费。及时的针砭——"

"谁是什么下层社会？"运送员大声斥责，"你自己才是什么下层社会！要是我刚才把你当作一个像模像样的贵族，我真不会让你搭车哩。"

这两句话是用毫不掩饰的厌恶口气说出来的；这一对显然意气不相投，即使像芬斯伯里先生这样一个无可救药的碎嘴子，再想谈下去也是不可能的了。他气呼呼地把步兵便帽的帽檐往下一拉，遮在眼睛上面，然后从最里边的口袋里掏出一本笔记簿和一支蓝铅笔，不久就全神贯注在计算题上了。

运送员这方面开始如释重负地吹起口哨来，如果他（偶然）对同车朋友瞧一眼的话，那是怀着亦喜亦惧的心理——喜的是他已经慑服了这个多话的怪物，惧的是生怕（由于什么意外）这怪物又开起口来。现在一阵骤雨落了下来，赶上了他们而又赶到前头去，即使在这当儿，两人仍旧默不作声地忍受着；他们也是这样默不作声地一直驶到南安普敦。

已是黄昏时分，商店里的灯光透过窗子照到这个古老的海港的街道上，住宅里也上灯吃晚饭了；芬斯伯里先生心里宽松舒畅，开始想起夜晚住宿的问题。他把簿子放开，清了清喉咙，怯生生地看看江德勒先生。

"你能客气一点，"他说，"给我介绍一家旅馆吗？"

江德勒沉思了一阵。

"嗯，"他终于说，"屈勒贡维尔·阿姆士不知怎么样。"

"屈勒贡维尔·阿姆士一定好得很，"老先生应声说，"要是那是一家清洁、便宜、住客都很客气的旅馆的话。"

"我并不怎么为你着想，"江德勒先生一边想一边回话，"我想到的是开那家旅馆的我的朋友瓦特；你不知道，去年我困难的时候，这个朋友帮了我的忙。我在想，这事情做得应该不应该呢，把你这样一个老头儿弄去麻烦他，你那套常识可能送掉他的命。对于我那位朋友说来，究竟是应该不应该呢？"江德勒先生以恳切的口气问着。

"听我说，"老先生冒火了，大声嚷着，"你不要钱，把我带到这儿，我很感谢；可是你并没有权利就这样随便糟蹋我。这一先令是酬谢你的；要是你不预备把我送到屈勒贡维尔·阿姆士下车，我可以自己去找。"

江德勒先生吃了一惊，有一点不知所措；一面含糊地说了些道歉的话，一面推辞了那一先令，一声不响地赶着马车，穿过几条错综曲折的小街陋巷，最后在一家灯火辉煌的旅馆门前停了车，高声呼喊："瓦特先生。"

"是你吗，詹姆？"一个充满热诚的声音从马房前的院子里传出来。"进来烤烤火呀。"

"我只在这儿停一停，"江德勒先生说明，"让一位要吃要住的老头儿下车。注意，我劝你要当心他，他可比禁酒会的宣传员还要叫人吃不消。"

芬斯伯里先生下车很费了一番劲，因为长途乘车使他筋肉失去了灵活性，火车出轨又叫他很受震动。友善的瓦特先生不顾运送员的介绍词不很中听，却以最周到的礼貌招待这位老先生，把他领到后客厅，那儿壁炉里正生着火，暖烘烘的。一会儿这房间就摆好了一张桌子，他又被请到桌旁坐下来，去对付一盆炖鸡——这盆鸡，之前曾经上过桌子，所以稍差一点——还有从酒桶里盛出来的一大锡镴杯麦酒。

吃完晚饭，他站起来的时候，就像是一个恢复了精神的巨人了；他移坐到一张靠近炉火的椅子上，为着寻求大发宏论的愉快，开始对别的住客从旁打量起来。在场的约有十二个人，都是男人，而且（约瑟夫很高兴地看出）都是手艺人。他已经常常感到应该感谢那些人有好胃口,愿意听东拉西扯和回环反复的言论,这特别是机匠们所喜欢的事。不过,即使要一群手艺人来做听众,也得下一番功夫才行,而对于这必修的艺术,没有谁比约瑟夫·芬斯伯里更为精通了。他把眼镜架在鼻梁上,从口袋里掏出一叠纸,摊在面前的桌子上。他一会儿把纸捏作一团,一会儿把纸展开抹抹平;一会儿一页页地看,对纸上的话显然很得意;一会儿皱着眉毛,敲敲铅笔,好像深思熟虑地推敲某一字句。他偷偷地向房间里四下望了一转,晓得自己的装腔作势已经获得成效;所有的眼睛都转到这位表演家的身上来了,嘴都张大着,烟斗都停在半中间;这些小鸟都入其彀中了。就在这时候,瓦特先生走进屋来,又给了他一个好机会。

"据我的观察,"他面对这位掌柜的说,一面又带着一种怂恿的神色向四周瞥了一眼,把一房间的人都划入他的听众范围之内,"据我的观察,这儿有几位先生,正在以好奇的眼光看着我;当然啰,在旅馆的一间公用客厅里,是不大看见有谁这样埋头研究文学和科学方面的事情的。这儿就是我今天上午得出的一些关于我国和别国生活费用的数字——也不用我说了,这是工人大众极感兴趣的一个话题。我做出一个每年收入八十、一百六十、二百和二百四十镑的生活费用比较表。我得承认收入八十镑的多少使我感到棘手,其他几项也不像我所希望的那样准确;因为外国各国的洗衣价格大有涨落,各种焦炭、煤块和柴的价钱也变动得厉害。我现在把研究的结果念出来,如果我由于疏忽或者欠缺知识,生出了不论多么小的错误,都希望你们毫不犹豫地指出来。先生们,我就从每年收入八十镑开始啦。"

于是这位老先生怀着比他对待野蛮的兽类还要少的怜悯心,公布了他全部引人入睡的统计数字。他不时把一种收入列出十种数字,把拟想中的人先后放在伦敦、巴黎、巴格达①、斯匹次卑尔根②、巴士拉③、赫尔戈兰④、锡利群岛⑤、布莱顿、辛辛那提⑥和下诺夫哥罗德⑦,在各个地区都给以适合当地情况的给养,这就难怪他的听众事后回想,认为那是他们生平所度过的最令人厌倦的一个夜晚。

在离芬斯伯里先生讲到以一百六十镑的收入生活在下诺夫哥罗德还差着一大段之前,听众已经减少,只剩几个豪饮的老年人和那个忍气吞声的瓦特陪伴他。络绎不绝地有顾客从各处来,但是他们一经受到招待,就匆匆忙忙地喝了酒,以最快的速度离开这儿,去找下一家旅馆。

等到那个一年收入二百镑的青年在锡利群岛混日子的时候,只有瓦特先生一个人陪着这位经济学家了;假想的青年还没有在布莱顿开始生活,这最后一个追随者也退出了

---

① 巴格达(Bagdad):伊拉克首都。
② 斯匹次卑尔根(Spitzbergen):群岛,濒北冰洋,属挪威。
③ 巴士拉(Bassorah,即 Basrah):伊拉克的一个海港,滨波斯湾。
④ 赫尔戈兰(Heligoland):靠近德国北海的海岛。
⑤ 锡利群岛(Scilly Islands):英国西南角的海岛。
⑥ 辛辛那提(Cincinnati):美国俄亥俄州西南部的一座城市。
⑦ 下诺夫哥罗德(Nijni-Novgorod):苏联时期名高尔基城,为俄罗斯一座大城,在莫斯科之东,位于伏尔加河畔。

这场东追西逐的游戏。

芬斯伯里先生经过白天这种种辛劳之后,睡得很好。他起身很迟,吃了一顿丰盛的早餐,吩咐开账。这时候,他发现了一桩许多人在以前和以后也发现的事:要账单和付账是凑合不到一块儿的两桩事情。各项费用都是低廉的,而且(这结果也少见)总数也小;然而,虽经最最仔细地搜遍每一只口袋,这老先生全部的流动资金总共似乎只有一先令九便士半。他请见瓦特先生。

"这是一张票面金额八百镑的汇到伦敦的汇票,"芬斯伯里先生在那位有身价的人来到的时候这样说,"除非你愿意自己贴现,否则怕得再过一两天才能去兑到现款。"

瓦特先生对这张汇票看了看,又翻过来,折了一个角。"还得过一两天?"他重复老先生的话,"你身边没有现钱?"

"只有一些零钱。"约瑟夫回答,"算不上什么的。"

"那你可以把钱寄来,我很乐于信任你。"

"不瞒你说,"老先生回答,"我很想待下去,我正等钱用。"

"假如借给你十先令可以够你需要的话,我可以效力。"瓦特急切地回答。

"不,我想我还是待下去,"老先生说,"并且请你把这张汇票贴现吧。"

"你决不能在我这儿待下去,"瓦特先生大声说,"你在屈勒贡维尔·阿姆士占一张床睡,是最后一次了。"

"我一定要待下去,"芬斯伯里先生怒气冲冲地回答,

"我要根据国会的法案待下去,谅你不敢把我赶走。"

"那么你付账啊。"瓦特先生说。

"把这个拿去。"老先生叫着,把汇票向他一扔。

"这不是法定货币,"瓦特先生回答,"你必须马上离开我这屋子。"

"你不知道我是多么瞧不起你,瓦特先生。"老先生说,在此情况下他束手无策了。"不过通过某一桩事情,我要让你知道我的一些厉害:我拒绝付账。"

"我不在乎你这笔账款,"瓦特先生回答,"我所要的是不要看见你。"

"这个要求行得通!"老先生一面说一面拿起步兵便帽往头上扣。"或许你已经蛮横过分,"他又说,"不愿意告诉我下一班到伦敦的火车几点钟开?"

"离开车时间还有三刻钟,"旅馆主人赶快回话,"你尽可以赶得上。"

约瑟夫的处境是相当尴尬的。一方面,最好避免乘火车这条捷径,因为他的两个侄儿可能守候在那儿把他重新抓走;另一方面,他又十分希望,甚至非常必要,把那张汇票在没有止付以前贴现。因此他决定就乘下一班火车到伦敦;那么只剩下一个问题需要考虑:火车票的钱怎么办。

约瑟夫的指甲缝里从来不干净,他吃饭的时候又差不多吃什么都用刀子送。你如果说他具有作为一个绅士的生活习惯,那我就不免怀疑;然而他却有着一种比生活习惯好的东西,那是一种并非造作的尊贵的气派。这是因为他在小亚细亚待过吗?这是因为顾客们有时候提到的芬斯伯里血统的传统特性吗?至少,当他去见了车站站长的时候,他的额手礼是纯粹东方式的,好像棕榈树已在这小小的办公室里长满了,同时还有阿拉伯的热风,或者夜莺——不过我还是把这个让给对于东方更熟悉的人去想象吧。此外,他的衣着对他也十分有利;那套法拉第爵士的制服,不管穿了多么不舒服,多么惹人注目,至少一个骗子穿了这套服装要想蒙混得过是不行的;一只贵重的表,一张票面金额八百镑的汇票,拿出来展览了一下,也把他仪表所发挥的初步作用推进至完全成功。一刻钟之后,火车开进了站,芬斯伯里先生就被介绍给一个管车人而被安置在一节头等车的车厢中,站长笑容可掬地承担了一切责任。

这位老先生坐着等车开动,这时候他眼见一桩事,这桩事意想不到地跟他一家的命运有关。约有十二个脚夫抬了一只大如巨怪的货箱,摇摇晃晃地沿着月台走来,最后搬上了行李车,一大群人看得津津有味。历史学家常常乐于做的事是提请人们注意冥冥之中的主宰的安排和(假如这样说可以不失恭敬的话)诡计。当约瑟夫被火车带着离开南安普敦东车站直向伦敦奔去的时候,在行李车里,这个故事的蛋(譬如这样说)正下在那儿等待孵化。那只庞大的货箱指明"存滑铁卢待领",领取人是"威廉·登特·皮特曼";紧挨着货箱的,是一只很好的大桶子,挤在行李车的角落里,签条上写着:"布鲁姆斯伯里,约翰街十六号,M.芬斯伯里收。运费付讫。"

这样并置在一起,这列火车的"火药"是预备好了,现在只少一个闲着没事做的人来把它点着了。

第四章　行李车里的司法官

温彻斯特城有几样出名的东西：一座大教堂、一位主教——只是他在几年前骑马不幸摔死了——一所公立学校、相当多的军队里各种各样的队伍和伦敦—西南铁路线上慢吞吞地开着的火车。这些和许多类似的联想无疑会纷纷涌上约瑟夫·芬斯伯里的心头；但他的灵魂这时候已飞出了火车的车厢，飞到一个天堂里，那儿有挤满了人的演讲厅和讲不完的演讲。他的躯体，在这期间，正蜷伏在椅垫中；步兵便帽撒娇般地歪戴在脑后，就像躺着等保姆来的小孩儿一样，可怜的老脸上表情恬静，一只手臂下夹着的《劳埃德每周新闻》贴在胸口。

就在他这样魂游天外的时候，有两位旅行者进来又出去了。这两个人本来差一步就赶不上这列火车的。他们一前一后像马车的纵列的马，以最快最快的速度往前直奔，到了车票间里来一阵简直好像抢劫一般的行动，再一口气狂奔，奔到月台上时正值机车喷着鼻息开动了。只有最后一节车厢他们还能赶得上。他们跳了上来，那领头的年岁较大的一个双脚刚刚落地，就看见了芬斯伯里先生。

"天呀！"他叫着，"约瑟夫叔叔！这绝对不行。"

他退了出去，差一点把同伴撞倒，他重新带上车厢门，让老长辈在里边睡觉。

一转眼，他们已经蹦到了行李车里。

"你的约瑟夫叔叔又怎么样呢？"那个年岁较轻的旅行者问，一面抹着前额。"他反对人家抽烟吗？"

"我倒说不上他怎么样。"对方回答，"我可以告诉你，我的约瑟夫叔叔绝不是一个难说话的人！他是很可敬的老绅士；有兴趣于皮革事业；曾经到过小亚细亚；没有家，没有财产——可是一张嘴，我亲爱的威克姆，比蛇的牙齿还厉害。"

"是个喜欢争吵的老人吧？"威克姆发问。

"一点也不是，"对方叫道，"只是个具有一种令人非常讨厌的天才的人。要是在荒岛上，我敢说那使人相当愉快，可是在乘着火车赶路的时候，这可受不了。你不得不听他大谈通蒂，就是首创'通蒂氏养老金法'的那个呆子。他讲起'通蒂'来，简直不可思议。"

"好家伙！"威克姆嚷着说，"这么说，你就是那些参加'通蒂会'的芬斯伯里会员之一了。我从来没有想到这个。"

"啊！"对方说，"你知道不知道车厢里那个老家伙对我说来值十万镑？他在那儿睡着了，除了你又没有旁人在！可是我饶了他，因为在政治上我是一个保守党党员。"

威克姆先生在行李车里很有怡然自得之感，他像只风度翩翩的蝴蝶，飞来飞去。

"天呀!"他叫起来,"这儿有件东西是给你的!'伦敦,布鲁姆斯伯里,约翰街十六号,M.芬斯伯里收。''M'代表迈克尔,你这滑头;你弄了两个公馆,是不是?"

"哦!那是莫里斯①,"迈克尔在行李车的另一头回答,他在那边把行李包当作一个舒服的座位,"他是我的堂弟。我倒喜欢他,因为他怕我。他是布鲁姆斯伯里的装饰品之一,他收藏了一些东西——鸟蛋啦,或者什么自认为稀奇的玩意儿。我相信这件东西与我的当事人毫不相干!"

"用这些地址标签来个捉迷藏该是多么好玩!"威克姆先生咯咯笑着。"真是,这儿就有一只钉锤!我们正可以像什么似的,把所有这些东西,瞎碰瞎撞地到处乱送!"

这时候,说话的声音惊动了警卫员,他开了他的小房间的门。

"你们最好到这儿来吧,两位先生。"听了他们讲的话之后,他说。

"你来不来,威克姆?"迈克尔问。

"我才不来哩——我愿意乘行李车旅行。"青年人回答。

于是这通路的门关上了;在以后的一段行程里,威克姆先生在这边独自一个人玩他的游戏,而在那边,迈克尔和警卫员关上门闲谈。

"这儿我可以给你找一间车厢,先生,"当火车快要进毕晓普斯多克城车站,渐渐慢下来的时候,这警卫员讲着,"你最好从我这儿的门里走出去,我再把你的朋友带来。"

---

① 莫里斯原文为 Morris,迈克尔原文为 Michael,两词头一个字母都是 M。

威克姆先生,我们刚才把他留在行李车里(精明的读者们已经猜中),让他着手叫标签"捉迷藏"。说起这位先生,他是位很有钱的年轻绅士,外表讨人喜欢,长了一脸的雀斑,有着一颗十分空虚的头脑。没有几个月以前,他竟自招惹了瓦拉几亚①总督家族的一个人向他讹诈,总督一家出于政治上的原因避居到欢乐的巴黎。他一个朋友(他曾对这朋友叹了苦情)认得迈克尔,就把他介绍给这位律师,律师一经掌握了事实,立即采取攻势,向瓦拉几亚队伍侧面袭击,三天之内,就称心满意地瞧着敌人溃败下来,向多瑙河方向奔逃。我们不必去跟踪他们这次退兵,因为这回事已承警察义不容辞地一口答应下来了。威克姆先生这样摆脱了他老是称为"保加利亚的祸事"之后,回到伦敦,心里对他的救主怀着无限的、发窘的感恩和崇拜的感情。这些情感并没有获得同类的或是同等程度的反应。实际上,迈克尔把自己跟这新当事人的友谊看得有点失身份,直到人家三邀四请,才到了温彻斯特的威克姆庄园;他毕竟是去了,而现在正从那儿回来。有一位贤明的思想家(可能是 J. F. 史密斯②)曾经说过,即使最卑贱的工具,上天也不鄙弃而不用;所以现在最愚钝的人也看得明明白白,威克姆先生和瓦拉几亚总督正是命运之神手中的活生生的工具。

---

① 瓦拉几亚(Wallachian):昔为一公国,自一八六一年起为罗马尼亚的一部。
② J. F. 史密斯(Joseph Fielding Smith,一八三八——一九一八):美国摩门教首领。

这青年绅士满心想要在迈克尔的眼前炫耀一番,表现自己是个有别出心裁的幽默和智能的人(他在本乡是一个司法官——多半是挂一个名的),一到他独自一个人在行李车里的时候,他就以改革家的热忱摆弄了那些标签;因之,当他在毕晓普斯多克城和这位律师重聚的时候,他脸上因为这番忙碌而发红,他那已经熄灭了的雪茄,差不多被他咬成了两段。

"真是,这真是好玩啊!"他叫着说。"我简直要把英国国内每一个人的东西都送错地方啦。你的堂弟们有了一个像屋子那么大的货箱啦。这整个事儿已经给我弄得一塌糊涂,芬斯伯里,如果这事传了出去,我怕我们准得受私刑。"

跟威克姆先生认真是没有用的。"小心点吧,"迈克尔说,"我对于你那种闹不完的事已经厌烦了;我的名誉已在受影响了。"

"你的名誉不用等到跟我搞完的时候就会丢光的,"他的同伴嬉皮笑脸地回答,"将来一并总算好了,我的朋友。'名誉完全损失,六先令八便士。'但是,"威克姆先生认真起来了,"我会因为这个小玩笑被委员会停职吗?我知道这是个小职司,但是我倒喜欢做一个司法官。从你职业上的角度来看,你想有没有什么危险?"

"这有什么分别?"迈克尔回答,"他们迟早总要把你撵出去。你似乎不像在做一个好的司法官。"

"我只想做一名律师,"他的同伴反驳道,"而不是一个可怜的倒霉的乡下绅士。我们两人来一个那种通蒂氏的办法怎么样？我每年付五百镑，你来保我除了疾病和结婚以外的一切灾难。"

"照我看来，"这律师若有所思地笑着说，一边点上一支雪茄，"照我看来，你实在是咱们这世界里一个该死的讨人厌的东西。"

"你真这么想吗，芬斯伯里？"这司法官跟着问，一边往后靠在椅垫上，把那句话当作赞美而喜不自胜。"是的，我想我是一个讨人厌的东西。可是，你得知道，在这个国家里也有我的地位的。好朋友，不要忘了这个。"

第五章　吉迪恩·福西斯先生和庞大的箱子

前面说过，茱莉娅在间或到伯恩茅斯去的时候，在那儿结识了几个朋友；不错，她向来只能在约翰街的重门叠户把俘虏们又关起来之前见着他们几眼，但是这几眼有时候就已令人不胜欣喜，同时随之而来的怅惘之感，也有着希望来冲淡它。一年前，她这样认识的朋友之中有一位是年轻的出庭律师①，名字叫作吉迪恩·福西斯。

就在司法官把标签乱搞一通的多事之日，在下午三点钟左右，福西斯先生带着几分抑郁烦闷的心情，信步走到了约翰街的转角上来；约莫在这时候，海士尔坦小姐也被一阵急促的、震天价响的敲门声叫到了第十六号住宅的门口。

吉迪恩·福西斯先生是个相当快乐的青年；要是他能够钱多一点、舅舅的干预少一点的话，那就会更快乐一些了。他一年的全部收入只有一百二十镑；不过舅舅爱德

---

① 出庭律师（barrister）：英国律师分出庭律师和撰状律师（solicitor）两种。凡有法律事件先交撰状律师研究办理。如向法庭起诉或辩诉，则由撰状律师推选出庭律师办理。

华·休·布洛姆菲尔德先生在这之外,还给他一笔很可观的零花钱和很多的劝告,可惜这种劝告的口气叫人听来,就是在一艘海盗船上,都可能觉得有点过火。布洛姆菲尔德先生在格莱斯顿①先生的时代里实在是个很特殊的人物;我们(在没有公认的适当名称的情况下)姑且称之为一个"乡绅激进派"吧。有了年纪,可是缺乏经验,因此他给政界里"激进派"这方面,带来了一种宴席过后乱嚷乱叫地发一通议论的激情,这种激情我们比较惯于把它跟凶猛却又老迈的保守党一派人联系起来。事实上,他不但有与布莱德劳先生②相同的主张,他还有那已经绝种的动物——乡绅——的脾气和爱好。他爱看拳斗,他带着一根惊人的橡木大手杖,他又是一个虔诚的国教信徒,如果遇到一个本该为国教辩护而未辩护的人,再遇到一个懒得参加国教圣餐礼的人,究竟谁更能激恼他,使他的脾气像火山一样爆发,那就很不容易猜测了。他还有些所向披靡的口头语,家里上上下下正是没有一个不怕的;当他不能过分强调某种措施是"不合国情"的时候,他可以(同样有效地)斥之为"不合实际"。吉迪恩常常受到这个比较轻的贬黜的处分。他对于研究法律的看法就曾被呵斥作"不合实际";那次谒见的时候,只听得喊声震天,橡木手杖擂地作响,仿佛在把一句一句话加上标点,吉迪恩得到训

---

① 格莱斯顿(William Ewart Gladstone,一八〇九——一八九八):英国政治家,曾数次出任首相。
② 布莱德劳(Charles Bradlaugh,一八三三——一八九一):英国激进派政治家。

示，如果不能再做努力，接一两件案子办办，那就不用想再拿到他舅舅的钱。

难怪吉迪恩闷闷不乐了。他丝毫不想改变他现在的习惯；但是可不能坚持己见了，因为如果布洛姆菲尔德先生真的取消零花钱，那会使他在习惯上起一种更激进的革命。他没有一点儿意思去熟研法律；他对这事已经划算过，觉着似乎得不偿失；不过在这一点上，他同样准备让步。老实说，他预备尽最大可能去迎合他这位"乡绅激进派"的舅舅的意见。然而这打算里有一部分似乎超出他的心力范围。怎样去弄到一件案子呢？这是一个问题。另外还有一个问题，而且更伤脑筋——就算他弄到一件，他能证明自己办得比别人更好吗？

忽然他发觉一群人挡住了他的去路。一辆光华四射的运货车后身对着人行道停着；可以看见从敞开的车尾露出了那只米德尔塞克斯郡①里最大的货箱的一端，一半架在地上，一半由几个肌肉闪光的运动家撑着；在那屋子的台阶上，赶车的彪形大汉和一个苗条的年轻姑娘像站在戏台上一般，正在争论着。

"这不是寄给我们的，"姑娘说，"我求求你把它带回去吧；就算你们有办法把它从货车上搬下来吧，这东西可弄不进这屋子里来啊。"

"那么，我把它搁在人行道上，M. 芬斯伯里可以跟教区会②商量商量办法，随便他怎么办。"运货人说。

---

① 米德尔塞克斯郡（Middlesex）：英国南部旧郡，滨泰晤士河。
② 教区会（Vestry）：英国教区纳税人的团体。

"可是我不是 M. 芬斯伯里呀。"姑娘正色相告。

"我管你是谁。"运货人说。

"请让我来帮你吧，海士尔坦小姐。"吉迪恩说着伸出手来。

茱莉娅惊喜地叫了一声。"哦，福西斯先生，"她喊道，"我见着你真开心；这东西送到这儿来，一定是送错了，却非要我们把这可怕的东西弄到屋子里来不可。这人说我们得把门拆了，或是把两扇窗户打通成一扇，要不然就会因为将东西放在人行道上，给教区会或关税局罚款，等等。"

这时候，那些人已经把箱子顺利地从运货车上卸了下来，他们砰的一声，将它扔在人行道上，然后斜倚着箱子站在那儿，或是眼睁睁地对着十六号的门呆看，显然带着躯体上的困顿和精神上的困惑。这整条街的窗口，好像被使了幻术似的，一下子塞满了大感兴趣和看得津津有味的观众。

吉迪恩尽量摆出一副深思的、有科学头脑的样子，用手杖测量门口，茱莉娅就把他所观测到的事项记录在一本绘画簿上。然后他再量那只箱子，又把这数字比较了一下，发现门口的宽度恰好能把它运进来。进一步，他脱掉了外衣和背心，帮着那些运货人拆下门上的铰链。最后，所有在旁看热闹的人都给拉来帮忙，这只货箱，由十五对摇摇晃晃的大腿支撑着，升上了石阶——擦着门道，吱嘎吱嘎地大声响着，挤了进来——终于，来了一下可怕的震动，这箱子就给摔在穿堂间的尽头，那穿堂间差不多全给堵住了。灰尘落定之后，功成业就的工人们不禁相视而笑。他们诚然砸碎了一座阿波罗神的半身雕像,并且把墙壁也犁上几道深槽,可是至少街上已经没有了那个伦敦城里的怪现象了。

"嘿,先生,"运货员说,"我从没干过这么一桩活。"

吉迪恩对这感想很有力地表示同意——塞了两个金镑到这人手里。

"就给三个吧,先生,我打算做个东道,请请这儿的全体人员!"这个人大声说;交涉这样办妥之后,那群自告奋勇的脚夫,全部蜂拥到运货车里,车子就驶向最近的一爿可靠的酒店去了。等他们走了,吉迪恩把门关上,转向苿莉娅;他们的目光相遇了;一阵不可抑制的喜悦袭上两人的心头,这幢房子里充满了他们的欢笑声。然后,苿莉娅的好奇心活动起来了,她走过去察看那只箱子,特别注意那标签。

"这事情真是再奇怪也没有了,"她说,又大笑着,"这的确是莫里斯的笔迹,而就在今天早上我收到他一封信,说有一只桶子要送来。你看待会儿还有一只桶子送来吗,福西斯先生?"

"雕像,当心,易碎,"吉迪恩念着箱子上用油漆写的警告的话,"那么这东西他一句也没有跟你提过吗?"

"没有。"苿莉娅回答。"哦,福西斯先生,你说我们可以偷看它一下吗?"

"当然可以,"吉迪恩说,"请给我一个锤子。"

"到下面来,我带你去拿,"苿莉娅说,"那架子太高,我够不到。"于是她开了通往厨房的楼梯的门,叫吉迪恩跟她走。他们找到了一个锤子和一把凿子,但是吉迪恩看不见一个用人的影子,很感诧异。他还发现了海士尔坦小姐的脚和脚踝长得小巧可爱,这个发现使他窘得很,于是很高兴能立即着手开那只货箱。

他竭力一心一意地工作着,他敲得像一个铁匠那样准确。茱莉娅这时静静地站在他身边,她所注意的与其说是这工作,不如说是这位工匠。他是一个美貌的男子,她跟自己说,她从来没有见过这样美的胳膊。突然间,好像他已经偷听到这些思想,他转过脸来朝着她笑。她也笑了,脸也红了;这双重变化和她配合得这样美好,吉迪恩都忘了把眼睛移开,他用力抡着锤子,狠命一下,却敲中了自己的指关节。他以一种很可钦佩的镇静态度压住一声诅咒,换用了一句没有毛病的评语:"这笨手!"然而这阵疼痛猛得很,他的神经都在震动,在做了一次半途而废的尝试之后,他知道不得不中止工作。

茱莉娅马上到食器室①去了,她端来了一盆水,拿着一块海绵,开始替他洗那只受伤的手。

"我非常抱歉,"吉迪恩甚感内疚,"我要是还懂得一点规矩的话,我应该先开了箱子,然后再把手砸伤。现在觉着好多啦,"他加上这句,"我不骗你,真是好多啦。"

"那么现在我想你是好多了,可以指挥工作了,"她说,"跟我讲要做些什么,我来做你的工匠。"

"一位非常美丽的工匠。"吉迪恩有点得意忘形地说。

---

① 食器室(pantry):储藏食物及刀叉盆碟等餐具的房间。

她掉过头来朝他看,似乎带点愠怒的神情;这唐突的青年私幸自己还能使她的视线转移到那只货箱上。大部分的工作已经做完;不久茱莉娅打穿了最后的障碍物,揭露出来一层稻草。他们立即并排跪着工作,好像两个弄干草的;更深一层,他们就得到了收获,瞥见一个白色的光滑的东西;进一步就明白无疑地出现了一条大理石的腿。

"他可真像个体育家呀。"茱莉娅说。

"我从没见过这种东西,"吉迪恩回答,"他的肌肉像一便士的面包卷那样鼓了出来。"

另一条腿也很快露了出来,然后好像还有第三条。不过,结果那是一根有结节的棍棒,支在一块台脚上。

"这是一座赫拉克勒斯①雕像,"吉迪恩喊着,"单看那腿肚子,我也可以猜到是他。我对于雕像可算相当偏爱,然而要说是赫拉克勒斯,那警察应当干涉的。我得说,"他接着说,一面鄙夷地对那硕大的大腿瞧了一眼,"这要算全欧洲最大最丑的了。它究竟为了什么跑到这儿来呢?"

"我想就没有第二个人愿意要他这个礼物,"茱莉娅说,"单从这点看,我觉得我们倒不如没有这怪物的好。"

"哦,别这么说,"吉迪恩表示异议,"这是我生平最有趣的经历之一哩。"

"我相信你不会忘得太快,"茱莉娅说,"你的手会提醒你的。"

"好了,我想我得走了。"吉迪恩说,可不是出于本心。

---

① 赫拉克勒斯(Hercules):希腊神话中的大力士。

"别走,"茱莉娅恳求着,"干吗要走?待着跟我吃茶吧。"

"我要是知道你真愿意我多待一会儿的话,"吉迪恩看着他的帽子说,"那当然是再高兴也没有啰。"

"你把我看作一个多么傻的人了吧!"这姑娘说,"是啊,我当然欢迎你;而且我还想要些蛋糕当点心,又没人可差。这是开门的钥匙。"

吉迪恩轻快地戴上帽子,向海士尔坦小姐瞟了一眼,又向赫拉克勒斯的两条腿瞟了一眼,开了门去办他的差事去了。

他带了一大纸袋极其精致的、令人馋涎欲滴的蛋糕和水果馅饼回来,看见茱莉娅正在穿堂间里铺摆一张小茶桌。

"那些房间里都搞得乱七八糟,"她嚷着,"所以我想倒不如就待在我们自己的穿堂间里,在我们自己的安乐窝中的雕像之下,这要更惬意、更舒服些呢。"

"这样好得多。"吉迪恩开心地叫着。

"哦,多么可爱的奶油水果馅饼啊!"茱莉娅说着打开了纸袋,"还有这最可爱的小樱桃饼,樱桃馅儿多得满出来,混到奶油里去了!"

"是呀,"吉迪恩遮掩着惊慌的神色说,"我知道它们和在一起和得很好,铺子里的那个女人刚才跟我这么说的。"

"现在呢,"茱莉娅在他们开始了这小小的欢宴的时候说,"我要给你看莫里斯的信,请你念出来,或许有些什么我疏漏了。"

吉迪恩拿了这封信，摊在他的膝上，这样念着：

> 亲爱的茱莉娅，我从百朗亭写这封信给你，我们要在这儿耽搁几天。那次惨祸我相信你一定已经在报上看到了，二伯父受的震动很厉害。明天我让约翰陪他留在这儿，我一个人先回来；在我回来之前你会收到一只桶子，里边装着给一个朋友的标本。无论如何不许打开它，要把它放在穿堂间里，等我回来办。
>
> M. 芬斯伯里匆草
>
> 又：一定要把桶子留在穿堂间里。

"没有，"吉迪恩说，"信里不像有什么讲到这座纪念像的话。"他朝着那两条大理石的腿说着，点着头。"海士尔坦小姐，"他继续说，"我问你几个问题没有关系吧？"

"当然没有关系，"茱莉娅回答，"如果你能使我明白为什么莫里斯送来一个赫拉克勒斯雕像，而不是一只装着送给朋友的标本的桶子，那我真是到死都要感谢你。再说，给朋友的标本究竟是什么呢？"

"我猜不出，"吉迪恩说，"一般说来，标本是一块块的石头，可是比我们这位朋友——这个纪念像，却要小得多。不过这不是我要问的。我要问的是这幢大房子里就只有你孤单单的一个人吗？"

"是的，我现在是这样，"茱莉娅回答，"我赶在他们之前回来把房子预备好,还要找一个用人。可是我找不到一个合适的。"

"那你绝对只是一个人啦,"吉迪恩惊讶地说,"你不害怕吗?"

"不,"茱莉娅英勇地回答,"我不懂为什么我就得比你更胆小;当然啰,我是弱一点,可是我一知道我得一个人睡在这屋子里,我就去买了一把手枪,很便宜的,还叫那个人教我怎样使用它。"

"你怎样使用它呢?"吉迪恩跟着问,觉得她胆大得很有趣。

"嗯,"她笑着说,"你把那上面的小扳机扳一下,把它瞄得很低,因为你开的时候枪会跳起来,再扳下面的小扳机,这就打出去了,跟男人打的一样好哩。"

"那你已经用了几次了?"吉迪恩问。

"哦,我还没有用过哩,"这位有气概的年轻小姐说,"可是我懂得怎样用,这就使我胆大得不得了,尤其是在我用了一只衣柜把门抵上的时候。"

"我非常开心他们快要回来了,"吉迪恩说,"这事我总觉得太不安全。假如还要些日子,我可以请我那位没出嫁的姑母来陪你,或者你喜欢的话,我的房东太太也可以。"

"借一位姑母给我呀!"茱莉娅叫着,"哦,那太慷慨了!我这倒想起来,要不就是你把赫拉克勒斯给送来的。"

"请你相信,"这青年嚷着说,"我万分仰慕你,怎么也不会送给你一个这样丑陋的美术品。"

茱莉娅正要回答,他们两个却都给敲门声怔住了。

"哦,福西斯先生!"

"别怕,我亲爱的小姐。"吉迪恩说,手轻轻地按住她的胳膊。

"我说这一定是警察,"她低声说,"他们是为雕像的事来派我们不是了。"

又传来一阵敲门声。比上次更响、更急。

"是莫里斯。"茱莉娅惊骇地叫着,就跑到门口,把门打开。

站在他们面前的正是莫里斯;可不是平日见到的莫里斯,而像是一个发了狂的人,苍白、憔悴,眼睛血红,下巴颏儿上长着两天没刮的胡子。

"桶子!"他喊着,"今天早上来的桶子在哪儿?"他瞪着眼向穿堂间四处打量,当他看到赫拉克勒斯雕像的大腿的时候,他的眼睛睁得老大。"那是什么啊?"他尖声直嚷,"那蜡像是怎么来的啊?说呀,你这笨蛋!那是什么啊?桶子呢——那只大水桶呢?"

"没有桶子送来,莫里斯,"茱莉娅冷静地回答,"送来的只是这个东西。"

"这个东西!"这苦恼的人直着嗓子叫,"我不相信!"

"这是照你亲笔写的地址送来的,"茱莉娅答复,"我们差一点把房子都拆了才把它弄了进来,这就是我所知道的一切。"

莫里斯瞪眼看着她,完全给弄糊涂了。他用手抹抹前额,靠住墙壁,好像快要晕倒似的。然后,他像开了闸,口若悬河,骂起这位姑娘来。那样的火气,那样的毫无顾忌,用了那样不文明的字眼,在从前,简直谁也不会想到莫里斯会这样骂人的;这位姑娘在他的盛怒之下,一直在战栗、退缩。

"你不准跟海士尔坦小姐这样说话,"吉迪恩严正地说,"这我决不能容忍。"

"我爱跟这姑娘怎样说就怎样说,"莫里斯回着话,又勃发一阵怒气,"我要跟这妞儿说她该听的话。"

"不准再说一个字,先生,一个字都不准。"吉迪恩喊着。"海士尔坦小姐,"他对这位年轻姑娘继续说,"你不能再跟这个不够男子汉的人待在一个屋子里,待一分钟都不行。你挽着我的手臂,让我带你到一个不会受到侮辱的地方去吧。"

"福西斯先生,"茱莉娅回答,"你说得对,我不能再在这儿待下去,而我知道我是把自己托付给一位正直的君子了。"

脸色苍白,态度坚决,吉迪恩请她挽臂同行,这一对踏阶而下,莫里斯却跟上来嚷着要前门的钥匙。

茱莉娅刚把钥匙交给莫里斯,就有一辆空的二轮轻马车敏捷地赶到约翰街来。有两个男子一同高唤这辆车,一等到赶车的人把顽强的马勒住了,莫里斯抢着跳进车子。

"车钱之外,多给六便士。"他只管这样叫,"滑铁卢车站,拼命赶。六个便士我另外赏!"

"就给一先令吧,老板,"赶车的说,龇着牙齿笑,"那两个人在先呀。"

"就一先令吧。"莫里斯叫苦,打算到了滑铁卢再说。赶车的把马抽上一鞭,二轮轻马车就从约翰街上消失了。

第六章　莫里斯的折磨：第一期

那辆二轮轻马车在伦敦的街道上疾驰而过，莫里斯在车子里打算提起精神好好想一想。装了尸体的水桶已经送错了地方，这非找回来不可。这一点是很清楚的；如果侥天之幸，它还在车站里的话，一切还能顺顺当当。如果已经被送走，已经落在什么人手里，那可凶多吉少了。一般人收到不知情由的包裹，总是渴望把它打开；眼前海士尔坦小姐的例子（他又骂了她一声），就使他想到这情形；如果已经有谁把这水桶打开了——"哦，天啊！"莫里斯想到这儿就叫了起来，摸摸潮腻腻的前额。人们对于一切违法的行动，暗地里总难免有兴奋的想法，因为这种作为（在开头想到的时候）总带有几分痛快、动人的色彩。可是一个罪犯后一部分的感想就完全不是滋味了，因为那得和警察发生关系。那个爱管闲事的部队（正如莫里斯现在开始觉着一样），在他着手干这冒险事业的时候，他是没有充分注意到的。"我得极其小心才是。"他想着，害怕得只觉脊背上起了一阵剧烈的震颤。

"到主线停,还是环线停①?"赶车人从天窗里问着。

"主线。"莫里斯回答,心里决定还是给这人一先令。"惹人注意,那是发疯的行为呀,"他想,"可是这事从头到尾要花我多少钱,已经像是个噩梦了!"

他穿过卖票间,在月台上没精打采地走着。这正是交通忙碌的一天里的一个喘息时间;月台上没有几个人,这些人又多半是静静地坐在长凳上。莫里斯似乎没有引起别人注意,这是好事;可是,另一方面,他要打听的事,也就没有一点进展。总得想个法子,总得冒点险;每一分钟过去,都增加他一分危险。他终于鼓足勇气,叫住了一名脚夫,问他,就他所记得的,今天早晨是否拿到过由火车带来的一只桶子;他渴望问到点消息,因为这桶子是一个朋友的。"这是有点重要的,"他加上一句,"因为里边装着标本。"

"我今儿早晨不在这儿,先生,"这脚夫有点不乐意地回答,"可是让我问问皮尔看。皮尔,你记得吧,今儿早晨是不是有一只从伯恩茅斯来的装着标本的桶子?"

"我不知道什么标本,"皮尔回答,"可是我得说,那个收到桶子的人可大闹了一阵。"

"什么?"莫里斯顿时激动得叫起来,同时塞了一便士到这人手里。

"你看,先生,桶子一点半钟到的,等到差不多三点钟还没有人来领。到了三点钟,一个小个儿、害着病似的先

---

① 主线(main line)指火车站火车轨道主线的进口处,环线(loop)指副线的进口处。

生（可能是一位副牧师）来了，他说，'你们这儿有寄给皮特曼的东西'，或是'威廉·本特[①]·皮特曼'，要是我记得不错的话。'我不大清楚，'我说，'不过我想那边桶子上有那个名字。'这小个儿的人走到桶子那儿，他一看到那地址，似乎大吃一惊，接着他就痛骂我们没有把他要的东西带来。'我才不管你要什么鬼东西，'我跟他说，'但是如果你就是威廉·本特·皮特曼，那么那个桶子就是你的。'"

"那么,他拿走了没有呢？"喘不过气来的莫里斯叫着。

"嗯，先生，"皮尔回答道，"看起来他要的是一只货箱。那货箱到是到了；那准没错，因为那是我生平看见过的最最大的一只货箱。这个皮特曼像是懊丧得厉害，他把管理员也叫了出来，他们又找了那运货人来——那个运货箱的人。哎，先生，"皮尔笑着继续说，"我从没见过谁弄成那副样子，那辆运货车上，除了马，全都喝得烂醉了。有那么一位先生（我听说是这样）给了这运货人一个金镑，所以你看，这就弄出麻烦来啦。"

"那么他说了什么呢？"莫里斯喘着气说。

"我倒不知道他说了什么，先生，"皮尔说，"不过他倒要跟这个皮特曼打一场,赌一壶啤酒。他把送件本子也丢了，收据簿子也丢了；他的伙伴们没有一个不跟他一样烂醉。哦，他们全都像——"皮尔停了停笑着——"像醉鬼啦！管理员当场开除了他们。"

[①] 本特（Bent）应为登特（Dent），此处表明脚夫皮尔误记。

"哦,算啦,那还算客气哩,"莫里斯说着,大声地叹了口气,"那么他记不记得把货箱送到哪儿去了?"

"他才不知道哩,"皮尔说,"他什么也不知道。"

"那么皮特曼怎么——怎么办呢?"莫里斯问。

"哦,他颤颤巍巍坐了四轮马车带了桶子走了。"皮尔回答。"我看这位先生身体像不太好。"

"嗯,那么这桶子是没有了。"莫里斯说,一半好像在对自己说。

"那准是没有了,先生,"脚夫回答,"可是你最好还是找管理员吧。"

"决不用这样,那东西没有关系,"莫里斯说,"里边不过是标本罢了。"他急急忙忙地走了。

重又安身在一辆二轮马车里边之后,他再度考虑起自己的处境来。假定(他想着),假定他认输了,立即宣布他二伯父的死亡怎么样呢?那他必定会丢了"通蒂会"的养老金,跟着,他的七千八百镑的最后一线希望也完了。然而在另一方面,自从他给了那赶车的一先令之后,他开始感到犯罪是要花很大的本钱的,自从丢了那只大水桶以后,觉得犯罪之后,前途也是茫然无把握的。他起先安静地、后来是越来越烦躁地想着,要是没有这些事情多么好。那免不了损失一些;然而(要是细想一下)到底不会损失这么多;只不过一笔"通蒂会"的养老金罢了,这本来是机会均等的东西,再说他也根本没有真正想要弄到这笔钱。他热切地提醒自己这一点,庆贺自己一贯是这样的淡泊。他实在从没有奢想过这笔养老金;他甚至从没有十分认真地想收回他的七千八百镑；只是因为迈克尔欺人太甚，才使他糊里糊涂地陷入这种种事情里去了。对啦，这种希望渺茫的冒险的事别干了，死心塌地干那皮革生意可能更好些——

"老天呀！"莫里斯叫了起来，在马车里就像一只小盒子里的洋娃娃那样乱蹦乱跳。"我不但没有弄着'通蒂会'的养老金——我还丢了皮革店哩！"

事实正是这样糟得要命。他的签字无效，连三十先令的支票他都不能开，在未能提供二伯父死亡的合法证据之前，他简直是个不名分文的流浪者——然而只要他一提供证据，就永远得不到那笔"通蒂会"的养老金了！莫里斯不能再迟疑，他一下子做出了决定：把"通蒂会"像一粒烫手的栗子那样甩开，把全副精力集中在皮革生意和其余价值虽小却是合法的遗产上。可是再一转眼，只见他灾难的全貌突然出现在面前。宣布他二伯父的死亡吗？不能呀！既然尸首丢了，约瑟夫（在法律上说来）就成为永生不死的了。

世上绝没有一部人造的车辆能够装载得下莫里斯和他的厄运。他付清了马车钱，漫无目的地走着。

"我这事好像做得太鲁莽了一点，"他沉思着，恨恨地叹了口气，"我怕这事对于像我这种脑子的人来说似乎头绪太纷繁了一点。"

这时，他忽然想起二伯父的一句话来：如果要想得清清楚楚，你得把事情全都写在纸上。"嗯，这老头儿倒是懂得一二，"莫里斯说，"我来试试看；可是我不信那种能使我头脑清醒的纸已经造出来了哩。"

他走进了一家公共娱乐场所,叫了面包和奶酪,还要了纸笔,闷沉沉地坐在它们前面。他试试那支笔,那是一支好笔,然而他写些什么呢?"有啦,"莫里斯嚷着,"鲁滨孙·克鲁索①和那对照记录。"他照那典型的格式把他的纸准备好了,这样写起来:

坏处	好处
一、二伯父的尸体,我已丢了。	一、可是皮特曼已把它找到。

"等一等,"莫里斯说,"我让正反对照法的兴味把我引入歧途啦。咱们从头来过吧。"

坏处	好处
一、二伯父的尸体,我已丢了。	一、可是我就用不着把它埋葬了。
二、那笔"通蒂会"的养老金,我已丢了。	二、可是只要皮特曼把尸体弄掉,只要我能找到一个敢作敢为的医生,那我还可能保得住这一笔钱。
三、皮革店和二伯父其他的继承权,我已丢了。	三、可是只要皮特曼把尸体交给警察,那就不会的。

"噢,要是那样,我就得坐牢。我倒把这点忘了。"莫

---

① 鲁滨孙·克鲁索(Robinson Cruseo):英国小说家丹尼尔·笛福(Daniel Defoe,一六六〇——一七三一)所写的小说《鲁滨孙漂流记》中的主角。这小说记载鲁滨孙航海触礁,漂流到一个无人的荒岛上住了二十八年,想出种种巧妙的方法,克服困难,生活下去。

里斯想着,"真的,我不知道自己尽是在这些假设上面转念头到底对不对;嘴上说说临危不惧很不错;可是碰着这一类的事情,一个人首先真要保持自己的头脑清醒才是。对于第三项没有别的答案了吗?这讨厌的一团糟的项目还可能有一点好的方面吗?当然一定要有的,要不然这个对照记录的玩意儿有什么用处?而且——天哪,我有啦!"他叫了起来,"这跟上一项简直一模一样呀!"于是他急急忙忙地把这一项重写。

坏处	好处
三、皮革店和二伯父其他的继承权,我已丢了。	三、可是只要我能找到一个敢作敢为的医生,那就不会的。

"这可以收买的医生看来是个万不可少的东西哩,"他沉思着,"第一,我要他给我一张证明书证明二伯父已死,使我可以拿到皮革店;然后,证明他是活着——可是这儿咱们又碰到利害冲突的两方了!"他这就再回到他的表格上来。

坏处	好处
四、我已差不多没有钱了。	四、可是有很多的钱存在银行里。
五、对是对的,但是我不能够向银行取钱。	五、唉,不幸的是,事情就是这样一种局面。
六、我让票面金额八百镑的汇票落在约瑟夫伯父的口袋里了。	六、只要皮特曼是个不规矩的人,他有这张汇票反而可以使他将这整个事情严格保密,而把那尸体扔到新闻河里去。

七、对是对的，可是皮特曼如果不规矩而又得到了那张汇票，他会晓得约瑟夫是谁，那就会向我讹诈。	七、不错，但是如果我对大伯父马斯特曼的看法对的话，我也可以讹诈迈克尔。
八、可是我不能讹诈迈克尔（而且这事做起来非常危险），除非把事查清楚了。	八、更糟！
九、皮革店很快就会要钱付现在的开支而我付不出。	九、但是皮革店是一艘正在沉下去的船。
十、是的，但是我也只有这一艘船。	十、事实如此。
十一、约翰就快向我要钱了，可是我拿不出。	
十二、还有那可以收买的医生总要预先付款的。	
十三、如果皮特曼是不规矩的，却又不把我送到监牢里去，他得要一大笔钱。	

"哦，这事儿太偏向一边啦，"莫里斯叫喊着，"这方法并不如我所想的那么有用。"他抟起纸来往地上一扔；可是，跟着又捡了起来，看一遍。"我的情况，好像在金钱这点上最是糟糕，"他沉思着，"完全没有法子筹款了吗？在偌大一个城市里，四周尽是文化的资财，这是不可思议的！咱们不要再慌张吧。难道我没有东西好卖？我收藏的印章戒指——"然而一想到要卖掉这些可爱的宝物，莫里斯的血液顿时涌上脸来。"我宁可死！"他叫喊着，把帽子往头上一扣，大踏步走到街上去了。

"我一定得筹款，"他想，"我的二伯父既然已经死了，那么银行里的钱就是我的了,可是,打我是一个孤儿,在一个商业学校里读书那时候起,那件不公正的事就一直拖累我,我该说,要不是这可恨的事,银行里的钱就是我的了。我知道别人会怎么办;基督教世界里随便哪一个人,处在我的地位,也会伪造签字的;虽然我真不明白,约瑟夫已经死了,这笔钱已经是我自己的,为什么我还要称之为冒签。当我想到这事,当我想到二伯父真的死了而我却不能证明出来,我对于这整个事儿的不公平,真是气得要死。我过去对于那七千八百镑一直是很痛心的;但现在像是很小的事了。啊,可不是么,前天我多少还是快乐的哩。"

莫里斯站在人行道上,又长长叹息了一声。

"另外还有一件事,"他继续想着,"我能吗?我做得了吗?我小时候为什么不练习写写各种不同的字体?一个人长大了,对于失掉的机会是多么后悔呀!可是有一点是令人心安的,这在道德上讲并没有错;我尽可以试试而问心无愧,即使给人发现,我也不太在乎——我是说在道德上讲。不过,如果我成功了,如果皮特曼却坚定如山——那就除了找一个可以收买的医生之外,没有别的办法了;在伦敦这样一个地方,这应当轻而易举。从各方面听到的,这些人在这城里正多着哩。当然啰,登报找寻腐败的医生是不成的;那是不高明的。不,我想只能自己沿街去找哪儿挂着红灯,窗户里摆着药草,你就进去,就——就——就老老实实跟他讲,虽然这一步似乎是一种精微细致的工作。"

他曲曲折折地漫游了好些地方之后,现在已经走到离家相近的地方,就转入约翰街来。当他把前门钥匙插进钥匙孔的时候,另一个痛心的感想直刺他的心坎。

"在我能证明他的死亡之前,连这幢房子也不是我的。"他咆哮着说,走了进去,把门使劲一关,连顶楼的窗户都被震得嘎嘎作响。

暮色早已降临,灯和店铺的窗户里早已闪着光,照着那无尽头的街道;穿堂间里乌漆墨黑;就像遇到鬼了,莫里斯的两个小腿竟自互碰一下,使他整个身体趴倒在赫拉克勒斯的台脚上。这一痛真是痛彻心扉;他的脾气已经完全抑制不住了;到末了还要加上一个不幸,他摔下去的时候,手正好抓着那把锤子;于是像小孩子发起一阵脾气一样,他回过头来就砸那惹恼了他的雕像。那儿就乒乒乓乓地响起了一阵破碎声。

"噢,天呀,我这又干下了什么啦?"莫里斯哭哭啼啼地说道,他摸索过去找一支蜡烛。他手里拿着火回来,站着看那被毁了的腿,腿上大概已有一磅肌肉给刲掉了。"啊,"他沉思着,"啊,我已经毁坏了一件真正的古物了;我可能要赔上好几千镑啦!"接着他胸中忽然涌起了一种夹着怒火的希望。"让我看,"他想,"茱莉娅已经给撵走了;那畜生福西斯跟我毫无关系;那些家伙那时都喝醉了的,而(更好的是)他们全都被开除了。哦,来吧,我看这又是一件需要道义上的勇气来干的事情啦!我将来就说这件事情我什么都不知道好啦。"

再一会儿,他又站在赫拉克勒斯雕像的面前,嘴唇紧紧地抿着,胳膊下面夹着砸煤的斧子和切肉的大菜刀。

又一会儿,他已经在动手对付那货箱了。它已经给吉迪恩毁得很厉害;他对准箱子猛击了几下,它已经摇摇晃晃,裂了缝;再来几下,就倒了,碎板一阵骤雨似的掉在莫里斯的四周,稻草大山崩雪似的跟着撒了出来。

现在皮革商才看到了他要进行的是什么样的工作,就在开头这么一眼,他已经泄了气。老实说,就是德·雷赛布①,带着他的全班人马去进攻巴拿马山岭,也比不上这只身一人的瘦小的年轻绅士来得伟大了,因为这位绅士并无开山采石的经验,却要面对这个矗立在台脚上的庞然巨怪。然而双方对垒倒也旗鼓相当:这一边呢,庞大——另一边呢,胸中真正是燃烧着英雄的怒火啊。

"你给我坍下来,你这个又大又粗又丑陋的畜生!"莫里斯大声吼叫,带着点曾经驱使混乱的巴黎民众汹涌到巴士底监狱围墙下②的那种慷慨激昂的情绪。"今晚你就得坍下来。我决不让像你这种东西待在我的穿堂间里。"

这脸,有丑八怪似的表情,尤其激发了我们这位偶像毁坏者的热忱;他就是要对着这脸开头一刀。这个半神半人是那么高——它不穿鞋子站着就有一英寻③半高——这就成了攻击它的头一道阻碍物。但是在这战事初次交锋的时候,智谋已开始战胜障碍。运来了一架图书室的短梯,

---

① 德·雷赛布(Ferdinand de Lesseps,一八〇五——一八九四):法国工程师,以开掘苏伊士运河闻名于世。一八八一年又开掘巴拿马运河,终因疟疾流行,很多工人病死,预算大大超标,工程难以为继,最后回到法国,悒郁而终。
② 指一七八九年的法国大革命。
③ 英寻(fathom):长度单位,约合一点八三米。

这受伤的户主占据了一个优势的地位；于是大挥砸煤的斧子，着手把这畜生的头砍掉。

两个钟头之后，那个曾经是一座直立的、巨大的，神奇地变成白皙肤色的运煤夫的塑像，现在已经粉身碎骨；这个无头无脚的塑像趴在台脚上；那塑像脸上带着淫荡的表情，对着下面厨房的楼梯斜视；腿、臂、手，甚至手指，在穿堂间里分散满地。再半个钟头之后，莫里斯费了九牛二虎之力把所有的碎石残片都运到厨房间里去了；莫里斯怀着胜利的陶然的心情，环顾那一片让人充满成就感的场地。是的，他现在可以咬定对这件事毫不知情了：这穿堂间，除了的确有一部分遭殃受损，并无赫拉克勒斯雕像曾经到过的痕迹。然而爬上床去的是一个筋疲力尽的莫里斯；他的胳膊和肩膀酸痛，两只手的掌心被那粗糙的砸煤的斧子磨过之后，发着烫，还有一只剧痛的手指，时常要偷跑到他的嘴里来。睡眠迟迟才来拜访这位瘫痪了的英雄，天刚一亮，它又丢下他跑了。

这天清早，好像是配合他的厄运似的，天色一发白天气就很恶劣。东方吹来的狂风在街上怒吼；一阵阵的暴雨，向着窗户猛打；当莫里斯穿衣的时候，从壁炉里吹来的风活泼泼地绕着他的腿边直打转。

"照我看来，"他不能自已地怨恨地说，"我有那么多的罪得受，他们也该让我有个好天气了吧。"

家里没有面包，因为海士尔坦小姐（和一般独自过活的妇女一样）完全靠蛋糕果腹。蛋糕倒找到一点，于是（再来一杯诗人们所谓的清凉的冷水）就胡乱凑成一顿早餐，这之后他就英勇果断地坐下来干他那细致的工作。

世上没有比研究签字更有意思的事情了,在吃饭之前和吃饭之后签,在不消化的时候和酒醉的时候签,在一个人为他的小孩的生命而战栗的时候签,或是在赢得了德比赛马①回来的时候签,在律师事务所里签,或是在情人的明眸注视之下签。在普通人看来,签字式(正是如此)绝不会是同样的;可是在专家、银行职员或是石印匠看来,签字乃是一成不变的事物,正如甲板上守夜的人看北极星一样,总可以辨认出来。

对于这种种,莫里斯是懂得的。说到他现在正从事的这种优雅的艺术的理论,我们这位兴致勃勃的皮革商人是无可訾议的。可是对于投资者说来,幸而伪造签字是一件需要练习的事。所以莫里斯坐在那儿,面前摆着他二伯父签字的式样,身边全是他自己一堆堆拙劣的成果,他不知不觉意志消沉了。风一阵一阵地在他背后的烟囱里打旋;带着乌云的暴风一阵一阵地刮过布鲁姆斯伯里的上空,弄得天色那么黑暗,他得站起来去把煤气灯点上;跟在一座荒凉的宅子里一样,他只觉得到处都是冷飕飕的寒气和杂乱无章的样子——光地板,沙发上用肮脏台布包上的簿子和账册堆得高高的,笔锈了,纸面上浮着一层厚厚的灰尘;然而这些也不过是惨状的旁证而已,真正使他垂头丧气的原因还是在他身旁堆在桌上那些见不得人的伪造签字里边。

---

① 德比赛马(Derby):英国萨里郡(Surrey)埃普瑟姆镇(Epsom)每年举行的赛马会。

"我听也没听到过这种怪事。"他自怨自艾。"看来就像我没有这种才能了。"他重新仔细检阅他的样张。"就是个抄写员看了也要嘲笑的。"他说,"好吧,除了依样画葫芦没有别的办法了。"

他等着,等到暴风吹过,窗外闪进来一线柔弱无力的日光。他走到窗玻璃前,在整个约翰街的面前影写着他二伯父的签字。影写得怎么好也还是拙劣的。"可是这不成也得成,"他说,站着忧郁地呆看他亲手完成的工作,"反正他已经死了。"于是他在支票上填写了几百镑的数字,就冲了出去,直奔英格兰-巴塔哥尼亚银行。

在那儿,莫里斯走到经常去处理业务的柜台前,尽量装着若无其事的样子,把那张冒签了字的支票交给那大个儿、红胡子的苏格兰籍出纳员。出纳员看着这张支票似乎有点惊讶;他把它翻来覆去,再三打量,甚至用放大镜来细看签字,他的惊讶的情绪高涨起来,变成了不满意。他请求让他走开一会儿,就退入银行最里边一部分去了;隔了好一会儿之后,他从那儿回来,跟来一位上级职员,上了一点年纪,头有一点秃,但很是温文尔雅,他们热切地谈着话。

"这位是莫里斯·芬斯伯里先生吧。"这位文雅的先生一面说,一面对着莫里斯在鼻梁上架上一副眼镜。

"这是我的名字,"莫里斯说着,直发抖,"有什么不对吗?"

"嗯,事实是,芬斯伯里先生,你知道我们收到这张支票觉得相当惊讶,"对方轻轻地弹着支票说,"账上已经没有什么钱了。"

"没有什么钱了?"莫里斯叫着,"怎么,如果我记得不错的话,我知道账上准有个二千八百镑。"

"二千七百六十四,我想,"这位文雅的人答复,"可是昨天已经被提走了。"

"被提走了!"莫里斯叫了起来。

"你的伯父自己来取的,先生,"对方跟着说,"不但如此,我们还给他贴现了一张汇票,那是——让我看——那是多少,贝尔先生!"

"八百,贾特金先生。"出纳员回答。

"本特·皮特曼!"莫里斯叫着,摇摇晃晃地往后退。

"对不起,你说什么?"贾特金先生说。

"这——这不过是一个感叹词。"莫里斯说。

"我希望没有出什么岔儿吧,芬斯伯里先生。"贝尔先生说。

"我只能跟你这么说,"莫里斯带着刺耳的笑声说,"就是这整个事儿都是不可能的。我的二伯父正在伯恩茅斯,动都动不了。"

"是真的吗?"贝尔先生叫着,又把支票从贾特金先生手上拿过来。"可是这张支票是在伦敦签的,而且是今天的日期,"他说,"你说这是什么道理,先生?"

"哦,我弄错了。"莫里斯说,从脸到脖子都涨红了。

"当然,当然。"贾特金先生说,可是还带着发问的眼神看着他的顾客。

"不过——不过——"莫里斯继续说,"就算账上没有钱——这也可算是笔很微小的透支——凭我们的店——凭芬斯伯里的名字,对于这样一个区区的小数目,总应当信得过吧。"

"当然,芬斯伯里先生,"贾特金先生回答,"如果你一定要,我可以把这事考虑一下;可是我很难认为——简括地说吧,芬斯伯里先生,就算别的没有什么,单说这签字,似乎也很难说是完全合乎我们期望的。"

"那没有关系,"莫里斯心神不定地答复,"我可以让我二伯父再签一张。事实是,"他继续说,耍着大胆的一手,"我的二伯父现在身体不好得很,他连签这张支票都不能没人帮忙,我怕是我给他把住笔,可能使这签字有点不同。"

贾特金先生用锐利的目光对莫里斯脸上盯了一眼,然后他转过来看着贝尔先生。

"嗯,"他说,"这么说,只怕我们好像被一个骗子骗过一次了。请你跟芬斯伯里先生说我们将立即请侦探侦查。至于你这张支票,我很抱歉,因为它是这样的签法,银行很难认为它——我怎么说呢?——合乎条件。"他这就把支票递过柜台交还给他。

莫里斯机械地捡了起来,他在想着另一些很不相同的事。

"对于这样一件案子,"他开始说,"我相信损失是应当由我们负担的;我的意思是由我二伯父和我负担。"

"不是这样的,先生,"贝尔先生回答,"银行是要负责任的,银行得追回这笔钱或是赔偿,你可以相信我们。"

莫里斯的脸沉了下来,随着又来了一线希望。

"我跟你说,"他说,"你把这事完全交给我好啦。我来彻查这事。无论怎样,我有个主意,而请这些侦探来,"他动人地加上一句,"费用是那么高。"

"银行方面不能答应这一点,"贾特金回复道,"银行方面恐怕要损失三四千镑;如果必要的话,我们不惜再花上这么些钱。一个没有查究出来的伪造签字者是个永久的危险。我们得把它弄个水落石出,芬斯伯里先生,这点你放心吧。"

"那么我愿意承担这个损失,"莫里斯大胆地说,"我命令你们放弃侦查。"他决意不要追究。

"请你原谅,"贾特金先生回答说,"在这桩事情上我们跟你毫无关系,这是你的伯父和我们之间的事。如果他有这样的意思,或是他自己到这儿来,或是让我到他病房里去看他——"

"绝不可能。"莫里斯叫着。

"好吧,你看,"贾特金先生说,"这是多么由不得我做主的事。这整个事得立刻交给警察办理。"

莫里斯机械地把支票折好,重新放回皮夹里。

"再会。"他说着就踉踉跄跄地跑出了银行。

"我不晓得他们疑心些什么,"他想,"我不懂他们,他们的一切举动都完全不像是正常的样子。然而这也无所谓,一切都完了。钱已经付掉了;警察要追踪了;两个钟头之内那个笨蛋皮特曼就会给抓起来——这尸体的整个故事就会登在晚报上了。"

如果他能听到他走了以后银行里说了些什么,他的惊骇就会减轻一点，羞愧的感觉或许更厉害一点。

"真是一件稀奇的事，贝尔先生。"贾特金先生说。

"是的，先生，"贝尔先生说，"但是我想我们已经吓了他一下。"

"哦，莫里斯·芬斯伯里先生不会再上门来了，"对方回答，"这是初犯，那爿店跟我们已经交易这么久，所以我刚才愿意从轻处理。可是我想，贝尔先生，昨天不会弄错吧？那位确是老芬斯伯里先生本人吧？"

"那不可能有什么疑问，"贝尔先生吃吃地笑着说，"他还给我讲解银行学原理啦。"

"好吧，好吧，"贾特金先生说，"下次他来，请他到我办公室里来。这事正应当好好儿跟他说说，叫他提防提防。"

第七章　威廉·登特·皮特曼向律师求计

和皇家大道相交的诺福克街——被皮特曼先生的房客们戏称为"诺福克岛"——是一条既不长,又不美,也不可爱的街道。龌龊的、身材矮小的杂役妇出现在这条街上喝啤酒,或是在这儿的人行道上一边徜徉,一边听取绵绵的情话。卖猫食的人每天走过两次。偶或有个手摇风琴师①荡来,却又大感嫌恶,荡走了。放假的日子里,这条街变成邻近一带的年轻小伙子的比武场,住户人家倒有了机会,好研究一下男子汉的自卫艺术。不过,诺福克街却有一点是可以称道的,就是它连一爿铺子也没有——除非你把街角上的酒馆算在内,它实在该算是皇家大道上的。

第七号的门上钉着一块铜牌,刻着这样的字:"W. D. 皮特曼,美术家"。那块铜牌并不怎么干净,而第七号住屋本身也不是一个怎么合人心意的处所。然而它却有着自己的特色,足可引起读者的好奇心。因为这儿是一位美术家

---

① 手摇风琴师(organ-grinder):摇手摇风琴(barrel organ)的艺人。手摇风琴为一种筒状风琴,用曲柄摇转,筒上有钉,摇转时能启动许多琴管小瓣。启动时风箱鼓风入管内,发出乐音。

的家——而且是一位卓越的、在失败这方面十分卓越的美术家——他的作品从来没有被那些有插图的杂志采用过。从来没有一位木刻家曾经翻刻过第七号的"后客厅之一角",或者"画室中之壁炉架";从来没有一位年轻的女作家曾经描述过皮特曼先生怎样在围绕着他的"宝物"堆中,带着一种"毫不矫饰的质朴"接见了她。这种疏漏我本来很愿意在这儿补充一下,但是我们现在要晓得的事只跟这幢风雅的房屋的后部和"后面的糟窝"有关。

那儿是一座花园,中间算是有个喷水池(从来没有喷过水),几只花盆里种着不好看的花,两三株新栽的树,虽然春之神拂照过切尔西①,可也没有显著的效果,还有两三座照古式仿制的雕像,森林之神②和山林水泽女神③都是一种坏得无以复加的雕塑艺术的作品。在一边,使这花园黯然失色的,是两间破烂的画室,那儿通常出租给更无名的年轻的以英国艺术为业的人。在另一边,是一幢高高的外屋,看起来造得比较精致,还算有着那么一条通往正屋的通路和一扇通往后弄的便门,这外屋里供奉着皮特曼先生的形形色色的作品。固然,白天的全部时间,他得在一所供青年女子读书的学校里教课;然而晚间至少是他自己的,因此他利用这时间直至夜深,一会儿涂一张"瀑布风景"的油画,一会儿自动为某社会名流雕一座半身像

---

① 切尔西(Chelsea):伦敦市西一区。
② 森林之神(Satyrs):希腊神话中半人半马或半人半羊的森林之神。
③ 山林水泽女神(Nymphs):神话中半神半人的少女,住在山林水泽之中。

（"用大理石雕的"，他会温文尔雅又扬扬自得地这样指出），一会儿弯腰凿的不过是一座"山林水泽女神"（"预备做楼梯边煤气灯支柱用的，先生"），或者是一座有婴儿那么大的"撒母耳婴儿"，是给一所教会的育婴堂做的。皮特曼先生从前在巴黎学画，又到罗马学画，他的慈爱的父亲供给费用，父亲后来因为有一次女人胸衣跌价而宣告破产；虽然谁都不信他有一点点儿的才能，但是有一个时期他却使人觉得他干得很不坏了。十八年的所谓"粉笔生涯"又把他从别人这危险的见解中拯救了出来。有时，他的那些美术家住客跟他理论；他们指出他在煤气灯光下作画，或者没有模特儿而雕刻一座大小相当的山林水泽女神像，是万万不行的。

"这个我知道，"他会这样回答，"住在诺福克街上的人谁也不比我知道得更清楚了；要是我有钱，我当然会雇几个伦敦最好的模特儿；不过既然这么穷哩，我已经学会不用模特儿来工作了。随便用一个模特儿反而会混淆我理想中的形象，那就实在成为我前途的障碍了。至于在煤气灯下作画哩，"他会继续说，"这正是一种我发觉必须掌握的诀窍，因为我白天的时间全部用在教书工作上了。"

说到这儿，我们必须让皮特曼出现在读者眼前，这时，他正在十月里一天的薄暮中，独自一个人待在画室里。他（不用说，当然带着一种"毫不矫饰的质朴"的神态）坐在一把温莎椅①上，帽顶低圆的黑呢帽搁在一旁；他是个

---

① 温莎椅（Windsor chair）：一种椅背弯曲、有扶手的椅子。

又黑又弱、可怜、无用、身材矮小的人，穿着像丧服一样颜色的衣服，上衣比凡夫俗子的长，颈间绕着一个没有领口的领子，领饰颜色灰暗而且系得马虎；他这整个外表，除了尖尖的胡子之外，简直可以冒充一个牧师。皮特曼头顶上的头发稀少，鬓发斑白。可怜的绅士啊，他已经不是青年了；年华虚度，穷困潦倒，加之连小小的壮志雄心也未得酬，他的境况是真够凄凉的了。

在他面前的门角落里，竖立着一只圆圆的大桶子；不管他把眼睛转到哪儿、思想转到哪儿，他的眼睛和思想总是又回到这只桶子上面来。

"我应该打开它吗？我应该把它送回去吗？我应该立刻就去通知山米托波立斯先生吗？"他想着。"不行，"他最后决定，"没有得到芬斯伯里先生的指点之前什么都不可以做。"于是他站起来，拿出一只破旧的皮"书桌"。这东西不用经过开锁的步骤就打开了，出现了深乳酪色的便笺，皮特曼先生惯用这种便笺写信给校董和学生的家长。他把"书桌"放在窗前一张桌子上，从壁炉架上拿来一颜料碟的黑墨水，很费劲地写成下面一封信：

"亲爱的芬斯伯里先生，"信上这样写着，"倘若不嫌太麻烦，能否请你今晚来舍间一谈？我要仰仗你鼎力相助的，并非一桩无足轻重的事，只消我说是关于山米托波立斯先生的赫拉克勒斯雕像的权益问题，你就知道这是够重要的了，是不是？我怀着十分焦急的心情写这封信给你，因为我已经四下打听过，我生怕这件古艺术品已经遗失。我还为另一桩事烦恼，这与上述一桩不无关系。祈请原谅我写得这样潦草,威廉·D.皮特曼匆上。"

拿了这封信,他拔脚就走到皇家大道二三三号,摁了门铃,这儿是迈克尔·芬斯伯里的私人住宅。从前他曾在切尔西某一次公共大聚会上遇见这位律师;这位迈克尔律师生性风趣,平易近人,因此他把这段友谊持续下去,到后来又觉得可笑,他就让这段友谊变成一种敷衍性质的。现在离他们第一次晤面已有四年,皮特曼等于是这位律师家里的一条狗了。

"不在家,"一个年老的女管家开了门,这样说,"迈克尔先生还没有回来。你看起来气色不怎么好,皮特曼先生。进来喝一杯白葡萄酒吧,先生,你会觉得好一点的。"

"不用了,谢谢你,女士。"美术家回答。"盛情至感,但是我现在简直没有兴致喝白葡萄酒。我只是来送一张条子给芬斯伯里先生,请他去找——到小巷里找那扇门,请你费心跟他说一声;我将整个晚上都等在画室里。"

他转身又走到街上,慢慢向家里走去。一爿理发店的橱窗引起了他的注意,橱窗摆设的正中间,转动着一个骄矜、高贵、穿着晚装的蜡制美人,他不禁全神贯注地凝视了很久。艺术家的心灵在他心里醒过来了,尽管眼前有着种种麻烦事。

"纵然有人诋毁做这类东西的人,"他嚷着,"但是这人像却有着一种——一种高傲的、难以形容的神态。这正是我想赋予我的'欧也妮皇后'①的神态呀。"他又说,叹

---

① 欧也妮皇后(Empress Eugenie,一八二六一一九二〇):法皇拿破仑三世的皇后。此处指皮特曼要做的这个皇后的雕像。

了一口气。

他一面思量着那种艺术品质,一面走回家去。"在巴黎,他们可不教给你这种叫人一看就动心的手法,"他想,"这是英国风格哩。嗯,我像是渐渐睡着了,我一定要醒过来,我一定要努力向上——努力向上!"这位小个儿的美术家自己对自己大声疾呼。他回家吃午茶,过后教他大儿子拉小提琴,在这整个时间里,他心中不再想到那种种麻烦事了,他已经陶醉在另一种优美的境地中;一教完小提琴,他就异常兴奋地向画室奔去。

即使那只大桶立在眼前,也不能完全使他沮丧了。他聚精会神、越来越起劲地摆弄他的作品——依据相片替格莱斯顿先生雕一座胸像;他把后脑部分这个难题解决了(做得异常成功),这后脑,除了一次在某公共集会中得了点模糊印象以外,他没有任何参考材料;对于衣领部分的处理,他也很得意。一直等到迈克尔·芬斯伯里在敲门,才把他唤回到人间的烦恼事上来。

"怎么,出了什么事?"迈克尔说,一边向壁炉走去。皮特曼知道他的朋友喜欢火生得旺,因此没有吝啬柴炭。"我想你是碰到什么伤脑筋的事了吧。"

"一言难尽,"美术家说,"山米托波立斯先生的雕像没有送到,我怕我得赔偿损失;不过我顾虑的实在不是这个——我所怕的,我亲爱的芬斯伯里先生,我所怕的——啊呀,我真不愿意说呀!——是真相暴露。那座赫拉克勒斯雕像是从意大利偷运出来的;这明明白白是桩错事,像我这样一个有原则、有地位的人,是万万(现在我才看到已经太迟）不该参与的。"

"这事看来难办得很，"律师说，"得多喝几杯酒才行，皮特曼。"

"我已经擅自——简单点说吧，为你预备好了。"美术家说，指着那一把水壶、一瓶杜松子酒、一只柠檬和几只玻璃杯。

迈克尔替自己调了一杯掺水的酒，抽出一支雪茄给美术家。

"谢谢你，我不抽烟，"皮特曼说，"我过去有个时候很喜欢抽抽，但是这气味熏到衣服上可真不好闻。"

"好吧，"律师说，"我现在舒服了。打开你的话匣子吧。"

皮特曼把他的心事相当详尽地说了一遍。他今天到滑铁卢车站，满指望可以拿到那庞大的赫拉克勒斯雕像，不料拿到的却是一只桶子，连一座铁饼掷手像①也装不下；然而桶子上的地址倒是他的在罗马的通信者所写（笔迹他完全认得出）。更奇怪的，同车运到了一只货箱，论重量、大小都像是装的赫拉克勒斯雕像；这只货箱被送到现在已经无法查明的地点。"那个送货人（说来气人）吃醉了酒，他说的话我是怎么也不能照样说一遍。铁路上的管理人员立即把他革职，那位管理人员一直用很正当的态度处理这事，还预备到南安普敦去调查这事情。在那时候，我做什么好呢？我只得留下我的住址，然后把这桶子带回家来；不过我总记着老古话，决定除非在我的律师面前，否则决

---

① 铁饼掷手像（Discobolus）：投掷铁饼者的雕像，原像为公元前五世纪的雕刻家米隆（Myron）所刻。

不打开它。"

"就是这桩事情吗?"迈克尔问。"我看不出有什么可愁的理由。赫拉克勒斯雕像准是耽误在路上。明后天就会送进家门;至于那只桶子,一定是你那些年轻淑女里哪一位的一点心意,里边装的可能是牡蛎。"

"哦,不要说得这么大声!"这小个儿的美术家嚷着。"要是人家以为我对年轻淑女们说话不敬,我的位子可能就保不住了;再说,又为什么从意大利带牡蛎来呢?而且,为什么这些牡蛎会得由理卡地先生亲笔写了地址送来给我呢?"

"好吧,我们打开来看看吧,"迈克尔说,"我们把它滚到亮处来。"

两个人把桶子从角落里滚到壁炉前,竖起来。

"像这样重,准是牡蛎。"迈克尔有把握地说。

"我们马上动手吗?"美术家问,在有了同伴、喝了杜松子酒的双重影响之下,他显而易见是愉快起来了;不等回答,他就开始脱去衣服,好像准备一场拳击比赛,牧师式的领子扔到了字纸篓里,牧师式的上衣挂在一根钉上,一只手拿着一柄凿子,另一只手拿着一把钉锤,敲出了这晚上的第一下。

"这样子不错,威廉·登特!"迈克尔大声说。"你花了钱可换到生火的东西了!桶里边也许是你那些年轻淑女里的一位给你来一次浪漫的访问——一种克利奥帕特拉①

---

① 克利奥帕特拉(Cleopatra,公元前六九—前三〇):埃及艳后。当恺撒率领罗马军队征服埃及的时候,她把自己裹在一条地毯里嘱人送给恺撒。本文引用了这段故事。

之类的事儿。小心别把克利奥帕特拉的头给打穿啦。"

然而看到了皮特曼这样矫健的身手，他自己也不禁手痒了。律师再也坐不安稳了。他把雪茄往炉火里一扔，从美术家的舍不得放的手里一把抢过工具，自己干起来。一会儿他又粗又浓的金黄色眉毛上就全沾上了汗珠；他的漂亮的裤子也给铁锈弄得面目全非，他那凿子的模样说明他白费了好多气力。

要打开一只桶子，即使你下手正确也不是一桩容易的事；倘若你下手错误呢，那么一定会整个儿散成碎片。而这正是这位美术家和这位律师所同样采取的方针。一转眼，最后一圈铁箍也撬开了——着力地添了两下，就叫一块块木板倒在地上——原来的那只桶子现在不过是一堆乱七八糟的不像个样子的碎片了。

在这些木板之中，有那么一件形象可怕的东西，用毛毯裹着的，还笔直地竖立了片刻，接着歪向一边，重重地倒在壁炉前。就在这东西倒地的时候，叮当一声，一块眼镜片落到地上，向着尖声叫喊的皮特曼滚过来。

"别叫！"迈克尔说。他一步冲到门边，把门锁上；然后，脸色发白，嘴唇紧咬，慢慢走过去，把裹着的毛毯掀开一角，发着抖，往后退。画室里静寂了好长一会儿。

"你跟我直说吧，"迈克尔低声说，"这事情你参与了没有？"他指着那尸体。

小个儿的美术家只能发出断断续续、上气不接下气的声音来。

迈克尔倒了些杜松子酒到玻璃杯里。"喝点酒，"他说，

"别怕我。我是能跟你共患难的朋友。"

皮特曼把杯子搁在一边,不想喝。

"我对天起誓,"他说,"这又是一桩不可思议的事。我做梦也想不到这样可怕的事。我是连一个吃奶的婴儿都不会碰一碰的。"

"那就好了,"迈克尔说,如释重负地叹了一口气,"我相信你,老朋友。"他热烈地握了握美术家的手。"我有那么片刻以为,"他又说,带着一种狰狞的微笑,"我有那么片刻以为你大概是把山米托波立斯先生干掉了。"

"即使我干掉了他,事情也不会两样,"皮特曼叹息说,"我一切都完啦。祸事已经临头了。"

"头一件要做的,"迈克尔说,"我们得把他弄走;因为老实跟你说,皮特曼,我不喜欢你这位朋友的脸。"一说到这儿律师就打着寒战。"我们能把它弄到哪儿去呢?"

"你可以把它藏在壁橱里——要是你不怕碰着它的话。"美术家回答。

"总得要有一个人做的,皮特曼,"律师说,"而且看情形是非我莫属。你到桌子跟前去吧,背过身来,给我调一杯掺水的酒。这样分工总公平啰。"

大约九十秒钟之后,就听见壁橱门咔嗒一声关上了。

"行了,"迈克尔说,"这样才比较像个家了。你可以转过身子来啦,我的面色苍白的皮特曼。这就是掺水的酒吗?"他跟着说:"老天饶了你吧,这是柠檬水呀!"

"不过,哦,芬斯伯里,那东西我们怎么处理才好呢?"美术家哀鸣着,一只手紧紧抓住律师的胳膊。

"怎么处理吗?"迈克尔重复一声,"把它埋在一个花坛里,再竖上你做的一座雕像做纪念碑。我跟你说,我们在暗淡的月光下面掘土,情调是怪浪漫的。喂,给我杯子里倒点儿杜松子酒。"

"我求求你,芬斯伯里先生,别拿我的苦恼事打趣了。"皮特曼嚷着说。"站在你面前的这个人,他的一生——我可以毫不犹豫地说——都是出人头地而受人尊敬的。即使在现在这严重的时刻,我也可以扪心自问而无愧色。除了偷盗赫拉克勒斯雕像这件小事之外(就是这件小事我现在也在低头忏悔),我的一生是没有一点不能公之于世的。我从来不怕亮光烛照,"那小个儿大声说,"可是现在——现在啊——!"

"不要难过了,老朋友,"迈克尔说,"我可以肯定地对你说,这类小小的意外在我的事务所里是不当一回事的;像这种事情谁都可能碰着;如果你真的跟这事一点干系没有——"

"要我说什么才能叫人——"皮特曼开始说。

"哦,那个我来处理,"迈克尔打断他的话,"你没有经验。但是关键在这儿:倘若——或者更确切地说,既然——你对这桩罪案一无所知,既然这个——这个壁橱里的东西——既非你的父亲,又非你的哥哥、你的债权人、你的岳母,或者人家所谓的一个被害的丈夫——"

"哦,我的好先生!"皮特曼接口说,害怕起来。

"总之,既然,"律师继续说,"你跟这桩罪案没有一点可能有的利害关系,那么摆在我们面前的路是再宽广自由也没有了,要怎么做也不用顾虑。真的,这问题实在引人入胜;我早已假设一件某某案子来思考这样一个问题,现在我终于在现实中碰到了,我就打算把你救出来。你听见了吗?——我打算把你救出来。让我看,我已经好久没有度过一个我所谓的实实在在的假期了,我明天通知事务所说有事不去。我们最好赶紧行动,"他意味深长地加上这句,"因为我们万万不能把另外一个人的生意搞砸了。"

"你说什么?"皮特曼问。"什么另外一个人?是说警察巡官吗?"

"滚他的警察巡官!"他的伙伴说。"你如果不愿意省点事,把这东西埋在你的后花园里,那么我们一定得另找一个愿意把这个埋在他的后花园里的人。简单地说,我们必须把这件事情交在一个顾虑少而计谋多的人的手里。"

"譬如一个私人侦探,是不是?"皮特曼提醒他。

"你有时候真叫我觉得你可怜。"律师说。"想起来了,皮特曼,"他换了一种声调说下去,"你这个巢穴里没有一架钢琴,我一直认为美中不足。即使你自己不弹,当你在胡搞些什么的时候,你的朋友们也可能想弹点小调子自娱一下的。"

"你要的话,我一定立刻弄一架来,"皮特曼又急又慌地说,一心想讨他的好,"我现在偶尔拉拉小提琴。"

"我知道你拉,"迈克尔说,"可是小提琴算得上什么——尤其像你那样的拉法?你该弄的是复音音乐。我来跟你说吧,既然这会儿你要买架钢琴已经来不及了,我把我那架给你吧。"

"谢谢你，"美术家迷惘地说，"你要把你那架给我吗？我知道你实在太好了。"

"是的，我要把我那架给你，"迈克尔继续说，"等警察巡官带来的那帮人在你后花园里开掘的时候，巡官可以弹着玩。"

皮特曼睁大眼睛看着他，又痛苦又惊愕。

"不，我没有疯。"迈克尔接着说下去，"我虽然在说着玩儿，可还是相当有条理的。听好，皮特曼，听我说半分钟。幸而我们确确实实是无辜的，这桩令人快慰的事实倒可以让我们利用一下；除了这儿藏着的那个——你知道那是什么——之外，就没有什么东西可以把我们牵连到这桩罪案里去了；只要我们一旦把它弄掉，也不管怎样的弄法，就不可能有任何线索追查到我们身上来了。嗯，我把我那架钢琴给你，我们就在今儿晚上把它搬来。明天我们把那些配件都拆掉，把那个——我们的朋友——放在里边，再把这整个东西嗨的一声装上一辆货车，送到一个我认得的年轻绅士的屋子里。"

"你认得的是谁？"皮特曼跟着问了一声。

"更好的是，"迈克尔自顾自讲下去，"我晓得他的屋子比他自己更清楚。我有一个朋友——为了方便起见，我称之为我的朋友；据我所知，他现在是在德梅拉拉①，而且（多半是）在监狱中——他从前住在那屋子里。我为他辩护过，并且替他脱了罪——救了他的一切，除了他的名

---

① 德梅拉拉（Demerara）：南美洲圭亚那（Guyana）的一条河。

誉；他的财产几乎等于零，但是他把所有的都给了我，可怜的人啊，其中有一件——是他屋子的钥匙。我打算在那地方安置那架钢琴和——可以这样说吗——克利奥帕特拉？"

"这似乎太莽撞了，"皮特曼说，"再说你认得的那位可怜的年轻绅士，他怎么办呢？"

"这会对他有好处，"迈克尔兴冲冲地说，"他正需要这个，好叫他磨炼磨炼。"

"可是，我亲爱的先生，这可能陷害了他，被控告——被控告谋杀。"美术家声音哽塞了。

"哼，他也不过会跟我们现在一样，"律师回答，"他是无罪的，你知道。我亲爱的皮特曼，人们犯了罪，只有碰得不巧的时候才会被处绞刑的呀。"

"不过，真的，真的，"皮特曼恳求说，"我总觉得这整个计划是太草率了。说实在的，去报告警察是不是更妥当一点呢？"

"闹一个满城风雨？"迈克尔反问。"'切尔西的奇案，皮特曼的辩白'？这一来，学院里会怎么说？"

"那我就可能被革职，"画师承认，"我不能否认这一点。"

"况且，"迈克尔说，"假如我花了钱而得不到娱乐，我是不想管这种事的。"

"哦，我的好先生，这想法难道是合情理的吗？"皮特曼高声说。

"哦，我只不过说着玩儿叫你兴奋起来，"不知羞的迈克尔说,"带点儿有分寸的轻率是再好不过的。不过这完全不必讨论。要是你决心听从我的办法,那么来吧,我们立刻去搬钢琴。要是你不听哩,那只要说一声,我就让你照你更好的打算去应付这整个事情。"

"你知道得很清楚,我完全要仰仗你的,"皮特曼回答说,"可是哦!这一夜,得跟那个——我画室里那个吓人的东西——在一起是什么滋味啊!我睡在枕头上会怎样地想到这东西啊!"

"不过,你知道,我的钢琴也要来的,"迈克尔说,"它可以替你分担一点儿。"

一小时后一辆货车进了那条小巷,律师的钢琴——一架庞大的布洛德伍德大钢琴——放到皮特曼先生的画室里边了。

第八章　迈克尔·芬斯伯里的假期

　　第二天早晨八时整,这位律师(遵照前约)在敲着画室的门了。他看见那可怜的美术家变得更不对了——苍白,两眼充血,面色如土——一副神经紧张的样子,而那两只下陷的失神的眼睛还在一下一下地向壁橱那边斜瞄过去。另一方面这位绘画教授看见了他朋友的样子,惊讶之情也并未减退。迈克尔平时最讲究穿着,总是带着一种商人味儿的豪华气派,或者最恰当的说法叫作时髦;照道理说,这并没有什么不对,只是他看来太像一个吃喜酒的客人,倒不怎样像一个绅士了。今天他可是从豪华的高空一落千丈。他穿了一件洗淡了颜色的牧童穿的格子花纹法兰绒衬衫,一套略带红色的粗花呢上衣和裤子,这种颜色的呢子,成衣匠们称作"杂色呢";围脖儿是黑色的,打了个松松的水手领结;一件很旧的长大衣遮住了这些好看的衣着的一部分;脚上穿的是粗劣的便靴。头上戴的是一顶旧的软毡帽,他进来的时候手那么美妙地一挥就把它脱掉了。

　　"我来啦,威廉·登特!"他高声说,一面从口袋里拿出两小绺红色的毛发,凑到两颊旁,好像长了络腮胡子,用舞女的飘飘欲仙的姿势在这画室里舞来舞去。

皮特曼苦笑着。"我真认不出你来了。"他说。

"原是不要你认出来呀。"迈克尔回话,重新把胡子放到口袋里。"现在我们得把你跟你的行头检查一番了,要把你彻底化装一下。"

"化装!"美术家叫起来。"我非得化装吗?已经到了这步田地了吗?"

"我的好人儿呀,"他的伙伴回答说,"化装是人生的调味品。法国一位哲学家热情地大声疾呼过,要是没有领略过从化装得到的乐趣,人生还有什么意思呢?我并不是说不论在何种情况下这都是风雅的,而且我也知道这与我们的职业并不相称;可是,意志消沉的画师,这有什么关系?我们不得不这样做。我们必须给好些人以一种不正确的印象,而尤其是要让吉迪恩·福西斯先生如此——就是我认得的那位年轻绅士——假定他竟然不知趣地耽在家里的话。"

"假定他在家的话呢?"美术家讷讷地说,"那一切都完啦。"

"一点儿鬼关系都没有。"迈克尔满不在乎地回答。"让我看看你那些衣服,我一下子就可以把你变成另外一个人。"

迈克尔由皮特曼立即带到卧室里来之后,以一种富于幽默的眼光查看皮特曼那只贫乏得可怜的衣橱,挑了一件黑羊驼呢的短上衣,同时又添上一条夏季穿的裤子,因为这样不伦不类,使他认为很对劲儿。于是,他拿了这些衣服在手里,盯着美术家仔细看。

"我不太喜欢那个牧师式的领圈,"他批评着,"你难道没有别的啦?"

这绘画教授考虑了一会儿,然后面露喜色。"我有两件低领的衬衫,"他说,"那是我在巴黎做学生的时候常穿的。只是颜色太触目了。"

"就是要这样的东西!"迈克尔脱口而出。"这一来你的样子才真能叫人讨厌。这儿还有鞋罩,"他继续说,一面掏出一副叫人皱眉头的小鞋罩,"鞋罩是非要不可的!好啦,你就用这些东西打扮起来,再到窗口去吹个调儿,吹它三刻钟的口哨。那之后,你可以回到那边光荣的战场上来跟我重聚。"

这样说过,迈克尔就回到画室里去。这是一个东风刮得很紧的早晨;风吹过花园里的雕像,发出嘘溜溜的尖啸声,又带着骤雨打着画室的天窗;差不多就当莫里斯在布鲁姆斯伯里研究他伯父的签字,再接再厉地做着第一百次的努力的时候,这方面迈克尔正在切尔西着手将那架布洛德伍德大钢琴里的钢丝拆掉。

三刻钟之后,皮特曼进了画室,看见壁橱门开着,里边的房客已经搬空了,而那架钢琴也很小心地合上了。

"这是一件特别重的乐器。"迈克尔评论着,然后他回过头来打量他朋友的化装。"你得把你那把胡子剃掉。"他说。

"我的胡子!"皮特曼叫着。"我不能把我的胡子剃掉。

我不能妄动我的面貌——我的那些上司要反对的。他们对于教授的面貌是有强烈的成见的——年轻淑女们是被人们看成那么浪漫的。我在那儿走来走去的时候,我的胡子被大家看作一个特色。她们都觉得,"美术家说着,脸红了起来,"她们都觉得不好看。"

"你可以把它再留起来,"迈克尔回答,"那时候你会变得奇丑,上司会加你薪水。"

"我可不要变得奇丑。"美术家喊着。

"别傻了,"迈克尔说,他最恨胡子,如果能够剃掉,他再开心也没有,"像个大丈夫的样子把它弄掉吧!"

"当然啰,要是你一定要这样。"皮特曼说,然后叹了口气,从厨房里拿了一点热水来,又把一面镜子摆在画架上边,先用剪子把胡子剪短了,再刮下巴。当他把自己打量了一下,不由得觉着他最后一点男子气概也全给牺牲了,可是迈克尔显然很高兴。

"一个崭新的人呀,我说!"他喊着,"等我把我口袋里这副玻璃窗式的眼镜给你戴上,那你简直就是一个典型的法国兜销员啦。"

皮特曼没有答话,一直对着镜子里自己的镜像垂头丧气地瞧着。

"你可知道,"迈克尔问,"南卡罗来纳州的州长跟北卡罗来纳州①的州长说了什么?'好一阵子没喝酒啦。'那位伟大的思想家这样说。你要是把手伸到我外衣左上首

---

① 南卡罗来纳州(South Carolina)、北卡罗来纳州(North Carolina)均在美国东南部。

的口袋里,据我料想,你或者可以找到一瓶白兰地。谢谢你,皮特曼。"他又说,同时给各人倒了一杯酒。"现在你说这酒怎么样?"

美术家伸手去拿水壶,可是被迈克尔制止住了。

"即使你跪着求,我也不会让你这样做!"他喊着。"这是全英国最醇的利久酒①类的白兰地。"

皮特曼用嘴唇试了试,却又放下杯子,叹了口气。

"嗯,我得说,作为假期里的一个伙伴,你是再糟也没有了!"迈克尔叫着。"要是你对白兰地的鉴赏力不过如此,那我就不再给你喝啦;我来把这瓶喝完,趁这时候你不如动手办事吧。"他忽然顿住,"我想起来了,我大大地弄错了一桩事:应当叫你在化装之前,先去叫一辆货车的呀。嘿,皮特曼,你这狗东西有什么用处?你怎么没有提醒我一声?"

"我根本不知道还要叫什么货车。"美术家说。"不过我可以把这个化装重新去掉。"他急切地提议。

"你要把胡子再装上可费事啦。"律师说。"不行,这一步走错了;往往就是这种毛病把人弄上绞刑架的,"他继续说,一面啜饮白兰地,显然兴致勃勃,"可是现在已经不能从头来过。你到马房去,把一切都接洽好吧;叫他们赶辆货车到这儿来把钢琴装走,运到维多利亚车站,在那儿送上火车运到加农街,摆在那儿,等一个叫作福气·丢·波司哥倍的人来取。"

---

① 利久酒(liqueur):一种芬芳甘味的烈酒,包括白兰地、薄荷酒、橘子酒等,常用以在晚餐后以小杯敬客。

"这个名字有点不伦不类吧?"皮特曼恳切地问。

"不伦不类?"迈克尔哼着鼻子嚷着,"还会把我们俩都送上绞刑架哩!还是'布朗'既比较妥当又比较容易念。就叫作'布朗'吧。"

"我希望,"皮特曼说,"为我设想,我希望你不要嘴上老是挂着绞刑架。"

"说说有什么关系,我的老朋友!"迈克尔回答。"拿了你的帽子去吧,可别忘了每样东西都得把钱先付啦。"

剩下他一个人了,律师就好一会儿以全力来应付那"利久"白兰地,这整个早晨他的兴致本来已经很好,现在更是大大高涨起来。他开始在镜子前面调理他的络腮胡子。"阔气得要命哪,"他一边研究自己的映像,一边说,"我真像一个出纳员的助手。"这时候,那副玻璃窗式的眼镜(他到现时为止是规定给皮特曼戴的)在他脑子里一闪,他把它戴上了,那股劲儿他立刻爱上了。"我正需要这个,"他说,"我不晓得现在像个什么样子?一个幽默小说家吧,我想不会错的。"于是他练习各种人的走法,一面走,一面跟自己报这种走法的名称:"幽默小说家的走法——不过这还得要一把伞;出纳员助手的走法;移民到澳大利亚的人重游童年旧地的走法;印度上校的走法,诸如此类,诸如此类。"当他正在学印度上校的时候(这个模拟,虽然跟他的化装不符,却非常好),他的目光落到那架钢琴上。这件乐器在顶上和琴盖上都装了锁,但是琴盖的钥匙已不知丢在哪儿了。迈克尔把它打了开来,他的手指在那哑无声息的琴键上抚弄一遍。"大好的乐器——声音洪亮深沉。"

他一面说，一面拖过一张凳子来。

皮特曼回到画室，一看见他的导师、哲学家、朋友，正在这无声的大钢琴上做着惊人的演奏，不禁大为惊愕。

"我的老天爷！"这个小个子心想，"我怕他是喝醉了吧！芬斯伯里先生。"他大声喊他。迈克尔并没有站起来，只把那张有点发红的脸转过来，这张脸被那丛红色的络腮胡子围绕着，并架上了眼镜。"《降B调狂想曲》，为送别朋友而作。"他说，继续演奏他那安静无声的音乐。

气愤开始在皮特曼的心里发作了。"那副眼镜该给我戴的，"他叫喊起来，"那是我化装里的重要部分。"

"我自己要戴了，"迈克尔回答，接着又加上一句，表示一些至理，"倘若我们两人都戴眼镜，那可能引起很多的怀疑。"

"噢，好吧，"皮特曼答应着说，"我本来准备用的，可是如果你一定要，那你戴吧。无论怎样，货车已经在门口了。"

当车工们在工作的时候，迈克尔躲在堆着桶子的残骸和钢琴的钢丝的壁橱里。等他们一走，风色正了，这两人立即扯起篷来从巷子里窜到皇家大道，跳上一辆二轮轻马车，很快地赶向城里去。天气还是那么寒冷彻骨，狂风暴雨还没有停息，雨点狠狠地打在他们脸上，但是迈克尔不让拉下玻璃窗来。他这时忽然自封为名胜古迹的向导，车子一路行来，他一路指点，详详细细地讲述伦敦那些壮观景象。

"我亲爱的朋友，"他说着，"你对于你这本乡本土的城市简直一无所知。我们去看伦敦塔楼①怎么样？不去？嗯，这大概要绕一点儿路。可是，不管——嘿，赶车的，从特拉法尔加广场②绕过去吧！"到了那个有历史意义的广场，他坚持停一下，评论了那些雕像，跟美术家讲了关于那些名人的很多（史乘所无的）离奇事迹。

皮特曼在车子里所受的罪真是难以形容：既冷又湿，又是吓得要死，又确实不能放心那个管辖他的指挥员，低领衬衫又教他觉得有失体统，胡子被剥夺了又叫他感到晦气。凡此种种，把他弄得心里乱七八糟。他们的车子远兜远转地走着，终于来到一家饭馆门前，这是第一桩令人心安的事。听见迈克尔定下了一间独用的房间，这是第二桩令人心安的事，而且比第一桩更令人心安。一个听不懂话的外国人给他们领路，走上楼梯的时候，他看到那儿只有寥寥可数的几个人，当然又是衷心庆幸，而且这些人大半是从法国流亡到这儿来的，这使他更为高兴。他想到这些人里边不会有谁跟那学院有关系，真是不胜欣慰。学院中那位法国教授，虽然大家知道他是一位罗马教徒，也实在

---

① 伦敦塔（the Tower）：伦敦泰晤士河畔一座高十九尺、四方形堡垒式的高楼。威廉一世（William the Conqueror，约一〇二八——一〇八七）于一〇六六年征服英国后所建。一半是堡垒，当时英国帝王常住其中；一半是监牢，许多皇室及名臣曾被监禁或处死于此。这是伦敦最古老而充满史实的伟大建筑物，现时专做博物馆之用。
② 特拉法尔加广场（Trafalgar Square）：在伦敦市中区，近滑铁卢桥，为纪念一八〇五年英国海军上将纳尔逊在特拉法尔加海岬大败法皇拿破仑的海军而建造的广场，中间建有高柱，柱顶矗立着纳尔逊的雕像。

难以相信他会时常光顾这样一个冶游之所的。

那个外国人把他们带到一间空空的小房间里来,那儿只有一张桌子、一只沙发和一簇鬼火似的炉火。迈克尔立即叫加煤,又叫了两杯白兰地和两杯苏打水。

"哦,不能,"皮特曼说,"真的不能——不能再喝了。"

"我不懂你是怎么一回事,"迈克尔悲叹地说,"我们显然需要来点什么的。在吃饭前又不应当抽烟——我以为这是不言而喻的事。你好像不懂卫生。"于是他拿出表来跟壁炉上的钟对时。

皮特曼陷入苦闷的沉思。他想:自己刮光了胡子,怪里怪气,化装得非驴非马,跟一个戴眼镜的醉汉做伴,在一个十足外国气派的饭馆子里等着一顿有香槟酒的午餐。要是给那几位上司看见的话,他们该怎样想?假定他们知道了他的悲剧色彩的欺人耳目之行,那又会怎样?

那个外国人拿来了白兰地和苏打水,这使他从这种种思虑中惊醒过来。迈克尔拿了一杯,叫侍者把另一杯递给他的朋友。

皮特曼挥手不受。"不要叫我丧尽了自尊心。"他说。

"为了朋友,我一切遵命。"迈克尔回答。"不过我不能一个人喝。嘿,"他向着侍者说,"你喝吧。"这一来,碰了碰杯。"祝吉迪恩·福西斯先生身体健康。"他说。

"祝葛登·波锡冼生[①]。"侍者应声说,咽了四口,把酒喝完。

---

① 此处原文表示外国侍者念人名及"先生"时都走了音。

"再来一杯？"迈克尔说，毫不掩饰他的兴趣。"我从没有见过谁喝得这样快。这使我恢复了对于人类的信心。"

可是侍者有礼貌地谢绝了，他由外边进来的一个人帮着，把午餐端了进来。

迈克尔吃了一顿很好的饭，这他是用一瓶海德西克牌无甜味的香槟酒送下去的。美术家可是太心烦意乱了，吃不下饭，但是他的伙伴除非他吃饭，否则硬是不分他一点香槟酒喝。

"我们俩总得有一个人是清醒的，"律师讲，"你就是给我一只松鸡腿，我也不会给你香槟酒。我得小心才是。"他以说知心话的口气加上一句："一个人喝醉，飘飘欲仙——两个人喝醉，万万不行。"

咖啡端了上来，侍者退了下去，这时可以看到迈克尔做了惊人的努力，装出一副庄重的神气。他直盯着他朋友的脸（一只眼睛许是斜着一点），重浊而严肃地发言。

"这样胡闹也闹够了，"这就是他并不怎么不恰当的引言，"干正经事吧。听好！我是澳大利亚人。我的名字是约翰·迪克逊，虽然从我那谦逊的面貌上你也许看不出来。你听了可以放心，我是有钱的，先生，非常有钱。这种事情，你不能太认真追究，皮特曼；整个诀窍只是做好准备，我一开头就把我的历史编好了，我本来现在就可以告诉你我是怎样的一个人，只是我已经忘记了。"

"也许我很笨——"皮特曼说。

"对啦！"迈克尔喊起来，"非常笨，可是也有钱——比我还有钱。我想你听了一定喜欢，皮特曼，因为我把你派作一个简直在钱堆里打滚的人。不过在另一方面,你只是一个美国人,而且只是一个制造橡胶套鞋的美国人。最糟的是——我为什么瞒着你——最糟的是你叫作以斯拉·托马斯。好啦,"迈克尔说着,神气真是严肃得可怕,"跟我说一遍我们是谁。"

这可怜的小个儿的人给他问来问去,直问得他背得出来才罢休。

"成啦!"律师叫着。"我们的计划全弄好了。前后吻合——这一点是最要紧的。"

"我可不懂。"皮特曼抗议着说。

"哦,你到那时自然会懂。"迈克尔说着就站起来。

"你的话里不像说了什么故事哩。"美术家说。

"我们一路走着就可以一路编一个。"律师回话。

"我可不会编,"皮特曼反对,"我一生一世也编不来。"

"你会知道非编不可,我的小朋友。"迈克尔轻描淡写地说,然后叫了侍者来,他立刻又跟他谈得很上劲。

跟在他后面走的是一个垂头丧气的小个子。"当然,他非常聪明,可是像他现在这样子,我能信任他吗?"他心里问。当他们又钻进了一辆二轮轻马车的时候,他打起精神来。

"你说,"他嗫嚅着,"把一切都盘算之后,这件事情拖两天办是不是比较妥善一些呢?"

"把今天能做的事情拖到明天去做吗?"迈克尔叫着,恼了,"从来没有听见过这种话!乐观点吧,什么问题都没有,迎上去,打个胜仗——这才是勇敢的皮特曼!"

到了加农街,他们问了布朗先生的钢琴,知道已经到了,他们再到近旁一家马车房去,在那儿租了一辆货车,他们在马具间火炉边待着,等货车准备起来。律师就在这儿靠在墙上浅浅睡着了;这一来皮特曼只好全靠自己的聪明来对付那些盯着他们看的游手好闲的人,那些人在没法弄到钱的日子里爱在马车房附近混时间。

"天气不好啊,先生,"其中一个说,"你要出远门吗?"

"是的,今天日子——日子相当不好。"美术家说。这之后,他觉着话题得改变一下,就接着说,"我的朋友是澳大利亚人,他是一个性子非常急的人。"

"一个澳大利亚人?"另一个说,"我倒也有一个弟兄在墨尔本①。你的朋友是从那儿来的吗?"

"不,离那儿有一点路,"美术家回答,他对于新荷兰②的地理有一点搞不清,"他住在里头老远的地方,是非常有钱的。"

这些流浪汉肃然起敬地向那个打瞌睡的殖民者盯着看。

"嗯,"第二个讲话的人评论说,"澳大利亚,那是个好大的地方啊。你也是从那儿来的吗?"

"不,我不是从那儿来的。"皮特曼说。"我不是从那

---

① 墨尔本(Melbourne):澳大利亚南方沿海的一大城市。
② 新荷兰(New Holland):澳大利亚的旧名。一六四二年荷兰航海家塔斯曼(A. G. Tasman,一六〇三——一六五九)发现澳大利亚南岸的大岛,这岛即称塔斯曼尼亚,北面的大陆就是澳大利亚,当时被称为新荷兰。

儿来的，也不想从那儿来。"他很不高兴地说。接着，他觉得需要把形势扭转一下，就转到迈克尔身上，把他摇醒。

"哈啰，"律师说，"什么事？"

"货车差不多准备好啦，"皮特曼严峻地说，"我不能让你睡了。"

"好吧——别生气，老朋友，"迈克尔回答，打着呵欠，"稍微睡一会儿对于谁都不碍事的，我现在觉着酒醒得差不多啦。可是干什么这么忙？"他又说，眼睛迟钝地四面看看。"我没有看见货车，我也忘了我们把钢琴放在哪儿了。"

律师这时候的一股劲儿可能叫他从心里说出什么话来，直到今天，皮特曼猜想起来还是不寒而栗。总算托天之福，这时候货车到了，迈克尔得集中精力，去做那更难做的事了。

"当然，车子得由你驾驶。"他一面爬上车子，一面跟他的伙伴说。

"我驾驶车子！"皮特曼叫唤起来。"我一生也没有干过这种事儿。我不会驾车。"

"很好，"迈克尔十分镇定地回答，"可是我现在眼睛看不清。不过随便你吧。为了朋友，我一切遵命。"

皮特曼看了一眼这位马夫阴沉的脸色，就做了决定。"好啦，"他把心一横，说，"你驾车子。我跟你讲怎么怎么走吧。"

至于迈克尔是怎样一个马车夫（既然现在不准备写一篇冒险故事），这里也不必说了。皮特曼两手抓得紧紧的，坐在车子里气喘吁吁地指点路途,对于迈克尔这段奇异的表演,他是独一无二的见证人,却也不知道该赞叹那驾驭人的勇气呢,还是该感谢他那不配有的好运气。不过至少一大半是仗着好运气,这货车没出一点事儿到了加农街;布朗先生的钢琴也很快很轻巧地弄上了货车。

"嗯,先生,"领头的脚夫说,心中揣摩手中一大把的零碎钱,微笑着,"这钢琴可重得要死呀。"

"那是因为声音洪亮而深沉呀。"迈克尔在赶着马车走的时候回答。

雨绵密地、静静地下着,从这儿到法学院①吉迪恩·福西斯先生事务所附近的地方只有一点路。迈克尔在一条寂无人影的旁街上把马勒住,交给一个垂头丧气的擦鞋人看管。这两个在货车上很不相称的人现在爬下车来,步行到对他们的冒险事业起决定性作用的地点去了。迈克尔这才头一次显出不安的样子。

"我的络腮胡子没有什么吧?"他问。"要是我给人家看出来,那就完蛋啦。"

"胡子挺好地待在原处,"皮特曼差不多没有看就回答,"可是我的化装是不是同样过得去呢?碰着我某些主顾的可能性是再大没有的。"

"哦,你胡子剃光了,谁还看得出你来?"迈克尔说,"你

---

① 法学院(the Temple):在伦敦中区,包括内院(Inner Temple)、中院(Middle Temple)、林肯院(Lincoln's Temple)及格雷院(Gray's Temple)。正式称谓为四法学协会(Inns of court),是英国有检定律师之权及出庭律师设立事务所的地方。

只消记住把话说慢点,你已经应该通过鼻子说话了。"

"我只希望那年轻人不在家。"皮特曼叹口气说。

"我可希望他只一个人在家,"律师回答,"这会省掉不知多少事。"

真是这样,他们敲了门,吉迪恩自己开门,把他们请到一间屋子里;那儿生着微微的火,刚够把里边暖和起来;书架一直高到天花板,装满了有关英国忒弥斯①的审判席上所用的著作,屋子里的陈设,除去一件特别事项之外,有力地提供了那位主人热心于法律的佐证。那件特别事项就是壁炉架上陈列了各式各样的板烟斗、板烟、雪茄烟盒,以及黄色书脊的法国小说。

"我想你就是福西斯先生吧?"迈克尔这样开始晤谈,"我们到这儿来麻烦你一件事情。我恐怕这不很合职业上的规矩——"

"恐怕应当通过一位撰状律师来委任我。"吉迪恩回答。

"嗯,嗯,你自己可以指定一位,这件事可以在明天完全按照规矩行事,"迈克尔回答,一面坐下来,同时示意皮特曼也坐,"不过,你知道,撰状律师我们一位也不认识;我们碰巧听见你的名字,而事情又逼得紧。"

"两位先生,我可否问一声,"吉迪恩问,"是谁推荐我的?"

"你问是可以问,"律师回答,傻笑了一下,"可是人家嘱咐我——在事情没有办完以前,先别跟你说。"

---

① 忒弥斯(Themis):希腊神话中掌管法律和正义的女神。

"一定是我的舅舅,毫无疑问。"这个出庭律师断定。

"我的名字是约翰·迪克逊,"迈克尔继续说,"在巴拉腊特城①里,这是人们相当熟悉的一个名字。我这位朋友是以斯拉·托马斯先生,从美国来的,一个有钱的制造橡胶套鞋的人。"

"请你停一会儿,让我记下来。"吉迪恩说。谁也会觉着他是一位老练的律师。

"也许我抽一支雪茄烟你不见怪吧?"迈克尔问。他进门的时候,已经打起了精神;可是现在他脑子里又起了一阵阵云雾似的不能自主的感觉和轻微的睡意;他希望(正如好多人在同样情况之下希望过的)吸支雪茄烟提提神。

"哦,当然啰,"吉迪恩殷勤地嚷着,"试一支我的;我可以很放心地把这烟介绍给你。"他把一盒烟递给他的当事人。

"假如我没有把话说得很清楚,"这澳大利亚人说,"也许最好还是跟你老实说,我刚才吃了午饭。这是谁都会有的事。"

"哦,当然啰,"出庭律师和颜悦色地回答,"请不要感到局促。我可以给你们,"他深思地看了看表,接着说——"对的,我可以给你们整个下午。"

"我到这儿来的事情,"澳大利亚人有兴味地继续说,"我可以跟你说,是一桩非常难以启齿的事情。我的朋友托马斯先生,他祖籍葡萄牙,是个美国人,对于我们的习

---

① 巴拉腊特(Ballarat):澳大利亚的一个城市。

俗尚不熟悉,他是一个富有的制造布洛德伍德钢琴——"

"布洛德伍德钢琴?"吉迪恩有点惊异地喊道,"天啊,那么托马斯先生是这公司的合股人吗?"

"噢,冒牌的布洛德伍德而已,"迈克尔回答,"我朋友经营的是美国布洛德伍德。"

"可是我以为你说,"吉迪恩提出异议,"我在摘记里的确是这样写的——你的朋友是制造橡胶套鞋的。"

"我知道一开头弄不清楚,"澳大利亚人说,满面堆着笑,"可是他——简言之,他兼营这两种生意。此外还有好些别的哩——好些、好些、好些别的哩。"迪克逊先生用了酒醉中的庄严神态重复地说。"托马斯先生的那些棉纺厂是塔拉哈西①的名胜之一;托马斯先生的烟厂是弗吉尼亚州里士满城所引以为荣的东西。简言之,他是我的最老的朋友之一,福西斯先生,我现在以激动的心情,把他的事情摊在你面前。"

这位出庭律师向托马斯先生看着,因为他那率直而有点紧张的面容和他那质朴而胆小的神气,已使他有了好感。"这种美国人是什么一种人哦!"他在想。"看这个紧张的、瘦弱的、质朴的、穿了低领衬衫的小家伙,谁会想到他竟然控制着那么伟大、看起来跟他那么不相称的事业!可是我们是否应当,"他说出声来,"我们是否应当谈谈事实?"

"先生,我看你真是个办事的人!"澳大利亚人说,"让

---

① 塔拉哈西(Tallahassee):美国佛罗里达州首府。

我们就来谈谈事实吧。这是一件破坏婚约的案子。"

这不幸的美术家再也没有想到会把他说成这样一回事,差点儿止不住叫喊起来。

"啊呀,"吉迪恩说,"这种事可能很麻烦。把一切情形讲给我听吧,"他很和气地又说,"你如果要我帮忙,一点都不要隐瞒。"

"你跟他讲,"迈克尔说,显然觉得已经尽了他的责任,"我的朋友会把这事从头到尾讲给你听。"他打了个呵欠,又对吉迪恩说。"原谅我把眼睛闭一会儿;一个朋友生病,我陪了他一夜。"

皮特曼直发愣,向屋子四周看看,愤怒和绝望在他无辜的心里沸腾着。逃跑的念头,甚至自杀的念头,在他的面前闪现。出庭律师一直在耐着性子等,可是这位美术家连一言半语毫无关系的话都寻不出。

"这是一件破坏婚约的案子,"他最后小声小气地说,"我——我,有人恐吓要告我破坏婚约。"说到这儿,为了迫不及待地向灵感求助,他伸手去抓胡子。他的手指抓着的却是不太熟悉的剃得光光的下巴;这一来,希望和勇气(假如在皮特曼身上这两个名词也安得上的话)联袂而逃了。他把迈克尔狠狠地摇了一下。"醒醒吧!"他带着真是恼了的口气叫着,"我办不了,你知道我办不了。"

"你得原谅我的朋友,"迈克尔说,"他不善于讲述一场剧变。事情很简单,"他说下去,"我的朋友是一个极端热情的人,他一向过着一种简单的、尊贵的生活。你听,事情是这样发生的:他不幸到欧洲来,跟着又不幸结识了一个冒充外国伯爵的人,那人有一位美丽的女儿。托马斯先生为她神魂颠倒;他向她求婚,竟被接受了,他写了情书——他当时所写的那许多话,我相信现在一定叫他后悔了。要是这些情书在法院里被提出来,先生,那托马斯先生的人格整个儿完啦。"

"是不是我可以理解为——"吉迪恩开始说。

"我亲爱的先生,"澳大利亚人郑重地说,"除非你亲自读到,否则那没法了解。"

"这种情况够痛苦的。"吉迪恩说。他对那罪人怜悯地看着,看到他脸上满是慌乱,又怜悯地把视线收回。

"这应该不算什么,"迪克逊先生严正地继续说,"不过我倒希望——先生,我打心底里希望我能说托马斯先生的一双手是干净的。但是他根本就不应该;因为那时候他已经订了婚——到现在仍然如此——未婚妻是咖的君士坦丁堡城的一个美人。我的朋友的行为简直比那班该死的野兽还不如。"

"咖?"吉迪恩欲知其详地重复说。

"这是现在通用的一种简称,"迈克尔说,"咖字代表佐治亚州[①],正像 Co. 代表'公司'[②]一样。"

"我晓得它有时候是这样写,"出庭律师回答,"可是它的念法并不是这样。"

"绝对无错,我可以向你保证。"迈克尔说,"你自己

---

① 佐治亚州(Georgia)简写作 Ga.。因为这是地名的简写,读音仍照原来的字,并不读"咖"。
② "公司"原文为 Company,简写作 Co.,读音照原来的字。

现在也可以看出来了，先生，如果要救这一个不幸的人，那必须来一手非常的、爽辣的办法才成。钱是有的，决不会舍不得用。托马斯先生明天就可以开一张十万镑的支票。而且，福西斯先生，另外还有比钱更好的东西哩。那个外国伯爵——塔诺伯爵，他这样称呼自己——从前是在贝斯沃特①做烟草商的，姓着卑贱的但是容易记得的姓：施密特；他的女儿——要是她是他的女儿的话——这又是一个要点——请你把这点记下来，福西斯先生——他的女儿那时候的的确确在店里帮过忙——而她现在倒说要和托马斯先生地位这么崇高的男人结婚！现在你可以了解我们这局棋了吧？我们知道他们正在琢磨下一着子儿，我们希望预先阻止它。要请你直接到汉普顿宫②，他们就住在那儿，去恐吓他们，或者拿钱动员他们，或者双管齐下，一定得把那些信取回来；要是你做不到的话，天哪，我们免不了上法庭，托马斯就要出丑。我和他也从此完蛋。"这个不讲义气的朋友加上这句话。

"这事看来有些成功的可能性，"吉迪恩说，"警察方面对于施密特多少晓得一点的吧？"

"我们希望如此，"迈克尔说，"我们有种种理由可以这样想。注意近边这地方——贝斯沃特！你觉得贝斯沃特很使人联想到什么吧？"

在这次稀奇的会谈中，吉迪恩恐怕已是第六次在诧异

---

① 贝斯沃特（Bayswater）：伦敦市西一地区。
② 汉普顿宫（Hampton Court）：距伦敦西南十五英里，部分为落魄贵族所居，部分供人游览。

迈克尔是不是兴奋过度。"这或许是他刚才用过午餐的缘故吧,"他想,接着他说出声来,"那么我得开出多少数目呢?"

"也许今天先开个五千就够了。"迈克尔说,"现在,先生,让我不要再耽搁你吧;天快晚了;到汉普顿去的火车有很多班次;我也用不着跟你说我的朋友多么着急。这是一张五镑的钞票,作为眼前的杂用,这是地址。"迈克尔开始写,却停住了,把纸撕了,把碎纸片塞到口袋里。"我来口述吧,"他说,"我的字写得这么不清楚。"

吉迪恩把地址抄了下来,"塔诺伯爵,汉普顿宫,苛诺尔别墅。"他又在一张纸上写了些别的东西。"你说你还没有找好一位撰状律师,"他说,"办这类案子,这是伦敦最好的一位。"他把那张纸交给了迈克尔。

"天啊!"迈克尔念着自己的地址失声喊着。

"哦,我敢说你看见过他的名字跟某些尴尬的案子发生过关系的,"吉迪恩说,"可是他自己却是一位完全诚实的人,而他的才能是人所公认的。现在呢,两位先生,我现在只要问一下跟你们通信的地方。"

"在蓝姆饭店,当然啰,"迈克尔回答,"到今晚为止。"

"到今晚为止,"吉迪恩带着笑说,"我可以在很迟的时间来看你们吧?"

"随便几点钟,随便几点钟。"这个影踪正在消逝的撰状律师喊着。

"嗯,他是一个有头脑的青年哩。"一走到街上,他跟皮特曼说。

只听见皮特曼含含糊糊地自言自语:"十足的傻瓜。"

"他一点也不是,"迈克尔回答,"他晓得伦敦最好的撰状律师是谁,这不是随便哪一个都说得出的。可是,我说,我那一套来得有劲吧?"

皮特曼没有回答。

"喂,"律师说着,停了一下,"受罪受了很久的皮特曼是怎么啦?"

"你没有权利把我说成那样子,"这美术家发作了,"你无论怎样也不该用那种字眼的;你使我伤痛得很厉害。"

"我一个字也没有讲到你,"迈克尔回答,"我讲的是以斯拉·托马斯;你得记住那是子虚乌有的一个人。"

"可一样难以忍受。"美术家说。

这时候他们已经走到这条旁路的拐弯角上了;那个忠诚的擦皮鞋的,装着神气十足、一本正经的样子,在那几匹马的头旁站着。那架钢琴,孤零零地待在货车上面,没有遮盖,雨点打湿了它,雨水顺着它那油漆得很华美的腿脚滴下来。

这擦皮鞋的又给征用到近边的酒店里去找五六个身强力壮的人来,于是这场战事的最后一仗开始了。可能在吉迪恩·福西斯先生还没有坐上那到汉普顿宫的火车之前,迈克尔已经开了他的房门,而那些哼哼唧唧的脚夫已经把布洛德伍德大钢琴放置在屋中央。

"那么现在,"律师把这些人打发走了之后说,"还有一桩事情得考虑到。我们得把钢琴的钥匙留给他,而且我们得想法子让他一定找到。让我看看。"他就在这乐器上面用雪茄堆成一座方形的塔,把钥匙丢在这中间。

"可怜的青年!"美术家说,他们一边走下楼梯来。

"他现在的处境确实糟不堪言,"迈克尔若无其事地表示同意,"这倒会叫他振作一下。"

"这叫我想起来了,"品行优良的皮特曼说,"我恐怕表现了一种不知好歹的脾气。我知道我没有权利来抱怨你说的话,不管那些话是怎样叫人受不了,因为那一点也不是对我而发的。"

"那没有关系,"迈克尔大声说,一面爬上了货车,"别再提啦,皮特曼。你有那种感觉是非常正常的。没有一个有自尊心的人能够站在一边,听任他的别名给人家侮辱。"

雨已经住了,迈克尔是相当清醒了,尸首已经给弄掉,两个朋友也已经和好如初。因此回到马车房的行程(比起这天冒险中前面那些阶段来)真够得上称作假期中的出游。他们把货车还了,从马车房的院子里走出来,没有给人查问,甚至也没有引起人家注意。皮特曼衷心愉快,深深地吸了一口气。

"哎,现在呢,"他说,"我们可以回家去了。"

"皮特曼,"律师说,突然停了脚步,"你这样漫不经心,真使我担忧。怎么!我们今天整整一大半时间全是淋得湿答答的,而你倒是全无心肝,马上提议回家!不成,先生——热的苏格兰酒①。"

于是他挽了朋友的手臂,态度坚决地带他到最近的一

---

① 苏格兰酒(Scotch):这里指苏格兰出产的有名的威士忌酒。

家酒店里去。皮特曼可也并非(我得抱憾地说)完全不愿。现在是和平重现、尸体已去的时候,这位美术家的举止里开始呈现出一些无忧无虑、活泼轻佻的样子;当他把他那冒着热气的杯子和迈克尔的杯子相碰的时候,他正像一个淘气的女学生在郊游中那样咻咻地大声傻笑。

第九章　迈克尔·芬斯伯里假期的辉煌成就

本人认识迈克尔·芬斯伯里。我的事情——我知道找上了这样一位律师多么糟糕——不过这已是老话了,而且一个人还应该懂得感谢。说得简单点吧,我的法律上的事情,虽然现在已经(我很高兴能够这样说)相当地风平浪静,可还是空悬在迈克尔手里。我有个毛病:没有记住地址的天才;我把每个朋友的一个住址牢记在心——这是我对朋友的特别贡献;可是那位朋友后来更换了住所,对我说来可就等于亡故了一样,我的记忆力追也追不到他了。因为情形是这样的,所以我写信给迈克尔从来都寄到他的事务所,而他在皇家大道的住所的门牌号码,我就不能肯定了。当然啰,我(像我的邻居们一样)也曾经在他的住所里吃过饭。近年来,自从他拥有巨资,对业务马马虎虎,又被选到俱乐部里之后,举办这种小型的宴乐已成为司空见惯的事。他在吸烟室里挑选少数几个朋友——全是潇洒文雅的人士——譬如我自己吧,只要他能幸而碰上我有空。一连串的轻马车（女王陛下可以看到）穿过圣詹姆斯公园①，热热闹闹地一路驶去；一刻钟之内这一伙人就围着备有伦敦最精美的山珍海味的餐桌之一，坐了下来。

我们写到这儿的时候，皇家大道上那所房屋里（让我们仍旧叫它为二三三号吧）却非常安静。迈克尔要大宴宾客，总是在尼各尔饭店或孚莱饭店召集他们，他私人住宅的大门则对朋友们关着。楼上一层阳光充足，专给他父亲住；客厅从来没有用过；饭厅才是迈克尔生活的园地。这是间很舒服的房间，金属线制成的窗帘遮住了皇家大道上的好奇的探视，四周密密围绕着这位律师收藏的无出其右的关于诗和刑事审案的图书，他和皮特曼度完了那个假期之后，我们就在这儿看见他坐下来进晚餐。一位瘦弱的老妇人，双目炯炯有神，嘴唇很滑稽地紧抿着，伺候着这位律师。她脸上的每一条皱纹都显示出她是一位老家人；她嘴里吐出的每一个字都夸示出苏格兰血统的光荣。这两种表现的有力合作能使最勇敢的人感到害怕，对于这一点，显然我们这位朋友也并非心中无数。那几杯热的苏格兰酒已经使海德西克的余烬多少复燃起来了，看着这位主人一副急惶惶的样子，在他仆人的目光下强作镇定，叫人真有点于心不忍。"我想，媞娜，我想喝点白兰地掺苏打水。"他说这句话，说得像一个对自己的口才没有信心的人一样，对方是否会照办，连一半把握都没有。

对方回答得很快："没有这种东西，迈克尔先生，红葡萄

---

① 圣詹姆斯公园（St. James's Park）：在伦敦中区，英王宫白金汉宫（Buckingham Palace）对面。

酒掺水。"

"好吧,好吧,媞娜,我知道你准没错。"主人说,"哦,事务所里这一天可累得很。"

"什么?"仆人说,"你连走都没有走近过你的事务所!"

"哦,怎么不?我在舰队街上跑来跑去不止一次哩。"迈克尔回答。

"那你今天玩得痛快啊!"她老人家幽默而又干脆地高声说。"当心——不要砸碎我的水晶!"正当律师差一点把桌上的杯子碰得掉下来的时候,她叫了起来。

"他怎么样?"迈克尔问。

"哦,还不是老样子,迈克尔先生,他一直到底都会是这个样子吧,这个好人!"这是答复。"不过今天你不是头一个问我这句话的人。"

"不是吗?"律师说,"还有谁?"

"嘿,这也是个笑话,"媞娜正颜厉色地说,"你的一位朋友:莫里斯先生。"

"莫里斯!这小要饭的来这儿干吗?"迈克尔问。

"要干什么吗?要看他,"管家人回答,大拇指往楼上指指,表明她的意思,"那是他的想法;可是我有我自己的主意。他想贿赂我,迈克尔先生。贿赂——我!"她重复说,她那种鄙夷的神情别人学也学不来。"简直不是一个年轻君子做的事。"

"他竟然这样吗?"迈克尔说,"我敢说他肯出的钱不多。"

"他不肯再多。"媞娜回答。后来的问话也没有能够从她那儿问出,那个节俭的皮革商究竟想拿出多少钱来腐蚀她。"我可把他撵走了,"她说,一副英雄气概,"他不会再冒冒失失地跑来了。"

"决不能让他见我的父亲,你知道的;这得留心!"迈克尔说,"我不打算对他那个小畜生开什么展览会。"

"放心,我不会依他的,"这靠得住的人回答,"可笑的是这个,迈克尔先生——你看,你把酱油打翻了,这是块干干净净的台布哪——顶可笑的是他猜想你的父亲已经死了,而你隐瞒着这件事。"

迈克尔吹起口哨来。"贼喊捉贼。"他说。

"我跟他讲的就是这句话!"这婆子高兴得直嚷嚷。

"为了这个,我得让他吃点苦头。"迈克尔说。

"你不能想办法告他吗?"媞娜好不狠心地建议。

"不,我想我不能,而且很明白自己不打算这样做,"迈克尔回答,"哎,我说,媞娜,我真的不相信这红葡萄酒有什么好;这不是一种可靠的醇酒。给咱们来点儿白兰地掺苏打水吧,好心眼儿的人哪。"媞娜的脸绷得像铁石一般。"那么,好吧,"律师气恼地说,"晚饭我就吃到这儿为止。"

"悉听尊便,迈克尔先生。"媞娜说着就泰然无事地动手把东西端开。

"我真愿媞娜不是一个忠于职守的仆人。"律师踏上了皇家大道,叹了口气。

雨已经停了;风还吹着,不过是清新爽快的;在这清澈的夜晚的黑暗中,这城市只有路灯闪着光,雨水积成的潭一亮一亮的。"啊,这才舒服些了。"律师自己心里想。

他往东走去,愉快地听着城市里辚辚的车轮声和无数的脚步声。

快走完这条皇家大道了,他又想起白兰地掺苏打水来,于是踅进一家灯光绚烂的酒店。里边有好些顾客,一个从马车停车处来的挑水夫①,五六个长年失业的人,一位先生(在这边角落里)从一只皮包中掏出些美术照片想卖给另外一位,又有一位年纪很轻的长着黄色山羊胡子的先生,还有一对情人在辩论一种细腻微妙的问题(在另一边角落里)。可是有极大吸引力的中心人物是一个小个子的老人,他穿了一件现成的黑色大礼服形大衣,那显然是新买的。在他面前的大理石台子上,一客三明治和一杯啤酒旁边放着一顶弄坏了的步兵便帽。他揎拳攘臂,飞舞着演讲的姿势;他的嗓子,本来就尖锐,显然更提高到在讲堂里所用的调门了。他用可以与那位"古舟子"②相媲美的艺术,使得酒吧姑娘、挑水夫和那四个失业者都像着了魔。

"我查看过伦敦所有的戏院,"他正在说,"我用脚步量量那些主要进出口,查明它们对于观众进出人数来说,是不成比例到可笑的程度。开门的方向先就开错了——一时我记不起哪一家,不过我家里有一个记录,在表演时间里门常常锁上,大厅里这时却简直挤满了英国的人民。你

---

① 挑水夫(waterman):马车停车处挑水给马饮的人。
② "古舟子"(Ancient Mariner):英国诗人柯勒律治(Samuel Taylor Coleridge,一七七二——一八三四)所作长诗《古舟子咏》(*The Rime of the Ancient Mariner*)中的人物。那首诗歌叙述古代一位舟子对一位要到某处参加结婚盛典的客人讲海上奇闻,使那听者好像着魔一般,直到听完才能走开。

们可能没有我那种机会把这个跟远在国外的地方的情形比较一下；不过我可以告诉你们，这种情形早已被认为是贵族掌权的政府的一种特征。你们想想看，在一个真正民治的国家里，这些弊病能够存在吗？你们自己的智慧，纵然没有经过怎样培养，也足以告诉你们这是不能存在的。就说奥地利吧，那个国家奴役人民可能比英国更要厉害一点。我亲身跟玲因剧院里一个老人谈过，虽然他的德国话说得不怎么好，他对这事的意见我却得到一个相当清楚的概念。不过，你们或许对这个更感兴趣，这是一张从维也纳报纸上剪下来的有关这个问题的剪报，我现在念给你们听，一边念一边翻译。你们可以亲眼看看，这是用德文印的。"他就把剪报递出去证实他的话，恰像一个变戏法的人把一只变戏法用的橘子拿给前排座位上的观众，传递过去一样。

"哈啰，老先生！你在这儿？"迈克尔说，把手搁在演说家的肩上。

这个躯体吓了一跳，转过来，现出约瑟夫·芬斯伯里先生的面貌。

"你，迈克尔！"他叫着，"没有别人跟你一起来吧，没有吧？"

"没有，"迈克尔回答，叫了白兰地掺苏打水，"我一个人。你以为还有谁？"

"我是想到莫里斯或者约翰。"这位老先生说，显然如释重负。

"我跟莫里斯或者约翰那些家伙有什么好来往的？"这侄子喊着。

"这话有点道理,"约瑟夫回应,"我相信我可以信任你。我相信你会站在我这一边。"

"我弄不懂你的意思,"律师说,"要是你缺钱的话,我倒有的是。"

"倒不是钱,我的好孩子,"叔父说,握握他的手,"待会儿我跟你从头谈一谈。"

"好的,"侄子回答说,"我请客,约瑟夫叔叔。你吃些什么?"

"既然你请客,"老先生回答说,"我就再来一客三明治吧。我敢说我叫你惊讶了,"他接着说,"竟然在一爿酒店里看到我;不过事实上我是按照我自己一种正确的而别人不大知道的原则行事——"

"哦,并不像你想象的那样,这种原则知道的人并不少,"迈克尔说着,啜了一口白兰地掺苏打水,"我自己要喝点酒的时候,就一直按照这原则行事。"

老先生竭力想讨好迈克尔,干笑了一声。"你的兴致这么好,"他说,"说实在的,我往往因此觉得很高兴。不过讲到我刚才打算说的原则——这原则是,如果命运使我们落到一个什么地方来,我们就得使自己适应这个地方的(不管是怎样卑微的)生活方式。譬如说吧,在法国,大家都到咖啡馆去吃饭;在美国呢,到所谓'两角五分食堂'①;在英国,我们就常到现在这样的场所来吃东西。吃点儿三明治、茶,有时再来杯苦啤酒。在伦敦,你每年花

---

① "两角五分食堂"(two-bit house):美国一种食堂,每餐只需美金两角五分。bit 是一角二分五,two-bit 是两角五分。

上十四镑十二先令，就可以过得舒舒服服。"

"是的，我知道，"迈克尔回答，"可是这不包括衣着、洗衣费，或靴子。一切东西在内，连雪茄烟和有时来几次痛饮，每年总得花掉我七百多镑。"

然而这是迈克尔末了一次的发言。以后的时间里都是他叔父的长篇大论，他很有涵养地静静听着，这篇演讲很快岔到政治改革，再从政治改革扯到晴雨表的理论，说了一段亚得里亚海里暴风雨的故事做例子；又从晴雨表的理论转到教授聋哑学生学数学的最好的方法。讲到这儿，三明治已经无影无踪，这才心满意足地走了；一会儿之后，这一对出现在皇家大道上。

"迈克尔，"他的叔父说，"我之所以来到这个地方，是因为我吃不消那两个侄子。我觉得他们真叫人受不了。"

"我敢说你没有说错，"迈克尔表示同意，"我跟他们一块儿待一分钟都受不了。"

"他们不让我说话，"老先生恨恨地又说下去，"我抽空儿从旁插一两句嘴都不许，他们会立刻用无礼的话叫我闭嘴。我想写点笔记，把再好玩也没有的趣事记下来，他们却克扣我的铅笔供应。他们提防我拿到每天的报纸，就像提防着娃娃给猩猩抓去一样。哦，你是了解我的,迈克尔。我活着，就是为了我的统计数字；我活着，就是为了我的错综复杂并且时刻变换的人生观。笔、纸以及种种通俗刊物，这些东西对于我来说就跟饮食一样重要哩。正当我的生活变得十分难受的时候，幸而百朗亭火车出了事，混乱中我逃了出来。他们一定以为我死了，为了得到'通蒂会'

的钱,一定在设法蒙骗世人。"

"说起来,你钱够用吧?"迈克尔善意地问。

"说到经济状况呢,我倒是富裕的,"老头儿愉快地回答,"我现在是按照一年花一百镑的等级生活着。笔跟纸要多少有多少;大英博物馆里有书看;还有所有我要看的报纸。在一个进步的时代里,一个对学问有兴趣的人,竟可以不必常去麻烦书本子,倒的确是奇怪的事。报纸把所有的结论全都供给你了。"

"我跟你说,"迈克尔说,"来跟我一起住吧。"

"迈克尔,"老先生说,"感谢你的好意,可是你差不多一点也不知道我的特殊处境。我碰到了银钱上的小纠纷,虽然是个监护人,我种种努力却不见得怎么顺利。也不必把事情原委细细说清了,我是完全在那可恶的混蛋莫里斯的手掌心里。"

"那你应当化装,"迈克尔急切地说,"我可以借给你一副窗玻璃片的眼镜,还有红色的络腮胡子。"

"我已经研究过这个办法,"老先生回答,"可是我怕惹起我那朴实无华的住处的人们的注意。至于那些贵族,我很晓得——"

"可是,哎,"迈克尔打断他的话,"你竟怎样弄到一点钱的呢?别把我当外人,约瑟夫叔叔;那件委托保管金钱的事,还有你把它弄得一团糟,以及你迫不得已做一个转让手续给莫里斯这些事我完全清楚。"

约瑟夫把他到银行去取钱的事讲了。

"哦,不过我看,这事不行,"律师喊着,"你弄糟了。

你没有权利那样做。"

"一切的一切都是我的,迈克尔,"老先生抗议着说,"完全是我苦心筹划,把那爿店创立起来、扩展起来的。"

"一点都不错,"律师说,"可是你做了一个转让手续,而且你是迫不得已做的;即使那时候你的处境已极端危险了。这一回哩,我亲爱的先生,这是吃官司的事。"

"这绝不可能,"约瑟夫叫喊着,"法律不能那么不公平!"

"事情妙就妙在——"迈克尔忽然放声大笑着接口说,"事情妙就妙在——你实在已经把这皮革店弄垮了!我不得不说,约瑟夫叔叔,你对于法律的见解是奇特的,不过我倒喜欢你的幽默感。"

"我看不出这有什么好笑的。"芬斯伯里先生尖刻地说。

"说到这桩事,我想问问莫里斯有没有出面给这店签字的权利?"迈克尔问。

"除了我没有别人。"约瑟夫回答。

"可怜的小鬼莫里斯!哦,可怜的小鬼莫里斯!"律师开心地叫起来,"他还要滑稽透顶地假装你待在家里呢!哦,莫里斯,老天可把你送到我的手里来啦!让我看看,约瑟夫叔叔,你看这皮革店值多少钱?"

"曾经值过十万镑,"约瑟夫恨恨地说,"那是它在我自己手里的时候。可是后来来了一个苏格兰人——他被认为有点儿本领——完全发挥在簿记上了——整个伦敦没有一个会计员能够懂他账簿上一个字。之后呢,就是莫里斯,他又完全不能称职。到现在这爿店已所值无几了。

去年莫里斯想把它卖掉,可是鲍格兰－贾利斯店只肯出四千镑。"

"我打算把我的精力转移到皮革方面。"迈克尔做了一个决定说。

"你?"约瑟夫问,"我劝你不要。整个商业界再也没有比皮革市场的波动更叫人吃惊的了。它的敏感性可以说是病态的。"

"那么现在,约瑟夫叔叔,你把那些钱都怎么处理了呢?"律师问。

"存到一家银行里去了,取出来二十镑。"芬斯伯里先生很快地回答,"干吗?"

"很好,"迈克尔说,"我明天差一个书记带一张一百镑的支票来,跟你换回那笔钱,还给英格兰－巴塔哥尼亚银行,同时附带一种解释,这解释我会给你措辞。这样一来就可以替你洗清了。再说莫里斯,他既然除了伪造签名之外无法动用分文,对于我这小小的计划也就不会有什么影响。"

"可是我怎么办呢?"约瑟夫问,"我不能喝西北风啊。"

"你没听见吗?"迈克尔回答,"我给你送来一张一百镑的支票,这多出的八十镑可以做你的用度。等到那笔钱用完了,你再问我要。"

"不管怎么说我还是不愿意受你的恩惠,"约瑟夫说,咬咬他的白胡子,"既然我自己有钱,我情愿用自己的。"

迈克尔一把抓住他的手臂。"难道你就相信不了,"他叫着,"我是在设法把你从达特穆尔^①救出来吗?"

他的诚恳使这老头儿激动起来。"我不得不把注意力转移到法律方面去了,"他说,"这将是一个新的园地;因为虽然理所当然我懂得它的一般原理,我可从来没有在细节上怎么用过心,以你对这事情的见解为例吧,那简直出乎我意料。不过你可能是对的,而且以我现在的年龄——因为我已经不再年轻了——真正长期的监禁当然是非常不利的。可是,我的好侄子,我不能向你要什么,你没有义务来赡养我。"

"那倒无所谓,"迈克尔说,"我很可能从皮革生意里得到补偿。"

迈克尔写下老先生的地址,就在街角和他分手了。

"一个多么有趣的老糊涂!"他心里想,"人生又是一个多么奇妙的东西!我好像是命里注定要替天行道似的。让我看看,我今儿都做了些什么?弄掉了一具尸首,救了皮特曼,救了我的约瑟夫叔叔,使福西斯振作起来,又喝了不知多少糟不堪言的酒。让我们以访问我的两个堂兄弟作为结束,来诚诚恳恳地替天行道吧。明天,我可以再去对付皮革店的事;今晚,我去用点温和的方法,叫他们兴奋一下。"

大约一刻钟之后,时钟正敲了十一下,这位替天行道的人从一辆二轮轻马车上跳下来,叫赶车的等着,就去敲约翰街十六号的大门。

---

① 达特穆尔(Dartmoor):指达特穆尔监狱,一所著名监狱,在德文郡(Devonshire)内。

莫里斯立刻开了门。

"哦,是你呀,迈克尔,"他说,有意把开着的一点缝儿挡住,"很晚啦。"

迈克尔一言不发,只管冲上来,热烈地抓住莫里斯的手,把它那么狠命地一握,使这位乖戾的户主直往后退。趁此时机,律师一步踏进了穿堂间,长驱直入,来到餐厅,莫里斯跟踪在后。

"我的约瑟夫叔叔在哪儿?"迈克尔问着,就在顶舒服的一把椅子上坐下来。

"他近来身体不大好,"莫里斯回答,"他现在待在百朗亭,约翰在照顾他。我就一个人在这儿,就像你看见的。"

迈克尔跟自己笑了一笑。"我有特别的事情要见他。"他说。

"你不让我看你的父亲,你也不用打算看我的二伯父。"莫里斯回答。

"胡扯,"迈克尔说,"我的父亲是我的父亲;可是约瑟夫是你的二伯父,却也是我的叔父啊;而且你无权扣押他这个人。"

"我没有做这种事,"莫里斯执拗地说,"他身体不好,他病得很厉害,谁都不能看他。"

"那么,我跟你说吧,"迈克尔说,"我要跟你坦坦白白地说。我是像一只负鼠①一样到这儿来的,莫里斯,我

----

① 负鼠(opossum):一种动物,产在美国南部,尾长能钩树枝,腹有袋,如袋鼠,遇见敌人的时候会蜷缩成团,假装已死,等有机会就跳走。

是来妥协的。"

可怜的莫里斯脸色变得死一样的灰白,然后对于人类命运的不公平激起了一阵愤怒,染得他两边鬓角都红了。"你这是什么话?"他叫着,"我一个字都不信!"等迈克尔保证他是诚心诚意的之后,"嗯,那么,"他鬓角又深深地红了一阵,叫着,"我不干,什么道理你自己慢慢去想吧。"

"哦嗬!"迈克尔怪声说,"你说你的二伯父病得很厉害,可是你又不愿意妥协?这里边很有点蹊跷。"

"你说什么?"莫里斯沙哑地喊着。

"我不过是说'脊鳍',"迈克尔回答,"那就是说,关于鱼族的。"

"你是不是话里有话啊?"莫里斯暴风雨般地吼着,试试自己的高压手段。

"话里有话?"迈克尔重复说,"哦,我们不要开始用不好听的字眼吧!让我们像两个和睦的本家那样,借着一瓶酒的力量把我们有分歧的意见消融掉吧。就是有时说是莎士比亚写的那《两个和睦的本家》①。"他这样往下说。

莫里斯脑子像水车一样转动着。"他疑心我吗?还是碰巧给他胡说说中了?我是要哄他一哄呢,还是跟他吵?哄他,"他下了结论,"这可以拖延点时间。好吧,"他说

---

① 与莎士比亚同时之英剧作家约翰·弗莱彻(John Fletcher,一五七九——一六二五)著有《两个高贵的本家》(*The Two Noble Kinsmen*),其中部分为莎士比亚所写。此处迈克尔讹为《两个和睦的本家》(*The Two Affable Kinsmen*)。

出声来，很难受地装出热诚的样子，"我们好久没有在一起消磨一个晚上了，迈克尔，虽然我平常很少喝酒（你是知道的），现在却很愿意破个例。对不起，请少坐一会儿，待我到地窖子里去拿瓶威士忌来。"

"别给我威士忌，"迈克尔说，"来一点不起气泡的陈香槟酒，不然什么也不必拿。"

莫里斯待了一会儿，不知如何是好，因为这酒太贵重了；然后他一声不响地走出这屋子。他灵敏的头脑已经想到了他的好机会；拿出地窖子里的上品来收服他，恐怕就会玩迈克尔于股掌之上。"一瓶？"他在想，"哼，我给他来两瓶！这时候不能讲省钱；只等这畜生一喝醉，我要不把他的秘密诈出来才怪。"

于是他拿了两瓶回来。酒杯已经摆好，莫里斯便慷慨地把酒杯斟满。

"我为你的健康干杯，堂哥哥！"他轻松愉快地叫着，"在我家里可别控制酒量啊。"

迈克尔站在桌旁，从容不迫地喝他那杯酒。然后他又斟满了一杯，回到原来的座位上，顺手把那瓶酒也带了来。

"战利品啊！"他带着歉意说，"弱者败北。很科学，莫里斯，很科学哪。"莫里斯想不出一句答话，沉寂就降临了好一会儿。可是两杯不起气泡的香槟酒却很快地使迈克尔发生了变化。

"你不够气魄，莫里斯，"他讲，"也许你是心计深的；可是要说你有气魄，我死也不相信。"

"何以见得我是心计深的呢？"莫里斯问，带着一种愉快的天真的神情。

"因为你不肯妥协,"律师说,"你是心计深的家伙,莫里斯,心计非常深的家伙,不妥协——真是一个工于心计的坏东西。这杯酒好得不得了;这是芬斯伯里家里唯一令人尊敬的地方,这酒比爵位还要难得——难得得多。嗯,地窖里有这样好的酒的人,我不懂为什么不肯妥协?"

"喂,从前你不肯妥协哩,你知道的,"堆上笑容的莫里斯说,"礼尚往来,这才是公平交易。"

"我不懂为什么我不肯妥协?我不懂为什么你又不肯?"迈克尔问着。"我不懂为什么我们各人都猜想对方不肯?这是太奇特——奇特的问题,"他又说,克服了说话的困难,显然不免有点自负,"很奇怪我们各人想些什么——你也奇怪?"

"你看我是因为什么呢?"莫里斯狡猾地问。

迈克尔朝他看看,眨了眨眼睛。"这倒好,"他说,"第二件事,你将会请求我把你从一团糟里救出来。我知道我是替天行道,但还不是那种天使!你得像伊索①跟另外那个人一样谋自救之道。对于一个四十岁的年轻孤儿说来,那一团糟一定糟得可怕——皮革店跟一切种种!"

"我实在不晓得你在说些什么。"莫里斯说。

"我自己也不一定知道,"迈克尔说,"这是很好的酒,先生——很好的酒。我不反对酗酒。就是一件事——现在一位贵重的叔叔失踪了。嗯,我要知道的就是:贵重的

---

① 伊索(Aesop,公元前六二〇—前五六〇):希腊的寓言小说家,足智多谋,后来死于国事。

叔叔在哪儿?"

"我已经告诉你了:他在百朗亭。"莫里斯回答,偷偷地抹抹前额,因为这些反复的讽示已经开始使他受罪。

"很容易说百朗——百朗地衣——结果倒并不怎么容易!"迈克尔叫着,"说说容易,随便什么事情说说容易,只要你能说得出。我所不满意的是一个叔叔彻头彻尾失踪。不是生意经。"于是他摇摇头。

"这是再简单没有了,"莫里斯回答,竭力保持镇定,"并没有什么神秘。他待在百朗亭,他因为火车出事受了震动。"

"啊!"迈克尔说,"震动得不得了!"

"你为什么这样说?"莫里斯尖声叫喊着说。

"有最好的根据。你自己这样告诉我啦,"律师说,"不过要是你现在跟我说相反的话,我当然非得或者相信这个说法,或者相信那个说法。问题是——我已经叫这酒瓶底朝天了,不起气泡的香槟是最好的东西,毛毯——问题是,贵重的叔叔是不是死了——而且——葬了?"

莫里斯从座位上蹦了起来。"你说什么?"他喘着气问。

"我说最好的东西毛毯,"迈克尔回答,一面站起来,"最好的东西有增进皮肤健康的作用。嗯,不管怎么说,全是一码事。给我问香槟叔叔好。"

"你打算走了吗?"莫里斯说。

"非常抱歉,老朋友。还得陪病朋友……陪他一夜。"摇摇摆摆的迈克尔说。

"你不把你那些讽示解释清楚不许走!"莫里斯凶狠

地回答,"你是什么意思?你到这儿来是想干什么?"

"不见怪吧,我相信,"律师说,一面开了房门,一面转过身来,"只是尽我替天行道的责任而已。"

他一路摸索到大门口,费了一点事才把大门打开,走下台阶,向那辆二轮轻马车走去。疲倦的赶车的见他来了,抬头问再到哪儿去。

迈克尔看到莫里斯跟着他走到台阶上,他心中闪来神妙的灵感。"只要能使他受罪,"他想着……"到伦敦警察厅。"他接着大声说了这句,扶着轮子让自己站得稳一点。"赶车的,那两个堂兄弟,有点事儿非常跷蹊。非得弄清楚不可!到伦敦警察厅去。"

"你不是这个意思吧,先生,"这人说,带着下层阶级的人对一个喝醉酒的绅士的一种天然存在的同情心,"我最好还是把你送回家吧,先生;你可以明天到伦敦警察厅去。"

"你是以朋友的立场,还是以职业上的立场,劝我今晚不要到伦敦警察厅去?"迈克尔问。"好吧,不用管伦敦警察厅吧,到快乐酒吧间去吧。"

"快乐酒吧间已经关门啦。"赶车的说。

"那么回家。"迈克尔说,依然是那样兴奋愉快。

"哪儿,先生?"

"我记不得了,说实话,"迈克尔说着上了车,"把车赶到伦敦警察厅去问吧。"

"不过你总有名片的,"赶车的对着车顶上的小洞里说,"把你的名片盒子给我。"

"好一个赶车人的想——想象力！"律师叫着，拿出名片盒子，交给赶车的。

这人借着路灯的光看着名片。"切尔西，皇家大道二三三号，迈克尔·芬斯伯里先生。是这儿吧，先生？"

"不错，"迈克尔喊着，"只要你还看得清楚路，就赶到那儿去吧。"

第十章　吉迪恩·福西斯和布洛德伍德大钢琴

　　读者或许看过 E. H. B 写的那本杰作《谁把时钟拨慢了?》，那本书在火车站的书摊上出现了几天，就此从地球上整个儿消失了。不知是否饕餮的"时间之神"以老版的书当作了它的主要食品；也不知是否老天为作家们制订了一项特别法规；也不知是否这班作家自己擅作主张，暗地里结成私党，提出某种口号，这口号我宁死也不泄露，而在一位活跃的领袖如詹姆士·潘恩[①]先生或沃尔特·比桑特[②]先生的领导之下，夜复一夜地蜂拥而出，去做那秘密的劫掠工作——无论怎么着，至少这是肯定的，就是老书不见了，让位给新出版的书了。说到证据，一般相信《谁把时钟拨慢了?》现在只存有三本：一本在大英博物馆里，因为登错了图书目录，隐藏得万无一失；一本在爱丁堡的

[①]　詹姆士·潘恩（James Payn，一八三〇——八九八）：英国小说家。
[②]　沃尔特·毕桑特（Sir Walter Besant，一八三六——九〇一）：英国小说家。

律师图书馆①的一个地窨子里（就是堆着乐谱的那个地窨子）；还有一本书面用摩洛哥皮装订的，却由吉迪恩·福西斯收藏着。要知道这第三本书为什么会有这样不同的命运，顶现成的说法是吉迪恩欣赏这书中的故事。至于要问到他怎么竟然会欣赏（对于凡是读过那本书的人说来），就似乎难解释得多了。要么只能说"癞痢头儿子自家的好"，因为吉迪恩（他幽默地借用了舅舅的姓名的起首字母②，但这个跟他舅舅无关）就是《谁把时钟拨慢了？》的作者。他从来没有承认过这一点，或者只在书还在校对的时候对几个亲密的朋友说过；等到它问世而遭到惨败之后，这位小说家的谦虚作风就更深了一层，因而这个秘密可能比《威弗莱》③的作者是谁，保守得更好。

这书有一本（因为我说的已是昨日的事）布满了尘埃，仍然冷冷清清地躺在滑铁卢车站的书摊上；当吉迪恩拿了到汉普顿宫去的火车票走过这书摊的时候，他对着他的思想的结晶轻蔑地微微一笑。那位作家是抱着何等渺茫的野心哪！这种小孩子的玩意儿他是应该怎样不屑为之啊！他抓紧了他的第一桩案子的卷宗，觉得自己毕竟是个男子汉了。那时有个在一桩有关风化的案子中担任主角的女神，

---

① 律师图书馆（Advocates' Library）：英国爱丁堡的一所大图书馆，始建于一六八二年，属于律师协会。
② 书中吉迪恩舅舅名为爱德华·休·布洛姆菲尔德（Edward Hugh Bloom-field）（见第五章），以头一字母简写为 E. H. B.。
③ 《威弗莱》(*Waverley*)：英国小说家和诗人沃尔特·司各特所著的一本小说，初版时（一八一四）作者未用真姓名，致引起很多猜测。

大概是个法国女人,打他身边飘过,回到赫利孔山①去会她的希腊姊妹,跟她们一起绕着泉水舞蹈。

一种生气勃勃的、从实际上着眼的想法使这年轻的出庭律师一路上觉得兴高采烈。他看中了大橡树林中孤岛似的一幢乡村别墅,一次又一次地盘算将来在那儿住家。他一边走过那儿,一边心中筹划怎样把那地方弄得更好一点,就像是个细心的屋主人了。这儿加一所马厩,那儿辟一个网球场,还有个地方想添间像样点的有乡间风味的船库。

"不就是一会儿之前的事么,"他不由自主地沉思着,"我还不过是像只但求温饱、无所用心的小狗一样!我只爱划划船,看看侦探小说,除此之外什么都不要。我真可以走过一幢古色古香的乡村别墅,有着大菜园、马厩、船库和宽敞的办公室的乡村别墅,连正眼都不瞧,更不用说去问那儿有没有排水道了。人是怎样跟着年龄成熟的呀!"

明智的读者一定会看出海士尔坦小姐的影响是多么厉害。吉迪恩那天把茱莉娅一直带到布洛姆菲尔德先生的家里;这位先生知道了她是个受欺压的遭难者之后,大嚷大闹着为她抱不平。他把自己直弄得热血沸腾!在这种情况之下,像他那种性格的人,采取一种行动是势所必然的。

"我不晓得哪一个更坏,"他喊着,"是那个欺诈人的老坏蛋呢,还是那个没有男子气的小子。我一定要写篇文章送到《蓓尔美尔杂志》去,把他们的事情揭露出来。岂有此理啊,先生,一定得把他们揭露出来!这是公民应尽

---

① 赫利孔山(Helicon):在希腊。据希腊神话是太阳神阿波罗和司文艺科学的女神住的地方。

的责任。你不是跟我说那家伙是个保守党员吗?哦,他伯父则是个激进派的演说家,是吧?毫无疑问,那伯父一定已经受到了粗暴的虐待。那么当然,正如你所说,这把情形改变了,这一来公民的责任就不见得怎样大了。"

他想着想着,立刻为他的活跃的劲儿找到了一条新的出路。海士尔坦小姐(他现在看来)必须被藏起来;他的住家船正泊在那儿,随时可上——一两天以前他刚结束了航行回来;要隐藏的话,再也没有比住家船更好的地方了。就在那天早上,冒着猛烈的东风,布洛姆菲尔德先生、夫人和茱莉娅·海士尔坦小姐开始了他们不合时宜的航行。吉迪恩恳求参加,可是被拒绝了。"不成,吉德,"舅舅说。"人家会注意你的,你必须避开我们。"这出庭律师却也不敢辩驳这奇怪的想法,因为他只怕如果在这雅人雅事上煞了他一点风景,布洛姆菲尔德先生就可能对这整个事情厌倦起来。他的审慎得到了回报,因为这位"乡绅激进派"把一只沉重的手按在外甥的肩膀上,加上了这几句值得注意的言论:"我知道你在追求什么,吉德。可是你要想得到这位姑娘的话,你必须去工作,先生。"

当这位出庭律师白天在事务所里看书的时候,这些悦耳的声音一直在鼓舞着他。当他奔驶到汉普顿宫去的时候,这些悦耳的声音一路上继续成为他那男子气概的思潮的基调。甚至在他下了火车,开始集中精力准备面对微妙的会谈的时候,内德[①]舅舅的声音和茱莉娅的眼睛他也没能忘

---

① 原文为 Ned,是爱德华(Edward)的简称。

得了。

可是现在令人惊讶的事纷至沓来了:在整个汉普顿宫,就没有一座奇诺尔别墅,也找不到塔诺伯爵,根本没有什么伯爵。这是怪事,不过只要想起他那前言不对后语的吩咐的话,或许就不怎么难以理解了,迪克逊先生那时已用过午餐,因此很可能把地址完全弄错。那么应当采取什么步骤才是彻底、敏捷、有男子气概而且是精明干练的样子呢?吉迪恩这样想,他立即答复自己:"打个电报,要言简意赅。"一会儿工夫,下面这个非常重要的信息在电线上闪了过去。"蓝姆饭店,迪克逊。别墅及人无着,地址或误;我下班车到。福西斯。"真的,不久之后,吉迪恩下了一辆热气腾腾的二轮轻马车,来到蓝姆饭店,眉宇间透出急匆匆的和殚精竭虑的神情。

我想吉迪恩再也不会忘记这个蓝姆饭店了。第一,这儿没有塔诺伯爵;第二,可也没有约翰·迪克逊,也没有以斯拉·托马斯其人。怎么搞的呢?什么缘故呢?怎么办呢?种种问题在他混乱的头脑里翻腾起伏;从我们戏称为人类智慧的中枢里,各种各样说法的报道,电报似的打来了。这一阵慌张的骚动还未完全平息,出庭律师不知不觉已经坐上了车子,拼命赶到他的事务所去了。至少那儿还是一个避难的山洞,至少那儿还是一处可以静下来想想的地方;他爬上楼梯,把钥匙插进锁眼,带点近乎希望的心情开了房门。

房间里漆黑一片,因为夜色降临已有一些时候了;不过吉迪恩熟悉自己的房间,他知道火柴放在壁炉架的一端;

因而大胆往前走去,哪晓得走过去就撞着了一件笨重的东西,那儿(这里把歌词稍稍改动一下)笨重东西原不该有。吉迪恩出去的时候那儿并没有什么东西,他出外去把门锁上,回家来门还是锁着,不可能有人进来,也不可能家具自己换地方。但是无可否认这儿是有一件什么东西。他在黑暗中伸出双手。不错,这儿是有件东西,有件大东西,光滑的东西,冷冰冰的东西。

"老天饶恕我吧!"吉迪恩说,"摸上去像是一架钢琴。"

再一会儿他记起背心口袋里有蜡火柴,就划着一根。果真是一架钢琴出现在他的半信半疑的眼光里了。一件庞大、昂贵的乐器,沾染了今天下午的雨点,有着新近剐蹭的痕迹。蜡火柴的光从漆得光溜溜的琴旁边木头上反射出来,正像静静的池水里的星光一般。在这屋子的另一端,这奇怪的不速之客的摇摇晃晃的影子在墙壁上显得很大。

那根火柴烧到吉迪恩的手指,于是一阵黑暗再一次地笼罩着他的惶惑。于是他双手颤抖着点上了灯,走近琴边。走近来看,走远去望,事实还是事实:这东西是钢琴。按照一切天理和人情,这东西万万不可能在这儿——可是那东西却是不讲道理地站在眼前。吉迪恩把琴盖打开,弹了一键。没有一点声音来打破屋中的沉寂。"难道我有点儿不对头吗?"他痛苦地想着。他拖了一张凳子过来,固执地非要敲破这沉寂不可,一下子弹了一段灿烂的分解和弦,一下子又弹了一段贝多芬的奏鸣曲,那一曲(在以往不倒霉的日子里）他晓得是这位强有力的作曲家的声音最洪亮的乐曲之一。可还是一点声音也没有。他握紧两只拳头，给那布洛德伍德砰砰两大下。一切仍然如同坟墓里一般无声无息。

这年轻的出庭律师蓦然站了起来。

"我简直完全疯了，"他大声喊着，"而且除了我自己谁也不知道。上帝最凶的灾祸降到我的头上来啦。"

他的手指碰着了表链，他立即拉出表来放到耳朵上。他听得见它在嘀嗒嘀嗒地响。

"我没有聋，"他大声地嚷着，"我只是疯了。我的理智永远离开我了。"

他不自在地向屋子四周看了一圈，然后目光无神地瞪视着迪克逊先生坐过的椅子。雪茄烟尾还在靠近椅子的炉围上。

"不，"他想，"我不相信那是一场梦。可是天晓得，我的智力在很快地衰退下来。譬如说，我似乎有点饿了，而这很可能又是一种幻觉。不过我还是不妨试试。我要好好地再吃一顿饭；我可以到乐雅咖啡馆去，从那儿就可能给直接送到疯人院去。"

他走下楼梯的时候，带着病态的兴趣，猜想自己开头会怎样泄露他这可怕的情况——他会去打一个侍者吗？或者吃玻璃吗？——他登上一辆马车，叫车夫把车赶到尼各尔咖啡馆，心里只怕没有这么一个地方。

这咖啡馆门口灯火辉煌，烟雾弥漫，使他心安下来了。他还认得出他素来喜欢的那个侍者，这使他更加高兴。他所叫的菜肴看起来一道一道，有条有理；晚餐端来了也很对口味，他吃得很满意。"老实说，"他想，"我差不多觉得有一种希望呢。我太性急一点了吧？我是不是做了罗伯特·希尔会做的事了？"罗伯特·希尔（我也不用说了）是《谁把时钟拨慢了?》的主角的姓名。这作者认为想出这个姓名是一种才气横溢、恰到好处的创造。有批判眼光的读者们都觉得罗伯特不配有那样的姓氏[①]；可是这类犯罪小说难免有个伤脑筋的地方，就是读者总比作者聪明不知多少倍。然而在这位创作者的心目中，他的罗伯特·希尔等于一句有魔力的话。这念头使他振奋并且鼓舞起来；那位杰出的人物会怎样做，吉迪恩也会怎样做的。如此想法并非少见。进退维谷的将军、受着诱惑的教士、踌躇彷徨的作家，他们在不同的情况之下，分别决定去做拿破仑、圣保罗、莎士比亚会怎样做的事。这样就只剩下一个小问题了：别人会怎样做呢？以吉迪恩的情形来说，有一件事情是清楚的：希尔是一个特别有决断力的人，他会立即采取某种（不管是什么）步骤，现在吉迪恩唯一能够想到的步骤是回到他的事务所去。

这一步完成之后，已经没有一点灵感来指示他下一步了，他张大眼睛，怪可怜地站在那儿，凝视着那件使他慌乱的乐器。他再也没有胆量去碰那些琴键了。不管它们保持上次的静默也好，或者用世界末日的喇叭声的音调来回答也好，一样会使他六神无主的。"这说不定是一个恶作

[①] 罗伯特是名，希尔是姓，希尔原文为 Skill，作"巧妙"解。

剧,"他想,"虽然这玩笑似乎既费事又费钱。可是还能是别的什么呢?这一定是恶作剧。"正在这时候,他的眼光落在一样东西上面,这东西好像进一步证明了这种看法似的;那就是迈克尔在临离开这事务所之前搭起来的雪茄烟宝塔。"这干吗?"吉迪恩想着。"这完全像是瞎胡闹。"他走了过来,小心谨慎地把它拆毁了。"一把钥匙。"他想着。"这干吗?为什么要这样触目地放着?"他绕着这件乐器走了一周,在后面看到一个锁孔。"啊哈!这把钥匙的用处在此啦,"他说,"他们要我看看里边。越来越奇怪。"于是他把钥匙插进去一转,把琴盖揭开。

吉迪恩当天晚上是在怎样让他哭笑不得的痛苦之中、怎样辗转反侧的苦思之中、怎样灰心至极的颓丧之中挨磨过去,是不忍细究的。

当伦敦屋檐下的小鸟啁啾呜哢地唱起小曲子迎接晨曦的时候,只见他瘫痪无力,缩成一团,两眼血红,脑子里还是空空如也,智穷才尽。他爬起身来,没精打采地看着外面遮上百叶窗的窗户、空无人影的街道以及那灰蒙蒙的曙光,其间点缀着一盏盏黄澄澄的路灯。有些日子里,这城市早晨醒来的时候似乎带着头痛的毛病,现在就是这样一个早晨,不过这些麻雀的喊喊喳喳的起床号还是打动了吉迪恩的心灵。

"已经是白天啦,"他想,"而我还是走投无路!决不能这样下去。"他把钢琴锁上,把钥匙放在口袋里,出去喝咖啡。他一路走去,他的脑子在一条恐怖、疑惧和悔恨的路上辛苦跋涉,推磨子似的兜了一百次圈子。报告警察,交出尸首，叫整个伦敦都贴满了缉拿约翰·迪克逊和以斯拉·托马斯的告示，叫所有的报纸都登上那么一段"法学院发生奇案——福西斯先生保释"，这是一条路，一条容易走的、安全的路；可是他越想越觉得不对——这并不是一条令人舒坦的路。因为，这不就得把他自己好些特别的行径公布于世吗？那两个冒险家编造的故事就是一个小孩子也定会识破的，而他竟然张着大口，生吞活剥地咽了下去。对于这样不按正规手续跑来的当事人，就是一个最不自爱的出庭律师也定会拒绝倾听的，而他却倾听了。哦，要是他只不过听听倒也罢了；他还给他们跑了腿哩——他，一个出庭律师，连撰状律师的影子也没来嘱托过他——却去跑了腿，做那只该一个暗探做的事。而且糟糕啊！——这里，他第一百次热血冲到眉毛上了——他还拿过他们的钱！"不成哪，"他说，"这事情跟圣保罗大教堂一样明摆在那儿。我一定会受到羞辱的！为了一张五镑的钞票，我把前途毁啦。"

在说不定会蒙受不白之冤而被处绞刑，以及可以肯定说是会遭受咎由自取的公众羞辱两者之间，凡是有点骨气的君子是不会长久迟疑不决的。吞了三大口那种热喷喷的、像鼻烟似的、混浊的饮料，那种在伦敦大街小巷里算是咖啡豆煎成的东西，吉迪恩心里决定下来了。他不想去找警察。他决意面对这种左右为难的境遇的另一面，真正做一个罗伯特·希尔。罗伯特·希尔会怎么做呢？一个君子该怎样处置一具平白无故跑来的尸首呢？他记起了那篇再好没有的驼子的故事①来。他把故事前前后后想了一遍，认为不足取法，便又撂开了。要把一具尸首停放在托特纳姆宫路的转角上而不引起过路人们致命的好奇心，那是不可能的；至于把它从伦敦哪一个烟囱里缒下去，体力上的困难却无法克服。把它带到火车上丢出去，或者弄到一辆公共汽车顶上丢掉，两者又同样想也不用想。把它搬到一艘游艇上抛入水中，倒是比较行得通一点；然而对于一个境遇平常的人说来，似乎太奢侈了。先不说游艇的租费需要考虑，只事后供应全体船员的费用（这似乎是必不可免的后果）也不堪设想。他的舅舅跟那艘住家船这时在他脑子里光芒四射地出现了。一个作曲家（譬如说，他叫作詹姆生吧）很可能像在他之前的贺加士俱乐部②里的音乐家一样，感到伦敦市里喧嚣烦扰。他很可能被限定时间，赶写一出歌剧——譬如说一出滑稽歌剧《橙香红茶③》吧——《橙香红茶》，詹姆生作曲——"这位音乐大师，是我们现代英国派之中最有希望的年轻音乐家之一"——开场是一阵雄武有力的擂鼓，等等——詹姆生这角色的整个形象和

---

① 驼子的故事：见《天方夜谭》中《小驼子的故事》(*The History of the Little Hunchback*)。叙述一个矮小的驼子，被某裁缝及其妻邀至家中吃饭，驼子不慎，鱼骨鲠喉而死。裁缝怕被鞫，将尸体偷送至犹太医生家中，医生又将尸体从天窗偷缒至苏丹王的侍者家中，侍者则乘夜将其置于街角。
② 贺加士俱乐部（Hogarth club）：伦敦一个艺术家的俱乐部，成立于一八七〇年。
③ 橙香红茶（Orange Pekoe）：印度和斯里兰卡产的一种红茶。此处作歌剧名。

他的音乐在吉迪恩的脑海里陡然升起。詹姆生带着一架大钢琴出现（譬如说，在百特微克吧），以及他独自一人带着他那未完成的《橙香红茶》的乐谱住在住家船上，还有什么比这更自然吗？他跟着失踪了，单单丢下一架钢琴的空壳，这或许比较难以交代。不过即使这点也有解释的可能。因为，假定詹姆生被一段"逃亡曲"弄得发了疯，因此毁掉造成这样丢脸的事情的帮凶，扔到欢迎它的河里去了，不也行吗？一般说来，对于一个现代音乐家，还有什么结局比这更近情理呢？

"哼，我就这么办，"吉迪恩嚷着，"就得要有詹姆生这角儿！"

第十一章 音乐大师詹姆生

爱德华·休·布洛姆菲尔德先生既然宣布他打算耽在梅登黑德①附近，那么音乐大师詹姆生如果脑筋转到百特微克，不是再自然也没有了吗？他记得曾在这可爱的傍河的村庄外，看见一艘肮脏老朽的住家船停泊在柳树丛下。他在那无忧无虑的日子里，还用着人们比较熟悉的名字，荡舟在这条河上，这艘住家船曾在他心里激起一种浪漫的遐思。他在心里已经把一篇美妙的故事的结构完全想好了，但又好像对待一只不知好歹的懒钟一样，把它差不多完全撂开，这是因为他要在小说里插上一章，在这章里罗伯特·希尔（他总是被人骗到什么地方去）规定要被白陆勋爵和美国无赖金·斯令诱骗到这艘孤零零的破船上。幸亏他又没有这样做，他想，因为这艘破船现在要做一项十分不同的用处了。

詹姆生穿了一身不显眼的衣服，但是带着一种胁肩谄笑的模样，他不怎么费事就找到了代管这艘住家船的人，

---

① 梅登黑德（Maidenhead）：英国城市，在伯克郡（Berkshire）内，傍泰晤士河，距伦敦市中心西二十五英里。

更不怎么费事就说动了这个人暂卸仔肩。租费几乎是有名无实,登船是立即可办,钥匙是预付不多不少一笔钱就移交了,于是,詹姆生当天下午就乘火车回到城里去接洽搬运钢琴的事。

"我准定明天来,"他肯定地说,"你知道,我的歌剧,人家等得急得要命哩。"

毫无差误,第二天中午,你就可以看见詹姆生在那条从百特微克到大哈浮罕的河边斜坡路上往上走。他一手拿着一篮食物,另一只手臂下夹着个皮包,装着(想来是)《橙香红茶》的乐谱。正是十月天气,灰色的天空中飞满了云雀,泰晤士河河面像铅色的镜子发着亮,映照着秋叶,栗子树上落下来的树叶在这位作曲家的脚步下吱吱唧唧。英国全年之中再也没有比这时候更令人精神振奋的了。詹姆生虽然不是没有他的烦恼,却是一面走,一面吹着口哨。

这条河在百特微克稍往上去一点的地方是非常寂静的。对岸一个私人花园里的树林把风景挡住了,那座宅第的一些烟囱在树丛顶上刚好钻了出来;这边河畔的小路的边缘上长着些柳树。就在这些柳树下停泊着那艘住家船,那东西被垂柳的泪水染得那么脏,寄生物长得那么多,又那么朽坏,那么破烂,那么无人照管,变成那样的一个老鼠窝,那么一望而知是个风湿症的痛苦的温床,一个要去住的人肯定会望而却步的。一块跳板充作活动的吊桥,连接着船跟河岸。詹姆生上了船,把这跳板拖了上来,这时候他看看自己孤孤单单一个人在这有碍健康的堡垒里,好不沮丧!他听得见老鼠在那非常可憎的船舱里急跑和跌扑的声响；钥匙在锁齿中间好像轧痛了似的直叫；那个起坐间里蒙着厚厚的灰尘，充斥着舱底污水的气味。即使对于一位沉浸在他热爱的工作里的作曲家说来，这也谈不上是一个惬意的地方。对于一个时时刻刻提心吊胆等着一具死尸到来的青年说来，这地方更是多么不对劲啊！

他坐了下来，把桌子上一块地方抹干净，就去进攻他篮子里的冷的午餐。为了避免招惹别人随后查问詹姆生的来踪去迹，还是少给人家看见为妙：换句话说，他就得整天待在船舱里。为了达到这个目的，并且为了供给他编造的故事以更好的证明起见，他皮包里不但带了写字的工具，另外还带了一令之多的大张乐谱用纸，他认为这才适合像詹姆生那样雄心勃勃的人之用。

"现在可以工作啦，"他把肚子填饱之后说，"咱们必须把这位可怜虫的劳动留下一点痕迹来才对。"于是他就用大字写了：

橙香红茶
作品第 17 号
J.B. 詹姆生
声乐与钢琴总谱

"我想他们从来不这样开头吧，"吉迪恩想着，"可是要我应付管弦乐总谱，那太不可能了，况且詹姆生是个多么不守陈规的人。加个题献会更能叫人相信，我想。'献给，'（让我看）'献给威廉·爱华特·格莱德士东，作曲者敬献.'好,现在写点音乐。我最好避免序曲,那看来不简单。咱们给男高音来一段抒情曲吧;调子——哦,来一种现代的!——七个升记号。"于是他在乐谱线上像模像样地画了个调号,这之后就停下来,把笔杆放在嘴里啃着。除了一张纸以外就没有其他更好的灵感的泉源,那么,一般说来,旋律是不会从一个玩票的脑子里自然而然地涌现出来的。而且七个升记号的调子对于缺乏经验的人,也不是一件怎么轻而易举的事。他把那一张扔了。"这会有益于詹姆生个性的培养。"吉迪恩说,于是重又小心侍奉着文艺科学女神,他试了种种调子,扔了若干纸张,可是结果全都这般不像样,叫他站在那儿直发呆。"这太奇怪了,"他想着,"我的幻想似乎没有我想象的那么丰富,要不然,我今天是心不在焉;不过詹姆生总得留下点东西来啊。"因此他又低下头来工作。

过了不多久,住家船里的刺骨的寒气开始直透到他心肝五脏里来了。他放弃了那毫无收获的尝试,他一边听着清晰可闻的老鼠骚扰声,一边在船舱里急急地来回直走。然而他还是觉得冷。"完全没有这回事,"他说,"这个危险我并不在意,我只是决不要患上感冒。我必须马上走出这个倒霉的地方。"

他登上甲板,走到船头那儿他登船的处所,向河面望了一眼。他愣住了。往上只有几百码的地方,另外还有一艘住家船泊在柳树下。那是一艘崭新的船,还有一条雅致的小划子拖在船尾,窗户都遮上了雪白的窗帘,旗杆上飘着一面船旗。吉迪恩越是盯着那面船旗看,他的厌恶的感觉之中越是夹杂着一种让他胆战心寒的惊讶。它很像他舅舅的那艘住家船;像得不得了——简直一模一样。要不是因为有两种情形,他真可以发誓说真就是那一艘。第一,他的舅舅已经到梅登黑德去了,这尚可解释为他的意志轻浮易变,在那些比一般人更有丈夫气概的人当中,这种性格是常见的。第二,无论如何,肯定是个问题:让一面船旗飘展在流动住宅上,这可丝毫不像布洛姆菲尔德先生所会做的;就算他要这样做的话,那面船旗也一定会染成适合于作标记用的颜色的。要知道这位乡绅激进派,正如那些更有丈夫气概的人里边最大多数的人一样,虽然在剑桥这知识的泉井里汲过水——他是一八五〇年的"木勺"①,然而住家船上这天下午在空中飘荡着的船旗,颜色却是代表那保守主义的中心、溥西主义②的摇篮、"糊涂老迈"的家乡牛津大学的。

可是很怪,那艘船还是像得很,吉迪恩想着。

他正在这样看着想着,那扇门打开了,一位年轻的姑娘走到甲板上来。出庭律师突然一溜溜进了自己的船舱——那是茱莉娅·海士尔坦!他从窗口看见她把那小划子拉了过来,爬上去,解了缆,朝着他这边顺流而下。

"好了,一切都完了。"他说着倒在一把椅子上。

---

① "木勺"(Wooden Spoon):英国剑桥大学每学年终了时有一个惯例:把一只大木勺送给末一名考试及格的学生。
② 溥西主义(Puseyism):溥西(E. B. Pusey,一八〇〇—一八八二)所领导的一种主义,又称"牛津运动",主张英国国教应当恢复某些旧制度和信条。

"午安，小姐。"水面上传来一个声音。吉迪恩晓得这是他的房东的口音。

"午安，"茱莉娅回答，"可是我不知道你是谁呀；你是谁呢？哦，是的，我知道啦。你就是让咱们在这破旧的住家船上画画儿的那个好人。"

吉迪恩吓得心直跳。

"不错，"这人回答，"我说哩，现在你不能再去画了。你知道，我已经把它出租了。"

"出租了！"茱莉娅叫起来。

"出租一个月，"这人说，"看来奇怪，是吧？真不懂那人要它干吗！"

"看来那人很罗曼蒂克，我想，"茱莉娅说，"他是怎样一个人？"

茱莉娅划着她的小划子，这房东摇着一条摆渡船，都靠近并且抓住了这住家船船舷的边缘，因此没有一个字漏过吉迪恩的耳朵。

"他是个弄音乐的，"这房东说，"至少他是这样跟我说的，小姐；他到这儿来写一本歌剧。"

"真的呀！"茱莉娅喊着，"我从来没有听过这么有意思的事情！嗯，咱们倒可以在晚上偷偷划过来听他即兴演奏啊！他叫什么名字？"

"詹姆生。"这人说。

"詹姆生？"茱莉娅重复说，盘查着自己的回忆，却是枉然。真的，咱们英国音乐的新兴学派里的音乐家真是车载斗量，非要其中哪个成了准男爵才得一闻其名不可。

"这名字你肯定没有弄错吗?"

"我叫他一个字一个字念给我听的,"这房东回答,"詹—姆—生——詹姆生,他的歌剧叫作——一种什么茶。"

"一种什么茶!"姑娘叫了起来,"用这个做歌剧的名字多么特别啊!这能说明什么呢?"吉迪恩听到她动听的笑声飘了开去。"咱们要想法子认识这位詹姆生先生,我晓得他一定是个好人。"

"嗯,小姐,我怕我得走啦。是啊,我得到哈浮罕去哩。"

"哦,可别让我耽搁你吧,你这位和善的人!"茱莉娅说,"再见。"

"再见,小姐。"

吉迪恩坐在船舱里,困扰在一些顶可怕的思潮之中。他现在是被拴牢在这艘正在腐烂的住家船上,不久那具尸首到了,他可更要被拴得牢而又牢了。在他的四周已经有了乡下人窃窃私语的嗡嗡声,可是年轻女郎又算计好了要在晚间来绕着他的屋子作乐。哼,这一来免不了要上绞刑架啦;他会多么喜欢这个吧。他现在感到痛苦的是茱莉娅的不堪言述的轻率。那姑娘简直会跟随便什么人交上朋友;她没有什么矜持,没有一点高贵妇女的金玉其外的仪表。她跟他的房东那样一个粗人都亲亲热热,她对詹姆生那样一个家伙都会立刻产生兴趣(她竟然不审慎得不知掩饰)!他甚至能想象她会跑来要詹姆生请她喝茶哩!而吉迪恩这样一个男子汉就是为了这样一个姑娘而——冷下去了,这颗男子汉的心!

他的思绪被一阵声响打断了,这声响使他猛然一跳跳到门背后。海士尔坦小姐已经踏上这艘住家船了。她的写生画是很有前途的;她看看这般寂静无声,以为詹姆生还没有来,便决定抓住时机完成一件艺术作品。于是她在船头上坐下来,拿出绘画板和水彩颜料,不一会儿就对着那(常被称为)"闺阁才艺"的东西唱着歌。她唱的歌时时中断,那是真的,因为她要在记忆里搜索一些可厌的小诀窍,这是玩这种东西所要用的——或者说在那卓越的旧时代里所要用的;人们说这个世界和作为这个世界的装饰品的年轻闺秀们,现在习气已经越来越深了;然而茱莉娅可能师从皮特曼,因此坚定不移地墨守旧规。

这时候,吉迪恩站在门背后,不敢动弹,不敢呼吸,也不敢想到必然会跟着来的事,拘束得苦死了,厌倦得要瘫倒在地上了。这个特别阶段,他感激涕零地觉得是不能永远这样下去的;不管事到临头要掉下什么来(即使是绞刑架吧,他痛心地思量着,但是也许想得不对),总比现在的痛苦轻些。他忽然想起做点开立方的数学,倒是一种巧妙的甚至有好处的方法,来逃避那折磨人的思想。于是他把全副精神都贯注到这枯燥无味的练习之中。

就是这样,这两个青年人各自忙着——吉迪恩在坚决地求取正确的数字,茱莉娅在使劲地把不调和的颜色用点彩法点上她的画板。正在这时候,老天爷差遣了一条汽艇,生哮喘病似的喘着气溯泰晤士河的河水开了来,一路上使两岸的水涨起来又落下去,弄得芦苇沙沙作响。这住家船,这静止不动的老东西,也忽然充满了生气,在它的碇泊所中活泼地颠簸起来,像一只海船开始航近港口沙洲的时候一般。冲激起来的水浪差不多已经平服了,汽艇急促的喘息声听来已模糊而遥远了,这时候茱莉娅的一声叫喊让吉迪恩吃了一惊。他从窗口偷偷看出去,只见她无可奈何地瞪视着那只顺流淌去、很快就要看不见了的小划子。出庭律师(不管他有什么缺点)这一次却表现出一种可跟他的英雄罗伯特·希尔相埒的机敏性,他脑筋一转就料到会有什么事情跟着发生,他身子一扭就跪到地板上,爬到桌子底下去了。

这一边,茱莉娅可还没有了解自己的处境。她是明白已经丢了那只小划子了,因此并不怎么十分热切地盼望再跟布洛姆菲尔德先生见面;可是她没有想到自己已经被囚禁在这儿了,因为她以为那跳板还在搭着桥。

她绕着船舱巡行一周,发现门开着,桥已经拆了。那么很显然,詹姆生一定来了;也很显然,他一定在船上了。他听任别人侵入他的住宅而没有一点反应,那一定是个很害羞的男人;这么一想,她更是勇气倍增。现在一定要他出来,她一定要逼着他从隐藏的地方钻出来,因为她一个人的气力动不了那块跳板;于是她在开着的门上敲敲。停一会儿,她又敲敲。

"詹姆生先生,"她喊着,"詹姆生先生!喂,来呀!——早点晚点,你知道,你非出来不可,因为没有你我走不了。哦,别这样傻得透顶呀!哦,求求你,来哪!"

依然是没有回音。

"如果他是在这儿,那他一定疯了。"她想着,有点儿害怕。再一会儿她想起他也许像自己一样坐了一只小船出去了。要是那样的话,她乐得看一看这艘住家船,她就把门推开得大些,走了进去。桌子下面,闷在灰尘里的吉迪恩的心停止了跳动。

那儿有詹姆生吃剩的午餐。"他喜欢吃些很不错的东西哩,"她想着,"哦,我相信他一定是个讨人喜欢的男人。我不知道他可像福西斯先生一样漂亮。詹姆生太太——我想这没有福西斯太太那么好听;不过'吉迪恩'这名字真是多么讨厌呀!哦,这是他的一些音乐;这可有意思。《橙香红茶》——哦,这就是他所说的什么茶了。"于是她开心得笑起来。"'极富表情的慢板','始终圆顺',"她这样念下去,(关于作曲家用语方面的事情,吉迪恩是很有一手的。)"写上这么些指示,可只有三四个音符,真是多么奇怪呀!哦,这是另外一张,又写了一些。'悲怆的行板'。"她开始浏览那乐谱。"哦,我的乖乖,"她想着,"他一定非常现代化!在我看来全篇都像是不和谐的乱调。咱们试试这支曲子看。非常奇怪,好像很耳熟。"她开始唱起那支曲子来,忽然中止了,大笑。"噢,这就是《汤米给你舅舅让开点》!"她大声嚷着,直使得吉迪恩心痛如绞。"什么'悲怆的行板'!这人一定就是一个骗子。"

正在这时候,桌子下面传来一阵乱糟糟的扭斗似的声响;声响很奇怪,好像一只鸡在动着一样,接着引出一阵像是爆炸似的喷嚏声;同时那受罪的人的头跟上面的桌板狠狠地碰撞了一下;而跟着喷嚏声来的是一阵重浊的呻吟。

茱莉娅一逃逃到门口,到了门口,却又带着勇士那种有益的本能转过身来,面对危险。一看并没有人追她。声响倒还在继续不断。桌子底下可以模糊地看出有个蜷缩的人影,正在跟欲待发作的喷嚏苦苦争斗——如此而已。

"这真是,"茱莉娅想,"太离奇的行为啦。他不可能是个见过世面的人!"

这时候,这位年轻的出庭律师的骚动,惊扰了多年沉积的灰尘;因此跟着那阵喷嚏之后,又发作了一阵凶猛剧烈的呛咳。

茱莉娅开始感到了一点兴趣。"我怕你真有些毛病啦。"她说着,走近了一点。"请别因为我,叫你为难吧,别待在桌子底下啦,詹姆生先生。真的,这对你不好呀。"

詹姆生先生的回答只是一阵苦恼的咳嗽;眼睛一眨这姑娘已经跪了下来,他们的脸差一点就在桌子下面撞在一起了。

"哎呀,不得了!"海士尔坦小姐惊喊着,蹦了起来。"福西斯先生疯啦!"

"我没有疯。"这位先生垂头丧气地说,从那地方脱身出来。"最亲爱的海士尔坦小姐,我给你跪着发誓,我没有疯!"

"你没有疯!"她喘着气大声说。

"我晓得,"他说,"从浮面上看,我的行为可能像是出乎寻常。"

"要说你没有疯,这可根本不成其为行为啊,"这姑娘叫着,脸上红了一阵,"而且显而易见你丝毫不顾及我心里会有什么感觉!"

"这真是罪该万死。我知道——我承认这个。"吉迪恩嚷着,竭力表现出一种大丈夫的正直坦白的精神。

"这种行为真是可恶极了!"茱莉娅着力地说。

"我知道这一定要叫你看不起,"出庭律师说,"不过,最亲爱的海士尔坦小姐,我求你把我的话听完。我的行为虽然看来奇怪,却并不是不能解释的;而且不论现在,还是将来,要是没有——没有我所爱慕的人的垂青,我绝对不能设法活下去的——我挑了这个时间说这些话,是不适当的,这点我很清楚;可是我要再说一遍——一位我所爱慕的人。"

海士尔坦小姐的脸上流露出一点感到有趣的神情。"好吧,"她说,"让我们走出这个冷得要命的地方,到甲板上去坐吧。"出庭律师愁眉苦脸地跟着她走。"现在,"她一面说,一面靠在船舱的一端,把自己安顿好,"说吧。我听你说完。"接着,看见他站在她面前的那副样子,显然表明对于这个任务提不起兴致来,她突然笑不可抑。茱莉娅的笑是一种能使情人心醉神迷的东西;她把她那婉转自如、起抑有致,好像画眉鸟的歌声一样的欢悦的旋律,传播到河上,又由对岸的回声照样播送一遍,那就好像是自然存在的东西,天空中本来有的声响。只有一个人听了不开心,那就是她的不幸的爱慕者。

"海士尔坦小姐,"他说,气恼得声音结结巴巴的,"我以诚恳的、希望你好的态度说这句话:这样子只能算是轻率。"

茱莉娅瞪眼看着他。

"我不会收回这个字眼,"他说,"我听见你跟那船夫那样毫无拘束地亲热地谈话,这已经给我带来了深切的伤痛。还有对于詹姆生也欠矜持——"

"可是詹姆生结果就是你啊。"茱莉娅争辩道。

"我决不否认这点,"出庭律师喊着,"可是你那时候并不知道这事情。詹姆生跟你有什么关系?詹姆生是什么人?海士尔坦小姐,我心如刀割。"

"我看这实在是太愚蠢啦,"茱莉娅正颜厉色地回答,"你这种做法太特别,太特别了。你自称能够解释你的行为,可是你不但不这样做,反而开始攻击我。"

"我十分了解这个,"吉迪恩回答,"我——我一定把事情一五一十地说出来。等你知道了种种情节,你就能够原谅我了。"

于是他在甲板上坐在她身旁,把他苦恼的遭遇和盘托出了。

"哦,福西斯先生,"他讲完之后她叫起来,"我是——多么——抱歉啊!我希望我没有嘲笑你——只是你知道,你实在太好笑啦。可是我希望我没有,要是我刚才晓得一丁点儿的话,我也不会了。"她把手给了他。

吉迪恩握住了她的手。"你不会因此对我印象坏一点吧?"他温存地问。

"因为你那么愚蠢,遭到了这样可怕的麻烦吗?你这可怜的孩子,不!"茱莉娅大声说,而在这一阵温情之中,她把另一只手也给了他。"你可以信赖我。"她紧接着说。

"真的吗?"吉迪恩说。

"真而又真。"这姑娘回答。

"那我就信赖你,我将来也一定信赖你。"这青年男子喊着。"我承认这时间是挑得不好,不过,我没有朋友——可以说得上是朋友的。"

"我也没有啊,"茱莉娅说,"可是你是否觉得,这也许是你应当把我的手还给我的时候了呢?"

"La ci darem la mano①,"出庭律师说,"再过一会儿吧!我的朋友那么少。"他紧接着说。

"我觉得一个年轻的男人没有朋友,人家是会瞧不起的。"茱莉娅说。

"哦,我的普通朋友可多着哩!"吉迪恩叫着,"我不是那个意思。我感到这时机挑得不好;可是,哦,茱莉娅,要是你心里能够明白——!"

"福西斯先生——"

"别叫我那个讨厌的名字!"这青年喊着。"叫我吉迪恩!"

"哦,那个绝对不能!"茱莉娅回答。"况且我们彼此认识只有这么短的时间。"

"一点不是这样!"吉迪恩抗议。"我们老早就在伯恩茅斯认得了。从那天起我就永远忘不了你。说你也永远忘不了我吧。说你永远忘不了我,叫我吉迪恩!"

"这不也是———种对詹姆生欠矜持的行动吗?"这姑娘问。

"哦,我知道我是一头蠢驴,"出庭律师叫着,"我一

---

① 法文:我们的手儿紧相握。

点儿也不在乎!我知道我是一头蠢驴,你尽可以痛痛快快地取笑我。"茱莉娅张嘴微笑的时候,他又一次浸沉到音乐里去了。"'那边是樱桃岛上的田园!'"他唱着,两只眼睛含情脉脉地瞅着她。

"这像是一出歌剧。"茱莉娅说,声音相当轻微了。

"不然是什么呢?"吉迪恩说。"我不是詹姆生吗?要是我不把我的爱情用小夜曲唱出来,这才奇怪哩。是的,我是诚心诚意地要说出'爱情'这两个字,我的茱莉娅,我非要赢得你的心不可。我是遭到了可怕的麻烦,我又是身无分文,我又弄成这副再愚蠢也没有的样子;可是我还是非要赢得你的心不可,茱莉娅。要是你能够的话,瞧着我,跟我说个'不'字!"

她瞧着他了;不管她的眼睛跟他说了些什么,想来他在那个眼色里是获得了快慰,因为他对着她的眼睛看了很久。

"当前内德舅舅会给我们一点钱用的。"他最后那么说。

"唔,我得说,这可胆大啊!"一个开心的声音在他耳边响起来。

吉迪恩和茱莉娅马上蹦了开来,动作之敏捷,可叹观止。后者着恼地发觉尽管他们俩坐下来之后并没有移动过,但是他们现在可是靠得很近哩。在爱德华·休·布洛姆菲尔德先生的眼里看来,这两个人脸上都现出火辣辣的颜色。那位绅士是坐了他的船在河里逆水行来的途中,抓住了那只私自溜逃的小划子,他猜到那是怎么回事,他原想偷偷跑来看看海士尔坦小姐的绘画。无意之中却一举两得,当他看着这一对绯红了脸、接不上气的罪犯的时候,人类做媒的善良本性把他的心软化了。

"嗯,我得说,这可胆大啊,"他重复说,"你似乎很拿得准内德舅舅会怎么样。可是,咳,吉德,我想,我曾经叫你不要来的吧?"

"你叫我不要到梅登黑德来,"吉德回答,"可是我怎么知道会在这儿碰到你们呢?"

"这倒有点道理,"布洛姆菲尔德先生承认,"你知道,我原先觉得,最好连你也不晓得我的地方;因为那些流氓,那几个芬斯伯里,会从你嘴里把这钩出来的。为了更叫他们找不出,我把那讨厌的船旗也挂上了。问题可不仅是这个,吉德;你答应我工作的呀,而我却看见你在百特微克做傻瓜。"

"求求你,布洛姆菲尔德先生,你不要难为福西斯先生了,"茱莉娅说,"可怜的孩子,他碰到了可怕的厄难了。"

"什么,吉德?"舅舅问。"你跟人打了架,还是银钱纠纷?"

在这位乡绅激进派看来,这两种是一个绅士在所难免的灾难;的确,这两种正是根据他自己的经历所得出来的结论。有一次他(只是名义上)在一个朋友办的报社里挂了个名,这事弄得他损失了整整一千镑。从此以后,这朋友来来去去都像怕死神降临一样,每次转过街角,从来没有不先察探一下他前面有没有布洛姆菲尔德先生和那根橡木手杖。至于打架,这位乡绅激进派老是险些跟人动起手来的。有一次他(正担任一个激进派俱乐部主席的职位)

把反对者撵出了演讲厅之后,他可更闹得大了。那保守党候选人霍尔特姆先生久久躺在病床上,打算去宣誓,咬定布洛姆菲尔德先生的罪状。"我一定要在不管哪个法院里为这事宣誓——是那个畜生动手把我打倒的。"布洛姆菲尔德接到报告说他这样说过。在他看来病势危殆的时候,大家知道他照那个意思写成了一份 ante-mortem①陈诉书。到后来霍尔特姆又能回到他的啤酒厂里办公去了,这位乡绅激进派才算松了一口气。

"比那两种更糟哪,"吉迪恩说,"是一种真正属于天意的种种不公平事件的组合———一种——实在是一个谋杀犯的集团,似乎看中了我有给他们弄掉他们犯罪的痕迹的潜在能力。这毕竟是一桩法律上值得研究的事,你知道!"接着这几句话,吉迪恩开始描绘那布洛德伍德大钢琴的冒险故事,这是一天里的第二遍。

"我一定要写信给《泰晤士报》。"布洛姆菲尔德先生喊着。

"你要把我的律师资格剥夺掉吗?"吉迪恩问。

"剥夺律师资格!嗯,不能那么严重吧。"他的舅舅说,"现在当政的是一个良好的、诚实的自由党政府。我要去说什么,他们一定会照办。谢谢上帝,保守党假公济私的日子总算结束啦。"

"这行不通,内德舅舅。"吉迪恩说。

"你还没有疯到,"布洛姆菲尔德先生嚷着,"坚持要

---

① 拉丁文:死亡前的。

自己设法把它弄掉那种程度吧？"

"我没有别的路可走啊。"吉迪恩说。

"这不近情理,我不答应。"布洛姆菲尔德先生喊着,"我断然命令你,吉德,不要再牵连到这桩罪案里去。"

"很好,我就把这事移交给你吧,"吉迪恩说,"你爱怎么处置这具尸首都行。"

"胡说八道!"这激进派俱乐部主席冲口而出,"这事我决不碰一碰。"

"那么你就必得准许我尽我最大能力去做了,"他的外甥回答,"你放心吧,我有特别的能耐来应付这种困难。"

"我们或许可以把它送到那传染病院,那保守党俱乐部里去,"布洛姆菲尔德先生说,"这或许能够损毁他们在他们选民心目中的地位;还可以利用它在本地报纸上大大宣传一番。"

"如果你在这件事情里边看到有什么可作为你政治资本的话,"吉迪恩说,"我可以把它转让给你。"

"不必要,不必要,吉德——绝对不必要,我是说你或许可以。这事情我决不沾手。想起来了,我跟海士尔坦小姐都太不宜于待在这儿了。人家可能看见我们,"这位主席说着,往河的上下方看看,"其后果,因为我在社会上的地位的关系,对于我党可能是很可悲的。而且不管怎么说,现在已经是晚餐时候啦。"

"什么?"吉迪恩叫了起来,伸手去掏他的表。"可不是嘛!天哪,钢琴早在几个钟头以前就该送到的呀!"

布洛姆菲尔德先生正在爬回他自己的船上去,可是这几句话使他打住了。

"我亲眼看见它运到火车站的;我雇了一个运货人,他得到别处兜个圈子,可是最迟四点钟也该到这儿,"这出庭律师嚷着,"无疑这钢琴是给打开了,尸首也给发现了。"

"你得立刻就逃,"布洛姆菲尔德先生喊着,"这是大丈夫唯一可行的一招。"

"可是假定没有事儿呢?"吉迪恩哀声说,"假定那架钢琴来了,而我却不在这儿收领呢?我得因为自己的懦怯惭愧无地了。不,内德舅舅,总得到百特微克打听打听;当然,我不敢去;然而你可以——你不妨到警察局那儿徘徊徘徊,你明白吗?"

"不,吉德——不,我亲爱的外甥,"布洛姆菲尔德先生如热锅上的蚂蚁,带着焦急的声音说,"我是以最神圣的爱心来看待你的;我还要谢谢上帝,我是一个英国人——以及诸如此类。可是不能——不能到警察局去,吉德。"

"那么你甩了我啦?"吉迪恩说。"明摆明地说出来吧。"

"决非如此!决非如此!"布洛姆菲尔德先生抗议着。"我只主张谨慎小心。常识,吉德,应当永远是英国人的导师。"

"你们可以让我说句话吗?"茱莉娅说。"我想吉迪恩最好离开这艘可怕的住家船,藏到那边柳树丛里等着。如果是钢琴来啦,他可以走出来拿;如果是警察来啦,他可以溜到我们的住家船上来,并且用不着再有什么詹姆生这个人。他可以爬上床去,我们可以在汽艇里把他的衣服烧掉(我们可以吧?)。这么一来,看来真的一切都没有问题了。布洛姆菲尔德先生是那么德高望重的,你知道,又是那样一位领袖人物,简直想象都不可能想象他跟这种事情有什么瓜葛。"

"这位年轻的小姐可极有常识啊!"乡绅激进派说。

"哦,我想我总不见得是个傻子。"茱莉娅自信地说。

"可是如果他们一个也不来呢?"吉迪恩问,"那我怎么办?"

"那么,"她说,"你最好在天黑之后到村子里去,我可以陪你去,这么一来,我相信人家再也不会疑心你。即使人家疑心你,我也可以跟他们说,那完全是误会。"

"我不能允许这样做——我决不能让海士尔坦小姐去。"布洛姆菲尔德先生嚷着。

"为什么呢?"茱莉娅问。

布洛姆菲尔德先生丝毫不想跟她说明原委,因为那只是一种怯懦,害怕把自己牵入这个纠纷里去;可是正如一个怀着内疚的人所常用的策略,他采取了高压手段。"万万不行,我亲爱的海士尔坦小姐,我提示一位小姐对于礼俗问题——"他开始说。

"哦,就因为这个啊?"茱莉娅打断他的话。"那么只得我们三个人都去啦。"

"这可逃不了啦!"乡绅激进派想着。

第十二章　布洛德伍德大钢琴的最后一瞥

英国被认为是个音乐不发达的国家；可是且不必详述我们对于手摇风琴师的栽培，也完全不用把普遍流行的犹太喇叭①找来作为论据，的的确确有一件乐器可以照字面意义不折不扣地称为"国粹"的。那金雀枝丛里的牧童，在乔叟②的时代已经很爱好音乐，就曾用这小小的笛子惊动了（也许是苦恼了）云雀。在那熟练的砌砖匠的手里，此物变成了喇叭，他吹出的（一般说来）不是《英国近卫步兵第一团》，就是《熟了樱桃》。后一种曲子正是吹这种便士笛的人的试金石和毕业证明书。我大胆猜想这曲子原来就是为这个乐器作的。真够奇怪，一个人凭着吹奏这种便士笛的本领，就能够混饭吃，甚至度过一段失业时期。更奇怪的是，那些以此为业的人几乎千篇一律地把才能限

---

① 犹太喇叭（jew's trump）：又称犹太口琴（jew's harp）。为一略似"凸"字形的铁框，中间直置一金属片，片的前端成直角形上翘。演奏时以铁框含口内，金属片的前端露口外，以手指弹之。
② 乔叟（Geoffrey Chaucer，约一三四三——一四〇〇）：英国最早的诗人之一。他的《坎特伯雷故事集》（*The Canterbury Tales*）为文学名著。

制在这曲《熟了樱桃》上。真的，关于这东西，奇怪的地方可多得像黑莓一样哩。譬如，为什么要把这笛子叫作"便士笛"呢？我想从来没有谁花一便士买到过。又为什么它的另一个名称是"白铁片笛子"呢？要真是用白铁片做的，我可大大受愚了。最后，那初学者是在哪一处听不见声音的地下墓窖里，哪一片不长耳朵的沙漠里，度过他那痛苦的学徒时期的呢？我们全都听见过人们练习钢琴、提琴和短号①，可是吹便士笛的小伙子却（像小鲑鱼一样）隐藏得看也看不见。除非他已精通此道，否则从来没有让人听见过。老天爷（或许被马洛克②先生的作品震惊了）保护了人类的听觉，不让听到他们对高音阶的尝试。

离开百特微克不远的地方，在一条绿色的小路上，有一桩值得注目的事在发展着。一辆运货车的坐板上坐着一个长着亚麻色头发、瘦瘦的、貌不惊人的小伙子。缰绳搁在膝上，鞭子放在他背后的车身里边。马儿自管自地往前走，没有人指挥，也没有人督促。这运货人（或者是运货人用的人）魂儿已经飞到高出他每日工作的境界里：他两眼观天，全神贯注着对付一只崭新的 D 调便士笛，毫无把握地努力着，想引出那支悦耳的曲子——《农家子》。任何一个善于观察的人，碰巧在这时候溜达到那条小路上的

---

① 短号（cornet）：一种吹管弯曲而用音栓之铜喇叭。
② 马洛克（William Hurrell Mallock，一八四九——一九二三）：英国作家，著有《新共和国》(*The New Republic*)、《人生有意义否?》(*Is Life Worth Living?*)、《寡头政治与改革》(*Aristocracy and Evolution*)、《信仰之重建》(*The Reconstruction of Belief*) 等书。

话,都会兴奋得直哆嗦。"到底,"他会这么说,"给我碰到一个初学者了。"

长着亚麻色头发的小伙子(他的名字叫哈克)刚刚第十九次叫自己"再来一个"的时候,蓦然发现并不是独自一人在这儿,他可被弄得慌乱到了极点。

"这回你成啦!"一个男子的声音从路旁传来。"这回我听得入耳啦。在节奏上或许稍稍油滑了一点。"这声音提示着,带着沉思的口气。"咱们再来一遍看看。"

哈克惭愧得无地自容,对那说话的人瞧了一眼。他瞧见的是个孔武有力,脸庞晒得黑黑的、修得光光的人。四十来岁的年纪,带着一种下士军人的神态,跟在货车旁大踏步走着,一面走一面在空中挥舞着一根手杖。这人衣衫褴褛,可是看来倒也清洁,有气度。

"我刚开始学哩,"红着脸的哈克喘着气说,"我没有想到竟然有谁听见我吹。"

"咳,这是什么话!"那一个回答。"你这样的初学者可真不错。来吧,我来给你开个门径。你边上给咱让个座儿。"

再一会儿这军人已经在货车上了,手里拿着那根笛子。他使那乐器的杆子发出一阵内行调弄时的呜噜噜的声响,就把嘴对着它,好像开始跟文艺科学女神通灵感似的停了一会儿,突然吹起《我断绝了的姑娘》。他可说是个伟大的,但不能说是个高超的演奏者。他缺少小鸟那般的珠圆玉润;他差不多不能把《熟了樱桃》里的甜汁完全榨出来;他不怕那乐器的尖锐刺耳的声音——他甚至夸张地演奏了,并且好像十分喜爱。可是那种火气、速度、准确、平稳和流利,那种接连的轻快的"抖调"——这是个专门术语,请你允许这样写,就跟风笛上发出来的鸟啭声相等,而最最动人的或许是那样的斜瞟一眼,他借此看到了演奏效果,并且(由于这是发于人类心灵的乞求)弥补了他表演上的缺憾。在上述种种方面,是没有人可以敌得过他的。哈克静静听着:《我断绝了的姑娘》使他不胜心灰意冷;《兵士的愉快》扫除了他嫉妒的心情,带他到那热情充溢的境地。

"这回该轮到你了。"这军人说着,把笛子递给他。

"哦,你吹过了,我怎能献丑!"哈克嚷着,"你是行家。"

"不是,"他的同伴说,"像你一样是空下来吹吹玩儿的。这是一种玩法,你的是另外一种,而我更喜欢你那种。不过,你知道,在我还是个孩子,还不懂得鉴赏的时候,我就开始玩了。你到了我这样的年纪,会把这东西玩得就跟吹的是短号一般了。那调子再吹给咱们听听看,怎么样来的?"于是他装作竭力在追忆那曲《农家子》。

一个怯生生的、疯狂的希望在哈克的心胸里涌现了。那是可能的吗?他的玩法里是有点道理的吗?真的哩,有时候他是好像觉着自己的玩意儿里有着一种完美的东西。难道他是个天才吗?在这中间,军人支离破碎地吹着那支曲子。

"不对,"哈克不愉快地说,"这不太像哩。是这样来的——我试给你听听。"

他把笛子凑在嘴唇上,自己的命运也就决定了。他吹了那支曲子,然后是第二遍、第三遍;军人再试了一次,却再失败了一次；哈克可看清楚了，自己这么个初出茅庐的腼腆角色，竟然在教导一个功力老到的吹笛家——而这位吹笛家在他的指导之下并没有卓越的进步——这个时候，我怎能形容？正如我怎能说得出，是什么样灿烂的光彩把那秋天的郊野点缀得如此明媚？这样，除非读者自己也是一个业余爱好者，我怎能形容这运货人在愚蠢的虚荣心理上所爬到的高度呀？一个很有意义的事实就足以形容这个情形：从这时候起是哈克在吹笛子，而那军人是在一边静听，一边称许。

当他在静听的时候，可并没有忘了军人那种警惕的习惯，他往后看看，又往前看看。往后看的时候，他算计了这运货人所装的东西能值多少，猜想那些棕色纸包和那堂皇的有盖的大篮子里全都是些什么，他又不假思索地认定那簇新的钢琴木箱里的大钢琴是件"难以脱手"的东西。往前看，他探察到这条绿荫夹道的小路的转角处有一爿小小的乡村酒店隐蔽在玫瑰花丛中。"我来试试看。"军人最后做了决定，大胆建议去喝一杯。

"呃，我不会喝酒。"哈克说。

"哎，你听呀，"对方接口就说，"告诉你我是谁吧，我是××部队的护旗中士白兰特。你这就可以知道我是不是一个会喝酒的人了。"可能如此，也可能并非如此，因而应该有古希腊戏剧中的合唱队插进来，走出戏台，指出那话里如何有着漏洞：没有说出为什么这中士穿得这样破烂，踯躅在乡下一条小路上；或者甚至议论他忽略自己的国防岗位一定已经有些时候，而（在这段时期里）可能转移精力到填麻絮①这方面来。可是那儿没有古希腊的合唱队。这军人接下去主张：喝酒是一回事，友谊上的一杯是另外一回事。

在"蓝狮"——这爿乡下酒店的名字——护旗中士白兰特对他的新朋友哈克先生推荐好几种巧妙的混合酒，算计好不会使人喝醉的。他解释这些酒是队里的"必需品"，可以使一个有自尊心的军官在阅兵的时候老是有一种样子，叫他的队伍觉得不胜光荣。几种方子里最有效的一种是拿一品脱的温和的淡啤酒掺上价值二便士的伦敦杜松子烧酒。我愿意将这个处方提交给有眼力的读者，他会发现即使在高尚文雅的场合里它也会发生作用；因为它在哈克身上产生的效果是具有革命性的。他必须让人搀扶才上得了他自己的货车，在车上他开始表现放纵于欢快和音乐之中的兴致，一会儿粗声粗气地笑，中士赶紧加入伴唱；一会儿又反反复复不连贯地吹起笛子来。军人这时候不动声色地掌握了缰绳。显然，他对于英国偏僻地方的风景之美特别有兴味；因为这货车在他的指挥之下虽然漫游了好些时候，可是从来不见它出现在尘土飞扬的大路上，行行复行行，总是在篱笆和沟渠之间，一大半时间还是在垂悬的树枝之下。而且显然，他是注意到哈克先生的真正的利益；因为货车虽然不止一次在各个酒店门口停下来，下地的只是中士自己，他配备了一夸脱瓶装的酒之后，就又继续他那乡村中的漫游。

---

① 填麻絮（oakum）：是水手的工作，用解开的旧麻绳等填塞甲板缝以防漏水。又，填麻絮过去为囚犯、穷人等的工作。

若要知道一点中士赶的路是怎样错综复杂,得印一幅米德尔塞克斯某一区的地图才行,可是我的出版者反对这笔费用。这且不提吧,单说夜色降临之后不多久,这辆货车在一处两旁树木森森的路上停住了;中士从纸包堆里抱起哈克那恹恹无生气的身体,轻轻放在路边。

"你要是在天亮之前就苏醒过来的话,"这中士想着,"那才怪呢。"

他从那安眠中的运货人的各个口袋里,和和气气地搜集了十七先令八便士。他重新上了货车,一面思索,一面赶车走。

"要是我能确切知道刚才是在什么地方的话,这桩事儿就做得好,"他默想着,"不管怎样,这儿拐弯了。"

他转了过去,发现自己到了河边。在他前面不远处,一艘住家船亮着荧荧的灯光。有三个人——一位女士,两位先生,正在不慌不忙地一步步走来,这时已经离得很近,无法避开他们的眼睛了。中士心想,夜色的暗黑便于隐蔽,也就向着他们赶车上前。两位先生里胖胖的一位,走到路中心来,接着举起一根手杖示意。

"嗨,你看见一个运货人驾着的一辆运货车没有?"他喊着。

虽然是那么黑,可是中士好像看到这两位先生里边瘦一点的那位做了个手势,叫另外那位不要说话,接着(他看到自己已经太迟)迅速地避到一边。在旁的时候,白兰特中士对于这样的事会比现在更加注意的;可是现在呢,他陷在进退维谷的危境中,已自顾不暇了。

"一个运货人驾着的一辆货车?"他说着,语音显然支支吾吾。"没有,先生。"

"啊!"胖胖的先生说,站在一边让中士过去。那女士好像往前弯着身子在细看这辆运货车,好奇心大得不得了的样子。那瘦瘦的先生还是待在后面。

"我不懂他们在搞什么鬼。"白兰特中士心想。他胆怯怯地回头一看,只见那三个人站在路中央,聚在一起,好像人们在商量事情那样。最勇敢的陆军英雄也不见得一直都有着虎胆或者永远保持住英名;而在某种离奇情况的刺激之下,就是从不知恐惧为何物的心胸里,也会有恐惧突然降临。可能听到"暗探"这两个字在中士的喉咙里咯咯作声,于是他使劲加上一鞭,在运货人那匹马的疾驰之下,顺着河边那条马路,直往大哈浮罕逃奔而去。住家船上的灯光照着了那一闪而过的货车;嘚嘚的马蹄声和辘辘的车轮声渐渐混合起来,又渐渐消失了;转瞬之间,静寂重新降临在这河边三人的四周。

"这件事真是再奇怪也没有了,"两位先生里瘦的那一位喊着,"就是那辆运货车呀!"

"而且我的确瞧见了一架钢琴。"这姑娘说。

"哦,就是那辆运货车,没有疑问;奇怪的是,这个人不对。"头一个人接着说。

"这个人一定没错,吉德,一定没错。"胖的说。

"那么他为什么要跑掉呢?"吉迪恩问。

"他的马不听指挥吧,我想。"乡绅激进派说。

"没有的事!我听见那鞭子像连枷^①一样打下去的,"吉迪恩说,"那简直是违反人性。"

"我跟你们说吧,"姑娘插嘴说,"他是从那儿拐弯过来的。假定我们去——书本儿上怎么说的?——追查其踪迹?那儿说不定有一幢房子,或者有刚才看见他的人,或者旁的什么。"

"好吧,就算我们为着好玩去的吧。"吉迪恩说。

好玩(看来是)就好玩在他自己跟海士尔坦小姐肩靠肩地靠得非常之紧。对内德舅舅说来,他是这种纯粹娱乐的局外人,这种远足从头就显见得没有什么希望;一幅新的夜景展现在面前,朦胧中,一边是黑黝黝的围栏,一边是篱笆跟沟渠,一点人烟庄宅的影子也不见,这时候,乡绅激进派打住不走了。

"这是水中捞月亮嘛。"他说。

脚步声停歇之后,另一种声响刺入他们的耳鼓。

"哦,那是什么?"茱莉娅叫着。

"我猜不出。"吉迪恩说。

乡绅激进派将他的手杖像一把剑那样高举了起来。"吉德,"他开始说,"吉德,我——"

"哦,福西斯先生!"姑娘叫着。"哦!别往前走,你不晓得那可能是什么——可能是可怕得不得了的东西。"

"可能正是魔鬼本身,"吉迪恩一面说着,一面释放自己,"可是我得去看个清楚。"

---

① 连枷(flail):一种打谷用的农具。

"别鲁莽,吉德。"他的舅舅喊着。

出庭律师走近那声响,它听来实在可怕。在音色上,它好像兼有母牛、雾角①和蚊子的声调。它发出来的那股可惊的劲儿,更使它恐怖到不可思议的程度。在沟渠的边上,好像有一个黑团团,样子跟神圣的人形不能说不像。

"那是一个人,"吉迪恩说,"不过是一个人罢了;他像是睡着了,在打呼。哈啰,"一会儿之后,他这样喊一声,"这人一定有什么不对吧,他叫不醒。"

吉迪恩拿出蜡火柴来,点上一根,在火光里他认出哈克的亚麻色头发。

"这就是那个运货人,"他说,"醉得像鬼一样。我明白这整个事情啦。"这时候他的两个同伴已经鼓起勇气来到他的身边,他就跟他们提出一套理论:那运货人和运货车是怎样脱离关系的,这倒也不能说不像事实。

"这醉鬼!"内德舅舅说,"我们把他带到一个抽水泵那儿去,让他受受他该受的。"

"绝对不成!"吉迪恩说。"他要是看见我们在一起,那是很不好的。真的呀,你们可知道,我得好好谢谢他,因为这事情这样发生,可说再幸运也没有了。照我看来——内德舅舅,照我看来,我可以告白于天下,我大概是没有事啦!"

"没有什么事呢?"乡绅激进派问。

"什么事都没有啦!"吉迪恩嚷着。"那人偷了那辆运

---

① 雾角(foghorn):船在雾中用来警告他船的号角。

货车跟尸首,真是个大傻瓜,他想把它怎么弄,我是既不知道也不管。我是一身轻松了,詹姆生不再存在了。去他的詹姆生。跟我握手吧,内德舅舅——茱莉娅,亲爱的姑娘,茱莉娅,我——"

"吉迪恩,吉迪恩!"他的舅舅说。

"哦,这没有什么不可以,舅舅,我们很快就要结婚了呀。"吉迪恩说。"你晓得你自己在住家船里这样说过哩。"

"我说过?"内德舅舅说,"我晓得我一定没有说过这种话。"

"恳求他,跟他说,他是说过的,在他的软心肠上下功夫。"吉迪恩说。"他真是一个好人,只要你在他的软心肠上下功夫。"

"亲爱的布洛姆菲尔德先生,"茱莉娅说,"我相信吉迪恩会成为一个非常好的孩子,而且他也答应过我,要研究许多许多法律,我也一定会照看他那样做。你知道这很能使年轻人好好地稳定下来,大家都承认这一点。虽则,当然啦,我知道我没有钱,布洛姆菲尔德先生。"她接着说了这句话。

"我亲爱的年轻小姐,这个坏东西今天在住家船上跟你说,内德舅舅有很多钱,"乡绅激进派说,"我再也不能忘了他是多么可耻地蒙骗了你。那么趁现在没有人看着,你最好让你的内德舅舅亲一亲吧。"布洛姆菲尔德先生在这典礼已经娴雅地举行了之后,继续说:"啊,你这滑头,这位十分美丽的年轻小姐是你的了,可是你太不配。现在呢,让我们回到住家船上去吧,把这汽艇的蒸汽弄起来,回到城里去。"

"这才对啦!"吉迪恩叫着说,"明天住家船没有了,詹姆生没有了,运货人的运货车没有了,还有那钢琴也没有了;等到哈克在沟渠边醒过来的时候,他可能要跟自己说这整个事情是一场梦。"

"啊哈!"内德舅舅说,"可是还有一个人他醒过来可不同啦。在运货车上的那个家伙他将会发觉自己聪明得过了头。"

"内德舅舅、茱莉娅,"吉迪恩说,"我开心得像鞑靼国王一般,我的心像一个三便士的银币,我的脚跟像翅膀一样轻飘。我已脱离了我所有的烦恼,茱莉娅许婚给我了。在这样的时候,除了欢快的情绪之外,还能有什么呢?真是,我的心里除了有天使心里的东西之外,简直不能再有别的哪!我想到那运货车里可怜的不幸的坏蛋,我就要在这夜里,站在这儿,诚心诚意地大声疾呼——上帝保佑他吧!"

"阿门[①]!"内德舅舅说。

[①] 阿门(amen):基督教祈祷或圣歌的结束语,意为"诚心所愿!"

第十三章 莫里斯的折磨：第二期

在文学上这个真正讲究文雅的时代里，我本来不屑于再回顾一下莫里斯那副愁眉苦脸的怪模样。不过这种研讨又合乎时代精神，而且可以使一种高度的、差不多令人作呕的善恶报应的道德面貌呈现出来，假如结果证明这也是一种办法，能防止一班可尊敬的然而阅历不深的先生去轻率地犯罪，即使是政治上的罪吧，这本书就没有白写了。

他跟迈克尔待了那一晚之后，第二天爬起来，从苦恼的昏睡中爬起来，两手直打战，两眼给眵目糊黏得睁不开，喉咙发干，胃口全无。"天知道这不是吃出来的！"莫里斯想着；他一面穿衣，一面从几个方面来重新考虑自己的处境。要描绘他现在正浮沉其中的苦海，最好的办法，莫过于把他那种种焦心事重温一下。我已经将这些焦心事（为读者方便起见）整理出一个眉目来；但是在我们那位可怜的人儿的心里，这些事儿却搅混在一起，像飓风里的灰尘一样旋转着。我又办了同样弥足称道的当务之急的事：替他每一种苦恼加上一个名目；人们将会带着怜悯的目光看到这些个名目都会印在供火车上阅读的小说的封面上，使它们显得光辉，从而吸引人们的注意。

焦心事之一：尸首在哪儿？或本特·皮特曼的秘密。现在已经清清楚楚，本特·皮特曼（从他那不吉利的称号[①]就可以看出）是属于刑事犯阶层里比较黑暗的一层的。一个诚实的人不会拿着那张汇票去兑现；一个心地仁厚的人不会不声不响地收下那大水桶里惨不忍睹的东西。一个人要不是早已积恶盈贯，不会有办法把这类东西神不知鬼不觉地弄掉。这样推论的结果，得出了那个怪物皮特曼的可怕的形象。毫无疑问，他早就把那具尸首弄掉了——把它从后厨房里的地板门里抛了下去，莫里斯猜着，模糊记起一本一便士的恐怖小说里的景象。毫无疑问，这人现在正靠了那张汇票的款子穷奢极侈地享受。到现在为止，一切尚属平安无事。可是像本特·皮特曼这个人的浪费习惯（他无疑还是一个驼子），八百镑在一个星期之内就可以很容易地化为乌有。等钞票全部消失了，他下一步可能做些什么呢？莫里斯胸膛里一个要命的声音回答道："讹诈我。"

焦心事之二："通蒂会"的骗局；或，大伯父死了没有？莫里斯把一切希望都寄托在这一点上，可是这一点却还是一个疑问。他曾试图吓唬媞娜，他曾试图贿赂她，可是全都没用。他心里依然确实相信自己猜想得不错；可是你不能用心里的猜想来讹诈一个精明的律师。而且，自从

[①] 本特·皮特曼原文为 Bent Pitman，字面上的意义是"弯腰的矿工"。他原名为 Dent（登特），滑铁卢车站的脚夫皮尔错记为"本特"，告诉了莫里斯，因此莫里斯一直以为他叫本特·皮特曼（参见第七十页脚注）。

他跟迈克尔会谈之后,这个主意显然是不那么动人了。迈克尔是一个可以去讹诈的人吗?而莫里斯又是做得了这种事的人吗?值得郑重考虑。"我并不是怕他。"莫里斯这下倒委屈地给自己再打打气了。"可是我自己脚步必须立得非常稳,糟糕的是,我简直看不出有什么办法好想。人生跟小说多么不同啊!要是在小说里,那我甚至还没有开始这件事,就会先在牛津路上遇着一个黑黑的、形容猥琐的家伙来做我的帮手,而且他对于怎样去干这种勾当完全内行。他可能在夜间闯进迈克尔的屋子,发现那儿存在的只不过是一座蜡像而已;然后就讹诈我,或者把我谋杀了。可是现在在现实生活里,尽管我在街上走得倒地而死,打家劫舍的好汉也不会有一个人走近来瞧我一眼。不过,这倒是真的,皮特曼总还好找到的。"他又深思地说。

焦心事之三:百朗亭的农舍;或,给养不足的共犯。他是有一个共犯,那个共犯正囊空如洗,好像一朵花在汉普郡的一个潮湿的农舍里,无人赏顾地开着。这事情怎么办呢?他实在应该给他寄点什么去;即使是邮汇五先令,也足以表示没有忘了他,也足以维持他的希望、啤酒,跟烟叶子。"可是能给你什么呢?"莫里斯想;满面愁容地把一个半克朗、一个弗罗林①和八便士的零钱倒在手里。这点钱光是给莫里斯一个人用已经是个笑话了:他的处境是他在跟整个社会作战,同时以毫无经验的手,指挥一桩范围很广、头绪纷繁的阴谋。约翰一定是骚然欲动了,这点

---

① 弗罗林(florin):英国银币,价值二先令。

毫无疑问。"不过,"那个要命的声音又问着,"约翰看来会忍受多久呢?"

焦心事之四:皮革店;或,终于倒闭,满城风雨。在这一个项目上,莫里斯没有资料。他还不敢就去访问他们家庭的这爿字号;可是他知道不能再拖,如果需要什么来使他对这点认识更深刻,那么迈克尔昨晚所提到的话,还在他耳朵里模模糊糊地响着呢。很好很好。城里是少不得要去的,可是到了那儿做些什么呢?他没有权利用他自己的名字签字;不管他的意志力怎样强,他可就是没有签他二伯父的名字的技能。在这种情形之下,莫里斯是无法拖延破产的。等这事情发生了,所有虎视眈眈的眼睛都开始注视他的一举一动,这时候,有两个问题,迟点早点儿,是不会不问到一个哑口无言、汗流浃背的破产者的。第一,约瑟夫·芬斯伯里先生在哪儿?第二,你到银行去的事怎么说?多么容易问的问题呀!——神灵在上,又是多么难以答复的问题呀!被他们问话的人一定得进监狱,而且——唉!什么?——可能上绞刑架哩。这个念头是在莫里斯剃胡子的时候,忽然钻到他心里的,于是他放下剃刀来。这一边是(照迈克尔的说法)一个值钱的叔叔完全不见了;另一边是一个侄儿处在无法解释自己的行为的时期之中,这侄儿和那老人相处七年以来没有一天不是横眉怒目的;那么遭受不白之冤是多么可能的一件事呀!"可是不会的,"莫里斯想,"他们不能,也不敢把这当作谋杀案。不能是那个。可是老实说,像君子对君子那样说话吧,在案件日程表上(除了'放火'以外)我看不出旁的哪一项罪名我好像没有犯过一点。然而我还是一个地地道道的可尊敬的人,从来没有想得我分外的东西。法律可不是好惹的。"

这个结论深深地印在莫里斯·芬斯伯里的脑海里,他便下楼走到这约翰街住宅的穿堂间里,胡子还只剃了一半。信箱里有一封信,他认得出那笔迹:是约翰!

"唉,我还以为我能免遭这个麻烦哩。"他辛酸地说,把它撕了开来。

"亲爱的莫里斯,"信上写着,"你这算什么意思?我在这儿不得了啦;我得赊账;可是这儿的一帮家伙并不欢迎这办法;他们不能,因为情形太明显,我是一文不名的。我连被单床毯都没有了,想想看吧,我一定要有点铜板呀,这整个儿的事简直是笑话,我不能再忍受下去了,谁也不能。要不然我早已一走了之,苦在我没有买火车票的钱。别发疯了,莫里斯,你好像不了解我这可怕的情况。我连这张邮票也是赊来的。这是事实。你亲爱的弟弟约·芬斯伯里。"

"连字都写得不像了①!"莫里斯想着,把那封信塞到口袋里,就离开这屋子。"我能替他做些什么呢?自己还得送点钱给理发师哩,我真是心烦!我怎么能够寄一个

---

① 原文是"连字都拼得不对"的意思。那封信上有几处拼字错误。

小钱给别人呢？这是逆境呀，我敢说，难道他以为我在享福不成？有一件事倒令人觉得安慰，"他好狠心地想起来，"他可不能甩手跑掉不管——他不得不耽下去；他像死人一样没有办法。"之后他忽然又说："口出怨言呀，他不是吗？他可从来没有听说过本特·皮特曼！要是他有我这些心事，那出出怨言还说得过去。"

可是这种说法不能说是无愧于心的，或者说不能完全无愧于心的；他的心里是有一番挣扎的。他瞒不了自己，他的弟弟约翰在百朗亭是过得很苦：没有消息，没有钱，没有被单床毯，也没有朋友或任何娱乐。等到他已经剃好胡子，又在一爿咖啡馆急急忙忙地吃了一点早餐之后，莫里斯决定采取一种权宜之计。

"可怜的约翰，"他跟自己说，"他是在一个很困难的境地之中！我不能寄钱给他，不过我跟你说我预备做些什么吧:寄一份《粉红报》去——这会使他开心起来的。而且，他能从邮局里拿到点东西，对于他的信用也是有帮助的。"

因此在莫里斯（依照他节俭的习惯）安步当车，走到皮革店去的时候，半路上买了并寄去了那一份能提精神、增气力的刊物。又因为突然袭来的一阵懊悔，胡乱加上了一本《雅典娜神庙》，一本《复兴信仰运动者》和一本一便士图画周刊。这样一来，约翰的文艺读物安排好了，同时莫里斯也给自己的良心敷上了镇痛剂。

像是给他一种奖励似的，他到了皮革字号里可得到了好消息。订货单雪片般飞进来；几种冷背货也有人抢着要，所以价格已经上涨。连那位经理都好像得意扬扬的。莫里斯呢，他差不多已经忘记了"好消息"作什么解释，这时他真想像一个小孩子一样呜呜啼哭起来。他简直要把那位经理（一个脸色苍白的人，眉宇间带着吃了一惊的神色）搂到怀里。在那慷慨的心情中他简直要给账房间里每一个抄写员一张（小数额的）支票。他坐在那儿拆阅来信的时候，一队虚无缥缈的合唱队，以最美妙的乐音，在他脑子里歌唱着："这爿老店还可能赚钱，还可能赚钱，还可能赚钱。"

在他轻松下来的这个温暖的时刻里，进来了一个债权人罗杰森先生，不过他的账，店里认为不必急于支付，因为他跟这爿店的关系维系很久，很正常。

"哦，芬斯伯里，"他说着，不免有点儿扭怩，"这当然只有跟你说明白才对——事情是这样的，银根略微紧张一点——我放了点票子在外边——这种事儿，大家都在抱怨——直截了当地说吧——"

"我们可从来没有这种规矩，罗杰森，"莫里斯说着，脸色变白了，"不过给我点时间转转身，看看有什么办法没有。我敢说我们能够给你点款子上上账。"

"哎，就是这事情。"罗杰森回答。"我被人家说动了，这笔账我已经转给了别人。"

"转给了别人？"莫里斯重复说了一遍。"这不免是在翻来覆去捉弄我们啦，罗杰森先生。"

"可是，转让这笔账我是十足收款的，"对方说，"拿了一张保付支票，立即支付。"

"十足收款！"莫里斯叫着。"啊，那就等于有百分之三十左右的利润哪。这倒是一件稀奇的事！那人是谁？"

"不认得这人,"这是回答,"叫什么摩西。"

"一个犹太人。"客人走了之后莫里斯这样想。一个犹太人要芬斯伯里的店铺子里的一笔欠账——他在账簿里查了一下数额——三百五十八镑十九先令十便士的欠账,他要这干吗?而且他为什么竟然十足付款?这数字证明罗杰森是讲义气的——连莫里斯也承认这点。可是这也不幸地证明了别的事——摩西的急切。一定是立刻要弄到这笔欠账的,当天要的,甚至于当天早晨要的。为什么呢?摩西的神秘配得上做皮特曼的神秘的尾声。"偏偏在一切都看来很顺手的时候会来这个!"莫里斯喊着,拍着桌子。差不多就在这个时候,摩西降临了。

摩西先生是一个容光焕发的希伯来①人,漂亮得简直要命,谦恭得叫人讨厌。从他的态度看来是代表第三者来办事的。他对于此事的情况一无所知;他的当事人是希望将其债权人的地位办个手续确定一下;不过他可以接受一张远期支票——两个月之后的,如果芬斯伯里先生愿意的话。

"可是我不懂这事,"莫里斯说,"你怎么会今天十足付款的呢?"

摩西先生一点也不晓得,他只知道所得到的命令。

"这整个事儿是彻底地不正常,"莫里斯说,"按照本行业的规矩,可不是在一年之中这个时候结账。假定我拒绝,你得到的指令是什么呢?"

---

① 希伯来(Hebrew):种族名。

"那我就要见约瑟夫·芬斯伯里先生,这爿店的首脑,"摩西先生说,"我奉命一定要这么办。意思是你在这儿并没有地位——这些并不是我的话。"

"你不能见约瑟夫先生,他不舒服。"莫里斯说。

"如果是那样的话,我就得把这事交到一个律师的手里去。让我看——"摩西先生说,他带着也许会令人起疑的小心的态度,把一本小摘记簿拿在正确的地方打了开来——"是的——迈克尔·芬斯伯里先生。可能是你一位亲戚吧?如果那样的话,我想,这事倒可以很顺利地办好。"

把事情弄到迈克尔的手里去,那是莫里斯受不了的。他投降了。一张两个月期的期票归根结底算不了什么。两个月之后,他说不定已经死了,或者无论怎样是进了监狱里去了。他叫那位经理给摩西先生一把椅子跟一张纸。"我去让芬斯伯里先生签一张支票,"他说,"他躺在约翰街生病哪。"

坐了一辆马车来的,又坐了一辆马车回去,他一点可怜的资产又得勾掉一笔啊!他算算这笔损失;跟摩西先生了结之后,他一股脑儿算在内,只剩下十二个半便士了。而更糟糕的是他给人家逼得把二伯父搬到布鲁姆斯伯里来了。"这一来用不着叫可怜的约翰耽在汉普郡啦,"他想着,"这出滑稽戏再怎样演下去,我可完全掌握不了。在百朗亭,事情还勉强可以掌控;在这布鲁姆斯伯里,就似乎不是人类的智慧所能应付得了的啦——虽然我看迈克尔倒有点办法。不过他有帮手——那个苏格兰人跟那一大帮家伙。啊,要是我也有帮手那多好!"

情急而后智生。在如此紧急的刺激之下,莫里斯的伪造签字新样品是那样修整和不费劲,连他自己也感到惊讶,在三刻钟之内他就把它交给了摩西先生。

"这好极了。"那位先生说着站了起来。"他们让我跟你说,这不会拿去取款的,不过还是请你小心点。"

这屋子绕着莫里斯直转。"什么——什么话啊!"他喊着,一把抓住桌子。再一会儿他才可悲地感觉到自己声音尖厉,脸色发白。"你是什么意思——不会拿去取款?为什么要请我小心点?这些是什么哑谜?"

"我不知道,芬斯伯里先生。"这带着笑脸的犹太人说。"这是要我带的信。这些话都是人家放在我嘴里的。"

"你的当事人叫什么名字?"莫里斯问。

"这在目前是个秘密。"摩西先生回答。

莫里斯把头朝他伸过去。"不是那家银行吧?"他嗓音沙哑地问。

"我无权再说什么了,芬斯伯里先生,"摩西先生回答,"请你让我祝你早安。"

"祝我早安!"莫里斯想。再一会儿,他抓起了帽子,像疯子似的逃出去。过了三条马路,他站住,呻吟着。"天哪!我应当向那经理借钱的呀!"他叫着。"可是现在太迟啦;再回去可太不好看;我是不名分文——简直不名分文——像个失业者一样。"

他回到家中,在那没有陈设的饭厅里坐下来,两手托着头。牛顿①也没有像这个穷于应付的牺牲者这样苦苦深思过,然而他还是想不通。"可能我的脑子有点毛病,"他嚷着,站了起来,"但是我看不出我得到的待遇是公道的。我碰到的晦气事真可以写到《泰晤士报》上登出来,这足够酿成一场革命。这整个情形,说得明白点,就是我必须立刻弄到钱才行。我现在是顾不了什么道德不道德了,我早已过了那个阶段。钱,我非得有不可,而唯一的希望,我看是在本特·皮特曼身上。本特·皮特曼是一个犯了罪的人,因此他的脚跟很不稳。那八百镑里,他一定还有点剩下来;要是有的话,我逼他均分;即使没有的话,我跟他讲那'通蒂会'的事,只要有个像皮特曼这样穷凶极恶的人来给我撑腰,我不成功才怪。"

很好,挺好。可是怎样才能捉到本特·皮特曼,除了登广告之外,那就看不出有什么办法了。就算这样办吧,用什么话来约会呢?什么理由呢?在什么地方呢?总不能在约翰街吧,因为像本特·皮特曼这样一个人,让他晓得你的真实住址可不得了。也不能就在皮特曼家里,在那霍洛韦的什么可怕的地方,后厨房里有一个地板门的。那种房子,你穿了一件单薄的夏季外衣跟亮油油的靴子进去,出来就可能变成好像菜篮子里的东西那样一团糟了。那是一个真正效率很高的帮犯的缺点,莫里斯想到这里,不免心寒。"我做梦也没有想到我竟然盼望要这种伙伴。"他想着。这时候,他忽然想到一个了不起的念头。滑铁卢车站,

---

① 牛顿(Issac Newton,一六四三——一七二七):英国著名物理学家兼数学家。

一个公共场所,可是每天在某些时候是冷清清的;而且,一提起这个地方,必定会使皮特曼心里一惊,会立即提示他,人家对于他最近干的亏心事的秘密都已经洞若观火。莫里斯拿起一张纸,拟了一张广告。

威廉·本特·皮特曼,见此广告请于下星期日下午二至四时,至滑铁卢车站主线尽头,出站月台,可得到好消息。

莫里斯再一次阅览这篇文艺小品,感到很得意。"简明扼要。"他想着,"好消息这句话并不太真实,可是这却能打动人心,也是别出心裁,况且一个人登广告又不需要宣誓。我现在需要的就是我自己吃饭跟登广告的现钱,还有——不,我不能在约翰身上乱花钱,可是我可以再给他寄一点报纸去。怎么筹款呢?"

他走近摆着印章戒指的陈列柜,然而这位收藏家打心底里不愿意起来了。"我决不!"他喊着,"没有东西可以诱使我残害我的收藏——我情愿盗窃!"于是他闯到楼上休息室里,动手拿了几件二伯父的古董:一双土耳其的拖鞋,一把士麦那①的扇子,一只水冷器②,一支保证是从以弗所的土匪手里夺来的毛瑟枪,还有满满一口袋离奇而不完整的海中的贝壳。

---

① 士麦那(Smyrna):伊兹密尔的旧称。土耳其西端濒地中海的商业大城市。
② 水冷器(water-cooler):一种不导热的水壶,中置冰块,可以冷却饮水。

第十四章　威廉·本特·皮特曼的好消息

星期日早上，威廉·登特·皮特曼在他平常起身的时间里爬起床来，不过比平常更勉强一点。昨天（这里应该解释一下），他家里增添了一个寄寓者。迈克尔·芬斯伯里是这事情的幕后主持人，并且担保每星期膳宿费如数照付。另一方面，由于迈克尔那强烈的好戏谑的脾性，起先一定把这个寄寓者的性格描绘成一种沉闷的典型。皮特曼先生因此总以为他的客人不是一个好朋友；他怀着戒心跟他接近，到后来发现那竟是一个天使般有趣的人物，他不胜欣喜。昨天吃茶的时候，他已大大地感到高兴；在画室里一直坐到将近第二天早上一点钟，出神地倾听着滔滔不绝的宏论，一点一滴地增长了种种知识。现在他一面漱洗，一面回味昨晚那不无裨益的消遣，更觉未来的日子正带着光明重现的动人风姿对他微笑着哩。"可不是吗，芬斯伯里先生真是可人。"他对自己这样说；走进小小的客厅的时候，早餐已经在桌上摆好了，他招呼得那样亲热，就是对一个老朋友也不过如此。

"我非常高兴看见你，先生，"——他的话是这样说的——"但愿你昨晚睡得很好。"

"像我这样的人,久已习惯于差不多永远变换的生活了。"这客人回答,"那些不大走动的人常常叫苦的事——譬如说,他们头一晚在睡到他们所谓的'新床'上去的时候所感到的不习惯,对我却完全不觉得有什么受不了。"

"我非常高兴听见这话,"绘画大师热切地说,"可是我打搅你看报啦。"

"星期日的报纸是这个时代里的一个特色,"芬斯伯里先生说,"在美国,我听说它就替代了其他一切文学,全国的中坚骨干都从其中满意地找到了他们所要的东西,成百行的栏目详尽地刊载了这个世界上的形形色色,例如旋风卷起的水柱、私奔、火灾,以及公众的娱乐。有那么一角是划给了政治、妇女工作、国际象棋、宗教,甚至文学。还有几篇锋利的评论来指导公众思想。这样庞大而驳杂的贮藏所,对于教育人民所起的作用是难以估量的。不过这(虽然本身很有兴味)好像已经有点离题了。我刚才要问你的是这个:你自己是不是每天看报?"

"报纸里没有多少东西能使一个美术家感兴趣。"皮特曼回答。

"要说兴趣,"约瑟夫又说,"最近两天里各种日报上出现了一条广告,今天又登了出来,你也许没有看到。那个名字,只差一些些就跟你的名字完全一样。啊,这就是。你爱听的话,我来念。'威廉·本特·皮特曼,见此广告请于下星期日下午二至四时,至滑铁卢车站主线尽头,出站月台,可得到好消息。'"

"有这样一条广告吗?"皮特曼叫了起来。"让我看看!本特?那一定是登特!可得到好消息?芬斯伯里先生,请你原谅我向你进一言,请你注意。我明白这在你听来会感到多么奇怪,可是因为有点家庭方面的缘故,这件小事也许最好只让你我二人知道。皮特曼太太——我亲爱的先生,我向你保证我要保守这个秘密是没有一点不光荣的;原因是家庭方面的,只是家庭方面;我只要向你保证,一切详情,我们的共同朋友,你的贤侄,迈克尔先生都知道得一清二楚,他却没有因此看不起我,这你就可以安心了。"

"君子一言,皮特曼先生。"约瑟夫说,致了个东方的敬礼。

半小时之后,这位绘画大师见到迈克尔正躺在床上看书,好一派赏心悦目、闲情逸致的景象。

"哈啰,皮特曼,"他说着把书放了下来,"什么事使你在这么不得当的时候到这儿来的?应该到教堂里去啊,我的孩子!"

"我今天没有心思到教堂里去了,芬斯伯里先生。"绘画大师说。"我面临着新的情况啦,先生。"他拿出那张广告来。

"嘿,这是什么?"迈克尔叫着,猛然坐了起来。他皱着眉头对那广告研究了半分钟。"皮特曼,我认为这文件没有一点道理。"他说。

"不过,这好歹要应付一下。"皮特曼说。

"照我看,你跟滑铁卢的关系已经够了,"这律师回答,"你开始有了一种病态的渴望吧?你自从剃掉胡子之后,向来不大正常。我现在相信你原来把心搁在那儿啦。"

"芬斯伯里先生,"绘画大师说,"我已经试着把这事情做了个分析,你爱听的话,我愿意把结果告诉你。"

"尽管说吧,"迈克尔说,"不过,皮特曼,请你记着今天是礼拜天,别叫咱们吵起嘴来才是。"

"我们面前有三种可能。"皮特曼开始说,"第一,这可能跟那大桶子有关。第二,这可能跟山米托波立斯先生的雕像有关。第三,这可能是我太太的兄弟刊登的,他原先到澳大利亚去了。关于第一种情形,这当然是可能的,但我认为最好让我们把它搁下不论。"

"在这一点上法院是支持你的,皮特曼业兄①。"迈克尔说。

"关于第二种,"对方继续说,"用尽一切方法来追回那遗失的古物,这显然是我的责任。"

"我亲爱的朋友,山米托波立斯简直做了一个老好人。他承担了那个损失,而把好处给了你。你还要什么呢?"律师问。

"我觉得,先生,说得不对的地方还请指正,我要说,山米托波立斯先生的宽厚使我觉得应该更加努力。"绘画大师说。"这整个事儿是不幸的;这是——我也用不着瞒你——这开头就是不合法的,因此更有理由要求我自己今后的行为像一个君子一样。"皮特曼红着脸总结说。

"对于这一点我没有意见,"律师回答,"我有时想想

---

① 原文为 brother。因为皮特曼的分析,很像一个律师的口吻,迈克尔就戏称他是律师界的同业弟兄。

我自己也愿意做一个正人君子,只是这想法太片面了,因为世界是这副样子,做律师又是这种职业啊。"

"那么,关于第三种,"绘画大师又说,"如果这是妻舅蒂姆登的,自然啰,那我们的好运是一定的了。"

"可是这不是妻舅蒂姆。"律师说。

"你没有注意到那非常显眼的句子吗?可得到好消息。"皮特曼精明地问。

"你这个天真的小傻子,"迈克尔说,"这是我们文字里最没有意思的俗套话,只不过证明登广告的人是一头蠢驴。让我立刻把你的空中楼阁毁了吧。难道妻舅蒂姆会把你的名字弄错吗?——这错误本身是美妙的,比起那粗劣的原名①,是一个很大的进步,我建议你在将来采用它。可是这像是妻舅蒂姆登的吗?"

"不,不像是他,"皮特曼承认,"不过他可能在巴拉腊特②那儿昏了头了。"

"你要是那么说的话,皮特曼,"迈克尔说,"登广告的,可能是维多利亚女王,一阵心血来潮要把你封做公爵。我问你这可能不可能,然而这跟宇宙的法则并不相悖啊。可是我们坐在这儿是要研究可能的事;请你海量放宽,我一开头就把女王陛下和妻舅蒂姆剔除不论了。接下来,我们要讨论你的第二个意见,就是说这跟雕像有关。也许吧,可是这样的话,谁是登广告的人呢?不会是理卡地,因为

---

① 皮特曼的名字登特原文为 Dent,照字面是"凹陷"的意思。
② 巴拉腊特(Ballarat):见前注第一〇三页。该地是墨尔本金矿区的中心,以产金著称于世。后文所述由此。

他知道你的地址；也不会是拿到那只箱子的人，因为他不知道你现在的姓名。那送货人，我听见你提到他曾经有过一段神志清醒的时期。他可能在车站那儿耳闻你的名字，可是弄错了；他又可能打听不到你的地址。我姑且假定是那送货人。不过有一个问题：你难道想去跟那送货人会面吗？"

"为什么不呢？"皮特曼反问。

"如果他要跟你会面，"迈克尔回答，"注意这点：这是因为他已经找到了他那本姓名住址簿，到收到那座雕像的人家去过，而且——注意这句话！——他背后是有那个谋杀犯在唆使！"

"要是这样的话，那我感到非常遗憾，"皮特曼说，"不过我还是要考虑我对于山米托波立斯先生的责任……"

"皮特曼，"迈克尔打断他的话，"这样可不行啊。别存心欺侮你的法律顾问；别冒充威灵顿公爵①，因为这你不在行。来吧，我跟你赌一顿饭，我知道你在想些什么。你还以为那是你的妻舅蒂姆。"

"芬斯伯里先生，"绘画大师说，脸上红了起来，"你不是一个处于穷困境地的人，你又没有家室之累。我呢，格温德琳长大了，一个大有希望的女孩子——她今年受了

---

① 威灵顿公爵（Duke of Wellington，一七六九——一八五二）：英国将军兼政治家，曾在滑铁卢打败拿破仑。"冒充威灵顿"意为装模作样冒充阔人。

坚信礼①；如果跟你说她还不懂什么跳舞，我想你定能体会我这做父亲的心里是什么滋味吧。两个男孩子在寄宿小学里念书，那种学校你照它们的标准看是很不错的了；至少，我是什么人，也配批评祖国的制度吗？可是我痴心妄想，希望哈罗德将来成为一个音乐家，小奥索则表现了做教会方面的事相当有才能。我并不能算是一个有多大野心的人……"

"嗯，嗯，"迈克尔打断他的话，"说清楚呀，你以为是你的妻舅蒂姆。"

"这可能是妻舅蒂姆，"皮特曼坚持着说，"如果是，而我错过了这次机会，那以后怎么再有脸见我的孩子们呢？我并不是要提到皮特曼太太……"

"不，你从来不。"迈克尔说。

"……可是如果她自己的兄弟从巴拉腊特回来了……"皮特曼跟着说。

"……带着昏了的头脑。"律师接上去说。

"……带着一大堆金子从巴拉腊特回来，她的不耐烦的心情那就只好意会而难于言传了。"皮特曼总结说。

"好吧，"迈克尔说，"就算这样吧。那么你打算怎么办呢？"

"我打算到滑铁卢去，"皮特曼说，"化着装去。"

"就你这小不点儿一个人去？"律师问。"嗯，我希望你能认为这样很安全吧。记着别忘了从警察局的拘留所里

---

① 坚信礼（confirmation）：一种宗教仪式。西方人幼时受洗礼，成为教徒，及长再受坚信礼。

给我捎个信来。"

"哦，芬斯伯里先生，我曾经大胆希望——也许可以请得动你也来——来参加。"皮特曼讷讷而言。

"叫我礼拜天把自己化装起来？"迈克尔喊着，"你太不了解我的原则啦！"

"芬斯伯里先生，要是允许我问你一个问题，我将简直无法表达我的感激之情。"皮特曼说，"如果我是一个很有钱的当事人，你也不肯冒这个险吗？"

"好厉害，好厉害，你不知道你说了什么！"迈克尔喊着。"嗨，老兄，你以为我老是把自己化装起来跟着当事人在伦敦乱窜吗？你以为钱就能叫我拿一根竿子来碰碰这桩事情吗？我对你郑重宣布，决不会的。然而我承认，我倒有极大的好奇心，想去瞧瞧你怎样应付这次会谈——这事情才吸引我；皮特曼，这比金子对我有更大的吸引力——这一定是出绝妙好戏。"迈克尔突然笑起来。"好吧，皮特曼，"他说，"你到画室里把一切胡闹的东西准备好吧。我去。"

在这重要的日子里，大约下午两点二十分的时候，广大而沉闷的滑铁卢车站的天棚下，像一座没有人前来朝拜的庙宇一样，寂静无人。稀稀拉拉地，在几处月台旁有火车静静地停靠着；稀稀拉拉地，有悠闲的脚步声回响着。车站外，拖着马车的马把蹄子在石子路上跺出惊人的响声；又或从近处的郊野的铁路线上传来机车鸣出的汽笛声。主线的出站月台跟别处一样，好像睡着了；车票间关着。哈格德①先生的小说，在平日总是排列在书架上，纹饰精美的书脊发着光，现在也小心谨慎地躲在暗淡的排门板后面。难得看到的一两个办事员，一望而知他们是在睡梦中走路。经常逗留在那儿游荡的人们，甚至穿着宽大衣②、挽着手提包的中年妇女，都逃到更相宜的地方去了。正如热带海岛深处的幽谷里可以觉着大海洋的颤动的余波一样，在这儿也感觉得到遍布伦敦四周每一个角落里的隐隐约约的嗡嗡声和震颤。

在上面所讲的时间里，凡是认得从巴拉腊特来的约翰·迪克逊和从美国来的以斯拉·托马斯的人，一定会高兴地看见他们从买票间那儿走了进来。

"我们用什么名字呢？"后面那个问，焦急地把这次让他用的窗玻璃做的眼镜摆一摆正。

"你不能随便乱挑，我的朋友，"迈克尔回答，"本特·皮特曼之外就没有别的。至于我呢，我想我的样子可以叫阿泼拜③；这阿泼拜带着点古老的地方的气息——有着德文郡④苹果酒的香味。说到这个，我看你还是润润喉吧？这

---

① 哈格德（Henry Rider Haggard，一八五六—一九二五）：英国小说家，著有《所罗门王的宝藏》(*King Solomon's Mines*)、《她》(*She*)、《克利奥佩特拉》(*Cleopatra*)等书。
② 宽大衣（Ulster）：或者称阿尔斯它大衣，通常指有腰带的宽松的长大衣。
③ 阿泼拜原文为 Appleby，是 apple(苹果)和 by(近旁)两字合成的。和这字发音相近的 apple-pie 是"苹果馅饼"的意思。另外，apple-pie order 是"齐齐整整"的意思。
④ 德文郡（Devonshire）：英国西南部一郡。

次会谈可能很费劲哩。"

"我想我还是等到事后吧,"皮特曼回答,"从整个事情看来,我想还是等到办完之后吧。我不晓得你对于这地方是不是跟我有同感:这地方好像人全走光了,那么静静的,芬斯伯里先生,而且又充满了非常奇怪的回声。"

"好像一种洋娃娃关在盒子里的滋味吗?"迈克尔问,"好像这些空车厢里装满了等着暗号的警察吗?而查尔斯·华伦爵士[①]是蹲在一根横梁上,嘴里衔着一只银哨子吗?这是犯罪,皮特曼。"

他们就怀着这样惴惴不安的心绪一直往前走。差不多走完了这条出站月台,到了西端的尽头,他们发觉一个瘦高个子正在那儿背靠柱子站着。那人显然是沉思得出了神,他没有觉着他们走近,只是在这晒着太阳的车站上往外边远远的地方愣着看。迈克尔站住了。

"哎呀!"他说,"难道这就是登广告找你的人吗?如果是他,我可完啦。"然后,再一转念,"也不见得,"他又比较高兴地说,"喂,你且转过身来。这样。把眼镜给我。"

"你答应让我用的嘛。"皮特曼提出抗议。

"啊,可是那个人认得我。"迈克尔说。

"他认得你?他叫什么名字?"皮特曼叫着。

"哦,我得讲义气,不泄露他的秘密。"律师回答,"不过我可以说一句话:如果他就是登广告找你的人(他可能是的,因为他好像得了犯刑事的人的那种疯病),你尽可

[①] 查尔斯·华伦爵士(Sir Charles Warren,一八四〇—一九二七):英国将军兼考古学家,于一八八六至一八八八年任伦敦警察局局长。

以心安理得地应付他,因为他已经逃不出我的手掌心了。"

眼镜换好,皮特曼也给这好消息安下了心,他们两人就走近莫里斯。

"你是在等威廉·本特·皮特曼先生吗?"绘画大师问,"我就是。"

莫里斯抬起头来。他看见站在面前说话的是一个无法形容的卑不足道的人,脚上罩着白鞋罩,身上穿一件领子低得不像话的衬衫。在他后面一点还站着一个较为粗壮的人,除了宽大衣、络腮胡子、眼镜和猎鹿者戴的帽子以外,倒也没有什么可以批评的。莫里斯自从决心向伦敦黑暗世界里的"鬼怪"发出召唤之后,心里早已完全准备好接受他们出现的可能。他现在的第一个感想,像嘉乐巴①初次看见大海一样,是一种失望。他的第二个感想对于目前这情景更恰当:他从来没有看见过一个穿得像这样子的人,他已经碰着一个新的阶层了。

"我得跟你单独谈话。"他说。

"你对阿泼拜先生可以不必在意,"皮特曼答话,"他全知道。"

"全知道?你知道我现在要说的是什么吗?"莫里斯问,"那个大桶子。"

皮特曼脸色变得苍白了,不过这是由于男子汉的愤慨。"你就是那个人!"他叫了起来。"你这个作恶多端的人!"

"你要我当着他的面说出来吗?"莫里斯问着,不理

---

① 嘉乐巴(Charoba):神话中的一个小天使。

这些严厉的话语。

"他一直在场,"皮特曼说,"他打开了那只大桶子;你的犯罪的秘密他已经晓得,就像创造你的上帝、就像我一样。"

"嗯,那么,"莫里斯说,"你把钱怎么弄了呢?"

"我一点也不晓得什么钱。"皮特曼说。

"你用不着装那一套,"莫里斯说,"我已经把你追捕到了;你亵渎神灵,化装成一个牧师到车站上来拿了我的桶子,打了开来,掠夺了死者身上的东西,把那张票据兑了现。我已经到银行里去过了,我告诉你吧!我曾经一步一步地追踪你,你的否认是幼稚的、愚蠢的。"

"喂,喂,莫里斯,脾气放好点吧。"阿泼拜先生说。

"迈克尔!"莫里斯叫了起来,"迈克尔也在这儿!"

"也在这儿,"律师学着他的话,"在这儿,在随便哪儿,我的好朋友。你走的每一步都给算计过了,训练有素的暗探像你的影子一样跟随着你,每三刻钟都有情报给我,什么费用都在所不惜的。"

莫里斯的脸布上了一层灰蒙蒙的色彩。"哼,我不管;我更不必客气啦。"他嚷着。"那个人把我的汇票兑了现,这是盗窃,我要拿回我的钱。"

"你想我会跟你说谎吗,莫里斯?"迈克尔问。

"我不晓得,"他的堂弟说,"我要我的钱。"

"碰着那尸首的只是我一个人。"迈克尔开始说。

"你?迈克尔!"莫里斯叫着,往后一退,"那么你为什么没有公布他的死讯呢?"

"你这胡话是什么意思?"迈克尔问。

"我疯了吗?还是你?"莫里斯叫着。

"我想一定是皮特曼。"迈克尔说。

这三个人你瞧瞧我,我瞧瞧你,眼睛疯狂似的瞪着。

"这真可怕,"莫里斯说,"可怕。你跟我说的话,我一句也不懂!"

"我跟你郑重地申明吧,我并不比你懂得多一些。"迈克尔说。

"那么老天爷,这胡子又为什么?"莫里斯叫着,带着一种鬼怪似的样子指着他的堂兄。"我的头脑在转吧?胡子是怎么回事?"

"哦,那是细节问题。"迈克尔说。

于是又静默了一阵子,这时候,莫里斯感到自己像坐在秋千上给一荡荡到圣保罗教堂①那么高,又一沉沉到贝克街车站②那么低。

"让我们把要点重述一下,"迈克尔说,"除非这真是一场梦;真是梦的话,我盼望媞娜会来叫我吃早饭。我的朋友皮特曼,就是这位,收到一只大桶子,而这东西现在看来应当是给你的。这大桶子里装了一个男人的尸首。你为什么而又怎样把他弄死的……"

"我从来没有碰过他,"莫里斯抗议着,"这就是我一

---

① 圣保罗教堂(St. Paul's Cathedral):在伦敦中区,高达三百六十五英尺。
② 贝克街车站(Baker Street Station):在贝克街上,距圣保罗教堂几条马路远。

直惧怕的一点。可是想想看,迈克尔!我不是那种人;虽然我有种种缺点,我连人家一根头发也不会碰,而这对我又是一笔无可补偿的损失。他是在那场倒霉的惨案里送了命的。"

突然间,迈克尔爆发了一阵狂笑,笑得那么久而又那么厉害,使得这两个同伴以为他一定神经错乱了。他一再挣扎着使自己恢复常态,可是那狂笑像潮水一样,一再把他压倒。在这整个癫狂的会谈中,再也没有比迈克尔这样的笑法更像是给鬼迷着的了。皮特曼和莫里斯由于共同的害怕心理而站到一条阵线上来了,彼此交换着焦急的眼光。

"莫里斯,"当这律师终于能发出声音来的时候,喘着气说,"等一等,我全懂了。我可以用一句话完全说清楚。这是关键:我在这以前从没有把它猜作约瑟夫叔叔。"

这句话使莫里斯紧张的心情暂时松弛下来;而皮特曼听了这句话,就好像最后一线希望和光明都给消灭了一样。约瑟夫叔叔?就在一个钟点以前还让他留在诺福克街家里的贴剪报的人?——是这个?——是这个尸首?——那么他,皮特曼是谁呢?那么这是滑铁卢车站呢,还是科尔尼·哈奇[①]?

"还用得着说吗!"莫里斯喊着,"尸首是毁得很厉害,我知道。你多傻!竟没有想到这个。好吧,那么一切都清楚啦;我亲爱的迈克尔,我跟你说——我们是得救啦,你我全得救啦。你得到'通蒂会'的养老金——我一点也不

---

① 科尔尼·哈奇(Colney Hatch):村名,在伦敦北,有著名的科尔尼·哈奇疯人院。通常即以这地名指该疯人院。

气不过你——我呢,得着皮革店,店里生意正在开始好转。立刻就宣布死亡的消息,一点不必以我为意,不必顾到我;宣布死亡的消息,我们都会很好的。"

"啊,可是我不能宣布哩。"迈克尔说。

"为什么不能?"莫里斯叫着。

"我拿不出那个尸体,莫里斯。我已经把它丢啦。"律师说。

"等一等,"这皮革商急惶惶地说,"这是怎么回事?这不可能。是我丢了呀。"

"呃,我也丢了呀,我的孩子。"迈克尔极端镇静地说。"没有把它认出来,你知道,而又疑惑它来路不明,我弄掉了——我们应该怎样说——立刻弄掉了那拿出来的东西。"

"你把那尸首弄掉啦?你为什么那样做啊?"莫里斯失声痛哭着说。"你还拿得回来吧?你知道尸首在哪儿吧?"

"我真希望我知道啊,莫里斯,你可以相信我,因为这只要花我口袋里一点钱而已;但是事实是我不知道。"迈克尔说。

"啊呀,"莫里斯呼天抢地地说,"啊呀,我丢掉了皮革店啦。"

迈克尔又笑得浑身筋肉直抖。

"你为什么笑啊,你这傻子?"他的堂弟嚷着,"你丢的比我多。你弄得比我更糟。你要是有一点儿感觉的话,你应该站在靴子里边气得发抖。可是我跟你讲一桩事情——我得要八百镑——拿到这笔钱,我就没事了——

无论怎样,这原本是我的,然而你的朋友一定伪签了汇票,取了款子。给我这八百,就在这儿这个月台上给我,要不然我就直接到警察总署把这整个丢脸的事儿兜底翻出来。"

"莫里斯,"迈克尔把手按着他的肩膀说,"你得讲理。我们并没有拿到钱,那是另外一个人。我们连那尸体都没有搜查过。"

"另外一个人?"莫里斯重复着说。

"是的,另外一个人。我们把约瑟夫叔叔塞给了另外一个人。"迈克尔说。

"你什么?你把他塞了出去?这倒确实是一种奇怪的说法。"莫里斯说。

"是的,把他充作钢琴塞了出去。"迈克尔十分天真地说。"声音特别洪亮深沉。"他跟着说。

莫里斯把手举到前额抹抹,又对手上看看,湿汗淋漓的。"发烧。"他说。

"不,那是一架布洛德伍德大钢琴,"迈克尔说,"皮特曼在这儿可以跟你说那是不是真货。"

"啊?哦!哦,是的,我相信那是一架真正的布洛德伍德大钢琴;这架琴我自己就弹过好几次哩,"皮特曼说,"那第三个音的 E 键是坏了的。"

"不要再说什么关于钢琴的事了,"莫里斯说,剧烈地战栗着,"我这人是不比从前了!这——这另外一个人——让我们讲他吧,只要我能想办法去追寻。他是谁?我到哪儿可以找到他?"

"啊,这就是难题了。"迈克尔说。"你所要的东西就在他手里，让我看——在星期三，差不多四点钟，而现在，我想他必定是在到爪哇岛和戈带岛的路上了。"

"迈克尔，"莫里斯恳求着说，"我现在是个一筹莫展的人，我求求你体恤一点同族弟兄。请再慢慢地说一遍，并且弄清楚你准没弄错尸首是什么时候落到他手里的？"

迈克尔把他的话重又说了一遍。

"是啦，这可再糟也没有啦。"莫里斯倒抽了一口冷气说。

"什么事情？"律师问。

"连这日期都荒谬透顶，"这皮革商说，"汇票是星期二兑现的。这整个事儿一点都说不通。"

一个年轻的绅士，已经走过这三个人的旁边，却突然一惊，转过身来，同时把手重重地按在迈克尔的肩膀上。

"啊哈，迪克逊先生在这儿啦？"他说。

宣判的喇叭声[①]刺到皮特曼跟这律师的耳朵里也不会像这样可怕了。对于莫里斯说来，这个错误的名字，看来不过是他久已经混迹其中的梦魇里少不了会有的东西。迈克尔甩脱了那生人的掌握，带着他那崭新的髯髯髻髻的络腮胡子转身就逃。那个怪模怪样、小个儿、剃光胡须、穿着低领衬衫的人，也像鸟儿一般尖叫了一声跟着他奔逃。这生人（看见别的俘虏全都逃掉了）就蛮不讲理地一把抓住了莫里斯，这时候，这位先生的心境，差不多可以用这句俗话来描写，正是："我不是早跟你说过了么！"

---

① 原文为 The trump of judgement，指宣告末日审判的喇叭声。

"这帮人里我总算逮着了一个。"吉迪恩·福西斯说。

"我不懂。"莫里斯没精打采地说。

"哦,我会叫你懂的。"吉迪恩冷酷地回答。

"无论什么东西,你要是能叫我弄个清楚,那你就是我的一个好朋友。"莫里斯突然怀着确信,有力地说。

"我不认得你的,是吧?"吉迪恩察看着这并不抵抗的囚犯说。"没有关系,我认得你那些朋友。他们是你的朋友,是吧?"

"我不懂你的意思。"莫里斯说。

"你说不定跟一架钢琴有关系吧?"吉迪恩提出。

"一架钢琴!"莫里斯叫了起来,抽筋似的抓住了吉迪恩的胳膊。"那你就是另外那个人!那东西在哪儿?那尸首在哪儿?你把汇票兑现了吗?"

"那尸首在哪儿?这倒非常奇怪啦,"吉迪恩默想着,"你要那尸首?"

"要吗?"莫里斯喊着,"我整个命运全靠这东西啊!我把它丢了。它在哪儿?领我到那儿去!"

"哦,你要它的,是吧?那么另外那个人,迪克逊——他要吗?"吉迪恩问。

"你说的迪克逊是谁?哦,迈克尔·芬斯伯里!嗨,他当然要!他也把它丢了。要是他还保有着的话,明天他就可以得到'通蒂会'的养老金。"

"迈克尔·芬斯伯里!不是那个撰状律师吧?"吉迪恩叫了起来。

"对的,就是那撰状律师。"莫里斯说,"可是那尸首在哪儿?"

"那么那就是他把案子送来的原因了!芬斯伯里先生的私人住址在哪儿?"吉迪恩问。

"皇家大道二三三号。什么案子?你上哪儿去?尸首在哪儿?"莫里斯嚷着,拉住吉迪恩的胳膊。

"我自己也把它丢了。"吉迪恩一面回答,一面跑出了车站。

第十五章 "伟大的万斯"回家了

莫里斯从滑铁卢车站回家来的时候,他那种心情可真难以描摹。他是个谦逊的人,从来不觉得自己有什么了不起的能耐。他知道自己写不出一本书,转不来一只餐巾环①,变不成一套戏法来在圣诞节的聚会上欢娱嘉宾——干不了(总而言之)任何这类通常归在"天才"名下出人头地的本事。他知道——也承认——自己的才具平平庸庸,然而他(直到最近为止)还以为,以这份才具应付人生总可以游刃有余。可是今天他认输了,迷离扑朔的人生中的事实占了他的上风。如果有任何办法能够溜掉,有任何地方可以遁逃,如果这个世界造得是另外一种样子,一个人可以像走出一处娱乐场所一样地离开它,那莫里斯会不假思索地放弃一切,不再追求这世上还会有的物质报酬和精神享受,而怀着不可言宣的满足的心情,告别世界。照眼前的事实,是这样一个标的在他面前放

---

① 餐巾环(table napkin-ring):一种用木或金属制成用来束餐巾的小环。西人餐食用毕后,将餐巾纳入环中套好,以便下次再用。各环式样或记号不同,以资识别。

着光芒:他还可以回家去。正像一条病狗可以爬到沙发底下一样,莫里斯还可以把约翰街上的那扇门关起来,独善其身。

他走近这个避难所,已经是暮色苍茫的时候了;他头一眼看到的是台阶上有个人影,一会儿拉拉门铃的把手,一会儿重重地敲着门上的嵌板。这个人没有戴帽子,衣服脏得可怕,样子像个采蛇麻草①的。然而莫里斯认得他,他是约翰。

哥哥心中头一个自发的念头是逃跑,但是接下来还是在绝望的空虚中静止不动。"现在还有什么关系呢?"他想着,一面掏出前门的钥匙,走上台阶。

约翰转过身来,他的脸可怕得很,疲乏,肮脏,怒形于色;他一看出走来的是他们的一家之主,就深深地、呼噜噜地倒抽一口冷气,眼睛里闪闪冒火。

"把门打开!"他说着,往后一站。

"我是要开。"莫里斯说,心里又跟自己说,"他简直像要杀人哪!"

这两兄弟来到穿堂间里,随手把大门关上了。突然间约翰抓住莫里斯两肩,像小猎狗摇撼一只老鼠一样摇撼着他。"你这个卑鄙龌龊的下流坯,"他说,"我就是把你的脑袋打得粉碎,你也是该受的!"这就又摇撼着他,摇得他牙齿嘎嘎直响,头往墙上直碰。

---

① 蛇麻草(hop):或称忽布,一种桑科蔓草,花带绿色,其雌蕊花长成球果。球果之已熟而干者称蛇麻子,用以酿制啤酒,可使啤酒带苦味。

"不要行凶,约翰,"莫里斯说,"这在现在没有一点用处啦。"

"你给我住口,"约翰说,"你听我说话的时候到啦。"

他大踏步走进饭厅,倒在一把安乐椅中,把走穿了口的便鞋脱掉一只,把脚抚摸了一阵,好像疼痛难忍的样子。"我这脚要瘸一生一世了。"他说,"晚饭有什么吃的?"

"什么也没有,约翰。"莫里斯说。

"什么也没有?你这是什么话?""伟大的万斯"问,"别跟我来这一套!"

"我是说,的的确确什么也没有,"哥哥说,"我没有什么吃的,也没有什么可以拿去买吃的。我自己这一整天只喝过一杯茶,吃过一客三明治。"

"只吃过一客三明治?""万斯"讥诮地说,"我看你再说下去就要叫苦啦。我看你还是小心点好:我已经到了忍无可忍的地步。我可以告诉你是怎么一回事,我一定要吃晚饭,而且要吃好的。拿出你的印章戒指来,把它们卖了。"

"今天我不能,"莫里斯抗议,"今天是礼拜天。"

"我跟你说我要吃晚饭嘛!"弟弟大喊着。

"可是要是办不到呢,约翰?"对方恳求着。

"你这个呆子!""万斯"喊着,"派克舅舅常到的那家旅馆,难道不知道我们吗?我们不是那儿的房东吗?你给我滚过去。可你要是半个钟头之内不回来,要是那顿晚饭不受用,我先要把你直打得不高兴吐气,然后径直跑到警察局去泄露秘密。你懂吧,莫里斯·芬斯伯里?要是你懂的话，你赶紧溜吧。"

这主意连可怜的莫里斯也觉得可喜，他自己也饿得发慌了。他赶紧去办这差事，回来时看到约翰还坐在安乐椅上摸脚。

"你要喝什么，约翰？"他体贴入微地问。

"香槟酒，"约翰说，"顶头的食物箱里那种深红色的劳什子，再来一瓶迈克尔喜欢的那种陈年红葡萄酒，好接下去喝；当心别把红葡萄酒摇晃了。还有，嗨，把火生起来；还有把煤气灯点起来，把窗帘拉下来；天气转冷了，天色渐渐黑了。还有，你可以把台布铺上。咳，我说，你呀！给我拿点衣服下来。"

等到晚餐端上来的时候，这屋子看来比较可以住人了。晚餐本身又好：肉汁浓汤，去骨箬鳎鱼，羊排加番茄汁，烤得很嫩的牛肉加烤番薯，葡萄干布丁，一块切斯特乳酪，还有些嫩芹菜——一顿地地道道的英国式的餐食，只不过分量十足。

"谢谢上帝！"约翰说，张开鼻孔嗅着，息息有声，自己也奇怪会玩这一下不习惯的谢恩礼仪。"现在我要坐在这把椅子上，把背对火烤着——这两晚霜结得很厚，我简直不能把寒气从我骨髓里赶出去；这芹菜正是对症下药的东西——我来坐在这儿，你去站在那儿，莫里斯·芬斯伯里，充个侍者。"

"可是，约翰，我自己也饿得发慌。"莫里斯恳求着说。

"你吃我剩下来的好啦，""万斯"说，"你才开始还你的债哩，我的宝货。我受你的恩可不小；你别招惹我这头英国狮子吧!""伟大的万斯"说这些话的时候,脸上跟嗓子里都带着一种非笔墨所能形容的威吓的神气,吓得莫里斯魂不附体。"喂,"这大吃大喝的人又说了,"先给咱们来杯香槟酒。肉汁汤!我还以为我不喜欢肉汁汤哩!你知道我是怎么回来的吗?"他问,又爆发了一阵愤怒。

"不知道,约翰。我怎么知道呢?"这卑躬屈膝的莫里斯说。

"我用十个脚指头走的!"约翰大声叫着。"从百朗亭一路走回来;一路讨着饭!我倒要看看你讨饭。没有你想象得那么容易。我讨着饭,装作一个从布莱斯来的沉船的遭难水手;我不知道勃力斯在哪儿,你知道吗?可是我觉得这地名听起来很自然。我向一个学童小畜生讨饭,他拿出一根短短的绳子,要我打一个酒瓶结①。我给他打了,我认为我是给他打了,可是他说不是的,他说那是蝴蝶结,说我就是人家说的'那一种人',要叫警察逮我。后来我向一个海军军官讨饭——他绝对没有麻烦我打结,可是他只给了我一份小册子。那是英国海军一篇很好的细账!——这之后,从一个卖棒棒糖的寡妇那儿才讨到了一大块面包。我另外碰着一个人,他说你要吃面包总不难;办法就是砸碎一块橱窗的厚玻璃,让人送到监狱里去。倒像是个了不起的办法。给我把牛肉端来。"

"你为什么不待在百朗亭呢?"莫里斯冒险询问。

"胡说!"约翰说。"靠什么过活啊?靠《粉红报》跟

---

① 酒瓶结(clove hitch):水手打的一种绳结。

一种毫无价值的宗教书吗?我不能不离开百朗亭。我非走不成,我跟你讲。我在一片酒店里赊了账,装得活像是'伟大的万斯'。你也会这样的,如果你也过着那种不是人过的日子!一张名片让我拿了好些麦酒跟别的东西,我们胡说八道地乱扯,讲到音乐厅和我歌唱所得的一大堆一大堆的钱。于是他们就怂恿我唱《我用神奇的网捉住美丽的她》,这么一来,他说我不可能是万斯,我可是死死咬定说我是的。当然啰,我去唱就是胡闹,不过我本来以为我可以老着脸皮混过那些村夫。这下子使我在那酒店里一切都完了。"约翰叹了口气说。"接着最后一件事就是那木匠——"

"我们的房东?"莫里斯问。

"正是那个人。"约翰说。"他到那地方来探头探脑的,后来就问水桶哪儿去了,还有被单床毯等等。我叫他滚开;你要是没话好说,你也会这样!他于是说,我把那些东西当掉了。问我难道不知道这是犯了重罪?这当口我要了很聪明的一手。我记得他是个聋子,我就很有礼貌地乱说了好些话,说得很轻,叫他一个字也听不见。'我听不见你的话。'他说。'我知道你听不见,我的大王爷,我原本不要你听见啊。'我像一个杂货商人那样笑嘻嘻地说。'我的耳朵不行啊。'他大声吼着。'如果你不是这样,那我就吃不消啰。'我说,一面做着手势,好像在解释一切似的。只要一直这样闹下去,倒也呱呱叫。'好吧,'他说,'我是很倒霉,聋子耳朵,可是我敢说警察能听见你的话。'他立刻朝一边跑去,我就朝另一边跑。结果他们得着了那盏酒精灯、《粉红报》、过期的宗教书,还有一本期刊,都是你寄给我的。我想你一定酒醉糊涂了——那名字就像二伯父常常搬出来的那种东西一样,里边则满是要命的关于诗的胡言乱语,还有地球仪的用法。这种东西没有人要看,要么疯人院里才有人看。《疯癫的神妙》,对啦,就是这名字!哼,一种什么书啊!"

"你说的想是《雅典娜神庙》①。"莫里斯说。

"我不管你把它叫作什么,"约翰说,"只要我用不着念它就行!啊,我觉着舒服些了。现在要把安乐椅挪到炉火边去坐。给我把乳酪端来,还有芹菜,还有那瓶红葡萄酒——不,我要盛香槟的酒杯,好多倒点。现在你可以开始啦;那儿还有一点鱼剩下来,还有一块排骨和一点香槟酒。啊,"这恢复了精神的赶路人叹口气说,"迈克尔对这红葡萄酒的评语是对的,的确是装在桶子里的陈年好酒!迈克尔这人我喜欢,他很聪明。而且念过很多书,还有《疯癫的神妙》等等。可是你跟他在一起不会觉得枯燥无味,他不像别人那样谈《疯癫的神妙》。嗯,大部分的人全会做些损人不利己的事!说到迈克尔,我可不会产生这个疑问,因为当然啦,我从头就知道这事情。是你把这事情弄糟的吧,啊?"

"是迈克尔把事情弄糟的。"莫里斯的脸涨得通红通红。

"他跟我们有什么关系呢?"约翰问。

"他把尸首丢了,这就是跟我们的关系。"莫里斯嚷着,"他把尸首丢了,这样,死亡就不能证实了。"

---

① 《雅典娜神庙》(*Athenaeum*):一种文字和艺术评论刊物,创立于一八二八年。十九世纪英国许多一流的作家都曾经为这一刊物写稿。

"等一等，"约翰说，"据我了解，你并不想要证实死亡，不是吗？"

"哦，我们早过了那一阶段啦，"哥哥说，"现在已经不是争'通蒂会'的养老金的问题，而是那皮革店啦，约翰。这是我们身上穿的衣服的事啦。"

"别这么牛皮糖的调调儿，"约翰说，"赶快把你的故事从头到尾说一遍。"

莫里斯照吩咐说了。"哼，看吧，我怎么跟你说的？""伟大的万斯"在对方说完之后嚷着。"可是我晓得一桩事，我不想叫我的财产给别人骗掉。"

"我倒要晓得你打算怎么办？"莫里斯说。

"我来跟你讲吧，"约翰怀着最大的决心说，"我要把有关我的利益的事，交到伦敦最聪明的律师的手里去；你会不会进监牢，不关我的事。"

"喂，约翰，我们是在一条船上的啊！"莫里斯分辩着说。

"是吗？"弟弟嚷着。"我敢说我们不是这样！我犯过伪造罪吗？我说过关于约瑟夫伯父的谎话吗？我在滑稽报纸上登过愚蠢的广告吗？我把人家的雕像砸碎过没有呢？我倒喜欢你的厚脸皮，莫里斯·芬斯伯里。不，我让你管我的事情管得太久了，现在这些事儿得交给迈克尔管啦。我本来就喜欢迈克尔，这已经是我应该懂得自己的处境的时候啦。"

正在此时，两弟兄的谈话给门铃声打断了。莫里斯小心翼翼地走到门口，从一个当差的手里接到一封信，姓名

地址是迈克尔的手笔。内容如下:

  莫里斯·芬斯伯里:见此条请于明日上午十时至法院街,我的事务所,可得到好消息。

迈克尔·芬斯伯里

  莫里斯已经被驯服得百依百顺,他匆匆看完了这封信,也不待问,就交给了约翰。
  "写信就得这样写,"约翰高声说,"除了迈克尔,没有人能写成这样子。"
  莫里斯甚至没有声明自己有首创之功。

第十六章　皮革店最后的改组

芬斯伯里两兄弟在第二天早上十点钟被领进了迈克尔事务所的一间大房间里。"伟大的万斯"已经恢复了一点精神,不像昨天那样软绵绵的了,不过一只脚上穿了拖鞋。莫里斯虽然没有真的瘫倒,可是比八天前离开伯恩茅斯的时候要老上十岁,他的脸上因焦灼而布满皱纹,黑发在鬓角上灰白了很多。

一张桌子边坐了三个人在等着他们,迈克尔居中,吉迪恩·福西斯在他的右手边,在他左面的是位年过古稀的绅士,戴着眼镜,满头银发。

"怪啦,这是二伯父约瑟夫!"约翰嚷着。

可是莫里斯带着苍白的脸色和一眨一眨的眼睛走近他的二伯父。

"我来说你干了什么事!"他嚷着,"你是逃跑啦!"

"早安,莫里斯·芬斯伯里,"约瑟夫回答,带着旗鼓相当的暴躁,"你的样子像是病得厉害。"

"现在不必找麻烦啦,"迈克尔说,"面对事实吧。你的二伯父,你可以亲眼看看,在那次火车事故里并没有受到怎样大的震动。像你这样富有仁爱心的人,定会感到高兴。"

"那么,果真是这样的话,"莫里斯突然说,"那个尸首是怎么回事?你们不见得在说,我苦心擘画的、为它出汗、亲手处理的东西,原来是一个根本不认得的人的尸首吧?"

"哦,不,我们不能说这句话,"迈克尔用安慰的口气说,"你可能在俱乐部里遇见过那个人。"

莫里斯重重地坐到一把椅子上。"要是那东西到了我家里,我定会查看个明白。"他抱怨着说。"为什么它没有送来呢?为什么送到皮特曼那儿去了呢?皮特曼有什么权利可以把它打开呢?"

"要是说到这个,那么你把那庞大的赫拉克勒斯雕像怎么弄了?"迈克尔问。

"他用斩肉的斧子①把它整个儿劈啦,"约翰说,"现在是乱七八糟地堆在后园子里。"

"哼,有一桩事儿,"莫里斯猝然说,"我这二伯父、我这欺诈了我的钱财的受托人又出现了。无论怎样,他是我的。'通蒂会'养老金也一样。我要这养老金,我现在就提出这个要求。我相信大伯父马斯特曼已经死了。"

"我得制止这种胡说八道,"迈克尔说,"而且永远制止。你说的十分近乎事实。在某一种意义上说,你的大伯父是死了,而且早已死了;那可并不是在'通蒂会'的意义上

---

① 前文为"砸煤的斧子"(coal-axe),见第七十七页。此处为"斩肉的斧子"(meat-axe)。并不一致。

说的，那笔养老金他多半还会活着赢得。约瑟夫叔叔今天早晨还看见过他，可以告诉你他还活着，可是脑筋已经不中用了。"

"他不认得我了。"约瑟夫说，他说这句的时候并不是无动于衷的，这倒要给他说句公平话。

"哦，你又搞错啦，莫里斯。"约翰说，"哎呀，你把自己弄成怎样一个傻瓜啊！"

"这就是你不肯妥协的原因了！"莫里斯说。

"至于你跟约瑟夫叔叔之间的荒谬关系，你们一直把自己弄得让人看了笑话，"迈克尔跟着说，"这早就应当告一个结束。我已经预备好一张适当的豁免全部债务的文件，你得给它签个字，作为一个开端。"

"什么！"莫里斯叫了起来，"叫我丢了那七千八百镑，还有那爿皮革店，还有那附带的利益，而什么也得不到吗？谢谢你啦！"

"你大概是要感激我的，莫里斯。"迈克尔开始说。

"哦，我知道向你吁请没有用，你这个会挖苦人的魔鬼！"莫里斯喊着。"可是这儿有一位生客，我不懂什么缘故，但是我要向他吁请。当我仅仅是一个幼小的孤儿，还在一个商业学校里念书的时候，我那笔钱就给骗走了。打那时候起，我除了一直想把自己的钱要回来之外，再也没有别的愿望。你可能听到好些关于我的闲话。无疑，有时候我是考虑得不周到。可是那是由于我境遇的凄惨，这是我要向你解释的。"

"莫里斯，"迈克尔插嘴说，"我真盼望你让我再加上一句话，因为我想这会影响你的思考。这句话也是'凄惨'的——既然你喜欢这文学上的修辞。"

"嗯，什么话呢？"莫里斯说。

"只是一个人的名字，他是你签字的见证人，莫里斯。"迈克尔回答。"他的名字是摩西，我亲爱的。"

一阵长久的沉寂。"我就想到一定是你！"莫里斯叫着。

"你签字吧，你不签吗？"迈克尔说。

"你可知道你做的是什么事？"莫里斯喊着。"你是在搞受到赔偿而不起诉的花样。"

"那好吧，我们不搞这一套也罢，莫里斯。"迈克尔回答。"看我是多么没有认清你那高尚正直的人格呀！我还以为你情愿这样办哩。"

"哎，迈克尔，"约翰说，"这一切都很好，很宽大；可是我怎么办？莫里斯是完啦，我知道；可是我没有完。而我也给人骗了，这要请你注意；而且也曾经同样是个孤儿，也曾经在那个宝贝学校里念书，跟他一样。"

"约翰，"迈克尔说，"你想你把这事儿交给我不更好吗？"

"我赞成你的意见，"约翰说，"我可以赌咒，你决不会蒙骗一个可怜的孤儿。莫里斯，签那张文件，要不然我就动手刺激一下你那脆弱的神经。"

莫里斯突然轻快起来，表示同意。书记被叫进来了，那张豁免债务的文件签订了，约瑟夫重又是个自由人了。

"现在，"迈克尔说，"听我建议怎样做。这儿，约翰和莫里斯，皮革店转让给你们，你们两人做合伙人。我把它尽可能按照最低的数额估了价,照鲍格兰－贾利斯店的估价。这是你的财产的余额的一张支票。你看,莫里斯,你从商业学校里出来,现在好从头做起了。既然你说过皮革店里生意正在好转起来,我想你可能不久就要结婚了吧。这是给你结婚的贺礼——一位摩西先生送的。"

莫里斯一扑就扑着他那张支票,脸涨得绯红。

"我看不懂这出戏。"约翰说。"这太美了,真叫人信都信不过来。"

"这不过是一种调整而已,"迈克尔解释道,"我承担了约瑟夫叔叔的债务;如果他得到'通蒂会'的养老金,那就得是我的;如果我的父亲得到呢,那反正也是我的,你懂吧。所以我是立于不败之地的。"

"莫里斯,我的脑筋转不过来的朋友呀,你可是给甩啦。"约翰这样评论。

"现在,福西斯先生,"迈克尔接着说,转过身来向着他那一直保持沉默的客人,"所有的罪犯都在你面前了,只有皮特曼一个人除外。我真不想断送他那学者的前途,可是你可以在他那小研究院里逮捕他——我知道他的时间。我们是都在这儿啦,样子可并不好看,你打算怎样处置我们呢?"

"什么都不要,芬斯伯里先生。"吉迪恩回答。"我好像觉得这位先生,"——指指莫里斯——"是这次骚扰的根源;而就我所了解的,他已付出了很大的代价。说实话,如果闹出笑话来,我不知道谁能占到什么便宜,至少我是不会的。此外,我得谢谢你给我的那桩案子。"

迈克尔脸红了。"给你找点业务,我不过是聊尽绵薄之意罢了。"他说。"可是另外还有一件事。我不希望你错看了不幸的皮特曼,世界上再也找不到像他那样一位好好先生。我希望今晚能请你去吃饭,看看这人的本来面目——在孚莱饭店怎么样?"

"我没有旁的约会,芬斯伯里先生,"吉迪恩回答,"高兴奉陪。然而——这得请你决定——我们能否为货车里那个人帮点忙?我感到良心上的责备。"

"没有办法,只有同情而已。"迈克尔说。

译者后记

史蒂文森是十九世纪末叶英国新浪漫主义的代表作家。十九世纪初叶，英国文学史上浪漫主义盛极一时，出现了拜伦、雪莱、济慈和司各特等伟大作家。到了狄更斯、萨克雷、勃朗特姐妹、盖斯凯尔夫人时期，英国的现实主义文学大放异彩。十九世纪后半期，现实主义传统由乔治·艾略特、梅瑞狄斯及哈代等继承；与此同时，史蒂文森则以其特有的风格独树一帜，为丰富的英国和世界文学宝库增添了一笔珍贵的遗产。

史蒂文森的全名是罗伯特·路易斯·贝尔福·史蒂文森（Robert Louis Balfour Stevenson），后来略去了其中的"贝尔福"，这是他母亲的姓氏。他于一八五〇年十一月十三日诞生于英国爱丁堡市。他的祖父罗伯特·史蒂文森、父亲汤玛斯·史蒂文森和几个叔父都是土木工程师，在英国沿海的灯塔建筑方面有特出的成就。汤玛斯还曾因为科学上的贡献，当选为爱丁堡皇家学会会长。他十分希望他的儿子继承自己的事业，一八六七年，便让十七岁的路易斯进了爱丁堡大学攻读土木工程学。可是路易斯从小对于文学艺术有特殊爱好。他后来说:"我整个儿童时代和青年时代,是出名的懒散,并被指为典型。然而我一直在为自己的目标忙着,那就是练习写作。我的口袋里总是装着两个本子,一本是阅读的书,一本是写作的簿子。"因此,进了大学两年以后,他便向他父亲提出要研读文学的想法。他的父亲大失所望,不允所请。作为折中的办法,让他改习法律。一八七五年,他通过毕业考试,取得了律师资格。但是,即使在律师图书馆里等待受理诉讼案件的时候,他还是忙于写作。学生时代,他已经发表了许多篇游记、评论和杂感。一八七七年,他发表了第一篇小说;第二年,出版了一本游记《内河航程》;又过一年,出版了两本书:《塞文山脉骑驴旅行记》和《人与书散论》。

史蒂文森自幼体弱多病,需要易地疗养,这对于他的律师业务是不利的;加上做律师本非其所愿,他在出版了几本书以后,终于放弃了律师业务,专门从事写作。

一八七六年,多次到法国旅居的史蒂文森在巴黎市郊遇见了美国人范妮·凡·德·格尔夫特女士。那时她是过着不愉快的家庭生活的奥斯本太太,带着一子一女不远千里到欧洲来为她自己和女儿求师学画。史蒂文森和她认识以后,发生了感情。过了四年,格尔夫特女士离了婚,终于在旧金山和远涉重洋、横越美国大陆赶来的史蒂文森结为夫妇。

从一八八〇年一直到一八九四年史蒂文森的一生的最后时刻,他们过着美满幸福的生活。但是胸膜炎、白喉、肺病交相袭扰着史蒂文森,使他们不得不经常在各地奔波,寻找适合疗养的地方。一八八八年，靠了《错箱记》这本书的收入的保证，他们租用了一艘九十五英尺长、载重量七十吨的纵帆船"卡斯科号"，雇请了一位船长、几位水手和一位中国厨师，从旧金山出发，在浩瀚无垠的太平洋上向南航行数千英里，在一年半的时间里，遍历了马克萨斯、塔希提、夏威夷等岛屿，最后于一八九一年定居在萨摩亚群岛的首府阿皮亚，在该地购置了一所住宅，取名"维利玛"，按该地土语这是"五条溪流"的意思。

萨摩亚当时受到英国、德国和美国殖民主义者的侵略，富有正义感的史蒂文森完全同情善良的土著人民。他斥责白人政务长官。"卑鄙、懦怯、寡廉鲜耻，这是对待野蛮的所谓文明的典型姿态。"他的正义立场开罪了殖民官吏，官吏们和某些白种居民对他敬而远之，甚至胁迫他。但是萨摩亚人民对他十分爱戴。有八位酋长去拜访了这位"图西塔拉"（土语是"文学家"的意思），提出替他修筑一条从公路通往他的住所的"感谢之路"。在这条路完工的纪念宴会上，史蒂文森发表了鼓舞当地人民反抗白人的热情洋溢的演说。他说："……这又是奸恶的白人伸出掠夺的双手来的时候了。手里拿着测量器的家伙一定会来到各位的村庄。考验各位的时机就从这时开始，到底是真金呢，还是铅屑？"

可是就在这以后不久，残酷的死神带走了这位正直和热情的文学家。那是一八九四年十二月三日的黄昏，史蒂文森和他的夫人正在游廊上一面说笑，一面准备晚餐。忽然他觉得头脑里有了毛病；他双手捧着头，口中喊道："这是怎么啦?……我可是脸色不对了?"便瘫跌下来。脑溢血夺去了他的生命。这年他才四十四岁。第二天,土著人民为这位"图西塔拉"在濒临太平洋的陡峭的瓦埃亚山上开辟了一条道路,把他抬到平如桌面的山顶上安葬。直至今日,那儿仍然立着他的坟墓。他的夫人在二十年后(一九一四年)去世,部分遗骨也运到那儿合葬。史蒂文森的墓碑上铭刻着一首著名的诗篇《安魂曲》,这是他于一八七九年的多病之秋写的:

> 在这寥廓的星空下面,
> 掘一座坟墓让我安眠:
> 我活得快乐,死也无怨,
> 躺下的时候我心甘情愿。
>
> 请把下面的诗句给我刻上:
> "他躺在自己心向往之的地方,
> 好像水手离开大海归故乡,
> 又像猎人下山回到了家园。"①

在指导他从事写作的文艺理论方面,史蒂文森认为,艺术家的任务是创造出有兴趣的画面,去满足人们对于罕见事物的憧憬,使人们的想象得到营养。他说,小说对于成人,应如戏剧对于儿童。他说,传奇故事能唤起"人类

---

① 译者曾为荣如德同志译的《金银岛》译出了这首诗。现在录在这里时已稍作了改动。

梦幻中的金碧辉煌的区域",可以避免人们整日在庸俗的现实中讨生活。

正是由于这种艺术主张,他的作品回避了现实的社会内容。他一生最后的十几年之中陆续出版的十多部小说都充满着浪漫的、传奇的、幻想的色彩。比如《新天方夜谭》(一八八二)、《金银岛》(一八八三)、《化身博士》(一八八六)、《诱拐》(一八八六)、《黑箭》(一八八八)、《巴伦特雷少爷》(一八八九)、《卡特丽娜》(一八九三)和《海岛夜谈》(一八九四)等都是。这些作品以其动人的情节、娴熟的技巧、精妙而有趣的描写、简练而典雅优美的文笔吸引着成年读者和青少年读者。他大概是希望用这些作品来照亮人们心灵中"金碧辉煌的区域",把人们带到一个神奇的罗曼蒂克的天地里。不论他的文艺思想是否能得到所有的评论家的赞赏,当时的和后世的许多读者在打开他的书,欣赏他在多病的、飘荡的一生里辛勤地创造的艺术品的时候,会感到惊喜;并且常常会从他的文章中包含的那种疾恶如仇的、乐观的、诙谐的、勇于冒险和进取的精神中得到有益的启示。

这本《错箱记》出版于一八八九年,是史蒂文森和他的养子劳埃德·奥斯本合作的三本小说中的一本。另外两本是《遭难船》(一八九二)和《退潮》(一八九四)。《错箱记》由十九岁的奥斯本写成初稿以后,再由史蒂文森作了全面修改。从这本书的主题思想和文章风格来看,都有着深深的史蒂文森的印记。当然,十九岁的少年的创造性必然也糅合其中,但是免不了受到当时已成为著名作家的史蒂文森的很大的影响。这本书不同于史蒂文森其他的主要作品,写的不是海外奇谈,不是荒岛探宝,也不是化身怪人,它写的是围绕一笔金钱展开的闹剧。

芬斯伯里三兄弟从小由父亲出钱,加入一种叫作"通蒂会"的养老金组织。按照规定,最后死者得到其公积金。入会时共有三十多个儿童,经过数十年时间的淘汰,活下来的只剩下芬斯伯里家的老大和老二两兄弟。老二约瑟夫曾经因亏空了老三一笔钱,老三的儿子莫里斯和约翰便把二伯父看管起来,怀着厌恶和憎恨的心情把他好生供养,切望他成为寿命马拉松竞赛中的冠军,好取回那笔欠款。约瑟夫受不住那种拘束的生活,趁一次火车失事之机溜之大吉。两个侄儿却误认了一具尸体,把它装在木桶里,企图封闭他们认为的二伯父的死亡的噩耗,以便保留取得那笔养老金的权利。老大的儿子律师迈克尔知道了其中奥秘,把他们大大捉弄一番。最后,整个故事以皆大欢喜的场面作为结束。

像这样的题材,本来也可以如同现实主义作家所做的那样,把它写成带有揭露社会问题、批判资本主义制度倾向的作品;但是这本书的两位作家还是把他们的材料作了史蒂文森式的处理。应该承认,他们的劳动的成果是值得称赞的。它的构思巧妙,结构完整,兴味浓郁,文笔生动,的确可以认为在这一类幽默小说中,是一个不可多得的艺术精品。无怪乎这本书在英美一再重印,也无怪乎直到这本书在开始问世的半个多世纪以后,还存在所谓"《错箱记》迷",他们在日常生活中还常常引用书中的隽言妙语。

虽然作者们把他们这本书只看作一幅山水画，一首轻音乐，或者一出热闹的喜剧，提供给人们作艺术欣赏，而不打算使它具备社会意义；但是我们仍然可以透过他们创造出来的万花筒式的引人的画面，得出自己的体会。那就是在金钱万能的社会里，人与人之间的关系能够变得多么荒谬和愚蠢，可笑和可怜。

在二十多年前，本人偶然购到这本原著，姚叔高教授和本人合作完成了这本书的翻译，并于一九五五年出版。姚教授毕业于清华大学和美国耶鲁大学，是一位法学专家，在英文方面，本人得到他很多教益。不幸，他已于一九七八年，七十八岁的时候病逝。修订工作只能由渐入老境的本人来独力完成了。人事沧桑，令人感叹。这次增译了二篇序文，增加了这篇译者后记，以期对读者了解史蒂文森、奥斯本及本书有所帮助。这些材料和关于史蒂文森生平的材料都是在译本初版以后，本人留意搜集到的。经过"文化大革命"的十年浩劫，居然能失而复得，真是一件幸事。

热诚期待读者们的批评指正。

吴钧陶

一九八一年四月二十八日。上海。

图书在版编目（CIP）数据

错箱记：汉英对照／（英）罗伯特·路易斯·史蒂文森，（美）劳埃德·奥斯本著；吴钧陶译．—南京：译林出版社，2022.4
（双语经典）
书名原文：The Wrong Box
ISBN 978-7-5447-8849-6

I.①错… II.①罗… ②劳… ③吴… III.①英语-汉语-对照读物 ②长篇小说-英国-近代 IV.①H319.4：I

中国版本图书馆 CIP 数据核字（2021）第 202595 号

错箱记 〔英国〕罗伯特·路易斯·史蒂文森
〔美国〕劳埃德·奥斯本／著 吴钧陶／译

责任编辑	陈绍敏
特约编辑	赵丽娟
装帧设计	鹏飞艺术
校　　对	刘文硕
责任印制	贺　伟

出版发行	译林出版社
地　　址	南京市湖南路1号A楼
邮　　箱	yilin@yilin.com
网　　址	www.yilin.com
市场热线	010-85376701
排　　版	鹏飞艺术
印　　刷	三河市中晟雅豪印务有限公司
开　　本	889毫米×1194毫米　1/32
印　　张	15.75
版　　次	2022年4月第1版
印　　次	2022年4月第1次印刷
书　　号	ISBN 978-7-5447-8849-6
定　　价	53.80元

版权所有·侵权必究

译林版图书若有印装错误可向出版社调换。质量热线：010-85376178

Bilingual Classics

THE WRONG BOX

Robert Louis Stevenson Lloyd Osbourne

CONTENTS

PREFACE ... 1

Chapter 1	In Which Morris Suspects	001
Chapter 2	In Which Morris Takes Action	018
Chapter 3	The Lecturer at Large	038
Chapter 4	The Magistrate in the Luggage Van	052
Chapter 5	Mr Gideon Forsyth and the Gigantic Box	058
Chapter 6	The Tribulations of Morris: Part the First	071
Chapter 7	In Which William Dent Pitman Takes Legal Advice	090
Chapter 8	In Which Michael Finsbury Enjoys a Holiday	105
Chapter 9	Glorious Conclusion of Michael Finsbury's Holiday	129
Chapter 10	Gideon Forsyth and the Broadwood Grand	148
Chapter 11	The Maestro Jimson	160
Chapter 12	Positively the Last Appearance of the Broadwood Grand	181
Chapter 13	The Tribulations of Morris: Part the Second	193

Chapter 14	William Bent Pitman Hears of Something to his Advantage	206
Chapter 15	The Return of the Great Vance	224
Chapter 16	Final Adjustment of the Leather Business	233

PREFACE

"Nothing like a little judicious levity," says Michael Finsbury in the text; nor can any better excuse be found for the volume in the reader's hand. The authors can but add that one of them is old enough to be ashamed of himself, and the other young enough to learn better.

R. L. S.
L. O.

Chapter 1   In Which Morris Suspects

How very little does the amateur, dwelling at home at ease, comprehend the labours and perils of the author, and, when he smilingly skims the surface of a work of fiction, how little does he consider the hours of toil, consultation of authorities, researches in the Bodleian, correspondence with learned and illegible Germans—in one word, the vast scaffolding that was first built up and then knocked down, to while away an hour for him in a railway train! Thus I might begin this tale with a biography of Tonti—birthplace, parentage, genius probably inherited from his mother, remarkable instance of precocity, etc.—and a complete treatise on the system to which he bequeathed his name. The material is all beside me in a pigeon-hole, but I scorn to appear vainglorious. Tonti is dead, and I never saw anyone who even pretended to regret him; and, as for the tontine system, a word will suffice for all the purposes of this unvarnished narrative.

A number of sprightly youths (the more the merrier) put

up a certain sum of money, which is then funded in a pool under trustees; coming on for a century later, the proceeds are fluttered for a moment in the face of the last survivor, who is probably deaf, so that he cannot even hear of his success—and who is certainly dying, so that he might just as well have lost. The peculiar poetry and even humour of the scheme is now apparent, since it is one by which nobody concerned can possibly profit; but its fine, sportsmanlike character endeared it to our grandparents.

When Joseph Finsbury and his brother Masterman were little lads in white-frilled trousers, their father—a well-to-do merchant in Cheapside—caused them to join a small but rich tontine of seven-and-thirty lives. A thousand pounds was the entrance fee; and Joseph Finsbury can remember to this day the visit to the lawyer's, where the members of the tontine—all children like himself—were assembled together, and sat in turn in the big office chair, and signed their names with the assistance of a kind old gentleman in spectacles and Wellington boots. He remembers playing with the children afterwards on the lawn at the back of the lawyer's house, and a battle-royal that he had with a brother tontiner who had kicked his shins. The sound of war called forth the lawyer from where he was dispensing cake and wine to the assembled parents in the office, and the combatants were separated, and Joseph's spirit (for he was the smaller of the two) commended by the gentleman in the Wellington boots, who vowed he had been just such another at the same age. Joseph wondered to himself if he had worn at that time little Wellingtons and a little bald head, and when, in bed at night, he grew tired of telling himself stories of sea-fights, he used to dress himself up as the old gentleman, and entertain other little boys and girls with cake and wine.

In the year 1840 the thirty-seven were all alive; in 1850 their number had decreased by six; in 1856 and 1857 business was more lively, for the Crimea and the Mutiny carried off no less than nine. There remained in 1870 but five of the original members, and at the date of my story, including the two Finsburys, but three.

By this time Masterman was in his seventy-third year; he had long complained of the effects of age, had long since retired from business, and now lived in absolute seclusion under the roof of his son Michael, the well-known solicitor. Joseph, on the other hand, was still up and about, and still presented but a semi-venerable figure on the streets in which he loved to wander. This was the more to be deplored because Masterman had led (even to the least particular) a model British life. Industry, regularity, respectability, and a preference for the four per cents are understood to be the very foundations of a green old age. All these Masterman had eminently displayed, and here he was, *ab agendo*, at seventy-three; while Joseph, barely two years younger, and in the most excellent preservation, had disgraced himself through life by idleness and eccentricity. Embarked in the leather trade, he had early wearied of business, for which he was supposed to have small parts. A taste for general information, not promptly checked, had soon begun to sap his manhood. There is no passion more debilitating to the mind, unless, perhaps, it be that itch of public speaking which it not infrequently accompanies or begets. The two were conjoined in the case of Joseph; the acute stage of this double malady, that in which the patient delivers gratuitous lectures, soon declared itself with severity, and not many years had passed over his head before he would have travelled thirty miles to address an infant school. He was no student; his reading was confined to elementary textbooks and the daily papers; he did not even fly as high as cyclopedias; life, he would say, was his volume. His lectures were not meant, he would declare, for college professors; they were addressed direct to "the great heart of the people", and the heart of the people must certainly be sounder than its head, for his lucubrations were received with favour. That entitled "How to Live Cheerfully on Forty Pounds a Year", created a sensation among the unemployed. "Education: Its Aims, Objects, Purposes, and Desirability", gained him the respect of the shallow-minded. As for his celebrated essay on "Life Insurance Regarded in its Relation to the Masses", read before the Working Men's Mutual Improvement Society, Isle of Dogs, it was received with a "literal ovation" by an unintelligent audience of both sexes, and so marked was the effect that he was next year elected honorary president of the institution, an office of less than no emolument—since the holder was expected to come down with a donation—but one which highly satisfied his self-esteem.

While Joseph was thus building himself up a reputation among the more cultivated portion of the ignorant, his domestic life was suddenly overwhelmed by orphans. The death of his younger brother Jacob saddled him with the charge of two boys, Morris and John; and in the course of the same year his family was still further swelled by the addition of a little girl, the daughter of John Henry Hazeltine, Esq., a gentleman of small property and fewer friends. He had met Joseph only once, at a lecture-hall in Holloway; but from that formative experience he returned home to make a new will, and consign his daughter and her fortune to the lecturer. Joseph had a kindly disposition; and yet it was not without reluctance that he accepted this new responsibility, advertised for a nurse, and purchased a second-hand perambulator. Morris and John he made more readily welcome; not so much because of the tie of consanguinity as because the leather business (in which he hastened to invest their fortune of thirty thousand pounds) had recently exhibited inexplicable symptoms of decline. A young but capable Scot was chosen as manager to the enterprise, and the cares of business never again afflicted Joseph Finsbury. Leaving his charges in the hands of the capable Scot (who was married), he began his extensive travels on the Continent and in Asia Minor.

With a polyglot Testament in one hand and a phrase-book in the other, he groped his way among the speakers of eleven European languages. The first of these guides is hardly applicable to the purposes of the philosophic traveller, and even the second is designed more expressly for the tourist than for the expert in life. But he pressed interpreters into his service—whenever he could get their services for nothing—and by one means and another filled many notebooks with the results of his researches.

In these wanderings he spent several years, and only returned to England when the increasing age of his charges needed his attention. The two lads had been placed in a good but economical school, where they had received a sound commercial education; which was somewhat awkward, as the leather business was by no means in a state to court enquiry. In fact, when Joseph went over his accounts preparatory to surrendering his trust, he was dismayed to discover that his brother's fortune had not increased by his stewardship; even by making over to his two wards every penny he had in the world, there would still be a deficit of seven thousand eight hundred pounds. When these facts were communicated to the two brothers in the presence of a lawyer, Morris Finsbury threatened his uncle with all the terrors of the law, and was only prevented from taking extreme steps by the advice of the professional man.

"You cannot get blood from a stone," observed the lawyer.

And Morris saw the point and came to terms with his uncle. On the one side, Joseph gave up all that he possessed, and assigned to his nephew his contingent interest in the tontine, already quite a hopeful speculation. On the other, Morris agreed to harbour his uncle and Miss Hazeltine (who had come to grief with the rest), and to pay to each of them one pound a month as pocket-money. The allowance was amply sufficient for the old man; it scarce appears how Miss Hazeltine contrived to dress upon it; but she did, and, what is more, she never complained. She was, indeed, sincerely attached to her incompetent guardian. He had never been unkind; his age spoke for him loudly; there was something appealing in his whole-souled quest of knowledge and innocent delight in the smallest mark of admiration; and, though the lawyer had warned her she was being sacrificed, Julia had refused to add to the perplexities of Uncle Joseph.

In a large, dreary house in John Street, Bloomsbury, these four dwelt together; a family in appearance, in reality a financial association. Julia and Uncle Joseph were, of course, slaves; John, a gentle man with a taste for the banjo, the music-hall, the Gaiety Bar, and the sporting papers, must have been anywhere a secondary figure; and the cares and delights of empire devolved entirely upon Morris. That these are inextricably intermixed is one of the commonplaces with which the bland essayist consoles the incompetent and the obscure, but in the case of Morris the bitter must have largely outweighed the sweet. He grudged no trouble to himself, he spared none to others; he called the servants in the morning, he served out the stores with his own hand, he took soundings of the sherry, he numbered the remainder biscuits; painful scenes took place over the weekly bills, and the cook was frequently impeached, and the tradespeople came and hectored with him in the back parlour upon a question of three farthings. The superficial might have deemed him a miser; in his own eyes he was simply a man who had been defrauded; the world owed him seven thousand eight hundred pounds, and he intended that the world should pay.

But it was in his dealings with Joseph that Morris's character particularly shone. His uncle was a rather gambling stock in which he had invested heavily; and he spared no pains in nursing the security. The old man was seen monthly by a physician, whether he was well or ill. His diet, his raiment, his occasional outings, now to Brighton, now to Bournemouth, were doled out to him like pap to infants. In bad weather he must keep the house. In good weather, by half-past nine, he must be ready in the hall; Morris would see that he had gloves and that his shoes were sound; and the pair would start for the leather business arm in arm. The way there was probably dreary enough, for there was no pretence of friendly feeling; Morris had never ceased to upbraid his guardian with his defalcation and to lament the burthen of Miss Hazeltine; and Joseph, though he was a mild enough soul, regarded his nephew with something very near akin to hatred. But the way there was nothing to the journey back; for the mere sight of the place of business, as well as every detail of its transactions, was enough to poison life for any Finsbury.

Joseph's name was still over the door; it was he who still signed the cheques; but this was only policy on the part of Morris, and designed to discourage other members of the tontine. In reality the business was entirely his; and he found it an inheritance of sorrows. He tried to sell it, and the offers he received were quite derisory. He tried to extend it, and it was only the liabilities he succeeded in extending; to restrict it, and it was only the profits he managed to restrict. Nobody had ever made money out of that concern except the capable Scot, who retired (after his discharge) to the neighbourhood of Banff and built a castle with his profits. The memory of this fallacious Caledonian Morris would revile daily, as he sat in the private office opening his mail, with old Joseph at another table, sullenly awaiting orders, or savagely affixing signatures to he knew not what. And when the man of the heather pushed cynicism so far as to send him the announcement of his second marriage (to Davida, eldest daughter of the Revd. Alexander McCraw), it was really supposed that Morris would have had a fit.

Business hours, in the Finsbury leather trade, had been cut to the quick; even Morris's strong sense of duty to himself was not strong enough to dally within those walls and under the shadow of that bankruptcy; and presently the manager and the clerks would draw a long breath, and compose themselves for another day of procrastination. Raw Haste, on the authority of my Lord Tennyson, is half-sister to Delay; but the Business

Habits are certainly her uncles. Meanwhile, the leather merchant would lead his living investment back to John Street like a puppy dog; and, having there immured him in the hall, would depart for the day on the quest of seal rings, the only passion of his life. Joseph had more than the vanity of man, he had that of lecturers. He owned he was in fault, although more sinned against (by the capable Scot) than sinning; but had he steeped his hands in gore, he would still not deserve to be thus dragged at the chariot-wheels of a young man, to sit a captive in the halls of his own leather business, to be entertained with mortifying comments on his whole career—to have his costume examined, his collar pulled up, the presence of his mittens verified, and to be taken out and brought home in custody, like an infant with a nurse. At the thought of it his soul would swell with venom, and he would make haste to hang up his hat and coat and the detested mittens, and slink upstairs to Julia and his notebooks. The drawing-room at least was sacred from Morris; it belonged to the old man and the young girl; it was there that she made her dresses; it was there that he inked his spectacles over the registration of disconnected facts and the calculation of insignificant statistics.

Here he would sometimes lament his connection with the tontine. "If it were not for that," he cried one afternoon, "he would not care to keep me. I might be a free man, Julia. And I could so easily support myself by giving lectures."

"To be sure you could," said she; "and I think it one of the meanest things he ever did to deprive you of that amusement. There were those nice people at the Isle of Cats (wasn't it?) who wrote and asked you so very kindly to give them an address. I did think he might have let you go to the Isle of Cats."

"He is a man of no intelligence," cried Joseph. "He lives here literally surrounded by the absorbing spectacle of life, and for all the good it does him, he might just as well be in his coffin. Think of his opportunities! The heart of any other young man would burn within him at the chance. The amount of information that I have it in my power to convey, if he would only listen, is a thing that beggars language, Julia."

"Whatever you do, my dear, you mustn't excite yourself," said Julia; "for you know, if you look at all ill, the doctor will be sent for."

"That is very true," returned the old man humbly, "I will compose myself with a little study." He thumbed his gallery of notebooks. "I wonder," he said, "I wonder (since I see your hands are occupied) whether it might not interest you—"

"Why, of course it would," cried Julia. "Read me one of your nice stories, there's a dear."

He had the volume down and his spectacles upon his nose instanter, as though to forestall some possible retraction. "What I propose to read to you," said he, skimming through the pages, "is the notes of a highly important conversation with a Dutch courier of the name of David Abbas, which is the Latin for Abbot. Its results are well worth the money it cost me, for, as Abbas at first appeared somewhat impatient, I was induced to (what is, I believe, singularly called) stand him drink. It runs only to about five-and-twenty pages. Yes, here it is." He cleared his throat, and began to read.

Mr Finsbury (according to his own report) contributed about four hundred and ninety-nine five-hundredths of the interview, and elicited from Abbas literally nothing. It was dull for Julia, who did not require to listen; for the Dutch courier, who had to answer, it must have been a perfect nightmare. It would seem as if he had consoled himself by frequent appliances to the bottle; it would even seem that (toward the end) he had ceased to depend on Joseph's frugal generosity and called for the flagon on his own account. The effect, at least, of some mellowing influence was visible in the record: Abbas became suddenly a willing witness; he began to volunteer disclosures; and Julia had just looked up from her seam with something like a smile, when Morris burst into the house, eagerly calling for his uncle, and the next instant plunged into the room, waving in the air the evening paper.

It was indeed with great news that he came charged. The demise was announced of Lieutenant-General Sir Glasgow Biggar, KCSI, KCMG, etc., and the prize of the tontine now lay between the Finsbury brothers. Here was Morris's opportunity at last. The brothers had never, it is true, been cordial. When word came that Joseph was in Asia Minor, Masterman had expressed himself with irritation. "I call it simply indecent," he had said. "Mark my words—we shall hear of him next at the North Pole." And these bitter expressions had been reported to the traveller on his return. What was worse, Masterman had refused to attend the lecture on "Education: Its Aims, Objects, Purposes, and Desirability", although invited to the platform. Since then the brothers had not met. On the other hand, they never had openly quarrelled; Joseph (by Morris's orders) was prepared to waive the advantage of his juniority; Masterman had enjoyed all through life the reputation of a man neither greedy nor unfair. Here, then, were all the elements of compromise assembled; and Morris, suddenly beholding his seven thousand eight hundred pounds restored to him, and himself dismissed from the vicissitudes of the leather trade, hastened the next morning to the office of his cousin Michael.

Michael was something of a public character. Launched upon the law at a very early age, and quite without protectors, he had become a trafficker in shady affairs. He was known to be the man for a lost cause; it was known he could extract testimony from a stone, and interest from a gold-mine; and his office was besieged in consequence by all that numerous class of persons who have still some reputation to lose, and find themselves upon the point of losing it; by those who have made undesirable acquaintances, who have mislaid a compromising correspondence, or who are blackmailed by their own butlers. In private life Michael was a man of pleasure; but it was thought his dire experience at the office had gone far to sober him, and it was known that (in the matter of investments) he preferred the solid to the brilliant. What was yet more to the purpose, he had been all his life a consistent scoffer at the Finsbury tontine.

It was therefore with little fear for the result that Morris presented himself before his cousin, and proceeded feverishly to set forth his scheme. For near upon a quarter of an hour the lawyer suffered him to dwell upon its manifest advantages uninterrupted. Then Michael rose from his seat, and, ringing for his clerk, uttered a single clause: "It won't do, Morris."

It was in vain that the leather merchant pleaded and reasoned, and returned day after day to plead and reason. It was in vain that he offered a bonus of one thousand, of two thousand, of three thousand pounds; in vain that he offered, in Joseph's name, to be content with only one-third of the pool. Still there came the same answer: "It won't do."

"I can't see the bottom of this," he said at last. "You answer none of my arguments; you haven't a word to say. For my part, I believe it's malice."

The lawyer smiled at him benignly. "You may believe one thing," said he. "Whatever else I do, I am not going to gratify any of your curiosity. You see I am a trifle more communicative today, because this is our last interview upon the subject."

"Our last interview!" cried Morris.

"The stirrup-cup, dear boy," returned Michael.

"I can't have my business hours encroached upon. And, by the by, have you no business of your own? Are there no convulsions in the leather trade?"

"I believe it to be malice," repeated Morris doggedly. "You always hated and despised me from a boy."

"No, no—not hated," returned Michael soothingly. "I rather like you than otherwise; there's such a permanent surprise about you, you look so dark and attractive from a distance. Do you know that to the naked eye you look romantic?—like what they call a man with a history? And indeed, from all that I can hear, the history of the leather trade is full of incident."

"Yes," said Morris, disregarding these remarks, "it's no use coming here. I shall see your father."

"O no, you won't," said Michael. "Nobody shall see my father."

"I should like to know why," cried his cousin.

"I never make any secret of that," replied the lawyer. "He is too ill."

"If he is as ill as you say," cried the other, "the more reason for accepting my proposal. I will see him."

"Will you?" said Michael, and he rose and rang for his clerk.

It was now time, according to Sir Faraday Bond, the medical baronet whose name is so familiar at the foot of bulletins, that Joseph (the poor Golden Goose) should be removed into the purer air of Bournemouth; and for that uncharted wilderness of villas the family now shook off the dust of Bloomsbury; Julia delighted, because at Bournemouth she sometimes made acquaintances; John in despair, for he was a man of city tastes; Joseph indifferent where he was, so long as there was pen and ink and daily papers, and he could avoid martyrdom at the office; Morris himself, perhaps, not displeased to pretermit these visits to the city, and have a quiet time for thought. He was prepared for any sacrifice; all he desired was to get his money again and clear his feet of leather; and it would be strange, since he was so modest in his desires, and the pool amounted to upward of a hundred and sixteen thousand pounds—it would be strange indeed if he could find no way of influencing Michael. "If I could only guess his reason," he repeated to himself; and by day, as he walked in Branksome Woods, and by night, as he turned upon his bed, and at meal-times, when he forgot to eat, and in the Bathing Machine, when he forgot to dress himself, that problem was constantly before him: Why had Michael refused?

At last, one night, he burst into his brother's room and woke him.

"What's all this?" asked John.

"Julia leaves this place tomorrow," replied Morris. "She must go up to town and get the house ready, and find servants. We shall all follow in three days."

"Oh, brayvo!" cried John. "But why?"

"I've found it out, John," returned his brother gently.

"It? What?" enquired John.

"Why Michael won't compromise," said Morris. "It's because he can't. It's because Masterman's dead, and he's keeping it dark."

"Golly!" cried the impressionable John. "But what's the use? Why does he do it, anyway?"

"To defraud us of the tontine," said his brother.

"He couldn't; you have to have a doctor's certificate," objected John.

"Did you never hear of venal doctors?" enquired Morris. "They're as common as blackberries: you can pick 'em up for three-pound-ten a head."

"I wouldn't do it under fifty if I were a sawbones," ejaculated John.

"And then Michael," continued Morris, "is in the very thick of it. All his clients have come to grief; his whole business is rotten eggs. If any man could arrange it, he could; and depend upon it, he has his plan all straight; and depend upon it, it's a good one, for he's clever, and be damned to him! But I'm clever too; and I'm desperate. I lost seven thousand eight hundred pounds when I was an orphan at school."

"O, don't be tedious," interrupted John. "You've lost far more already trying to get it back."

Chapter 2 In Which Morris Takes Action

Some days later, accordingly, the three males of this depressing family might have been observed (by a reader of G. P. R. James) taking their departure from the East Station of Bournemouth. The weather was raw and changeable, and Joseph was arrayed in consequence according to the principles of Sir Faraday Bond, a man no less strict (as is well known) on costume than on diet. There are few polite invalids who have not lived, or tried to live, by that punctilious physician's orders. "Avoid tea, madam," the reader has doubtless heard him say, "avoid tea, fried liver, antimonial wine, and bakers' bread. Retire nightly at 10:45; and clothe yourself (if you please) throughout in hygienic flannel. Externally, the fur of the marten is indicated. Do not forget to procure a pair of health boots at Messrs Dail and Crumbie's." And he has probably called you back, even after you have paid your fee, to add with stentorian emphasis: "I had forgotten one caution: avoid kippered sturgeon as you would the very devil." The unfortunate Joseph was cut to the pattern of Sir Faraday in every button; he was shod with the health boot; his suit was of genuine ventilating cloth; his shirt of hygienic flannel, a somewhat dingy fabric; and he was draped to the knees in the inevitable greatcoat of marten's fur. The very railway porters at Bournemouth (which was a favourite station of the doctor's) marked the old gentleman for a creature of Sir Faraday. There was but one evidence of personal taste, a vizarded forage cap; from this form of headpiece, since he had fled from a dying jackal on the plains of Ephesus, and weathered a bora in the Adriatic, nothing could divorce our traveller.

The three Finsburys mounted into their compartment, and fell immediately to quarrelling, a step unseemly in itself and (in this case) highly unfortunate for Morris. Had he lingered a moment longer by the window, this tale need never have been written. For he might then have observed (as the porters did not fail to do) the arrival of a second passenger in the uniform of Sir Faraday Bond. But he had other matters on hand, which he judged (God knows how erroneously) to be more important.

"I never heard of such a thing," he cried, resuming a discussion which had scarcely ceased all morning. "The bill is not yours; it is mine."

"It is payable to me," returned the old gentleman, with an air of bitter obstinacy. "I will do what I please with my own property."

The bill was one for eight hundred pounds, which had been given him at breakfast to endorse, and which he had simply pocketed.

"Hear him, Johnny!" cried Morris. "His property! the very clothes upon his back belong to me."

"Let him alone," said John. "I am sick of both of you."

"That is no way to speak of your uncle, sir," cried Joseph. "I will not endure this disrespect. You are a pair of exceedingly forward, impudent, and ignorant young men, and I have quite made up my mind to put an end to the whole business."

"O skittles!" said the graceful John.

But Morris was not so easy in his mind. This unusual act of insubordination had already troubled him; and these mutinous words now sounded ominously in his ears. He looked at the old gentleman uneasily. Upon one occasion, many years before, when Joseph was delivering a lecture, the audience had revolted in a body; finding their entertainer somewhat dry, they had taken the question of amusement into their own hands; and the lecturer (along with the board schoolmaster, the Baptist clergyman, and a working-man's candidate, who made up his bodyguard) was ultimately driven from the scene. Morris had not been present on that fatal day; if he had, he would have recognized a certain fighting glitter in his uncle's eye, and a certain chewing movement of his lips, as old acquaintances. But even to the inexpert these symptoms breathed of something dangerous.

"Well, well," said Morris. "I have no wish to bother you further till we get to London."

Joseph did not so much as look at him in answer; with tremulous hands he produced a copy of the *British Mechanic*, and ostentatiously buried himself in its perusal.

"I wonder what can make him so cantankerous?" reflected the nephew. "I don't like the look of it at all." And he dubiously scratched his nose.

The train travelled forth into the world, bearing along with it the customary freight of obliterated voyagers, and along with these old Joseph, affecting immersion in his paper, and John slumbering over the columns of the Pink Un, and Morris revolving in his mind a dozen grudges, and suspicions, and alarms. It passed Christchurch by the sea, Herne with its pinewoods, Ringwood on its mazy river. A little behind time, but not much for the South-Western, it drew up at the platform of a station, in the midst of the New Forest, the real name of which (in case the railway company "might have the law of me") I shall veil under the alias of Browndean.

Many passengers put their heads to the window, and among the rest an old gentleman on whom I willingly dwell, for I am nearly done with him now, and (in the whole course of the present narrative) I am not in the least likely to meet another character so decent. His name is immaterial, not so his habits. He had passed his life wandering in a tweed suit on the continent of Europe; and years of Galignani's Messenger having at length undermined his eyesight, he suddenly remembered the rivers of Assyria and came to London to consult an oculist. From the oculist to the dentist, and from both to the physician, the step appears inevitable; presently he was in the hands of Sir Faraday, robed in ventilating cloth and sent to Bournemouth; and to that domineering baronet (who was his only friend upon his native soil) he was now returning to report. The case of these tweed-suited wanderers is unique. We have all seen them entering the table d'hote (at Spezzia, or Gräz, or Venice) with a genteel melancholy and a faint appearance of having been to India and not succeeded. In the offices of many hundred hotels they are known by name; and yet, if the whole of this wandering cohort were to disappear tomorrow, their absence would be wholly unremarked. How much more, if only one—say this one in the ventilating cloth—should vanish! He had paid his bills at Bournemouth; his worldly effects were all in the van in two portmanteaux, and these after the proper interval would be sold as unclaimed baggage to a Jew; Sir Faraday's butler would be a half-crown poorer at the year's end, and the hotelkeepers of Europe about the same date would be mourning a small but quite observable decline in profits. And that would be literally all. Perhaps the old gentleman thought something of the sort, for he looked melancholy enough as he pulled his bare, grey head back into the carriage, and the train smoked under the bridge, and forth, with ever quickening speed, across the mingled heaths and woods of the New Forest.

Not many hundred yards beyond Browndean, however, a sudden jarring of brakes set everybody's teeth on edge, and there was a brutal stoppage. Morris Finsbury was aware of a confused uproar of voices, and sprang to the window. Women were screaming, men were tumbling from the windows on the track, the guard was crying to them to stay where they were; at the same time the train began to gather way and move very slowly backward toward Browndean; and the next moment—all these various sounds were blotted out in the apocalyptic whistle and the thundering onslaught of the down express.

The actual collision Morris did not hear. Perhaps he fainted. He had a wild dream of having seen the carriage double up and fall to pieces like a pantomime trick; and sure enough, when he came to himself, he was lying on the bare earth and under the open sky. His head ached savagely; he carried his hand to his brow, and was not surprised to see it red with blood. The air was filled with an intolerable, throbbing roar, which he expected to find die away with the return of consciousness; and instead of that it seemed but to swell the louder and to pierce the more cruelly through his ears. It was a raging, bellowing thunder, like a boiler-riveting factory.

And now curiosity began to stir, and he sat up and looked about him. The track at this point ran in a sharp curve about a wooded hillock; all of the near side was heaped with the wreckage of the Bournemouth train; that of the express was mostly hidden by the trees; and just at the turn, under clouds of vomiting steam and piled about with cairns of living coal, lay what remained of the two engines, one upon the other. On the heathy margin of the line were many people running to and fro, and crying aloud as they ran, and many others lying motionless like sleeping tramps.

Morris suddenly drew an inference. "There has been an accident," thought he, and was elated at his perspicacity. Almost at the same time his eye lighted on John, who lay close by as white as paper. "Poor old John! Poor old cove!" he thought, the schoolboy expression popping forth from some forgotten treasury, and he took his brother's hand in his with childish tenderness. It was perhaps the touch that recalled him; at least John opened his eyes, sat suddenly up, and after several ineffectual movements of his lips, "What's the row?" said he, in a phantom voice.

The din of that devil's smithy still thundered in their ears. "Let us get away from that," Morris cried, and pointed to the vomit of steam that still spouted from the broken engines. And the pair helped each other up, and stood and quaked and wavered and stared about them at the scene of death.

Just then they were approached by a party of men who had already organized themselves for the purposes of rescue.

"Are you hurt?" cried one of these, a young fellow with the sweat streaming down his pallid face, and who, by the way he was treated, was evidently the doctor.

Morris shook his head, and the young man, nodding

grimly, handed him a bottle of some spirit.

"Take a drink of that," he said; "your friend looks as if he needed it badly. We want every man we can get," he added; "there's terrible work before us, and nobody should shirk. If you can do no more, you can carry a stretcher."

The doctor was hardly gone before Morris, under the spur of the dram, awoke to the full possession of his wits.

"My God!" he cried. "Uncle Joseph!"

"Yes," said John, "where can he be? He can't be far off. I hope the old party isn't damaged."

"Come and help me to look," said Morris, with a snap of savage determination strangely foreign to his ordinary bearing; and then, for one moment, he broke forth. "If he's dead!" he cried, and shook his fist at heaven.

To and fro the brothers hurried, staring in the faces of the wounded, or turning the dead upon their backs. They must have thus examined forty people, and still there was no word of Uncle Joseph. But now the course of their search brought them near the centre of the collision, where the boilers were still blowing off steam with a deafening clamour. It was a part of the field not yet gleaned by the rescuing party. The ground, especially on the margin of the wood, was full of inequalities—here a pit, there a hillock surmounted with a bush of furze. It was a place where many bodies might lie concealed, and they beat it like pointers after game. Suddenly Morris, who was leading, paused and reached forth his index with a tragic gesture.

John followed the direction of his brother's hand.

In the bottom of a sandy hole lay something that had once been human. The face had suffered severely, and it was unrecognizable; but that was not required. The snowy hair, the coat of marten, the ventilating cloth, the hygienic flannel—everything down to the health boots from Messrs Dail and Crumbie's, identified the body as that of Uncle Joseph. Only the forage cap must have been lost in the convulsion, for the dead man was bareheaded.

"The poor old beggar!" said John, with a touch of natural feeling; "I would give ten pounds if we hadn't chivvied him in the train!"

But there was no sentiment in the face of Morris as he gazed upon the dead. Gnawing his nails, with introverted eyes, his brow marked with the stamp of tragic indignation and tragic intellectual effort, he stood there silent. Here was a last injustice; he had been robbed while he was an orphan at school, he had been lashed to a decadent leather business, he had been saddled with Miss Hazeltine, his cousin had been defrauding him of the tontine, and he had borne all this, we might almost say, with dignity, and now they had gone and killed his uncle!

"Here!" he said suddenly, "take his heels, we must get him into the woods. I'm not going to have anybody find this."

"O, fudge!" said John, "where's the use?"

"Do what I tell you," spirted Morris, as he took the corpse by the shoulders. "Am I to carry him myself?"

They were close upon the borders of the wood; in ten or twelve paces they were under cover; and a little further back, in a sandy clearing of the trees, they laid their burthen down, and stood and looked at it with loathing.

"What do you mean to do?" whispered John.

"Bury him, to be sure," responded Morris, and he opened his pocket-knife and began feverishly to dig.

"You'll never make a hand of it with that," objected the other.

"If you won't help me, you cowardly shirk," screamed Morris, "you can go to the devil!"

"It's the childishest folly," said John; "but no man shall call me a coward," and he began to help his brother grudgingly.

The soil was sandy and light, but matted with the roots of the surrounding firs. Gorse tore their hands; and as they baled the sand from the grave, it was often discoloured with their blood. An hour passed of unremitting energy upon the part of Morris, of lukewarm help on that of John; and still the trench was barely nine inches in depth. Into this the body was rudely flung; sand was piled upon it, and then more sand must be dug, and gorse had to be cut to pile on that; and still from one end of the sordid mound a pair of feet projected and caught the light upon their patent-leather toes. But by this time the nerves of both were shaken; even Morris had enough of his grisly task; and they skulked off like animals into the thickest of the neighbouring covert.

"It's the best that we can do," said Morris, sitting down.

"And now," said John, "perhaps you'll have the politeness to tell me what it's all about."

"Upon my word," cried Morris, "if you do not understand for yourself, I almost despair of telling you."

"O, of course it's some rot about the tontine," returned the other. "But it's the merest nonsense. We've lost it, and there's an end."

"I tell you," said Morris, "Uncle Masterman is dead. I know it, there's a voice that tells me so."

"Well, and so is Uncle Joseph," said John.

"He's not dead, unless I choose," returned Morris.

"And come to that," cried John, "if you're right, and Uncle Masterman's been dead ever so long, all we have to do is to tell the truth and expose Michael."

"You seem to think Michael is a fool," sneered Morris. "Can't you understand he's been preparing this fraud for years? He has the whole thing ready: the nurse, the doctor, the undertaker, all bought, the certificate all ready but the date! Let him get wind of this business, and you mark my words, Uncle Masterman will die in two days and be buried in a week. But see here, Johnny; what Michael can do, I can do. If he plays a game of bluff, so can I. If his father is to live forever, by God, so shall my uncle!"

"It's illegal, ain't it?" said John.

"A man must have SOME moral courage," replied Morris

with dignity.

"And then suppose you're wrong? Suppose Uncle Masterman's alive and kicking?"

"Well, even then," responded the plotter, "we are no worse off than we were before; in fact, we're better. Uncle Masterman must die some day; as long as Uncle Joseph was alive, he might have died any day; but we're out of all that trouble now: there's no sort of limit to the game that I propose—it can be kept up till Kingdom Come."

"If I could only see how you meant to set about it," sighed John. "But you know, Morris, you always were such a bungler."

"I'd like to know what I ever bungled," cried Morris; "I have the best collection of signet rings in London."

"Well, you know, there's the leather business," suggested the other. "That's considered rather a hash."

It was a mark of singular self-control in Morris that he suffered this to pass unchallenged, and even unresented.

"About the business in hand," said he, "once we can get him up to Bloomsbury, there's no sort of trouble. We bury him in the cellar, which seems made for it; and then all I have to do is to start out and find a venal doctor."

"Why can't we leave him where he is?" asked John.

"Because we know nothing about the country," retorted Morris. "This wood may be a regular lovers' walk. Turn your mind to the real difficulty. How are we to get him up to Bloomsbury?"

Various schemes were mooted and rejected. The railway station at Browndean was, of course, out of the question, for it would now be a centre of curiosity and gossip, and (of all things) they would be least able to dispatch a dead body without remark. John feebly proposed getting an ale-cask and sending it as beer, but the objections to this course were so overwhelming that Morris scorned to answer. The purchase of a packing-case seemed equally hopeless, for why should two gentlemen without baggage of any kind require a packing-case? They would be more likely to require clean linen.

"We are working on wrong lines," cried Morris at last. "The thing must be gone about more carefully. Suppose now," he added excitedly, speaking by fits and starts, as if he were thinking aloud, "suppose we rent a cottage by the month. A householder can buy a packing-case without remark. Then suppose we clear the people out today, get the packing-case tonight, and tomorrow I hire a carriage or a cart that we could drive ourselves—and take the box, or whatever we get, to Ringwood or Lyndhurst or somewhere; we could label it 'specimens,' don't you see? Johnny, I believe I've hit the nail at last."

"Well, it sounds more feasible," admitted John.

"Of course we must take assumed names," continued Morris. "It would never do to keep our own. What do you say to 'Masterman' itself? It sounds quiet and dignified."

"I will NOT take the name of Masterman," returned his

brother; "you may, if you like. I shall call myself Vance—the Great Vance; positively the last six nights. There's some go in a name like that."

"Vance?" cried Morris. "Do you think we are playing a pantomime for our amusement? There was never anybody named Vance who wasn't a music-hall singer."

"That's the beauty of it," returned John; "it gives you some standing at once. You may call yourself Fortescue till all's blue, and nobody cares; but to be Vance gives a man a natural nobility."

"But there's lots of other theatrical names," cried Morris. "Leybourne, Irving, Brough, Toole—"

"Devil a one will I take!" returned his brother. "I am going to have my little lark out of this as well as you."

"Very well," said Morris, who perceived that John was determined to carry his point, "I shall be Robert Vance."

"And I shall be George Vance," cried John, "the only original George Vance! Rally round the only original!"

Repairing as well as they were able the disorder of their clothes, the Finsbury brothers returned to Browndean by a circuitous route in quest of luncheon and a suitable cottage. It is not always easy to drop at a moment's notice on a furnished residence in a retired locality; but fortune presently introduced our adventurers to a deaf carpenter, a man rich in cottages of the required description, and unaffectedly eager to supply their wants. The second place they visited, standing, as it did, about a mile and a half from any neighbours, caused them to exchange a glance of hope. On a nearer view, the place was not without depressing features. It stood in a marshy-looking hollow of a heath; tall trees obscured its windows; the thatch visibly rotted on the rafters; and the walls were stained with splashes of unwholesome green. The rooms were small, the ceilings low, the furniture merely nominal; a strange chill and a haunting smell of damp pervaded the kitchen; and the bedroom boasted only of one bed.

Morris, with a view to cheapening the place, remarked on this defect.

"Well," returned the man; "if you can't sleep two abed, you'd better take a villa residence."

"And then," pursued Morris, "there's no water. How do you get your water?"

"We fill THAT from the spring," replied the carpenter, pointing to a big barrel that stood beside the door. "The spring ain't so VERY far off, after all, and it's easy brought in buckets. There's a bucket there."

Morris nudged his brother as they examined the water-butt. It was new, and very solidly constructed for its office. If anything had been wanting to decide them, this eminently practical barrel would have turned the scale. A bargain was promptly struck, the month's rent was paid upon the nail, and about an hour later the Finsbury brothers might have been observed returning to the blighted cottage, having along with them the key, which was the symbol of their tenancy, a spirit-lamp, with which they fondly told themselves they would be able to cook, a pork pie of suitable dimensions, and a quart of the worst whisky in Hampshire. Nor was this all they had effected; already (under the plea that they were landscape-painters) they had hired for dawn on the morrow a light but solid two-wheeled cart; so that when they entered in their new character, they were able to tell themselves that the back of the business was already broken.

John proceeded to get tea; while Morris, foraging about the house, was presently delighted by discovering the lid of the water-butt upon the kitchen shelf. Here, then, was the packing-case complete; in the absence of straw, the blankets (which he himself, at least, had not the smallest intention of using for their present purpose) would exactly take the place of packing; and Morris, as the difficulties began to vanish from his path, rose almost to the brink of exultation. There was, however, one difficulty not yet faced, one upon which his whole scheme depended. Would John consent to remain alone in the cottage? He had not yet dared to put the question.

It was with high good-humour that the pair sat down to the deal table, and proceeded to fall-to on the pork pie. Morris retailed the discovery of the lid, and the Great Vance was pleased to applaud by beating on the table with his fork in true music-hall style.

"That's the dodge," he cried. "I always said a water-butt

was what you wanted for this business."

"Of course," said Morris, thinking this a favourable opportunity to prepare his brother, "of course you must stay on in this place till I give the word; I'll give out that uncle is resting in the New Forest. It would not do for both of us to appear in London; we could never conceal the absence of the old man."

John's jaw dropped.

"O, come!" he cried. "You can stay in this hole yourself. I won't."

The colour came into Morris's cheeks. He saw that he must win his brother at any cost.

"You must please remember, Johnny," he said, "the amount of the tontine. If I succeed, we shall have each fifty thousand to place to our bank account; ay, and nearer sixty."

"But if you fail," returned John, "what then? What'll be the colour of our bank account in that case?"

"I will pay all expenses," said Morris, with an inward struggle; "you shall lose nothing."

"Well," said John, with a laugh, "if the ex-s are yours, and half-profits mine, I don't mind remaining here for a couple of days."

"A couple of days!" cried Morris, who was beginning to get angry and controlled himself with difficulty; "why, you would do more to win five pounds on a horse-race!"

"Perhaps I would," returned the Great Vance; "it's the artistic temperament."

"This is monstrous!" burst out Morris. "I take all risks; I pay all expenses; I divide profits; and you won't take the slightest pains to help me. It's not decent; it's not honest; it's not even kind."

"But suppose," objected John, who was considerably impressed by his brother's vehemence, "suppose that Uncle Masterman is alive after all, and lives ten years longer; must I rot here all that time?"

"Of course not," responded Morris, in a more conciliatory tone; "I only ask a month at the outside; and if Uncle Masterman is not dead by that time you can go abroad."

"Go abroad?" repeated John eagerly. "Why shouldn't I go at once? Tell 'em that Joseph and I are seeing life in Paris."

"Nonsense," said Morris.

"Well, but look here," said John; "it's this house, it's such a pigsty, it's so dreary and damp. You said yourself that it was damp."

"Only to the carpenter," Morris distinguished, "and that was to reduce the rent. But really, you know, now we're in it, I've seen worse."

"And what am I to do?" complained the victim. "How can I entertain a friend?"

"My dear Johnny, if you don't think the tontine worth a little trouble, say so, and I'll give the business up."

"You're dead certain of the figures, I suppose?" asked John. "Well"—with a deep sigh—"send me the Pink Un and all the comic papers regularly. I'll face the music."

As afternoon drew on, the cottage breathed more thrillingly of its native marsh; a creeping chill inhabited its chambers; the fire smoked, and a shower of rain, coming up from the channel on a slant of wind, tingled on the window-panes. At intervals, when the gloom deepened toward despair, Morris would produce the whisky-bottle, and at first John welcomed the diversion—not for long. It has been said this spirit was the worst in Hampshire; only those acquainted with the county can appreciate the force of that superlative; and at length even the Great Vance (who was no connoisseur) waved the decoction from his lips. The approach of dusk, feebly combated with a single tallow candle, added a touch of tragedy; and John suddenly stopped whistling through his fingers—an art to the practice of which he had been reduced—and bitterly lamented his concessions.

"I can't stay here a month," he cried. "No one could. The thing's nonsense, Morris. The parties that lived in the Bastille would rise against a place like this."

With an admirable affectation of indifference, Morris proposed a game of pitch-and-toss. To what will not the diplomatist condescend! It was John's favourite game; indeed his only game—he had found all the rest too intellectual—and he played it with equal skill and good fortune. To Morris himself, on the other hand, the whole business was detestable; he was a bad pitcher, he had no luck in tossing, and he was one who suffered torments when he lost. But John was in a dangerous humour, and his brother was prepared for any sacrifice.

By seven o'clock, Morris, with incredible agony, had lost a couple of half-crowns. Even with the tontine before his eyes, this was as much as he could bear; and, remarking that he would take his revenge some other time, he proposed a bit of supper and a grog.

Before they had made an end of this refreshment it was time to be at work. A bucket of water for present necessities was withdrawn from the water-butt, which was then emptied and rolled before the kitchen fire to dry; and the two brothers set forth on their adventure under a starless heaven.

Chapter 3   The Lecturer at Large

Whether mankind is really partial to happiness is an open question. Not a month passes by but some cherished son runs off into the merchant service, or some valued husband decamps to Texas with a lady help; clergymen have fled from their parishioners; and even judges have been known to retire. To an open mind, it will appear (upon the whole) less strange that Joseph Finsbury should have been led to entertain ideas of escape. His lot (I think we may say) was not a happy one. My friend, Mr Morris, with whom I travel up twice or thrice a week from Snaresbrook Park, is certainly a gentleman whom I esteem; but he was scarce a model nephew. As for John, he is of course an excellent fellow; but if he was the only link that bound one to a home, I think the most of us would vote for foreign travel. In the case of Joseph, John (if he were a link at all) was not the only one; endearing bonds had long enchained the old gentleman to Bloomsbury; and by these expressions I do not in the least refer to Julia Hazeltine (of whom, however, he was fond enough), but to that collection of manuscript notebooks in which his life lay buried. That he should ever have made up his mind to separate himself from these collections, and go forth upon the world with no other resources than his memory supplied, is a circumstance highly pathetic in itself, and but little creditable to the wisdom of his nephews.

The design, or at least the temptation, was already some months old; and when a bill for eight hundred pounds, payable to himself, was suddenly placed in Joseph's hand, it brought matters to an issue. He retained that bill, which, to one of his frugality, meant wealth; and he promised himself to disappear among the crowds at Waterloo, or (if that should prove impossible) to slink out of the house in the course of the evening and melt like a dream into the millions of London. By a peculiar interposition of Providence and railway mismanagement he had not so long to wait.

He was one of the first to come to himself and scramble to his feet after the Browndean catastrophe, and he had no sooner remarked his prostrate nephews than he understood his opportunity and fled. A man of upwards of seventy, who has just met with a railway accident, and who is cumbered besides with the full uniform of Sir Faraday Bond, is not very likely to flee far, but the wood was close at hand and offered the fugitive at least a temporary covert. Hither, then, the old gentleman skipped with extraordinary expedition, and, being somewhat winded and a good deal shaken, here he lay down in a convenient grove and was presently overwhelmed by slumber. The way of fate is often highly entertaining to the looker-on, and it is certainly a pleasant circumstance, that while Morris and John were delving in the sand to conceal the body of a total stranger, their uncle lay in dreamless sleep a few hundred yards deeper in the wood.

He was awakened by the jolly note of a bugle from the neighbouring high road, where a char-a-banc was bowling by with some belated tourists. The sound cheered his old heart, it directed his steps into the bargain, and soon he was on the highway, looking east and west from under his vizor, and doubtfully revolving what he ought to do. A deliberate sound of wheels arose in the distance, and then a cart was seen approaching, well filled with parcels, driven by a good-natured looking man on a double bench, and displaying on a board the legend, "I Chandler, carrier". In the infamously prosaic mind of Mr Finsbury, certain streaks of poetry survived and were still efficient; they had carried him to Asia Minor as a giddy youth of forty, and now, in the first hours of his recovered freedom, they suggested to him the idea of continuing his flight in Mr Chandler's cart. It would be cheap; properly broached, it might even cost nothing, and, after years of mittens and hygienic flannel, his heart leaped out to meet the notion of exposure.

Mr Chandler was perhaps a little puzzled to find so old a gentleman, so strangely clothed, and begging for a lift on so retired a roadside. But he was a good-natured man, glad to do a service, and so he took the stranger up; and he had his own idea of civility, and so he asked no questions. Silence, in fact, was quite good enough for Mr Chandler; but the cart had scarcely begun to move forward ere he found himself involved in a one-sided conversation.

"I can see," began Mr Finsbury, "by the mixture of parcels and boxes that are contained in your cart, each marked with its individual label, and by the good Flemish mare you drive, that you occupy the post of carrier in that great English system of transport which, with all its defects, is the pride of our country."

"Yes, sir," returned Mr Chandler vaguely, for he hardly knew what to reply; "them parcels posts has done us carriers a world of harm."

"I am not a prejudiced man," continued Joseph Finsbury. "As a young man I travelled much. Nothing was too small or too obscure for me to acquire. At sea I studied seamanship, learned the complicated knots employed by mariners, and acquired the technical terms. At Naples, I would learn the art of making macaroni; at Nice, the principles of making candied fruit. I never went to the opera without first buying the book of the piece, and making myself acquainted with the principal airs by picking them out on the piano with one finger."

"You must have seen a deal, sir," remarked the carrier, touching up his horse; "I wish I could have had your advantages."

"Do you know how often the word whip occurs in the Old

Testament?" continued the old gentleman. "One hundred and (if I remember exactly) forty-seven times."

"Do it indeed, sir?" said Mr Chandler. "I never should have thought it."

"The Bible contains three million five hundred and one thousand two hundred and forty-nine letters. Of verses I believe there are upward of eighteen thousand. There have been many editions of the Bible; Wycliff was the first to introduce it into England about the year 1300. The 'Paragraph Bible,' as it is called, is a well-known edition, and is so called because it is divided into paragraphs. The 'Breeches Bible' is another well-known instance, and gets its name either because it was printed by one Breeches, or because the place of publication bore that name."

The carrier remarked drily that he thought that was only natural, and turned his attention to the more congenial task of passing a cart of hay; it was a matter of some difficulty, for the road was narrow, and there was a ditch on either hand.

"I perceive," began Mr Finsbury, when they had successfully passed the cart, "that you hold your reins with one hand; you should employ two."

"Well, I like that!" cried the carrier contemptuously. "Why?"

"You do not understand," continued Mr Finsbury. "What I tell you is a scientific fact, and reposes on the theory of the lever, a branch of mechanics. There are some very interesting little shilling books upon the field of study, which I should think a man in your station would take a pleasure to read. But I am afraid you have not cultivated the art of observation; at least we have now driven together for some time, and I cannot remember that you have contributed a single fact. This is a very false principle, my good man. For instance, I do not know if you observed that (as you passed the hay-cart man) you took your left?"

"Of course I did," cried the carrier, who was now getting belligerent; "he'd have the law on me if I hadn't."

"In France, now," resumed the old man, "and also, I believe, in the United States of America, you would have taken the right."

"I would not," cried Mr Chandler indignantly. "I would have taken the left."

"I observe again," continued Mr Finsbury, scorning to reply, "that you mend the dilapidated parts of your harness with string. I have always protested against this carelessness and slovenliness of the English poor. In an essay that I once read before an appreciative audience—"

"It ain't string," said the carrier sullenly, "it's pack-thread."

"I have always protested," resumed the old man, "that in their private and domestic life, as well as in their labouring career, the lower classes of this country are improvident, thriftless, and extravagant. A stitch in time—"

"Who the devil ARE the lower classes?" cried the carrier. "You are the lower classes yourself! If I thought you were a blooming aristocrat, I shouldn't have given you a lift."

The words were uttered with undisguised ill-feeling; it was plain the pair were not congenial, and further conversation, even to one of Mr Finsbury's pathetic loquacity, was out of the question. With an angry gesture, he pulled down the brim of the forage-cap over his eyes, and, producing a notebook and a blue pencil from one of his innermost pockets, soon became absorbed in calculations.

On his part the carrier fell to whistling with fresh zest; and if (now and again) he glanced at the companion of his drive, it was with mingled feelings of triumph and alarm—triumph because he had succeeded in arresting that prodigy of speech, and alarm lest (by any accident) it should begin again. Even the shower, which presently overtook and passed them, was endured by both in silence; and it was still in silence that they drove at length into Southampton.

Dusk had fallen; the shop windows glimmered forth into the streets of the old seaport; in private houses lights were kindled for the evening meal; and Mr Finsbury began to think complacently of his night's lodging. He put his papers by, cleared his throat, and looked doubtfully at Mr Chandler.

"Will you be civil enough," said he, "to recommend me to an inn?"

Mr Chandler pondered for a moment.

"Well," he said at last, "I wonder how about the 'Tregonwell Arms'."

"The 'Tregonwell Arms' will do very well," returned the old man, "if it's clean and cheap, and the people civil."

"I wasn't thinking so much of you," returned Mr Chandler thoughtfully. "I was thinking of my friend Watts as keeps the 'ouse; he's a friend of mine, you see, and he helped me through my trouble last year. And I was thinking, would it be fair-like on Watts to saddle him with an old party like you, who might be the death of him with general information. Would it be fair to the 'ouse?" enquired Mr Chandler, with an air of candid appeal.

"Mark me," cried the old gentleman with spirit. "It was kind in you to bring me here for nothing, but it gives you no right to address me in such terms. Here's a shilling for your trouble; and, if you do not choose to set me down at the 'Tregonwell Arms', I can find it for myself."

Chandler was surprised and a little startled; muttering something apologetic, he returned the shilling, drove in silence through several intricate lanes and small streets, drew up at length before the bright windows of an inn, and called loudly for Mr Watts.

"Is that you, Jem?" cried a hearty voice from the stableyard. "Come in and warm yourself."

"I only stopped here," Mr Chandler explained, "to let down an old gent that wants food and lodging. Mind, I warn you agin him; he's worse nor a temperance lecturer."

Mr Finsbury dismounted with difficulty, for he was cramped with his long drive, and the shaking he had received in the accident. The friendly Mr Watts, in spite of the carter's scarcely agreeable introduction, treated the old gentleman with the utmost courtesy, and led him into the back parlour, where there was a big fire burning in the grate. Presently a table was spread in the same room, and he was invited to seat himself before a stewed fowl—somewhat the worse for having seen service before—and a big pewter mug of ale from the tap.

He rose from supper a giant refreshed; and, changing his seat to one nearer the fire, began to examine the other guests with an eye to the delights of oratory. There were near a dozen present, all men, and (as Joseph exulted to perceive) all working men. Often already had he seen cause to bless that appetite for disconnected fact and rotatory argument which is so marked a character of the mechanic. But even an audience of working men has to be courted, and there was no man more deeply versed in the necessary arts than Joseph Finsbury. He placed his glasses on his nose, drew from his pocket a bundle of papers, and spread them before him on a table. He crumpled them, he smoothed them out; now he skimmed them over, apparently well pleased with their contents; now, with tapping pencil and contracted brows, he seemed maturely to consider some particular statement. A stealthy glance about the room assured him of the success of his manoeuvres; all eyes were turned on the performer, mouths were open, pipes hung suspended; the birds were charmed. At the same moment the entrance of Mr Watts afforded him an opportunity.

"I observe," said he, addressing the landlord, but taking at the same time the whole room into his confidence with an encouraging look, "I observe that some of these gentlemen are looking with curiosity in my direction; and certainly it is unusual to see anyone immersed in literary and scientific labours in the public apartment of an inn. I have here some calculations I made this morning upon the cost of living in this and other countries—a subject, I need scarcely say, highly interesting to the working classes. I have calculated a scale of living for incomes of eighty, one hundred and sixty, two hundred, and two hundred and forty pounds a year. I must confess that the income of eighty pounds has somewhat baffled me, and the others are not so exact as I could wish; for the price of washing varies largely in foreign countries, and the different cokes, coals and firewoods fluctuate surprisingly. I will read my researches, and I hope you won't scruple to point out to me any little errors that I may have committed either from oversight or ignorance. I will begin, gentlemen, with the income of eighty pounds a year."

Whereupon the old gentleman, with less compassion than he would have had for brute beasts, delivered himself of all his tedious calculations. As he occasionally gave nine versions of a single income, placing the imaginary person in London, Paris, Bagdad, Spitzbergen, Bassorah, Heligoland, the Scilly Islands, Brighton, Cincinnati, and Nijni-Novgorod, with an appropriate outfit for each locality, it is no wonder that his hearers look back on that evening as the most tiresome they ever spent.

Long before Mr Finsbury had reached Nijni-Novgorod with the income of one hundred and sixty pounds, the company had dwindled and faded away to a few old topers and the bored but affable Watts. There was a constant stream of customers from the outer world, but so soon as they were served they drank their liquor quickly and departed with the utmost celerity for the next public-house.

By the time the young man with two hundred a year was vegetating in the Scilly Islands, Mr Watts was left alone with the economist; and that imaginary person had scarce commenced life at Brighton before the last of his pursuers desisted from the chase.

Mr Finsbury slept soundly after the manifold fatigues of the day. He rose late, and, after a good breakfast, ordered the bill. Then it was that he made a discovery which has been made by many others, both before and since: that it is one thing to order your bill, and another to discharge it. The items were moderate and (what does not always follow) the total small; but, after the most sedulous review of all his pockets, one and nine-pence-halfpenny appeared to be the total of the old gentleman's available assets. He asked to see Mr Watts.

"Here is a bill on London for eight hundred pounds," said Mr Finsbury, as that worthy appeared. "I am afraid, unless you choose to discount it yourself, it may detain me a day or two till I can get it cashed."

Mr Watts looked at the bill, turned it over, and dogs-eared it with his fingers. "It will keep you a day or two?" he said, repeating the old man's words. "You have no other money with you?"

"Some trifling change," responded Joseph. "Nothing to speak of."

"Then you can send it me; I should be pleased to trust you."

"To tell the truth," answered the old gentleman, "I am more than half inclined to stay; I am in need of funds."

"If a loan of ten shillings would help you, it is at your service," responded Watts, with eagerness.

"No, I think I would rather stay," said the old man, "and get my bill discounted."

"You shall not stay in my house," cried Mr Watts. "This is the last time you shall have a bed at the 'Tregonwell Arms'."

"I insist upon remaining," replied Mr Finsbury, with spirit; "I remain by Act of Parliament; turn me out if you dare."

"Then pay your bill," said Mr Watts.

"Take that," cried the old man, tossing him the negotiable bill.

"It is not legal tender," replied Mr Watts. "You must leave my house at once."

"You cannot appreciate the contempt I feel for you, Mr Watts," said the old gentleman, resigning himself to circumstances. "But you shall feel it in one way: I refuse to pay my bill."

"I don't care for your bill," responded Mr Watts. "What I want is your absence."

"That you shall have!" said the old gentleman, and, taking up his forage cap as he spoke, he crammed it on his head. "Perhaps you are too insolent," he added, "to inform me of the time of the next London train?"

"It leaves in three-quarters of an hour," returned the innkeeper with alacrity. "You can easily catch it."

Joseph's position was one of considerable weakness. On the one hand, it would have been well to avoid the direct line of railway, since it was there he might expect his nephews to lie in wait for his recapture; on the other, it was highly desirable, it was even strictly needful, to get the bill discounted ere it should be stopped. To London, therefore, he decided to proceed on the first train; and there remained but one point to be considered, how to pay his fare.

Joseph's nails were never clean; he ate almost entirely with his knife. I doubt if you could say he had the manners of a gentleman; but he had better than that, a touch of genuine dignity. Was it from his stay in Asia Minor? Was it from a strain in the Finsbury blood sometimes alluded to by customers? At least, when he presented himself before the station-master, his salaam was truly Oriental, palm-trees appeared to crowd about the little office, and the simoom or the bulbul—but I leave this image to persons better acquainted with the East. His appearance, besides, was highly in his favour; the uniform of Sir Faraday, however inconvenient and conspicuous, was, at least, a costume in which no swindler could have hoped to prosper; and the exhibition of a valuable watch and a bill for eight hundred pounds completed what deportment had begun. A quarter of an hour later, when the train came up, Mr Finsbury was introduced to the guard and installed in a first-class compartment, the station-master smilingly assuming all responsibility.

As the old gentleman sat waiting the moment of departure, he was the witness of an incident strangely connected with the fortunes of his house. A packing-case of cyclopean bulk was borne along the platform by some dozen of tottering porters, and ultimately, to the delight of a considerable crowd, hoisted on board the van. It is often the cheering task of the historian to direct attention to the designs and (if it may be reverently said) the artifices of Providence. In the luggage van, as Joseph was borne out of the station of Southampton East upon his way to London, the egg of his romance lay (so to speak) unhatched. The huge packing-case was directed to lie at Waterloo till called for, and addressed to one "William Dent Pitman;" and the very next article, a goodly barrel jammed into the corner of the van, bore the superscription, "M. Finsbury, 16 John Street, Bloomsbury. Carriage paid."

In this juxtaposition, the train of powder was prepared; and there was now wanting only an idle hand to fire it off.

Chapter 4 The Magistrate in the Luggage Van

The city of Winchester is famed for a cathedral, a bishop—but he was unfortunately killed some years ago while riding—a public school, a considerable assortment of the military, and the deliberate passage of the trains of the London and South-Western line. These and many similar associations would have doubtless crowded on the mind of Joseph Finsbury; but his spirit had at that time flitted from the railway compartment to a heaven of populous lecture-halls and endless oratory. His body, in the meanwhile, lay doubled on the cushions, the forage-cap rakishly tilted back after the fashion of those that lie in wait for nursery-maids, the poor old face quiescent, one arm clutching to his heart Lloyd's Weekly Newspaper.

To him, thus unconscious, enter and exeunt again a pair of voyagers. These two had saved the train and no more. A tandem urged to its last speed, an act of something closely bordering on brigandage at the ticket office, and a spasm of running, had brought them on the platform just as the engine uttered its departing snort. There was but one carriage easily within their reach; and they had sprung into it, and the leader and elder already had his feet upon the floor, when he observed Mr Finsbury.

"Good God!" he cried. "Uncle Joseph! This'll never do."

And he backed out, almost upsetting his companion, and once more closed the door upon the sleeping patriarch.

The next moment the pair had jumped into the baggage van.

"What's the row about your Uncle Joseph?" enquired the younger traveller, mopping his brow. "Does he object to smoking?"

"I don't know that there's anything the row with him," returned the other. "He's by no means the first comer, my Uncle Joseph, I can tell you! Very respectable old gentleman; interested in leather; been to Asia Minor; no family, no assets—and a tongue, my dear Wickham, sharper than a serpent's tooth."

"Cantankerous old party, eh?" suggested Wickham.

"Not in the least," cried the other; "only a man with a solid talent for being a bore; rather cheery I dare say, on a desert island, but on a railway journey insupportable. You should hear him on Tonti, the ass that started tontines. He's incredible on Tonti."

"By Jove!" cried Wickham, "then you're one of these Finsbury tontine fellows. I hadn't a guess of that."

"Ah!" said the other, "do you know that old boy in the carriage is worth a hundred thousand pounds to me? There he was asleep, and nobody there but you! But I spared him, because I'm a Conservative in politics."

Mr Wickham, pleased to be in a luggage van, was flitting to and fro like a gentlemanly butterfly.

"By Jingo!" he cried, "here's something for you! 'M. Finsbury, 16 John Street, Bloomsbury, London.' M. stands for Michael, you sly dog; you keep two establishments, do you?"

"O, that's Morris," responded Michael from the other end of the van, where he had found a comfortable seat upon some sacks. "He's a little cousin of mine. I like him myself, because he's afraid of me. He's one of the ornaments of Bloomsbury, and has a collection of some kind—birds' eggs or something that's supposed to be curious. I bet it's nothing to my clients!"

"What a lark it would be to play billy with the labels!" chuckled Mr Wickham. "By George, here's a tack-hammer! We might send all these things skipping about the premises like what's-his-name!"

At this moment, the guard, surprised by the sound of voices, opened the door of his little cabin.

"You had best step in here, gentlemen," said he, when he had heard their story.

"Won't you come, Wickham?" asked Michael.

"Catch me—I want to travel in a van," replied the youth.

And so the door of communication was closed; and

for the rest of the run Mr Wickham was left alone over his diversions on the one side, and on the other Michael and the guard were closeted together in familiar talk.

"I can get you a compartment here, sir," observed the official, as the train began to slacken speed before Bishopstoke station. "You had best get out at my door, and I can bring your friend."

Mr Wickham, whom we left (as the reader has shrewdly suspected) beginning to "play billy" with the labels in the van, was a young gentleman of much wealth, a pleasing but sandy exterior, and a highly vacant mind. Not many months before, he had contrived to get himself blackmailed by the family of a Wallachian Hospodar, resident for political reasons in the gay city of Paris. A common friend (to whom he had confided his distress) recommended him to Michael; and the lawyer was no sooner in possession of the facts than he instantly assumed the offensive, fell on the flank of the Wallachian forces, and, in the inside of three days, had the satisfaction to behold them routed and fleeing for the Danube. It is no business of ours to follow them on this retreat, over which the police were so obliging as to preside paternally. Thus relieved from what he loved to refer to as the Bulgarian Atrocity, Mr Wickham returned to London with the most unbounded and embarrassing gratitude and admiration for his saviour. These sentiments were not repaid either in kind or degree; indeed, Michael was a trifle ashamed of his new client's friendship; it had taken many invitations to get him to Winchester and Wickham Manor; but he had gone at last, and was now returning. It has been remarked by some judicious thinker (possibly J. F. Smith) that Providence despises to employ no instrument, however humble; and it is now plain to the dullest that both Mr Wickham and the Wallachian Hospodar were liquid lead and wedges in the hand of Destiny.

Smitten with the desire to shine in Michael's eyes and show himself a person of original humour and resources, the young gentleman (who was a magistrate, more by token, in his native county) was no sooner alone in the van than he fell upon the labels with all the zeal of a reformer; and, when he rejoined the lawyer at Bishopstoke, his face was flushed with his exertions, and his cigar, which he had suffered to go out was almost bitten in two.

"By George, but this has been a lark!" he cried. "I've sent the wrong thing to everybody in England. These cousins of yours have a packing-case as big as a house. I've muddled the whole business up to that extent, Finsbury, that if it were to get out it's my belief we should get lynched."

It was useless to be serious with Mr Wickham. "Take care," said Michael. "I am getting tired of your perpetual scrapes; my reputation is beginning to suffer."

"Your reputation will be all gone before you finish with me," replied his companion with a grin. "Clap it in the bill, my boy. 'For total loss of reputation, six and eightpence.' But," continued Mr Wickham with more seriousness, "could I be bowled out of the Commission for this little jest? I know it's small, but I like to be a JP Speaking as a professional man, do you think there's any risk?"

"What does it matter?" responded Michael, "they'll chuck you out sooner or later. Somehow you don't give the effect of being a good magistrate."

"I only wish I was a solicitor," retorted his companion, "instead of a poor devil of a country gentleman. Suppose we start one of those tontine affairs ourselves; I to pay five hundred a year, and you to guarantee me against every misfortune except illness or marriage."

"It strikes me," remarked the lawyer with a meditative laugh, as he lighted a cigar, "it strikes me that you must be a cursed nuisance in this world of ours."

"Do you really think so, Finsbury?" responded the magistrate, leaning back in his cushions, delighted with the compliment. "Yes, I suppose I am a nuisance. But, mind you, I have a stake in the country: don't forget that, dear boy."

Chapter 5   Mr Gideon Forsyth and the Gigantic Box

It has been mentioned that at Bournemouth Julia sometimes made acquaintances; it is true she had but a glimpse of them before the doors of John Street closed again upon its captives, but the glimpse was sometimes exhilarating, and the consequent regret was tempered with hope. Among those whom she had thus met a year before was a young barrister of the name of Gideon Forsyth.

About three o'clock of the eventful day when the magistrate tampered with the labels, a somewhat moody and distempered ramble had carried Mr Forsyth to the corner of John Street; and about the same moment Miss Hazeltine was called to the door of No. 16 by a thundering double knock.

Mr Gideon Forsyth was a happy enough young man; he would have been happier if he had had more money and less uncle. One hundred and twenty pounds a year was all his store; but his uncle, Mr Edward Hugh Bloomfield, supplemented this with a handsome allowance and a great deal of advice, couched in language that would probably have been judged intemperate on board a pirate ship. Mr Bloomfield was indeed a figure quite peculiar to the days of Mr Gladstone; what we may call (for the lack of an accepted expression) a Squirradical. Having acquired years without experience, he carried into the Radical side of politics those noisy, after-dinner-table passions, which we are more accustomed to connect with Toryism in its severe and senile aspects. To the opinions of Mr Bradlaugh, in fact, he added the temper and the sympathies of that extinct animal, the Squire; he admired pugilism, he carried a formidable oaken staff, he was a reverent churchman, and it was hard to know which would have more volcanically stirred his choler—a person who should have defended the established church, or one who should have neglected to attend its celebrations. He had besides some levelling catchwords, justly dreaded in the family circle; and when he could not go so far as to declare a step un-English, he might still (and with hardly less effect) denounce it as unpractical. It was under the ban of this lesser excommunication that Gideon had fallen. His views on the study of law had been pronounced unpractical; and it had been intimated to him, in a vociferous interview punctuated with the oaken staff, that he must either take a new start and get a brief or two, or prepare to live on his own money.

No wonder if Gideon was moody. He had not the slightest wish to modify his present habits; but he would not stand on that, since the recall of Mr Bloomfield's allowance would revolutionize them still more radically. He had not the least desire to acquaint himself with law; he had looked into it already, and it seemed not to repay attention; but upon this also he was ready to give way. In fact, he would go as far as he could to meet the views of his uncle, the Squirradical. But there was one part of the programme that appeared independent of his will. How to get a brief? there was the question. And there was another and a worse. Suppose he got one, should he prove the better man?

Suddenly he found his way barred by a crowd. A garishly illuminated van was backed against the kerb; from its open stern, half resting on the street, half supported by some glistening athletes, the end of the largest packing-case in the county of Middlesex might have been seen protruding; while, on the steps of the house, the burly person of the driver and the slim figure of a young girl stood as upon a stage, disputing.

"It is not for us," the girl was saying. "I beg you to take it away; it couldn't get into the house, even if you managed to get it out of the van."

"I shall leave it on the pavement, then, and M. Finsbury can arrange with the Vestry as he likes," said the vanman.

"But I am not M. Finsbury," expostulated the girl.

"It doesn't matter who you are," said the vanman.

"You must allow me to help you, Miss Hazeltine," said Gideon, putting out his hand.

Julia gave a little cry of pleasure. "O, Mr Forsyth," she cried, "I am so glad to see you; we must get this horrid thing, which can only have come here by mistake, into the house. The man says we'll have to take off the door, or knock two of our windows into one, or be fined by the Vestry or Custom House or something for leaving our parcels on the pavement."

The men by this time had successfully removed the box from the van, had plumped it down on the pavement, and now stood leaning against it, or gazing at the door of No. 16, in visible physical distress and mental embarrassment. The windows of the whole street had filled, as if by magic, with interested and entertained spectators.

With as thoughtful and scientific an expression as he could assume, Gideon measured the doorway with his cane, while Julia entered his observations in a drawing-book. He then measured the box, and, upon comparing his data, found that there was just enough space for it to enter. Next, throwing off his coat and waistcoat, he assisted the men to take the door from its hinges. And lastly, all bystanders being pressed into the service, the packing-case mounted the steps upon some fifteen pairs of wavering legs—scraped, loudly grinding, through the doorway—and was deposited at length, with a formidable convulsion, in the far end of the lobby, which it almost blocked. The artisans of this victory smiled upon each other as the dust subsided. It was true they had smashed a bust of Apollo and ploughed the wall into deep ruts; but, at least, they were no longer one of the public spectacles of London.

"Well, sir," said the vanman, "I never see such a job."

Gideon eloquently expressed his concurrence in this sentiment by pressing a couple of sovereigns in the man's hand.

"Make it three, sir, and I'll stand Sam to everybody here!" cried the latter, and, this having been done, the whole body of volunteer porters swarmed into the van, which drove off in the direction of the nearest reliable public-house. Gideon closed the door on their departure, and turned to Julia; their eyes met; the most uncontrollable mirth seized upon them both, and they made the house ring with their laughter. Then curiosity awoke in Julia's mind, and she went and examined the box, and more especially the label.

"This is the strangest thing that ever happened," she said, with another burst of laughter. "It is certainly Morris's handwriting, and I had a letter from him only this morning, telling me to expect a barrel. Is there a barrel coming too, do you think, Mr Forsyth?"

"Statuary with Care, Fragile," read Gideon aloud from the painted warning on the box. "Then you were told nothing about this?"

"No," responded Julia. "O, Mr Forsyth, don't you think we might take a peep at it?"

"Yes, indeed," cried Gideon. "Just let me have a hammer."

"Come down, and I'll show you where it is," cried Julia. "The shelf is too high for me to reach;" and, opening the door of the kitchen stair, she bade Gideon follow her. They found both the hammer and a chisel; but Gideon was surprised to see no sign of a servant. He also discovered that Miss Hazeltine had a very pretty little foot and ankle; and the discovery embarrassed him so much that he was glad to fall at once upon the packing-case.

He worked hard and earnestly, and dealt his blows with the precision of a blacksmith; Julia the while standing silently by his side, and regarding rather the workman than the work. He was a handsome fellow; she told herself she had never seen such beautiful arms. And suddenly, as though he had overheard these thoughts, Gideon turned and smiled to her. She, too, smiled and coloured; and the double change became her so prettily that Gideon forgot to turn away his eyes, and, swinging the hammer with a will, discharged a smashing blow on his own knuckles. With admirable presence of mind he crushed down an oath and substituted the harmless comment, "Butter fingers!" But the pain was sharp, his nerve was shaken, and after an abortive trial he found he must desist from further operations.

In a moment Julia was off to the pantry; in a moment she was back again with a basin of water and a sponge, and had begun to bathe his wounded hand.

"I am dreadfully sorry!" said Gideon apologetically. "If I had had any manners I should have opened the box first and smashed my hand afterward. It feels much better," he added. "I assure you it does."

"And now I think you are well enough to direct operations," said she. "Tell me what to do, and I'll be your workman."

"A very pretty workman," said Gideon, rather forgetting himself. She turned and looked at him, with a suspicion of a frown; and the indiscreet young man was glad to direct her attention to the packing-case. The bulk of the work had been accomplished; and presently Julia had burst through the last barrier and disclosed a zone of straw. in a moment they were kneeling side by side, engaged like haymakers; the next they were rewarded with a glimpse of something white and polished; and the next again laid bare an unmistakable marble leg.

"He is surely a very athletic person," said Julia.

"I never saw anything like it," responded Gideon. "His muscles stand out like penny rolls."

Another leg was soon disclosed, and then what seemed to be a third. This resolved itself, however, into a knotted club resting upon a pedestal.

"It is a Hercules," cried Gideon; "I might have guessed that from his calf. I'm supposed to be rather partial to statuary, but when it comes to Hercules, the police should interfere. I should say," he added, glancing with disaffection at the swollen leg, "that this was about the biggest and the worst in Europe. What in heaven's name can have induced him to come here?"

"I suppose nobody else would have a gift of him," said Julia. "And for that matter, I think we could have done without the monster very well."

"O, don't say that," returned Gideon. "This has been one of the most amusing experiences of my life."

"I don't think you'll forget it very soon," said Julia. "Your hand will remind you."

"Well, I suppose I must be going," said Gideon reluctantly.

"No," pleaded Julia. "Why should you? Stay and have tea with me."

"If I thought you really wished me to stay," said Gideon, looking at his hat, "of course I should only be too delighted."

"What a silly person you must take me for!" returned the girl. "Why, of course I do; and, besides, I want some cakes for tea, and I've nobody to send. Here is the latchkey."

Gideon put on his hat with alacrity, and casting one look at Miss Hazeltine, and another at the legs of Hercules, threw open the door and departed on his errand.

He returned with a large bag of the choicest and most tempting of cakes and tartlets, and found Julia in the act of spreading a small tea-table in the lobby.

"The rooms are all in such a state," she cried, "that I thought we should be more cosy and comfortable in our own lobby, and under our own vine and statuary."

"Ever so much better," cried Gideon delightedly.

"O what adorable cream tarts!" said Julia, opening the bag, "and the dearest little cherry tartlets, with all the cherries spilled out into the cream!"

"Yes," said Gideon, concealing his dismay, "I knew they

would mix beautifully; the woman behind the counter told me so."

"Now," said Julia, as they began their little festival, "I am going to show you Morris's letter; read it aloud, please; perhaps there's something I have missed."

Gideon took the letter, and spreading it out on his knee, read as follows:

> DEAR JULIA, I write you from Browndean, where we are stopping over for a few days. Uncle was much shaken in that dreadful accident, of which, I dare say, you have seen the account. Tomorrow I leave him here with John, and come up alone; but before that, you will have received a barrel CONTAINING SPECIMENS FOR A FRIEND. Do not open it on any account, but leave it in the lobby till I come.
>
> Yours in haste,
M. FINSBURY.
>
> P. S. —Be sure and leave the barrel in the lobby.

"No," said Gideon, "there seems to be nothing about the monument," and he nodded, as he spoke, at the marble legs. "Miss Hazeltine," he continued, "would you mind me asking a few questions?"

"Certainly not," replied Julia; "and if you can make me understand why Morris has sent a statue of Hercules instead of a barrel containing specimens for a friend, I shall be grateful till my dying day. And what are specimens for a friend?"

"I haven't a guess," said Gideon. "Specimens are usually bits of stone, but rather smaller than our friend the monument. Still, that is not the point. Are you quite alone in this big house?"

"Yes, I am at present," returned Julia. "I came up before them to prepare the house, and get another servant. But I couldn't get one I liked."

"Then you are utterly alone," said Gideon in amazement. "Are you not afraid?"

"No," responded Julia stoutly. "I don't see why I should be more afraid than you would be; I am weaker, of course, but when I found I must sleep alone in the house I bought a revolver wonderfully cheap, and made the man show me how to use it."

"And how do you use it?" demanded Gideon, much amused at her courage.

"Why," said she, with a smile, "you pull the little trigger thing on top, and then pointing it very low, for it springs up as you fire, you pull the underneath little trigger thing, and it goes off as well as if a man had done it."

"And how often have you used it?" asked Gideon.

"O, I have not used it yet," said the determined young lady; "but I know how, and that makes me wonderfully courageous, especially when I barricade my door with a chest of drawers."

"I'm awfully glad they are coming back soon," said Gideon. "This business strikes me as excessively unsafe; if it goes on much longer, I could provide you with a maiden aunt of mine, or my landlady if you preferred."

"Lend me an aunt!" cried Julia. "O, what generosity! I begin to think it must have been you that sent the Hercules."

"Believe me," cried the young man, "I admire you too much to send you such an infamous work of art."

Julia was beginning to reply, when they were both startled by a knocking at the door.

"O, Mr Forsyth!"

"Don't be afraid, my dear girl," said Gideon, laying his hand tenderly on her arm.

"I know it's the police," she whispered. "They are coming to complain about the statue."

The knock was repeated. It was louder than before, and more impatient.

"It's Morris," cried Julia, in a startled voice, and she ran to the door and opened it.

It was indeed Morris that stood before them; not the Morris of ordinary days, but a wild-looking fellow, pale and haggard, with bloodshot eyes, and a two-days' beard upon his chin.

"The barrel!" he cried. "Where's the barrel that came this morning?" And he stared about the lobby, his eyes, as they fell upon the legs of Hercules, literally goggling in his head. "What is that?" he screamed. "What is that waxwork? Speak, you fool! What is that? And where's the barrel—the water-butt?"

"No barrel came, Morris," responded Julia coldly. "This is the only thing that has arrived."

"This!" shrieked the miserable man. "I never heard of it!"

"It came addressed in your hand," replied Julia; "we had nearly to pull the house down to get it in, that is all that I can tell you."

Morris gazed at her in utter bewilderment. He passed his hand over his forehead; he leaned against the wall like a man about to faint. Then his tongue was loosed, and he overwhelmed the girl with torrents of abuse. Such fire, such directness, such a choice of ungentlemanly language, none had ever before suspected Morris to possess; and the girl trembled and shrank before his fury.

"You shall not speak to Miss Hazeltine in that way," said Gideon sternly. "It is what I will not suffer."

"I shall speak to the girl as I like," returned Morris, with a fresh outburst of anger. "I'll speak to the hussy as she deserves."

"Not a word more, sir, not one word," cried Gideon. "Miss Hazeltine," he continued, addressing the young girl, "you cannot stay a moment longer in the same house with this unmanly fellow. Here is my arm; let me take you where you will be secure from insult."

"Mr Forsyth," returned Julia, "you are right; I cannot stay here longer, and I am sure I trust myself to an honourable gentleman."

Pale and resolute, Gideon offered her his arm, and the pair descended the steps, followed by Morris clamouring for the latchkey.

Julia had scarcely handed the key to Morris before an empty hansom drove smartly into John Street. It was hailed by both men, and as the cabman drew up his restive horse, Morris made a dash into the vehicle.

"Sixpence above fare," he cried recklessly. "Waterloo Station for your life. Sixpence for yourself!"

"Make it a shilling, guv'ner," said the man, with a grin; "the other parties were first."

"A shilling then," cried Morris, with the inward reflection that he would reconsider it at Waterloo. The man whipped up his horse, and the hansom vanished from John Street.

Chapter 6 The Tribulations of Morris: Part the First

As the hansom span through the streets of London, Morris sought to rally the forces of his mind. The water-butt with the dead body had miscarried, and it was essential to recover it. So much was clear; and if, by some blest good fortune, it was still at the station, all might be well. If it had been sent out, however, if it were already in the hands of some wrong person, matters looked more ominous. People who receive unexplained packages are usually keen to have them open; the example of Miss Hazeltine (whom he cursed again) was there to remind him of the circumstance; and if anyone had opened the water-butt—"O Lord!" cried Morris at the thought, and carried his hand to his damp forehead. The private conception of any breach of law is apt to be inspiriting, for the scheme (while yet inchoate) wears dashing and attractive colours. Not so in the least that part of the criminal's later reflections which deal with the police. That useful corps (as Morris now began to think) had scarce been kept sufficiently in view when he embarked upon his enterprise. "I must play devilish close," he reflected, and he was aware of an exquisite thrill of fear in the region of the spine.

"Main line or loop?" enquired the cabman, through the scuttle.

"Main line," replied Morris, and mentally decided that the man should have his shilling after all. "It would be madness to attract attention," thought he. "But what this thing will cost me, first and last, begins to be a nightmare!"

He passed through the booking-office and wandered disconsolately on the platform. It was a breathing-space in the day's traffic. There were few people there, and these for the most part quiescent on the benches. Morris seemed to attract no remark, which was a good thing; but, on the other hand, he was making no progress in his quest. Something must be done, something must be risked. Every passing instant only added to his dangers. Summoning all his courage, he stopped a porter, and asked him if he remembered receiving a barrel by the morning train. He was anxious to get information, for the barrel belonged to a friend. "It is a matter of some moment," he added, "for it contains specimens."

"I was not here this morning, sir," responded the porter, somewhat reluctantly, "but I'll ask Bill. Do you recollect, Bill, to have got a barrel from Bournemouth this morning containing specimens?"

"I don't know about specimens," replied Bill; "but the party as received the barrel I mean raised a sight of trouble."

"What's that?" cried Morris, in the agitation of the moment pressing a penny into the man's hand.

"You see, sir, the barrel arrived at one-thirty. No one claimed it till about three, when a small, sickly-looking gentleman (probably a curate) came up, and sez he, 'Have you got anything for Pitman?' or 'Wili'm Bent Pitman,' if I recollect right. 'I don't exactly know,' sez I, 'but I rather fancy that there barrel bears that name.' The little man went up to the barrel, and seemed regularly all took aback when he saw the address, and then he pitched into us for not having brought what he wanted. 'I don't care a damn what you want,' sez I to him, 'but if you are Will'm Bent Pitman, there's your barrel.'"

"Well, and did he take it?" cried the breathless Morris.

"Well, sir," returned Bill, "it appears it was a packing-case he was after. The packing-case came; that's sure enough, because it was about the biggest packing-case ever I clapped eyes on. And this Pitman he seemed a good deal cut up, and he had the superintendent out, and they got hold of the vanman—him as took the packing-case. Well, sir," continued Bill, with a smile, "I never see a man in such a state. Everybody about that van was mortal, bar the horses. Some gen'leman (as well as I could make out) had given the vanman a sov.; and so that was where the trouble come in, you see."

"But what did he say?" gasped Morris.

"I don't know as he SAID much, sir," said Bill. "But he offered to fight this Pitman for a pot of beer. He had lost his book, too, and the receipts, and his men were all as mortal as himself. O, they were all like"—and Bill paused for a simile—"like lords! The superintendent sacked them on the spot."

"O, come, but that's not so bad," said Morris, with a bursting sigh. "He couldn't tell where he took the packing-case, then?"

"Not he," said Bill, "nor yet nothink else."

"And what—what did Pitman do?" asked Morris.

"O, he went off with the barrel in a four-wheeler, very trembling like," replied Bill. "I don't believe he's a gentleman as has good health."

"Well, so the barrel's gone," said Morris, half to himself.

"You may depend on that, sir," returned the porter. "But you had better see the superintendent."

"Not in the least; it's of no account," said Morris. "It only contained specimens." And he walked hastily away.

Ensconced once more in a hansom, he proceeded to reconsider his position. Suppose (he thought), suppose he should accept defeat and declare his uncle's death at once? He should lose the tontine, and with that the last hope of his seven thousand eight hundred pounds. But on the other hand, since the shilling to the hansom cabman, he had begun to see that crime was expensive in its course, and, since the loss of the water-butt, that it was uncertain in its consequences. Quietly at first, and then with growing heat, he reviewed the advantages of backing out. It involved a loss; but (come to think of it) no such great loss after all; only that of the tontine, which had been always a toss-up, which at bottom he had never really expected. He reminded himself of that eagerly; he congratulated himself upon his constant moderation. He had never really expected the tontine; he had never even very definitely hoped to recover his seven thousand eight hundred pounds; he had been hurried into the whole thing by Michael's obvious dishonesty. Yes, it would probably be better to draw back from this high-flying venture, settle back on the leather business—

"Great God!" cried Morris, bounding in the hansom like a Jack-in-a-box. "I have not only not gained the tontine—I have lost the leather business!"

Such was the monstrous fact. He had no power to sign; he could not draw a cheque for thirty shillings. Until he could produce legal evidence of his uncle's death, he was a penniless outcast—and as soon as he produced it he had lost the tontine! There was no hesitation on the part of Morris; to drop the tontine like a hot chestnut, to concentrate all his forces on the leather business and the rest of his small but legitimate inheritance, was the decision of a single instant. And the next, the full extent of his calamity was suddenly disclosed to him. Declare his uncle's death? He couldn't! Since the body was lost Joseph had (in a legal sense) become immortal.

There was no created vehicle big enough to contain Morris

and his woes. He paid the hansom off and walked on he knew not whither.

"I seem to have gone into this business with too much precipitation," he reflected, with a deadly sigh. "I fear it seems too ramified for a person of my powers of mind."

And then a remark of his uncle's flashed into his memory: If you want to think clearly, put it all down on paper. "Well, the old boy knew a thing or two," said Morris. "I will try; but I don't believe the paper was ever made that will clear my mind."

He entered a place of public entertainment, ordered bread and cheese, and writing materials, and sat down before them heavily. He tried the pen. It was an excellent pen, but what was he to write? "I have it," cried Morris. "Robinson Crusoe and the double columns!" He prepared his paper after that classic model, and began as follows:

Bad.	Good.
1. I have lost my uncle's body.	1. But then Pitman has found it.

"Stop a bit," said Morris. "I am letting the spirit of antithesis run away with me. Let's start again."

Bad.	Good.
1. I have lost my uncle's body.	1. But then I no longer require to bury it.
2. I have lost the tontine.	2. But I may still save that if Pitman disposes of the body, and if I can find a physician who will stick at nothing.

3. I have lost the leather business and the rest of my uncle's succession.	3. But not if Pitman gives the body up to the police.

"O, but in that case I go to gaol; I had forgot that," thought Morris. "Indeed, I don't know that I had better dwell on that hypothesis at all; it's all very well to talk of facing the worst; but in a case of this kind a man's first duty is to his own nerve. Is there any answer to No. 3? Is there any possible good side to such a beastly bungle? There must be, of course, or where would be the use of this double-entry business? And—by George, I have it!" he exclaimed; "it's exactly the same as the last!" And he hastily re-wrote the passage:

Bad.	Good.
3. I have lost the leather business and the rest of my uncle's succession.	3. But not if I can find a physician who will stick at nothing.

"This venal doctor seems quite a desideratum," he reflected. "I want him first to give me a certificate that my uncle is dead, so that I may get the leather business; and then that he's alive—but here we are again at the incompatible interests!" And he returned to his tabulation:

Bad.	Good.
4. I have almost no money.	4. But there is plenty in the bank.
5. Yes, but I can't get the money in the bank.	5. But—well, that seems unhappily to be the case.

Bad.	Good.
6. I have left the bill for eight hundred pounds in Uncle Joseph's pocket.	6. But if Pitman is only a dishonest man, the presence of this bill may lead him to keep the whole thing dark and throw the body into the New Cut.
7. Yes, but if Pitman is dishonest and finds the bill, he will know who Joseph is, and he may blackmail me.	7. Yes, but if I am right about Uncle Masterman, I can blackmail Michael.
8. But I can't blackmail Michael (which is, besides, a very dangerous thing to do) until I find out.	8. Worse luck!
9. The leather business will soon want money for current expenses, and I have none to give.	9. But the leather business is a sinking ship.
10. Yes, but it's all the ship I have.	10. A fact.
11. John will soon want money, and I have none to give.	11.
12. And the venal doctor will want money down.	12.
13. And if Pitman is dishonest and don't send me to gaol, he will want a fortune.	13.

"O, this seems to be a very one-sided business," exclaimed Morris. "There's not so much in this method as I was led to think." He crumpled the paper up and threw it down; and then, the next moment, picked it up again and ran it over. "It seems it's on the financial point that my position is weakest," he reflected. "Is there positively no way of raising the wind? In a vast city like this, and surrounded by all the resources of civilization, it seems not to be conceived! Let us have no more precipitation. Is there nothing I can sell? My collection of signet—" But at the thought of scattering these loved treasures the blood leaped into Morris's check. "I would rather die!" he exclaimed, and, cramming his hat upon his head, strode forth into the streets.

"I MUST raise funds," he thought. "My uncle being dead, the money in the bank is mine, or would be mine but for the cursed injustice that has pursued me ever since I was an orphan in a commercial academy. I know what any other man would do; any other man in Christendom would forge; although I don't know why I call it forging, either, when Joseph's dead, and the funds are my own. When I think of that, when I think that my uncle is really as dead as mutton, and that I can't prove it, my gorge rises at the injustice of the whole affair. I used to feel bitterly about that seven thousand eight hundred pounds; it seems a trifle now! Dear me, why, the day before yesterday I was comparatively happy."

And Morris stood on the sidewalk and heaved another sobbing sigh.

"Then there's another thing," he resumed; "can I? Am I able? Why didn't I practise different handwritings while I was young? How a fellow regrets those lost opportunities when he grows up! But there's one comfort: it's not morally wrong; I can try it on with a clear conscience, and even if I was found out, I wouldn't greatly care—morally, I mean. And then, if I succeed, and if Pitman is staunch, there's nothing to do but find a venal doctor; and that ought to be simple enough in a place like London. By all accounts the town's alive with them. It wouldn't do, of course, to advertise for a corrupt physician; that would be impolitic. No, I suppose a fellow has simply to spot along the streets for a red lamp and herbs in the window, and then you go in and—and—and put it to him plainly; though it seems a delicate step."

He was near home now, after many devious wanderings, and turned up John Street. As he thrust his latchkey in the lock, another mortifying reflection struck him to the heart.

"Not even this house is mine till I can prove him dead," he snarled, and slammed the door behind him so that the windows in the attic rattled.

Night had long fallen; long ago the lamps and the shop-fronts had begun to glitter down the endless streets; the lobby was pitch-dark; and, as the devil would have it, Morris barked his shins and sprawled all his length over the pedestal of Hercules. The pain was sharp; his temper was already thoroughly undermined; by a last misfortune his hand closed on the hammer as he fell; and, in a spasm of childish irritation, he turned and struck at the offending statue. There was a splintering crash.

"O Lord, what have I done next?" wailed Morris; and he groped his way to find a candle. "Yes," he reflected, as he stood with the light in his hand and looked upon the mutilated leg, from which about a pound of muscle was detached. "Yes, I have destroyed a genuine antique; I may be in for thousands!" And then there sprung up in his bosom a sort of angry hope. "Let me see," he thought. "Julia's got rid of—, there's nothing to connect me with that beast Forsyth; the men were all drunk, and (what's better) they've been all discharged. O, come, I think this is another case of moral courage! I'll deny all knowledge of the thing."

A moment more, and he stood again before the Hercules, his lips sternly compressed, the coal-axe and the meat-cleaver under his arm. The next, he had fallen upon the packing-case. This had been already seriously undermined by the operations of Gideon; a few well-directed blows, and it already quaked and gaped; yet a few more, and it fell about Morris in a shower of boards followed by an avalanche of straw.

And now the leather-merchant could behold the nature of his task, and at the first sight his spirit quailed. It was, indeed, no more ambitious a task for De Lesseps, with all his men and horses, to attack the hills of Panama, than for a single, slim young gentleman, with no previous experience of labour in a quarry, to measure himself against that bloated monster on his pedestal. And yet the pair were well encountered: on the one side, bulk—on the other, genuine heroic fire.

"Down you shall come, you great big, ugly brute!" cried Morris aloud, with something of that passion which swept the Parisian mob against the walls of the Bastille. "Down you shall come, this night. I'll have none of you in my lobby."

The face, from its indecent expression, had particularly animated the zeal of our iconoclast; and it was against the face that he began his operations. The great height of the demigod—for he stood a fathom and half in his stocking-feet—offered a preliminary obstacle to this attack. But here, in the first skirmish of the battle, intellect already began to triumph over matter. By means of a pair of library steps, the injured householder gained a posture of advantage; and, with great swipes of the coal-axe, proceeded to decapitate the brute.

Two hours later, what had been the erect image of a gigantic coal-porter turned miraculously white, was now no more than a medley of disjected members; the quadragenarian torso prone against the pedestal; the lascivious countenance leering down the kitchen stair; the legs, the arms, the hands, and even the fingers, scattered broadcast on the lobby floor. Half an hour more, and all the debris had been laboriously carted to the kitchen; and Morris, with a gentle sentiment of triumph, looked round upon the scene of his achievements. Yes, he could deny all knowledge of it now: the lobby, beyond the fact that it was partly ruinous, betrayed no trace of the passage of Hercules. But it was a weary Morris that crept up to bed; his arms and shoulders ached, the palms of his hands burned from the rough kisses of the coal-axe, and there was one smarting finger that stole continually to his mouth. Sleep long delayed to visit the dilapidated hero, and with the first peep of day it had again deserted him.

The morning, as though to accord with his disastrous fortunes, dawned inclemently. An easterly gale was shouting in the streets; flaws of rain angrily assailed the windows; and as Morris dressed, the draught from the fireplace vividly played about his legs.

"I think," he could not help observing bitterly, "that with all I have to bear, they might have given me decent weather."

There was no bread in the house, for Miss Hazeltine (like all women left to themselves) had subsisted entirely upon cake. But some of this was found, and (along with what the poets call a glass of fair, cold water) made up a semblance of a morning meal, and then down he sat undauntedly to his delicate task.

Nothing can be more interesting than the study of signatures, written (as they are) before meals and after, during indigestion and intoxication; written when the signer is trembling for the life of his child or has come from winning the Derby, in his lawyer's office, or under the bright eyes of his sweetheart. To the vulgar, these seem never the same; but to the expert, the bank clerk, or the lithographer, they are constant quantities, and as recognizable as the North Star to the night-watch on deck.

To all this Morris was alive. In the theory of that graceful art in which he was now embarking, our spirited leather-merchant was beyond all reproach. But, happily for the investor, forgery is an affair of practice. And as Morris sat surrounded by examples of his uncle's signature and of his own incompetence, insidious depression stole upon his spirits. From time to time the wind wuthered in the chimney at his back; from time to time there swept over Bloomsbury a squall so dark that he must rise and light the gas; about him was the chill and the mean disorder of a house out of commission—the floor bare, the sofa heaped with books and accounts enveloped in a dirty table-cloth, the pens rusted, the paper glazed with a thick film of dust; and yet these were but adminicles of misery, and the true root of his depression lay round him on the table in the shape of misbegotten forgeries.

"It's one of the strangest things I ever heard of," he complained. "It almost seems as if it was a talent that I didn't possess." He went once more minutely through his proofs. "A clerk would simply gibe at them," said he. "Well, there's nothing else but tracing possible."

He waited till a squall had passed and there came a blink of scowling daylight. Then he went to the window, and in the face of all John Street traced his uncle's signature. It was a poor thing at the best. "But it must do," said he, as he stood gazing woefully on his handiwork. "He's dead, anyway." And he filled up the cheque for a couple of hundred and sallied forth for the Anglo-Patagonian Bank.

There, at the desk at which he was accustomed to transact business, and with as much indifference as he could assume, Morris presented the forged cheque to the big, red-bearded Scots teller. The teller seemed to view it with surprise; and as he turned it this way and that, and even scrutinized the signature with a magnifying-glass, his surprise appeared to warm into disfavour. Begging to be excused for a moment, he passed away into the rearmost quarters of the bank; whence, after an appreciable interval, he returned again in earnest talk with a superior, an oldish and a baldish, but a very gentlemanly man.

"Mr Morris Finsbury, I believe," said the gentlemanly man, fixing Morris with a pair of double eye-glasses.

"That is my name," said Morris, quavering. "Is there anything wrong?"

"Well, the fact is, Mr Finsbury, you see we are rather surprised at receiving this," said the other, flicking at the cheque. "There are no effects."

"No effects?" cried Morris. "Why, I know myself there must be eight-and-twenty hundred pounds, if there's a penny."

"Two seven six four, I think," replied the gentlemanly man; "but it was drawn yesterday."

"Drawn!" cried Morris.

"By your uncle himself, sir," continued the other. "Not only that, but we discounted a bill for him for—let me see—how much was it for, Mr Bell?"

"Eight hundred, Mr Judkin," replied the teller.

"Bent Pitman!" cried Morris, staggering back.

"I beg your pardon," said Mr Judkin.

"It's—it's only an expletive," said Morris.

"I hope there's nothing wrong, Mr Finsbury," said Mr Bell.

"All I can tell you," said Morris, with a harsh laugh, "is that the whole thing's impossible. My uncle is at Bournemouth, unable to move."

"Really!" cried Mr Bell, and he recovered the cheque from Mr Judkin. "But this cheque is dated in London, and today," he observed. "How d' ye account for that, sir?"

"O, that was a mistake," said Morris, and a deep tide of colour dyed his face and neck.

"No doubt, no doubt," said Mr Judkin, but he looked at his customer enquiringly.

"And—and—" resumed Morris, "even if there were no effects—this is a very trifling sum to overdraw—our firm—the name of Finsbury, is surely good enough for such a wretched sum as this."

"No doubt, Mr Finsbury," returned Mr Judkin; "and if you insist I will take it into consideration; but I hardly think—in short, Mr Finsbury, if there had been nothing else, the signature seems hardly all that we could wish."

"That's of no consequence," replied Morris nervously. "I'll get my uncle to sign another. The fact is," he went on, with a bold stroke, "my uncle is so far from well at present that he was unable to sign this cheque without assistance, and I fear that my holding the pen for him may have made the difference in the signature."

Mr Judkin shot a keen glance into Morris's face; and then turned and looked at Mr Bell.

"Well," he said, "it seems as if we had been victimized by a swindler. Pray tell Mr Finsbury we shall put detectives on at once. As for this cheque of yours, I regret that, owing to the way it was signed, the bank can hardly consider it—what shall I say?—businesslike," and he returned the cheque across the counter.

Morris took it up mechanically; he was thinking of something very different.

"In a—case of this kind," he began, "I believe the loss falls on us; I mean upon my uncle and myself."

"It does not, sir," replied Mr Bell; "the bank is responsible, and the bank will either recover the money or refund it, you may depend on that."

Morris's face fell; then it was visited by another gleam of hope.

"I'll tell you what," he said, "you leave this entirely in my hands. I'll sift the matter. I've an idea, at any rate; and detectives," he added appealingly, "are so expensive."

"The bank would not hear of it," returned Mr Judkin. "The bank stands to lose between three and four thousand pounds; it will spend as much more if necessary. An undiscovered forger is a permanent danger. We shall clear it up to the bottom, Mr Finsbury; set your mind at rest on that."

"Then I'll stand the loss," said Morris boldly. "I order you to abandon the search." He was determined that no enquiry should be made.

"I beg your pardon," returned Mr Judkin, "but we have nothing to do with you in this matter, which is one between your uncle and ourselves. If he should take this opinion, and will either come here himself or let me see him in his sick-room—"

"Quite impossible," cried Morris.

"Well, then, you see," said Mr Judkin, "how my hands are tied. The whole affair must go at once into the hands of the police."

Morris mechanically folded the cheque and restored it to his pocket-book.

"Good-morning," said he, and scrambled somehow out of the bank.

"I don't know what they suspect," he reflected; "I can't make them out, their whole behaviour is thoroughly unbusinesslike. But it doesn't matter; all's up with everything. The money has been paid; the police are on the scent; in two hours that idiot Pitman will be nabbed—and the whole story of the dead body in the evening papers."

If he could have heard what passed in the bank after his departure he would have been less alarmed, perhaps more mortified.

"That was a curious affair, Mr Bell," said Mr Judkin.

"Yes, sir," said Mr Bell, "but I think we have given him a fright."

"O, we shall hear no more of Mr Morris Finsbury,"

returned the other; "it was a first attempt, and the house have dealt with us so long that I was anxious to deal gently. But I suppose, Mr Bell, there can be no mistake about yesterday? It was old Mr Finsbury himself?"

"There could be no possible doubt of that," said Mr Bell with a chuckle. "He explained to me the principles of banking."

"Well, well," said Mr Judkin. "The next time he calls ask him to step into my room. It is only proper he should be warned."

Chapter 7 In Which William Dent Pitman Takes Legal Advice

Norfolk Street, King's Road—jocularly known among Mr Pitman's lodgers as "Norfolk Island"—is neither a long, a handsome, nor a pleasing thoroughfare. Dirty, undersized maids-of-all-work issue from it in pursuit of beer, or linger on its sidewalk listening to the voice of love. The cat's-meat man passes twice a day. An occasional organ-grinder wanders in and wanders out again, disgusted. In holiday-time the street is the arena of the young bloods of the neighbourhood, and the householders have an opportunity of studying the manly art of self-defence. And yet Norfolk Street has one claim to be respectable, for it contains not a single shop—unless you count the public-house at the corner, which is really in the King's Road.

The door of No. 7 bore a brass plate inscribed with the legend "W. D. Pitman, Artist". It was not a particularly clean brass plate, nor was No. 7 itself a particularly inviting place of residence. And yet it had a character of its own, such as may well quicken the pulse of the reader's curiosity. For here was the home of an artist—and a distinguished artist too, highly distinguished by his ill-success—which had never been made the subject of an article in the illustrated magazines. No wood-engraver had ever reproduced "a corner in the back drawing-room" or "the studio mantelpiece" of No. 7; no young lady author had ever commented on "the unaffected simplicity" with which Mr Pitman received her in the midst of his "treasures". It is an omission I would gladly supply, but our business is only with the backward parts and "abject rear" of this aesthetic dwelling.

Here was a garden, boasting a dwarf fountain (that never played) in the centre, a few grimy-looking flowers in pots, two or three newly planted trees which the spring of Chelsea visited without noticeable consequence, and two or three statues after the antique, representing Satyrs and Nymphs in the worst possible style of sculptured art. On one side the garden was overshadowed by a pair of crazy studios, usually hired out to the more obscure and youthful practitioners of British art. Opposite these another lofty out-building, somewhat more carefully finished, and boasting of a communication with the house and a private door on the back lane, enshrined the multifarious industry of Mr Pitman. All day, it is true, he was engaged in the work of education at a seminary for young ladies; but the evenings at least were his own, and these he would prolong far into the night, now dashing off "A landscape with waterfall" in oil, now a volunteer bust ("in marble", as he would gently but proudly observe) of some public character, now stooping his chisel to a mere "Nymph for a gasbracket on a stair, sir", or a life-size "Infant Samuel" for a religious nursery. Mr Pitman had studied in Paris, and he had studied in Rome, supplied with funds by a fond parent who went subsequently bankrupt in consequence of a fall in corsets; and though he was never thought to have the smallest modicum of talent, it was at one time supposed that he had learned his business. Eighteen years of what is called "tuition" had relieved him of the dangerous knowledge. His artist lodgers would sometimes reason with him; they would point out to him how impossible it was to paint by gaslight, or to sculpture life-sized Nymphs without a model.

"I know that," he would reply. "No one in Norfolk Street knows it better; and if I were rich I should certainly employ the best models in London; but, being poor, I have taught myself to do without them. An occasional model would only disturb my ideal conception of the figure, and be a positive impediment in my career. As for painting by an artificial light," he would continue, "that is simply a knack I have found it necessary to acquire, my days being engrossed in the work of tuition."

At the moment when we must present him to our readers, Pitman was in his studio alone, by the dying light of the October day. He sat (sure enough with "unaffected simplicity") in a Windsor chair, his low-crowned black felt hat by his side; a dark, weak, harmless, pathetic little man, clad in the hue of mourning, his coat longer than is usual with the laity, his neck enclosed in a collar without a parting, his neckcloth pale in hue and simply tied; the whole outward man, except for a pointed beard, tentatively clerical. There was a thinning on the top of Pitman's head, there were silver hairs at Pitman's temple. Poor gentleman, he was no longer young; and years, and poverty, and humble ambition thwarted, make a cheerless lot.

In front of him, in the corner by the door, there stood a portly barrel; and let him turn them where he might, it was always to the barrel that his eyes and his thoughts returned.

"Should I open it? Should I return it? Should I communicate with Mr Sernitopolis at once?" he wondered. "No," he concluded finally, "nothing without Mr Finsbury's advice." And he arose and produced a shabby leathern desk. It opened without the formality of unlocking, and displayed the thick cream-coloured notepaper on which Mr Pitman was in the habit of communicating with the proprietors of schools and the parents of his pupils. He placed the desk on the table by the window, and taking a saucer of Indian ink from the chimney-piece, laboriously composed the following letter:

"My dear Mr Finsbury," it ran, "would it be presuming on your kindness if I asked you to pay me a visit here this evening? It is in no trifling matter that I invoke your valuable assistance, for need I say more than it concerns the welfare of Mr

Semitopolis's statue of Hercules? I write you in great agitation of mind; for I have made all enquiries, and greatly fear that this work of ancient art has been mislaid. I labour besides under another perplexity, not unconnected with the first. Pray excuse the inelegance of this scrawl, and believe me yours in haste, William D. Pitman."

Armed with this he set forth and rang the bell of No. 233 King's Road, the private residence of Michael Finsbury. He had met the lawyer at a time of great public excitement in Chelsea; Michael, who had a sense of humour and a great deal of careless kindness in his nature, followed the acquaintance up, and, having come to laugh, remained to drop into a contemptuous kind of friendship. By this time, which was four years after the first meeting, Pitman was the lawyer's dog.

"No," said the elderly housekeeper, who opened the door in person, "Mr Michael's not in yet. But ye're looking terribly poorly, Mr Pitman. Take a glass of sherry, sir, to cheer ye up."

"No, I thank you, ma'am," replied the artist. "It is very good in you, but I scarcely feel in sufficient spirits for sherry. Just give Mr Finsbury this note, and ask him to look round—to the door in the lane, you will please tell him; I shall be in the studio all evening."

And he turned again into the street and walked slowly homeward. A hairdresser's window caught his attention, and he stared long and earnestly at the proud, high-born, waxen lady in evening dress, who circulated in the centre of the show. The artist woke in him, in spite of his troubles.

"It is all very well to run down the men who make these things," he cried, "but there's a something—there's a haughty, indefinable something about that figure. It's what I tried for in my 'Empress Eugenie'," he added, with a sigh.

And he went home reflecting on the quality. "They don't teach you that direct appeal in Paris," he thought. "It's British. Come, I am going to sleep, I must wake up, I must aim higher— aim higher," cried the little artist to himself. All through his tea and afterward, as he was giving his eldest boy a lesson on the fiddle, his mind dwelt no longer on his troubles, but he was rapt into the better land; and no sooner was he at liberty than he hastened with positive exhilaration to his studio.

Not even the sight of the barrel could entirely cast him down. He flung himself with rising zest into his work—a bust of Mr Gladstone from a photograph; turned (with extraordinary success) the difficulty of the back of the head, for which he had no documents beyond a hazy recollection of a public meeting; delighted himself by his treatment of the collar; and was only recalled to the cares of life by Michael Finsbury's rattle at the door.

"Well, what's wrong?" said Michael, advancing to the grate, where, knowing his friend's delight in a bright fire, Mr Pitman had not spared the fuel. "I suppose you have come to grief somehow."

"There is no expression strong enough," said the artist. "Mr

Semitopolis's statue has not turned up, and I am afraid I shall be answerable for the money; but I think nothing of that—what I fear, my dear Mr Finsbury, what I fear—alas that I should have to say it! is exposure. The Hercules was to be smuggled out of Italy; a thing positively wrong, a thing of which a man of my principles and in my responsible position should have taken (as I now see too late) no part whatever."

"This sounds like very serious work," said the lawyer. "It will require a great deal of drink, Pitman."

"I took the liberty of—in short, of being prepared for you," replied the artist, pointing to a kettle, a bottle of gin, a lemon, and glasses.

Michael mixed himself a grog, and offered the artist a cigar.

"No, thank you," said Pitman. "I used occasionally to be rather partial to it, but the smell is so disagreeable about the clothes."

"All right," said the lawyer. "I am comfortable now. Unfold your tale."

At some length Pitman set forth his sorrows. He had gone today to Waterloo, expecting to receive the colossal Hercules, and he had received instead a barrel not big enough to hold Discobolus; yet the barrel was addressed in the hand (with which he was perfectly acquainted) of his Roman correspondent. What was stranger still, a case had arrived by the same train, large enough and heavy enough to contain the Hercules; and this case had been taken to an address now undiscoverable. "The vanman (I regret to say it) had been drinking, and his language was such as I could never bring myself to repeat. He was at once discharged by the superintendent of the line, who behaved most properly throughout, and is to make enquiries at Southampton. In the meanwhile, what was I to do? I left my address and brought the barrel home; but, remembering an old adage, I determined not to open it except in the presence of my lawyer."

"Is that all?" asked Michael. "I don't see any cause to worry. The Hercules has stuck upon the road. It will drop in tomorrow or the day after; and as for the barrel, depend upon it, it's a testimonial from one of your young ladies, and probably contains oysters."

"O, don't speak so loud!" cried the little artist. "It would cost me my place if I were heard to speak lightly of the young ladies; and besides, why oysters from Italy? and why should they come to me addressed in Signor Ricardi's hand?"

"Well, let's have a look at it," said Michael. "Let's roll it forward to the light."

The two men rolled the barrel from the corner, and stood it on end before the fire.

"It's heavy enough to be oysters," remarked Michael judiciously.

"Shall we open it at once?" enquired the artist, who had grown decidedly cheerful under the combined effects of company and gin; and without waiting for a reply, he began to strip as if for a prize-fight, tossed his clerical collar in the wastepaper basket, hung his clerical coat upon a nail, and with a chisel in one hand and a hammer in the other, struck the first blow of the evening.

"That's the style, William Dent," cried Michael. "There's fire for—your money! It may be a romantic visit from one of the young ladies—a sort of Cleopatra business. Have a care and don't stave in Cleopatra's head."

But the sight of Pitman's alacrity was infectious. The lawyer could sit still no longer. Tossing his cigar into the fire, he snatched the instrument from the unwilling hands of the artist, and fell to himself. Soon the sweat stood in beads upon his large, fair brow; his stylish trousers were defaced with iron rust, and the state of his chisel testified to misdirected energies.

A cask is not an easy thing to open, even when you set about it in the right way; when you set about it wrongly, the whole structure must be resolved into its elements. Such was the course pursued alike by the artist and the lawyer. Presently the last hoop had been removed—a couple of smart blows tumbled the staves upon the ground—and what had once been a barrel was no more than a confused heap of broken and distorted boards.

In the midst of these, a certain dismal something, swathed in blankets, remained for an instant upright, and then toppled to one side and heavily collapsed before the fire. Even as the thing subsided, an eyeglass tingled to the floor and rolled toward the screaming Pitman.

"Hold your tongue!" said Michael. He dashed to the house door and locked it; then, with a pale face and bitten lip, he drew near, pulled aside a corner of the swathing blanket, and recoiled, shuddering. There was a long silence in the studio.

"Now tell me," said Michael, in a low voice: "Had you any hand in it?" and he pointed to the body.

The little artist could only utter broken and disjointed sounds.

Michael poured some gin into a glass. "Drink that," he said. "Don't be afraid of me. I'm your friend through thick and thin."

Pitman put the liquor down untasted.

"I swear before God," he said, "this is another mystery to me. In my worst fears I never dreamed of such a thing. I would not lay a finger on a sucking infant."

"That's all square," said Michael, with a sigh of huge relief. "I believe you, old boy." And he shook the artist warmly by the hand. "I thought for a moment," he added with rather a ghastly smile, "I thought for a moment you might have made away with Mr Semitopolis."

"It would make no difference if I had," groaned Pitman. "All is at an end for me. There's the writing on the wall."

"To begin with," said Michael, "let's get him out of sight; for to be quite plain with you, Pitman, I don't like your friend's appearance." And with that the lawyer shuddered. "Where can we put it?"

"You might put it in the closet there—if you could bear to touch it," answered the artist.

"Somebody has to do it, Pitman," returned the lawyer; "and it seems as if it had to be me. You go over to the table, turn your back, and mix me a grog; that's a fair division of labour."

About ninety seconds later the closet-door was heard to shut.

"There," observed Michael, "that's more homelike. You can turn now, my pallid Pitman. Is this the grog?" he ran on. "Heaven forgive you, it's a lemonade."

"But, O, Finsbury, what are we to do with it?" wailed the artist, laying a clutching hand upon the lawyer's arm.

"Do with it?" repeated Michael. "Bury it in one of your flowerbeds, and erect one of your own statues for a monument. I tell you we should look devilish romantic shovelling out the sod by the moon's pale ray. Here, put some gin in this."

"I beg of you, Mr Finsbury, do not trifle with my misery," cried Pitman. "You see before you a man who has been all his life—I do not hesitate to say it—imminently respectable. Even in this solemn hour I can lay my hand upon my heart without a blush. Except on the really trifling point of the smuggling of the Hercules (and even of that I now humbly repent), my life has been entirely fit for publication. I never feared the light," cried the little man; "and now—now—!"

"Cheer up, old boy," said Michael. "I assure you we should count this little contretemps a trifle at the office; it's the sort of thing that may occur to any one; and if you're perfectly sure you had no hand in it—"

"What language am I to find—" began Pitman.

"O, I'll do that part of it," interrupted Michael, "you have no experience. But the point is this: If—or rather since—you know nothing of the crime, since the—the party in the closet—is neither your father, nor your brother, nor your creditor, nor your mother-in-law, nor what they call an injured husband—"

"O, my dear sir!" interjected Pitman, horrified.

"Since, in short," continued the lawyer, "you had no possible interest in the crime, we have a perfectly free field before us and a safe game to play. Indeed, the problem is really entertaining; it is one I have long contemplated in the light of an A. B. case; here it is at last under my hand in specie; and I mean to pull you through. Do you hear that?—I mean to pull you through. Let me see: it's a long time since I have had what I call a genuine holiday; I'll send an excuse tomorrow to the office. We had best be lively," he added significantly; "for we must not spoil the market for the other man."

"What do you mean?" enquired Pitman. "What other man? The inspector of police?"

"Damn the inspector of police!" remarked his companion. "If you won't take the short cut and bury this in your back garden, we must find some one who will bury it in his. We must place the affair, in short, in the hands of some one with fewer scruples and more resources."

"A private detective, perhaps?" suggested Pitman.

"There are times when you fill me with pity," observed the lawyer. "By the way, Pitman," he added in another key, "I have always regretted that you have no piano in this den of yours. Even if you don't play yourself, your friends might like to entertain themselves with a little music while you were mudding."

"I shall get one at once if you like," said Pitman nervously, anxious to please. "I play the fiddle a little as it is."

"I know you do," said Michael; "but what's the fiddle—above all as you play it? What you want is polyphonic music. And I'll tell you what it is—since it's too late for you to buy a piano I'll give you mine."

"Thank you," said the artist blankly. "You will give me yours? I am sure it's very good in you."

"Yes, I'll give you mine," continued Michael, "for the inspector of police to play on while his men are digging up your back garden."

Pitman stared at him in pained amazement.

"No, I'm not insane," Michael went on. "I'm playful, but quite coherent. See here, Pitman: follow me one half minute. I mean to profit by the refreshing fact that we are really and truly innocent; nothing but the presence of the—you know what—connects us with the crime; once let us get rid of it, no matter how, and there is no possible clue to trace us by. Well, I give you my piano; we'll bring it round this very night. Tomorrow we rip the fittings out, deposit the—our friend—inside, plump the whole on a cart, and carry it to the chambers of a young gentleman whom I know by sight."

"Whom do you know by sight?" repeated Pitman.

"And what is more to the purpose," continued Michael, "whose chambers I know better than he does himself. A friend of mine—I call him my friend for brevity; he is now, I understand, in Demerara and (most likely) in gaol—was the previous occupant. I defended him, and I got him off too—all saved but honour; his assets were nil, but he gave me what he had, poor gentleman, and along with the rest—the key of his chambers. It's there that I propose to leave the piano and, shall we say, Cleopatra?"

"It seems very wild," said Pitman. "And what will become of the poor young gentleman whom you know by sight?"

"It will do him good,"—said Michael cheerily. "Just what he wants to steady him."

"But, my dear sir, he might be involved in a charge of—a charge of murder," gulped the artist.

"Well, he'll be just where we are," returned the lawyer. "He's innocent, you see. What hangs people, my dear Pitman, is the unfortunate circumstance of guilt."

"But indeed, indeed," pleaded Pitman, "the whole scheme appears to me so wild. Would it not be safer, after all, just to send for the police?"

"And make a scandal?" enquired Michael. "'The Chelsea Mystery; alleged innocence of Pitman'? How would that do at the Seminary?"

"It would imply my discharge," admitted the drawing-master. "I cannot deny that."

"And besides," said Michael, "I am not going to embark in such a business and have no fun for my money."

"O, my dear sir, is that a proper spirit?" cried Pitman.

"O, I only said that to cheer you up," said the unabashed Michael. "Nothing like a little judicious levity. But it's quite needless to discuss. If you mean to follow my advice, come on, and let us get the piano at once. If you don't, just drop me the word, and I'll leave you to deal with the whole thing according to your better judgement."

"You know perfectly well that I depend on you entirely," returned Pitman. "But O, what a night is before me with that—horror in my studio! How am I to think of it on my pillow?"

"Well, you know, my piano will be there too," said Michael. "That'll raise the average."

An hour later a cart came up the lane, and the lawyer's piano—a momentous Broadwood grand—was deposited in Mr Pitman's studio.

Chapter 8   In Which Michael Finsbury Enjoys a Holiday

Punctually at eight o'clock next morning the lawyer rattled (according to previous appointment) on the studio door. He found the artist sadly altered for the worse—bleached, bloodshot, and chalky—a man upon wires, the tail of his haggard eye still wandering to the closet. Nor was the professor of drawing less inclined to wonder at his friend. Michael was usually attired in the height of fashion, with a certain mercantile brilliancy best described perhaps as stylish; nor could anything be said against him, as a rule, but that he looked a trifle too like a wedding guest to be quite a gentleman. Today he had fallen altogether from these heights. He wore a flannel shirt of washed-out shepherd's tartan, and a suit of reddish tweeds, of the colour known to tailors as "heather mixture"; his neckcloth was black, and tied loosely in a sailor's knot; a rusty ulster partly concealed these advantages; and his feet were shod with rough walking boots. His hat was an old soft felt, which he removed with a flourish as he entered.

"Here I am, William Dent!" he cried, and drawing from his pocket two little wisps of reddish hair, he held them to his cheeks like side whiskers and danced about the studio with the filmy graces of a ballet-girl.

Pitman laughed sadly. "I should never have known you," said he.

"Nor were you intended to," returned Michael, replacing his false whiskers in his pocket. "Now we must overhaul you and your wardrobe, and disguise you up to the nines."

"Disguise!" cried the artist. "Must I indeed disguise myself. Has it come to that?"

"My dear creature," returned his companion, "disguise is the spice of life. What is life, passionately exclaimed a French philosopher, without the pleasures of disguise? I don't say it's always good taste, and I know it's unprofessional; but what's the odds, downhearted drawing-master? It has to be. We have to leave a false impression on the minds of many persons, and in particular on the mind of Mr Gideon Forsyth—the young gentleman I know by sight—if he should have the bad taste to be at home."

"If he be at home?" faltered the artist. "That would be the end of all."

"Won't matter a d—," returned Michael airily. "Let me see your clothes, and I'll make a new man of you in a jiffy."

In the bedroom, to which he was at once conducted,

Michael examined Pitman's poor and scanty wardrobe with a humorous eye, picked out a short jacket of black alpaca, and presently added to that a pair of summer trousers which somehow took his fancy as incongruous. Then, with the garments in his hand, he scrutinized the artist closely.

"I don't like that clerical collar," he remarked. "Have you nothing else?"

The professor of drawing pondered for a moment, and then brightened; "I have a pair of low-necked shirts," he said, "that I used to wear in Paris as a student. They are rather loud."

"The very thing!" ejaculated Michael. "You'll look perfectly beastly. Here are spats, too," he continued, drawing forth a pair of those offensive little gaiters. "Must have spats! And now you jump into these, and whistle a tune at the window for (say) three-quarters of an hour. After that you can rejoin me on the field of glory."

So saying, Michael returned to the studio. It was the morning of the easterly gale; the wind blew shrilly among the statues in the garden, and drove the rain upon the skylight in the studio ceiling; and at about the same moment of the time when Morris attacked the hundredth version of his uncle's signature in Bloomsbury, Michael, in Chelsea, began to rip the wires out of the Broadwood grand.

Three-quarters of an hour later Pitman was admitted, to find the closet-door standing open, the closet untenanted, and the piano discreetly shut.

"It's a remarkably heavy instrument," observed Michael, and turned to consider his friend's disguise. "You must shave off that beard of yours," he said.

"My beard!" cried Pitman. "I cannot shave my beard. I cannot tamper with my appearance—my principals would object. They hold very strong views as to the appearance of the professors—young ladies are considered so romantic. My beard was regarded as quite a feature when I went about the place. It was regarded," said the artist, with rising colour, "it was regarded as unbecoming."

"You can let it grow again," returned Michael, "and then you'll be so precious ugly that they'll raise your salary."

"But I don't want to be ugly," cried the artist.

"Don't be an ass," said Michael, who hated beards and was delighted to destroy one. "Off with it like a man!"

"Of course, if you insist," said Pitman; and then he sighed, fetched some hot water from the kitchen, and setting a glass upon his easel, first clipped his beard with scissors and then shaved his chin. He could not conceal from himself, as he regarded the result, that his last claims to manhood had been sacrificed, but Michael seemed delighted.

"A new man, I declare!" he cried. "When I give you the window glass spectacles I have in my pocket, you'll be the beau ideal of a French commercial traveller."

Pitman did not reply, but continued to gaze disconsolately on his image in the glass.

"Do you know," asked Michael, "what the Governor of South Carolina said to the Governor of North Carolina? 'It's a long time between drinks,' observed that powerful thinker; and if you will put your hand into the top left-hand pocket of my ulster, I have an impression you will find a flask of brandy. Thank you, Pitman," he added, as he filled out a glass for each. "Now you will give me news of this."

The artist reached out his hand for the water-jug, but Michael arrested the movement.

"Not if you went upon your knees!" he cried. "This is the finest liqueur brandy in Great Britain."

Pitman put his lips to it, set it down again, and sighed.

"Well, I must say you're the poorest companion for a holiday!" cried Michael. "If that's all you know of brandy, you shall have no more of it; and while I finish the flask, you may as well begin business. Come to think of it," he broke off, "I have made an abominable error: you should have ordered the cart before you were disguised. Why, Pitman, what the devil's the use of you? why couldn't you have reminded me of that?"

"I never even knew there was a cart to be ordered," said the artist. "But I can take off the disguise again," he suggested eagerly.

"You would find it rather a bother to put on your beard," observed the lawyer. "No, it's a false step; the sort of thing that hangs people," he continued, with eminent cheerfulness, as he sipped his brandy; "and it can't be retraced now. Off to the mews with you, make all the arrangements; they're to take the piano from here, cart it to Victoria, and dispatch it thence by rail to Cannon Street, to lie till called for in the name of Fortune du Boisgobey."

"Isn't that rather an awkward name?" pleaded Pitman.

"Awkward?" cried Michael scornfully. "It would hang us both! Brown is both safer and easier to pronounce. Call it Brown."

"I wish," said Pitman, "for my sake, I wish you wouldn't talk so much of hanging."

"Talking about it's nothing, my boy!" returned Michael. "But take your hat and be off, and mind and pay everything beforehand."

Left to himself, the lawyer turned his attention for some time exclusively to the liqueur brandy, and his spirits, which had been pretty fair all morning, now prodigiously rose. He proceeded to adjust his whiskers finally before the glass. "Devilish rich," he remarked, as he contemplated his reflection. "I look like a purser's mate." And at that moment the window glass spectacles (which he had hitherto destined for Pitman) flashed into his mind; he put them on, and fell in love with the effect. "Just what I required," he said. "I wonder what I look like now? A humorous novelist, I should think," and he began to practise divers characters of walk, naming them to himself as—he proceeded. "Walk of a humorous novelist—but that would require an umbrella. Walk of a purser's mate. Walk of an Australian colonist revisiting the scenes of childhood. Walk of Sepoy colonel, ditto, ditto. And in the midst of the Sepoy colonel (which was an excellent assumption, although inconsistent with the style of his make-up), his eye lighted on the piano. This instrument was made to lock both at the top and at the keyboard, but the key of the latter had been mislaid. Michael opened it and ran his fingers over the dumb keys. "Fine instrument—full, rich tone," he observed, and he drew in a seat.

When Mr Pitman returned to the studio, he was appalled to observe his guide, philosopher, and friend performing miracles of execution on the silent grand.

"Heaven help me!" thought the little man, "I fear he has been drinking! Mr Finsbury," he said aloud; and Michael, without rising, turned upon him a countenance somewhat flushed, encircled with the bush of the red whiskers, and bestridden by the spectacles. "Capriccio in B-flat on the departure of a friend," said he, continuing his noiseless evolutions.

Indignation awoke in the mind of Pitman. "Those spectacles were to be mine," he cried. "They are an essential part of my disguise."

"I am going to wear them myself," replied Michael; and he added, with some show of truth, "There would be a devil of a lot of suspicion aroused if we both wore spectacles."

"O, well," said the assenting Pitman, "I rather counted on them; but of course, if you insist. And at any rate, here is the cart at the door."

While the men were at work, Michael concealed himself in the closet among the debris of the barrel and the wires of the piano; and as soon as the coast was clear the pair sallied forth by the lane, jumped into a hansom in the King's Road, and were driven rapidly toward town. It was still cold and raw and boisterous; the rain beat strongly in their faces, but Michael refused to have the glass let down; he had now suddenly donned the character of cicerone, and pointed out and lucidly commented on the sights of London, as they drove.

"My dear fellow," he said, "you don't seem to know anything of your native city. Suppose we visited the Tower? No? Well, perhaps it's a trifle out of our way. But, anyway—Here, cabby, drive round by Trafalgar Square!" And on that historic battlefield he insisted on drawing up, while he criticized the statues and gave the artist many curious details (quite new to history) of the lives of the celebrated men they represented.

It would be difficult to express what Pitman suffered in the cab: cold, wet, terror in the capital degree, a grounded distrust of the commander under whom he served, a sense of imprudency in the matter of the low-necked shirt, a bitter sense of the decline and fall involved in the deprivation of his beard, all these were among the ingredients of the bowl. To reach the restaurant, for which they were deviously steering, was the first relief. To hear Michael bespeak a private room was a second and a still greater. Nor, as they mounted the stair under the guidance of an unintelligible alien, did he fail to note with gratitude the fewness of the persons present, or the still more cheering fact that the greater part of these were exiles from the land of France. It was thus a blessed thought that none of them would be connected with the Seminary; for even the French professor, though admittedly a Papist, he could scarce imagine frequenting so rakish an establishment.

The alien introduced them into a small bare room with a single table, a sofa, and a dwarfish fire; and Michael called promptly for more coals and a couple of brandies and sodas.

"O, no," said Pitman, "surely not—no more to drink."

"I don't know what you would be at," said Michael plaintively. "It's positively necessary to do something; and one shouldn't smoke before meals. I thought that was understood. You seem to have no idea of hygiene." And he compared his watch with the clock upon the chimney-piece.

Pitman fell into bitter musing; here he was, ridiculously shorn, absurdly disguised, in the company of a drunken man in spectacles, and waiting for a champagne luncheon in a restaurant painfully foreign. What would his principals think, if they could see him? What if they knew his tragic and deceitful errand?

From these reflections he was aroused by the entrance of the alien with the brandies and sodas. Michael took one and bade the waiter pass the other to his friend.

Pitman waved it from him with his hand. "Don't let me lose all self-respect," he said.

"Anything to oblige a friend," returned Michael. "But I'm not going to drink alone. Here," he added to the waiter, "you take it." And, then, touching glasses, "The health of Mr Gideon Forsyth," said he.

"Meestare Gidden Borsye," replied the waiter, and he tossed off the liquor in four gulps.

"Have another?" said Michael, with undisguised interest. "I never saw a man drink faster. It restores one's confidence in the human race.

But the waiter excused himself politely, and, assisted by some one from without, began to bring in lunch.

Michael made an excellent meal, which he washed down with a bottle of Heidsieck's dry monopole. As for the artist, he was far too uneasy to eat, and his companion flatly refused to let him share in the champagne unless he did.

"One of us must stay sober," remarked the lawyer, "and I won't give you champagne on the strength of a leg of grouse. I have to be cautious," he added confidentially. "One drunken man, excellent business—two drunken men, all my eye."

On the production of coffee and departure of the waiter, Michael might have been observed to make portentous efforts after gravity of mien. He looked his friend in the face (one eye perhaps a trifle off), and addressed him thickly but severely.

"Enough of this fooling," was his not inappropriate exordium. "To business. Mark me closely. I am an Australian. My name is John Dickson, though you mightn't think it from my unassuming appearance. You will be relieved to hear that I am rich, sir, very rich. You can't go into this sort of thing too thoroughly, Pitman; the whole secret is preparation, and I can get up my biography from the beginning, and I could tell it you now, only I have forgotten it."

"Perhaps I'm stupid—" began Pitman.

"That's it!" cried Michael. "Very stupid; but rich too—richer than I am. I thought you would enjoy it, Pitman, so I've arranged that you were to be literally wallowing in wealth. But then, on the other hand, you're only an American, and a maker of india-rubber overshoes at that. And the worst of it is—why should I conceal it from you?—the worst of it is that you're called Ezra Thomas. Now," said Michael, with a really appalling seriousness of manner, "tell me who we are."

The unfortunate little man was cross-examined till he knew these facts by heart.

"There!" cried the lawyer. "Our plans are laid. Thoroughly consistent—that's the great thing."

"But I don't understand," objected Pitman.

"O, you'll understand right enough when it comes to the point," said Michael, rising.

"There doesn't seem any story to it," said the artist.

"We can invent one as we go along," returned the lawyer.

"But I can't invent," protested Pitman. "I never could invent in all my life."

"You'll find you'll have to, my boy," was Michael's easy

comment, and he began calling for the waiter, with whom he at once resumed a sparkling conversation.

It was a downcast little man that followed him. "Of course he is very clever, but can I trust him in such a state?" he asked himself. And when they were once more in a hansom, he took heart of grace.

"Don't you think," he faltered, "it would be wiser, considering all things, to put this business off?"

"Put off till tomorrow what can be done today?" cried Michael, with indignation. "Never heard of such a thing! Cheer up, it's all right, go in and win—there's a lion-hearted Pitman!"

At Cannon Street they enquired for Mr Brown's piano, which had duly arrived, drove thence to a neighbouring mews, where they contracted for a cart, and while that was being got ready, took shelter in the harness-room beside the stove. Here the lawyer presently toppled against the wall and fell into a gentle slumber; so that Pitman found himself launched on his own resources in the midst of several staring loafers, such as love to spend unprofitable days about a stable.

"Rough day, sir," observed one. "Do you go far?"

"Yes, it's a—rather a rough day," said the artist; and then, feeling that he must change the conversation, "My friend is an Australian; he is very impulsive," he added.

"An Australian?" said another. "I've a brother myself in Melbourne. Does your friend come from that way at all?"

"No, not exactly," replied the artist, whose ideas of the

geography of New Holland were a little scattered. "He lives immensely far inland, and is very rich."

The loafers gazed with great respect upon the slumbering colonist.

"Well," remarked the second speaker, "it's a mighty big place, is Australia. Do you come from thereaway too?"

"No, I do not," said Pitman. "I do not, and I don't want to," he added irritably. And then, feeling some diversion needful, he fell upon Michael and shook him up.

"Hullo," said the lawyer, "what's wrong?"

"The cart is nearly ready," said Pitman sternly. "I will not allow you to sleep."

"All right—no offence, old man," replied Michael, yawning. "A little sleep never did anybody any harm; I feel comparatively sober now. But what's all the hurry?" he added, looking round him glassily. "I don't see the cart, and I've forgotten where we left the piano."

What more the lawyer might have said, in the confidence of the moment, is with Pitman a matter of tremulous conjecture to this day; but by the most blessed circumstance the cart was then announced, and Michael must bend the forces of his mind to the more difficult task of rising.

"Of course you'll drive," he remarked to his companion, as he clambered on the vehicle.

"I drive!" cried Pitman. "I never did such a thing in my life. I cannot drive."

"Very well," responded Michael with entire composure, "neither can I see. But just as you like. Anything to oblige a friend."

A glimpse of the ostler's darkening countenance decided Pitman. "All right," he said desperately, "you drive. I'll tell you where to go."

On Michael in the character of charioteer (since this is not intended to be a novel of adventure) it would be superfluous to dwell at length. Pitman, as he sat holding on and gasping counsels, sole witness of this singular feat, knew not whether most to admire the driver's valour or his undeserved good fortune. But the latter at least prevailed, the cart reached Cannon Street without disaster; and Mr Brown's piano was speedily and cleverly got on board.

"Well, sir," said the leading porter, smiling as he mentally reckoned up a handful of loose silver, "that's a mortal heavy piano."

"It's the richness of the tone," returned Michael, as he drove away.

It was but a little distance in the rain, which now fell thick and quiet, to the neighbourhood of Mr Gideon Forsyth's chambers in the Temple. There, in a deserted by-street, Michael drew up the horses and gave them in charge to a blighted shoeblack; and the pair descending from the cart, whereon they had figured so incongruously, set forth on foot for the decisive scene of their adventure. For the first time Michael displayed a shadow of uneasiness.

"Are my whiskers right?" he asked. "It would be the devil and all if I was spotted."

"They are perfectly in their place," returned Pitman, with scant attention. "But is my disguise equally effective? There is nothing more likely than that I should meet some of my patrons."

"O, nobody could tell you without your beard," said Michael. "All you have to do is to remember to speak slow; you speak through your nose already."

"I only hope the young man won't be at home," sighed Pitman.

"And I only hope he'll be alone," returned the lawyer. "It will save a precious sight of manoeuvring."

And sure enough, when they had knocked at the door, Gideon admitted them in person to a room, warmed by a moderate fire, framed nearly to the roof in works connected with the bench of British Themis, and offering, except in one particular, eloquent testimony to the legal zeal of the proprietor. The one particular was the chimney-piece, which displayed a varied assortment of pipes, tobacco, cigar-boxes, and yellow-backed French novels.

"Mr Forsyth, I believe?" It was Michael who thus opened the engagement. "We have come to trouble you with a piece of business. I fear it's scarcely professional—"

"I am afraid I ought to be instructed through a solicitor,"

replied Gideon.

"Well, well, you shall name your own, and the whole affair can be put on a more regular footing tomorrow," replied Michael, taking a chair and motioning Pitman to do the same. "But you see we didn't know any solicitors; we did happen to know of you, and time presses."

"May I enquire, gentlemen," asked Gideon, "to whom it was I am indebted for a recommendation?"

"You may enquire," returned the lawyer, with a foolish laugh; "but I was invited not to tell you—till the thing was done."

"My uncle, no doubt," was the barrister's conclusion.

"My name is John Dickson," continued Michael; "a pretty well-known name in Ballarat; and my friend here is Mr Ezra Thomas, of the United States of America, a wealthy manufacturer of india-rubber overshoes."

"Stop one moment till I make a note of that," said Gideon; any one might have supposed he was an old practitioner.

"Perhaps you wouldn't mind my smoking a cigar?" asked Michael. He had pulled himself together for the entrance; now again there began to settle on his mind clouds of irresponsible humour and incipient slumber; and he hoped (as so many have hoped in the like case) that a cigar would clear him.

"Oh, certainly," cried Gideon blandly. "Try one of mine; I can confidently recommend them." And he handed the box to his client.

"In case I don't make myself perfectly clear," observed the Australian, "it's perhaps best to tell you candidly that I've been lunching. It's a thing that may happen to any one."

"O, certainly," replied the affable barrister. "But please be under no sense of hurry. I can give you," he added, thoughtfully consulting his watch—"yes, I can give you the whole afternoon."

"The business that brings me here," resumed the Australian with gusto, "is devilish delicate, I can tell you. My friend Mr Thomas, being an American of Portuguese extraction, unacquainted with our habits, and a wealthy manufacturer of Broadwood pianos—"

"Broadwood pianos?" cried Gideon, with some surprise. "Dear me, do I understand Mr Thomas to be a member of the firm?"

"O, pirated Broadwoods," returned Michael. "My friend's the American Broadwood."

"But I understood you to say," objected Gideon, "I certainly have it so in my notes—that your friend was a manufacturer of india-rubber overshoes."

"I know it's confusing at first," said the Australian, with a beaming smile. "But he—in short, he combines the two professions. And many others besides—many, many, many others," repeated Mr Dickson, with drunken solemnity. "Mr Thomas's cotton-mills are one of the sights of Tallahassee; Mr Thomas's tobacco-mills are the pride of Richmond, Va.; in short, he's one of my oldest friends, Mr Forsyth, and I lay his case before you with emotion."

The barrister looked at Mr Thomas and was agreeably prepossessed by his open although nervous countenance, and the simplicity and timidity of his manner. "What a people are these Americans!" he thought. "Look at this nervous, weedy, simple little bird in a low-necked shirt, and think of him wielding and directing interests so extended and seemingly incongruous! But had we not better," he observed aloud, "had we not perhaps better approach the facts?"

"Man of business, I perceive, sir!" said the Australian. "Let's approach the facts. It's a breach of promise case."

The unhappy artist was so unprepared for this view of his position that he could scarce suppress a cry.

"Dear me," said Gideon, "they are apt to be very troublesome. Tell me everything about it," he added kindly; "if you require my assistance, conceal nothing."

"You tell him," said Michael, feeling, apparently, that he had done his share. "My friend will tell you all about it," he added to Gideon, with a yawn. "Excuse my closing my eyes a moment; I've been sitting up with a sick friend."

Pitman gazed blankly about the room; rage and despair seethed in his innocent spirit; thoughts of flight, thoughts even of suicide, came and went before him; and still the barrister patiently waited, and still the artist groped in vain for any form of words, however insignificant.

"It's a breach of promise case," he said at last, in a low voice. "I—I am threatened with a breach of promise case." Here, in desperate quest of inspiration, he made a clutch at his beard; his fingers closed upon the unfamiliar smoothness of a shaven chin; and with that, hope and courage (if such expressions could ever have been appropriate in the case of Pitman) conjointly fled. He shook Michael roughly. "Wake up!" he cried, with genuine irritation in his tones. "I cannot do it, and you know I can't."

"You must excuse my friend," said Michael; "he's no hand as a narrator of stirring incident. The case is simple," he went on. "My friend is a man of very strong passions, and accustomed to a simple, patriarchal style of life. You see the thing from here: unfortunate visit to Europe, followed by unfortunate acquaintance with sham foreign count, who has a lovely daughter. Mr Thomas was quite carried away; he proposed, he was accepted, and he wrote—wrote in a style which I am sure he must regret today. If these letters are produced in court, sir, Mr Thomas's character is gone."

"Am I to understand—" began Gideon.

"My dear sir," said the Australian emphatically, "it isn't possible to understand unless you saw them."

"That is a painful circumstance," said Gideon; he glanced pityingly in the direction of the culprit, and, observing on his countenance every mark of confusion, pityingly withdrew his eyes.

"And that would be nothing," continued Mr Dickson sternly, "but I wish—I wish from my heart, sir, I could say that Mr Thomas's hands were clean. He has no excuse; for he was engaged at the time—and is still engaged—to the belle of Constantinople, Ga.. My friend's conduct was unworthy of the brutes that perish."

"Ga.?" repeated Gideon enquiringly.

"A contraction in current use," said Michael. "Ga. for Georgia, in The same way as Co. for Company."

"I was aware it was sometimes so written," returned the barrister, "but not that it was so pronounced."

"Fact, I assure you," said Michael. "You now see for yourself, sir, that if this unhappy person is to be saved, some devilish sharp practice will be needed. There's money, and no desire to spare it. Mr Thomas could write a cheque tomorrow for a hundred thousand. And, Mr Forsyth, there's better than money. The foreign count—Count Tarnow, he calls himself—was formerly a tobacconist in Bayswater, and passed under the humble but expressive name of Schmidt; his daughter—if she is his daughter—there's another point—make a note of that, Mr Forsyth—his daughter at that time actually served in the shop—and she now proposes to marry a man of the eminence of Mr Thomas! Now do you see our game? We know they contemplate a move; and we wish to forestall 'em. Down you go to Hampton Court, where they live, and threaten, or bribe, or both, until you get the letters; if you can't, God help us, we must go to court and Thomas must be exposed. I'll be done with him for one," added the unchivalrous friend.

"There seem some elements of success," said Gideon. "Was Schmidt at all known to the police?"

"We hope so," said Michael. "We have every ground to think so. Mark the neighbourhood—Bayswater! Doesn't Bayswater occur to you as very suggestive?"

For perhaps the sixth time during this remarkable interview, Gideon wondered if he were not becoming light-headed. "I suppose it's just because he has been lunching," he thought; and then added aloud, "To what figure may I go?"

"Perhaps five thousand would be enough for today," said Michael. "And now, sir, do not let me detain you any longer; the afternoon wears on; there are plenty of trains to Hampton Court; and I needn't try to describe to you the impatience of my friend. Here is a five-pound note for current expenses; and here is the address." And Michael began to write, paused, tore up the paper, and put the pieces in his pocket. "I will dictate," he said, "my writing is so uncertain."

Gideon took down the address, "Count Tarnow, Kurnaul Villa, Hampton Court." Then he wrote something else on a sheet of paper. "You said you had not chosen a solicitor," he said. "For a case of this sort, here is the best man in London." And he handed the paper to Michael.

"God bless me!" ejaculated Michael, as he read his own address.

"O, I daresay you have seen his name connected with some rather painful cases," said Gideon. "But he is himself a perfectly honest man, and his capacity is recognized. And now, gentlemen, it only remains for me to ask where I shall communicate with you."

"The Langham, of course," returned Michael. "Till tonight."

"Till tonight," replied Gideon, smiling. "I suppose I may knock you up at a late hour?"

"Any hour, any hour," cried the vanishing solicitor.

"Now there's a young fellow with a head upon his shoulders," he said to Pitman, as soon as they were in the street.

Pitman was indistinctly heard to murmur, "Perfect fool."

"Not a bit of him," returned Michael. "He knows who's the best solicitor in London, and it's not every man can say the same. But, I say, didn't I pitch it in hot?"

Pitman returned no answer.

"Hullo!" said the lawyer, pausing, "what's wrong with the long-suffering Pitman?"

"You had no right to speak of me as you did," the artist broke out; "your language was perfectly unjustifiable; you have wounded me deeply."

"I never said a word about you," replied Michael. "I spoke of Ezra Thomas; and do please remember that there's no such party."

"It's just as hard to bear," said the artist.

But by this time they had reached the corner of the by-street; and there was the faithful shoeblack, standing by the horses' heads with a splendid assumption of dignity; and there was the piano, figuring forlorn upon the cart, while the rain beat upon its unprotected sides and trickled down its elegantly varnished legs.

The shoeblack was again put in requisition to bring five or six strong fellows from the neighbouring public-house; and the last battle of the campaign opened. It is probable that Mr Gideon Forsyth had not yet taken his seat in the train for Hampton Court, before Michael opened the door of the chambers, and the grunting porters deposited the Broadwood grand in the middle of the floor.

"And now," said the lawyer, after he had sent the men about their business, "one more precaution. We must leave him the key of the piano, and we must contrive that he shall find it. Let me see." And he built a square tower of cigars upon the top of the instrument, and dropped the key into the middle.

"Poor young man," said the artist, as they descended the stairs.

"He is in a devil of a position," assented Michael drily. "It'll brace him up."

"And that reminds me," observed the excellent Pitman, "that I fear I displayed a most ungrateful temper. I had no right, I see, to resent expressions, wounding as they were, which were in no sense directed."

"That's all right," cried Michael, getting on the cart. "Not a word more, Pitman. Very proper feeling on your part; no man of self-respect can stand by and hear his alias insulted."

The rain had now ceased, Michael was fairly sober, the body had been disposed of, and the friends were reconciled. The return to the mews was therefore (in comparison with previous stages of the day's adventures) quite a holiday outing; and when they had returned the cart and walked forth again from the stable-yard, unchallenged, and even unsuspected, Pitman drew a deep breath of joy.

"And now," he said, "we can go home."

"Pitman," said the lawyer, stopping short, "your recklessness fills me with concern. What! we have been wet through the greater part of the day, and you propose, in cold blood, to go home! No, sir—hot Scotch."

And taking his friend's arm he led him sternly towards the nearest public-house. Nor was Pitman (I regret to say) wholly unwilling. Now that peace was restored and the body gone, a certain innocent skittishness began to appear in the manners of the artist; and when he touched his steaming glass to Michael's, he giggled aloud like a venturesome schoolgirl at a picnic.

Chapter 9   Glorious Conclusion of Michael Finsbury's Holiday

I know Michael Finsbury personally; my business—I know the awkwardness of having such a man for a lawyer—still it's an old story now, and there is such a thing as gratitude, and, in short, my legal business, although now (I am thankful to say) of quite a placid character, remains entirely in Michael's hands. But the trouble is I have no natural talent for addresses; I learn one for every man—that is friendship's offering; and the friend who subsequently changes his residence is dead to me, memory refusing to pursue him. Thus it comes about that, as I always write to Michael at his office, I cannot swear to his number in the King's Road. Of course (like my neighbours), I have been to dinner there. Of late years, since his accession to wealth, neglect of business, and election to the club, these little festivals have become common. He picks up a few fellows in the smoking-room—all men of Attic wit—myself, for instance, if he has the luck to find me disengaged; a string of hansoms may be observed (by Her Majesty) bowling gaily through St. James's Park; and in a quarter of an hour the party surrounds one of the best appointed boards in London.

But at the time of which we write the house in the King's Road (let us still continue to call it No. 233) was kept very quiet; when Michael entertained guests it was at the halls of Nichol or Verrey that he would convene them, and the door of his private residence remained closed against his friends. The upper storey, which was sunny, was set apart for his father; the drawing-room was never opened; the dining-room was the scene of Michael's life. It is in this pleasant apartment, sheltered from the curiosity of King's Road by wire blinds, and entirely surrounded by the lawyer's unrivalled library of poetry and criminal trials, that we find him sitting down to his dinner after his holiday with Pitman. A spare old lady, with very bright eyes and a mouth humorously compressed, waited upon the lawyer's needs; in every line of her countenance she betrayed the fact that she was an old retainer; in every word that fell from her lips she flaunted the glorious circumstance of a Scottish origin; and the fear with which this powerful combination fills the boldest was obviously no stranger to the bosom of our friend. The hot Scotch having somewhat warmed up the embers of the Heidsieck. It was touching to observe the master's eagerness to pull himself together under the servant's eye; and when he remarked, "I think, Teena, I'll take a brandy and soda," he spoke like a man doubtful of his elocution, and not half certain of obedience.

"No such a thing, Mr Michael," was the prompt return. "Clar't and water."

"Well, well, Teena, I daresay you know best," said the master. "Very fatiguing day at the office, though."

"What?" said the retainer, "ye never were near the office!"

"O, yes, I was though; I was repeatedly along Fleet Street," returned Michael.

"Pretty pliskies ye've been at this day!" cried the old lady, with humorous alacrity; and then, "Take care—don't break my crystal!" she cried, as the lawyer came within an ace of knocking the glasses off the table.

"And how is he keeping?" asked Michael.

"O, just the same, Mr Michael, just the way he'll be till the end, worthy man!" was the reply. "But ye'll not be the first that's asked me that the day."

"No?" said the lawyer. "Who else?"

"Ay, that's a joke, too," said Teena grimly. "A friend of yours: Mr Morris."

"Morris! What was the little beggar wanting here?" enquired Michael.

"Wanting? To see him," replied the housekeeper, completing her meaning by a movement of the thumb toward the upper storey. "That's by his way of it; but I've an idee of my own. He tried to bribe me, Mr Michael. Bribe—me!" she repeated, with inimitable scorn. "That's no kind of a young gentleman."

"Did he so?" said Michael. "I bet he didn't offer much."

"No more he did," replied Teena; nor could any subsequent questioning elicit from her the sum with which the thrifty leather merchant had attempted to corrupt her. "But I sent him about his business," she said gallantly. "He'll not come here again in a hurry."

"He mustn't see my father, you know; mind that!" said Michael. "I'm not going to have any public exhibition to a little beast like him."

"No fear of me lettin' him," replied the trusty one. "But the joke is this, Mr Michael—see, ye're upsettin' the sauce, that's a clean tablecloth—the best of the joke is that he thinks your father's dead and you're keepin' it dark."

Michael whistled. "Set a thief to catch a thief," said he.

"Exac'ly what I told him!" cried the delighted dame.

"I'll make him dance for that," said Michael.

"Couldn't ye get the law of him some way?" suggested Teena truculently.

"No, I don't think I could, and I'm quite sure I don't want to," replied Michael. "But I say, Teena, I really don't believe this claret's wholesome; it's not a sound, reliable wine. Give us a brandy and soda, there's a good soul." Teena's face became like adamant. "Well, then," said the lawyer fretfully, "I won't eat any more dinner."

"Ye can please yourself about that, Mr Michael," said Teena, and began composedly to take away.

"I do wish Teena wasn't a faithful servant!" sighed the

lawyer, as he issued into Kings's Road.

The rain had ceased; the wind still blew, but only with a pleasant freshness; the town, in the clear darkness of the night, glittered with street-lamps and shone with glancing rain-pools. "Come, this is better," thought the lawyer to himself, and he walked on eastward, lending a pleased ear to the wheels and the million footfalls of the city.

Near the end of the King's Road he remembered his brandy and soda, and entered a flaunting public-house. A good many persons were present, a waterman from a cab-stand, half a dozen of the chronically unemployed, a gentleman (in one corner) trying to sell aesthetic photographs out of a leather case to another and very youthful gentleman with a yellow goatee, and a pair of lovers debating some fine shade (in the other). But the centre-piece and great attraction was a little old man, in a black, ready-made surtout, which was obviously a recent purchase. On the marble table in front of him, beside a sandwich and a glass of beer, there lay a battered forage cap. His hand fluttered abroad with oratorical gestures; his voice, naturally shrill, was plainly tuned to the pitch of the lecture room; and by arts, comparable to those of the Ancient Mariner, he was now holding spellbound the barmaid, the waterman, and four of the unemployed.

"I have examined all the theatres in London," he was saying; "and pacing the principal entrances, I have ascertained them to be ridiculously disproportionate to the requirements of their audiences. The doors opened the wrong way—I forget at this moment which it is, but have a note of it at home; they were frequently locked during the performance, and when the auditorium was literally thronged with English people. You have probably not had my opportunities of comparing distant lands; but I can assure you this has been long ago recognized as a mark of aristocratic government. Do you suppose, in a country really self-governed, such abuses could exist? Your own intelligence, however uncultivated, tells you they could not. Take Austria, a country even possibly more enslaved than England. I have myself conversed with one of the survivors of the Ring Theatre, and though his colloquial German was not very good, I succeeded in gathering a pretty clear idea of his opinion of the case. But, what will perhaps interest you still more, here is a cutting on the subject from a Vienna newspaper, which I will now read to you, translating as I go. You can see for yourselves; it is printed in the German character." And he held the cutting out for verification, much as a conjuror passes a trick orange along the front bench.

"Hullo, old gentleman! Is this you?" said Michael, laying his hand upon the orator's shoulder.

The figure turned with a convulsion of alarm, and showed the countenance of Mr Joseph Finsbury.

"You, Michael!" he cried. "There's no one with you, is there?"

"No," replied Michael, ordering a brandy and soda, "there's

nobody with me; whom do you expect?"

"I thought of Morris or John," said the old gentleman, evidently greatly relieved.

"What the devil would I be doing with Morris or John?" cried the nephew.

"There is something in that," returned Joseph. "And I believe I can trust you. I believe you will stand by me."

"I hardly know what you mean," said the lawyer, "but if you are in need of money I am flush."

"It's not that, my dear boy," said the uncle, shaking him by the hand. "I'll tell you all about it afterwards."

"All right," responded the nephew. "I stand treat, Uncle Joseph; what will you have?"

"In that case," replied the old gentleman, "I'll take another sandwich. I daresay I surprise you," he went on, "with my presence in a public-house; but the fact is, I act on a sound but little-known principle of my own—"

"O, it's better known than you suppose," said Michael sipping his brandy and soda. "I always act on it myself when I want a drink."

The old gentleman, who was anxious to propitiate Michael, laughed a cheerless laugh. "You have such a flow of spirits," said he, "I am sure I often find it quite amusing. But regarding this principle of which I was about to speak. It is that of accommodating one's-self to the manners of any land (however humble) in which our lot may be cast. Now, in France, for instance, every one goes to a cafe for his meals; in America, to what is called a 'two-bit house'; in England the people resort to such an institution as the present for refreshment. With sandwiches, tea, and an occasional glass of bitter beer, a man can live luxuriously in London for fourteen pounds twelve shillings per annum."

"Yes, I know," returned Michael, "but that's not including clothes, washing, or boots. The whole thing, with cigars and occasional sprees, costs me over seven hundred a year."

But this was Michael's last interruption. He listened in good-humoured silence to the remainder of his uncle's lecture, which speedily branched to political reform, thence to the theory of the weather-glass, with an illustrative account of a bora in the Adriatic; thence again to the best manner of teaching arithmetic to the deaf-and-dumb; and with that, the sandwich being then no more, explicuit valde feliciter. A moment later the pair issued forth on the King's Road.

"Michael," said his uncle, "the reason that I am here is because I cannot endure those nephews of mine. I find them intolerable."

"I daresay you do," assented Michael, "I never could stand them for a moment."

"They wouldn't let me speak," continued the old gentleman bitterly; "I never was allowed to get a word in edgewise; I was shut up at once with some impertinent remark. They kept me on short allowance of pencils, when I wished to make notes of the most absorbing interest; the daily newspaper was guarded from me like a young baby from a gorilla. Now, you know me, Michael. I live for my calculations; I live for my manifold and ever-changing views of life; pens and paper and the productions of the popular press are to me as important as food and drink; and my life was growing quite intolerable when, in the confusion of that fortunate railway accident at Browndean, I made my escape. They must think me dead, and are trying to deceive the world for the chance of the tontine."

"By the way, how do you stand for money?" asked Michael kindly.

"Pecuniarily speaking, I am rich," returned the old man with cheerfulness. "I am living at present at the rate of one hundred a year, with unlimited pens and paper; the British Museum at which to get books; and all the newspapers I choose to read. But it's extraordinary how little a man of intellectual interest requires to bother with books in a progressive age. The newspapers supply all the conclusions."

"I'll tell you what," said Michael, "come and stay with me."

"Michael," said the old gentleman, "it's very kind of you, but you scarcely understand what a peculiar position I occupy. There are some little financial complications; as a guardian, my efforts were not altogether blessed; and not to put too fine a point upon the matter, I am absolutely in the power of that vile fellow, Morris."

"You should be disguised," cried Michael eagerly; "I will

lend you a pair of window-glass spectacles and some red side-whiskers."

"I had already canvassed that idea," replied the old gentleman, "but feared to awaken remark in my unpretentious lodgings. The aristocracy, I am well aware—"

"But see here," interrupted Michael, "how do you come to have any money at all? Don't make a stranger of me, Uncle Joseph; I know all about the trust, and the hash you made of it, and the assignment you were forced to make to Morris."

Joseph narrated his dealings with the bank.

"O, but I say, this won't do," cried the lawyer. "You've put your foot in it. You had no right to do what you did."

"The whole thing is mine, Michael," protested the old gentleman. "I founded and nursed that business on principles entirely of my own."

"That's all very fine," said the lawyer; "but you made an assignment, you were forced to make it, too; even then your position was extremely shaky; but now, my dear sir, it means the dock."

"It isn't possible," cried Joseph; "the law cannot be so unjust as that?"

"And the cream of the thing," interrupted Michael, with a sudden shout of laughter, "the cream of the thing is this, that of course you've downed the leather business! I must say, Uncle Joseph, you have strange ideas of law, but I like your taste in humour."

"I see nothing to laugh at," observed Mr Finsbury tartly.

"And talking of that, has Morris any power to sign for the firm?" asked Michael.

"No one but myself," replied Joseph.

"Poor devil of a Morris! O, poor devil of a Morris!" cried the lawyer in delight. "And his keeping up the farce that you're at home! O, Morris, the Lord has delivered you into my hands! Let me see, Uncle Joseph, what do you suppose the leather business worth?"

"It was worth a hundred thousand," said Joseph bitterly, "when it was in my hands. But then there came a Scotsman—it is supposed he had a certain talent—it was entirely directed to bookkeeping—no accountant in London could understand a word of any of his books; and then there was Morris, who is perfectly incompetent. And now it is worth very little. Morris tried to sell it last year; and Pogram and Jarris offered only four thousand."

"I shall turn my attention to leather," said Michael with decision.

"You?" asked Joseph. "I advise you not. There is nothing in the whole field of commerce more surprising than the fluctuations of the leather market. Its sensitiveness may be described as morbid."

"And now, Uncle Joseph, what have you done with all that money?" asked the lawyer.

"Paid it into a bank and drew twenty pounds," answered

Mr Finsbury promptly. "Why?"

"Very well," said Michael. "Tomorrow I shall send down a clerk with a cheque for a hundred, and he'll draw out the original sum and return it to the Anglo-Patagonian, with some sort of explanation which I will try to invent for you. That will clear your feet, and as Morris can't touch a penny of it without forgery, it will do no harm to my little scheme."

"But what am I to do?" asked Joseph; "I cannot live upon nothing."

"Don't you hear?" returned Michael. "I send you a cheque for a hundred; which leaves you eighty to go along upon; and when that's done, apply to me again."

"I would rather not be beholden to your bounty all the same," said Joseph, biting at his white moustache. "I would rather live on my own money, since I have it."

Michael grasped his arm. "Will nothing make you believe," he cried, "that I am trying to save you from Dartmoor?"

His earnestness staggered the old man. "I must turn my attention to law," he said; "it will be a new field; for though, of course, I understand its general principles, I have never really applied my mind to the details, and this view of yours, for example, comes on me entirely by surprise. But you may be right, and of course at my time of life—for I am no longer young—any really long term of imprisonment would be highly prejudicial. But, my dear nephew, I have no claim on you; you have no call to support me."

"That's all right," said Michael; "I'll probably get it out of the leather business."

And having taken down the old gentleman's address, Michael left him at the corner of a street.

"What a wonderful old muddler!" he reflected, "and what a singular thing is life! I seem to be condemned to be the instrument of Providence. Let me see; what have I done today? Disposed of a dead body, saved Pitman, saved my Uncle Joseph, brightened up Forsyth, and drunk a devil of a lot of most indifferent liquor. Let's top off with a visit to my cousins, and be the instrument of Providence in earnest. Tomorrow I can turn my attention to leather; tonight I'll just make it lively for 'em in a friendly spirit."

About a quarter of an hour later, as the clocks were striking eleven, the instrument of Providence descended from a hansom, and, bidding the driver wait, rapped at the door of No. 16 John Street.

It was promptly opened by Morris.

"O, it's you, Michael," he said, carefully blocking up the narrow opening: "it's very late."

Michael without a word reached forth, grasped Morris warmly by the hand, and gave it so extreme a squeeze that the sullen householder fell back. Profiting by this movement, the lawyer obtained a footing in the lobby and marched into the dining-room, with Morris at his heels.

"Where's my Uncle Joseph?" demanded Michael, sitting

down in the most comfortable chair.

"He's not been very well lately," replied Morris; "he's staying at Browndean; John is nursing him; and I am alone, as you see."

Michael smiled to himself. "I want to see him on particular business," he said.

"You can't expect to see my uncle when you won't let me see your father," returned Morris.

"Fiddlestick," said Michael. "My father is my father; but Joseph is just as much my uncle as he's yours; and you have no right to sequestrate his person."

"I do no such thing," said Morris doggedly. "He is not well, he is dangerously ill and nobody can see him."

"I'll tell you what, then," said Michael. "I'll make a clean breast of it. I have come down like the opossum, Morris; I have come to compromise."

Poor Morris turned as pale as death, and then a flush of wrath against the injustice of man's destiny dyed his very temples. "What do you mean?" he cried, "I don't believe a word of it." And when Michael had assured him of his seriousness, "Well, then," he cried, with another deep flush, "I won't; so you can put that in your pipe and smoke it."

"Oho!" said Michael queerly. "You say your uncle is dangerously ill, and you won't compromise? There's something very fishy about that."

"What do you mean?" cried Morris hoarsely.

"I only say it's fishy," returned Michael, "that is, pertaining to the finny tribe."

"Do you mean to insinuate anything?" cried Morris stormily, trying the high hand.

"Insinuate?" repeated Michael. "O, don't let's begin to use awkward expressions! Let us drown our differences in a bottle, like two affable kinsmen. *The Two Affable Kinsmen*, sometimes attributed to Shakespeare," he added.

Morris's mind was labouring like a mill. "Does he suspect? or is this chance and stuff? Should I soap, or should I bully? Soap," he concluded. "It gains time. Well," said he aloud, and with rather a painful affectation of heartiness, "it's long since we have had an evening together, Michael; and though my habits (as you know) are very temperate, I may as well make an exception. Excuse me one moment till I fetch a bottle of whisky from the cellar."

"No whisky for me," said Michael; "a little of the old still champagne or nothing."

For a moment Morris stood irresolute, for the wine was very valuable: the next he had quitted the room without a word. His quick mind had perceived his advantage; in thus dunning him for the cream of the cellar, Michael was playing into his hand. "One bottle?" he thought. "By George, I'll give him two! This is no moment for economy; and once the beast is drunk, it's strange if I don't wring his secret out of him."

With two bottles, accordingly, he returned. Glasses were

produced, and Morris filled them with hospitable grace.

"I drink to you, cousin!" he cried gaily. "Don't spare the wine-cup in my house."

Michael drank his glass deliberately, standing at the table; filled it again, and returned to his chair, carrying the bottle along with him.

"The spoils of war!" he said apologetically. "The weakest goes to the wall. Science, Morris, science." Morris could think of no reply, and for an appreciable interval silence reigned. But two glasses of the still champagne produced a rapid change in Michael.

"There's a want of vivacity about you, Morris," he observed. "You may be deep; but I'll be hanged if you're vivacious!"

"What makes you think me deep?" asked Morris with an air of pleased simplicity.

"Because you won't compromise," said the lawyer. "You're deep dog, Morris, very deep dog, won't compromise—remarkable deep dog. And a very good glass of wine; it's the only respectable feature in the Finsbury family, this wine; rarer thing than a title—much rarer. Now a man with glass wine like this in cellar, I wonder why won't compromise?"

"Well, YOU wouldn't compromise before, you know," said the smiling Morris. "Turn about is fair play."

"I wonder why I wouldn't compromise? I wonder why YOU wouldn't?" enquired Michael. "I wonder why we each think the other wouldn't? It is quite a remarrable—remarkable problem," he added, triumphing over oral obstacles, not without obvious pride. "Wonder what we each think—don't you?"

"What do you suppose to have been my reason?" asked Morris adroitly.

Michael looked at him and winked. "That's cool," said he. "Next thing, you'll ask me to help you out of the muddle. I know I'm emissary of Providence, but not that kind! You get out of it yourself, like Aesop and the other fellow. Must be dreadful muddle for young orphan o' forty; leather business and all!"

"I am sure I don't know what you mean," said Morris.

"Not sure I know myself," said Michael. "This is exc'lent vintage, sir—exc'lent vintage. Nothing against the tipple. Only thing: here's a valuable uncle disappeared. Now, what I want to know: where's valuable uncle?"

"I have told you: he is at Browndean," answered Morris, furtively wiping his brow, for these repeated hints began to tell upon him cruelly.

"Very easy say Brown—Browndee—not so easy after all!" cried Michael. "Easy say; anything's easy say, when you can say it. What I don' like's total disappearance of an uncle. Not businesslike." And he wagged his head.

"It is all perfectly simple," returned Morris, with laborious calm. "There is no mystery. He stays at Browndean, where he got a shake in the accident."

"Ah!" said Michael, "got devil of a shake!"

"Why do you say that?" cried Morris sharply.

"Best possible authority. Told me so yourself," said the lawyer. "But if you tell me contrary now, of course I'm bound to believe either the one story or the other. Point is I've upset this bottle, still champagne's exc'lent thing carpet—point is, is valuable uncle dead—an'—bury?"

Morris sprang from his seat. "What's that you say?" he gasped.

"I say it's exc'lent thing carpet," replied Michael, rising. "Exc'lent thing promote healthy action of the skin. Well, it's all one, anyway. Give my love to Uncle Champagne."

"You're not going away?" said Morris.

"Awf'ly sorry, ole man. Got to sit up sick friend," said the wavering Michael.

"You shall not go till you have explained your hints," returned Morris fiercely. "What do you mean? What brought you here?"

"No offence, I trust," said the lawyer, turning round as he opened the door; "only doing my duty as shemishery of Providence."

Groping his way to the front-door, he opened it with some difficulty, and descended the steps to the hansom. The tired driver looked up as he approached, and asked where he was to go next.

Michael observed that Morris had followed him to the

steps; a brilliant inspiration came to him. "Anything t' give pain," he reflected.... "Drive Shcotlan' Yard," he added aloud, holding to the wheel to steady himself; "there's something devilish fishy, cabby, about those cousins. Mush' be cleared up! Drive Shcotlan' Yard."

"You don't mean that, sir," said the man, with the ready sympathy of the lower orders for an intoxicated gentleman. "I had better take you home, sir; you can go to Scotland Yard tomorrow."

"Is it as friend or as perffessional man you advise me not to go Shcotlan' Yard t' night?" enquired Michael. "All righ, never min' Shcotlan' Yard, drive Gaiety bar."

"The Gaiety bar is closed," said the man.

"Then home," said Michael, with the same cheerfulness.

"Where to, sir?"

"I don't remember, I'm sure," said Michael, entering the vehicle, "drive Shcotlan' Yard and ask."

"But you'll have a card," said the man, through the little aperture in the top, "give me your card-case."

"What imagi—imagination in a cabby!" cried the lawyer, producing his card-case, and handing it to the driver.

The man read it by the light of the lamp. "Mr Michael Finsbury, 233 King's Road, Chelsea. Is that it, sir?"

"Right you are," cried Michael, "drive there if you can see way."

Chapter 10   Gideon Forsyth and the Broadwood Grand

The reader has perhaps read that remarkable work, *Who Put Back the Clock?* by E. H. B., which appeared for several days upon the railway bookstalls and then vanished entirely from the face of the earth. Whether eating Time makes the chief of his diet out of old editions; whether Providence has passed a special enactment on behalf of authors; or whether these last have taken the law into their own hand, bound themselves into a dark conspiracy with a password, which I would die rather than reveal, and night after night sally forth under some vigorous leader, such as Mr James Payn or Mr Walter Besant, on their task of secret spoliation—certain it is, at least, that the old editions pass, giving place to new. To the proof, it is believed there are now only three copies extant of *Who Put Back the Clock?*, one in the British Museum, successfully concealed by a wrong entry in the catalogue; another in one of the cellars (the cellar where the music accumulates) of the Advocates' Library at Edinburgh;

and a third, bound in morocco, in the possession of Gideon Forsyth. To account for the very different fate attending this third exemplar, the readiest theory is to suppose that Gideon admired the tale. How to explain that admiration might appear (to those who have perused the work) more difficult; but the weakness of a parent is extreme, and Gideon (and not his uncle, whose initials he had humorously borrowed) was the author of *Who Put Back the Clock?*. He had never acknowledged it, or only to some intimate friends while it was still in proof; after its appearance and alarming failure, the modesty of the novelist had become more pressing, and the secret was now likely to be better kept than that of the authorship of *Waverley*.

A copy of the work (for the date of my tale is already yesterday) still figured in dusty solitude in the bookstall at Waterloo; and Gideon, as he passed with his ticket for Hampton Court, smiled contemptuously at the creature of his thoughts. What an idle ambition was the author's! How far beneath him was the practice of that childish art! With his hand closing on his first brief, he felt himself a man at last; and the muse who presides over the police romance, a lady presumably of French extraction, fled his neighbourhood, and returned to join the dance round the springs of Helicon, among her Grecian sisters.

Robust, practical reflection still cheered the young barrister upon his journey. Again and again he selected the little country-house in its islet of great oaks, which he was to make his future home. Like a prudent householder, he projected improvements as he passed; to one he added a stable, to another a tennis-court, a third he supplied with a becoming rustic boathouse.

"How little a while ago," he could not but reflect, "I was a careless young dog with no thought but to be comfortable! I cared for nothing but boating and detective novels. I would have passed an old-fashioned countryhouse with large kitchen-garden, stabling, boathouse, and spacious offices, without so much as a look, and certainly would have made no enquiry as to the drains. How a man ripens with the years!"

The intelligent reader will perceive the ravages of Miss Hazeltine. Gideon had carried Julia straight to Mr Bloomfield's house; and that gentleman, having been led to understand she was the victim of oppression, had noisily espoused her cause. He worked himself into a fine breathing heat; in which, to a man of his temperament, action became needful.

"I do not know which is the worse," he cried, "the fraudulent old villain or the unmanly young cub. I will write to the *Pall Mall* and expose them. Nonsense, sir; they must be exposed! It's a public duty. Did you not tell me the fellow was a Tory? O, the uncle is a Radical lecturer, is he? No doubt the uncle has been grossly wronged. But of course, as you say, that makes a change; it becomes scarce so much a public duty."

And he sought and instantly found a fresh outlet for his alacrity. Miss Hazeltine (he now perceived) must be kept out of the way; his houseboat was lying ready—he had returned but a day or two before from his usual cruise; there was no place like a houseboat for concealment; and that very morning, in the teeth of the easterly gale, Mr and Mrs Bloomfield and Miss Julia Hazeltine had started forth on their untimely voyage. Gideon pled in vain to be allowed to join the party. "No, Gid," said his uncle. "You will be watched; you must keep away from us." Nor had the barrister ventured to contest this strange illusion; for he feared if he rubbed off any of the romance, that Mr Bloomfield might weary of the whole affair. And his discretion was rewarded; for the Squirradical, laying a heavy hand upon his nephew's shoulder, had added these notable expressions: "I see what you are after, Gid. But if you're going to get the girl, you have to work, sir."

These pleasing sounds had cheered the barrister all day, as he sat reading in chambers; they continued to form the groundbase of his manly musings as he was whirled to Hampton Court; even when he landed at the station, and began to pull himself together for his delicate interview, the voice of Uncle Ned and the eyes of Julia were not forgotten.

But now it began to rain surprises: in all Hampton Court there was no Kurnaul Villa, no Count Tarnow, and no count. This was strange; but, viewed in the light of the incoherency of his instructions, not perhaps inexplicable; Mr Dickson had been lunching, and he might have made some fatal oversight in the address. What was the thoroughly prompt, manly, and businesslike step? thought Gideon; and he answered himself at once: "A telegram, very laconic." Speedily the wires were flashing the following very important missive: "Dickson, Langham Hotel. Villa and persons both unknown here, suppose erroneous address; follow self next train.—Forsyth." And at the Langham Hotel, sure enough, with a brow expressive of dispatch and intellectual effort, Gideon descended not long after from a smoking hansom.

I do not suppose that Gideon will ever forget the Langham Hotel. No Count Tarnow was one thing; no John Dickson and no Ezra Thomas, quite another. How, why, and what next, danced in his bewildered brain; from every centre of what we playfully call the human intellect incongruous messages were telegraphed; and before the hubbub of dismay had quite subsided, the barrister found himself driving furiously for his chambers. There was at least a cave of refuge; it was at least a place to think in; and he climbed the stair, put his key in the lock and opened the door, with some approach to hope.

It was all dark within, for the night had some time fallen; but Gideon knew his room, he knew where the matches stood on the end of the chimney-piece; and he advanced boldly, and in so doing dashed himself against a heavy body; where (slightly altering the expressions of the song) no heavy body should have been. There had been nothing there when Gideon went out; he had locked the door behind him, he had found it locked on his return, no one could have entered, the furniture could not have changed its own position. And yet undeniably there was a something there. He thrust out his hands in the darkness. Yes, there was something, something large, something smooth, something cold.

"Heaven forgive me!" said Gideon, "it feels like a piano."

And the next moment he remembered the vestas in his waistcoat pocket and had struck a light. It was indeed a piano that met his doubtful gaze; a vast and costly instrument, stained with the rains of the afternoon and defaced with recent scratches. The light of the vesta was reflected from the varnished sides, like a staice in quiet water; and in the farther end of the room the shadow of that strange visitor loomed bulkily and wavered on the wall.

Gideon let the match burn to his fingers, and the darkness closed once more on his bewilderment. Then with trembling hands he lit the lamp and drew near. Near or far, there was no doubt of the fact: the thing was a piano. There, where by all the laws of God and man it was impossible that it should be—there the thing impudently stood. Gideon threw open the keyboard and struck a chord. Not a sound disturbed the quiet of the room. "Is there anything wrong with me?" he thought, with a pang; and drawing in a seat, obstinately persisted in his attempts to ravish silence, now with sparkling arpeggios, now with a sonata of Beethoven's which (in happier days) he knew to be one of the loudest pieces of that powerful composer. Still not a sound. He gave the Broadwood two great bangs with his clenched first. All was still as the grave.

The young barrister started to his feet.

"I am stark-staring mad," he cried aloud, "and no one knows it but myself. God's worst curse has fallen on me."

His fingers encountered his watch-chain; instantly he had plucked forth his watch and held it to his ear. He could hear it ticking.

"I am not deaf," he said aloud. "I am only insane. My mind has quitted me for ever."

He looked uneasily about the room, and—gazed with lacklustre eyes at the chair in which Mr Dickson had installed himself. The end of a cigar lay near on the fender.

"No," he thought, "I don't believe that was a dream; but God knows my mind is failing rapidly. I seem to be hungry, for instance; it's probably another hallucination. Still I might try. I shall have one more good meal; I shall go to the Cafe Royal, and may possibly be removed from there direct to the asylum."

He wondered with morbid interest, as he descended the stairs, how he would first betray his terrible condition—would he attack a waiter? or eat glass?—and when he had mounted into a cab, he bade the man drive to Nichol's, with a lurking fear that there was no such place.

The flaring, gassy entrance of the cafe speedily set his mind at rest; he was cheered besides to recognize his favourite waiter; his orders appeared to be coherent; the dinner, when it came, was quite a sensible meal, and he ate it with enjoyment.

"Upon my word," he reflected, "I am about tempted to indulge a hope. Have I been hasty? Have I done what Robert Skill would have done?" Robert Skill (I need scarcely mention) was the name of the principal character in *Who Put Back the Clock*?. It had occurred to the author as a brilliant and probable invention; to readers of a critical turn, Robert appeared scarce upon a level with his surname; but it is the difficulty of the police romance, that the reader is always a man of such vastly greater ingenuity than the writer. In the eyes of his creator, however, Robert Skill was a word to conjure with; the thought braced and spurred him; what that brilliant creature would have done Gideon would do also. This frame of mind is not uncommon; the distressed general, the baited divine, the hesitating author, decide severally to do what Napoleon, what St Paul, what Shakespeare would have done; and there remains only the minor question, What is that? In Gideon's case one thing was clear: Skill was a man of singular decision, he would have taken some step (whatever it was) at once; and the only step that Gideon could think of was to return to his chambers.

This being achieved, all further inspiration failed him, and he stood pitifully staring at the instrument of his confusion. To touch the keys again was more than he durst venture on; whether they had maintained their former silence, or responded with the tones of the last trump, it would have equally dethroned his resolution. "It may be a practical jest," he reflected, "though it seems elaborate and costly. And yet what else can it be? It MUST be a practical jest." And just then his eye fell upon a feature which seemed corroborative of that view: the pagoda of cigars which Michael had erected ere he left the chambers. "Why that?" reflected Gideon. "It seems entirely irresponsible." And drawing near, he gingerly demolished it. "A key," he thought. "Why that? And why so conspicuously placed?" He made the circuit of the instrument, and perceived the keyhole at the back. "Aha! this is what the key is for," said he. "They wanted me to look inside. Stranger and stranger." And with that he turned the key and raised the lid.

In what antics of agony, in what fits of flighty resolution, in what collapses of despair, Gideon consumed the night, it would be ungenerous to enquire too closely.

That trill of tiny song with which the eaves-birds of London welcome the approach of day found him limp and rumpled and bloodshot, and with a mind still vacant of resource. He rose and looked forth unrejoicingly on blinded windows, an empty street, and the grey daylight dotted with the yellow lamps. There are mornings when the city seems to awake with a sick headache; this was one of them; and still the twittering reveille of the sparrows stirred in Gideon's spirit.

"Day here," he thought, "and I still helpless! This must come to an end." And he locked up the piano, put the key in his pocket, and set forth in quest of coffee. As he went, his mind trudged for the hundredth time a certain mill-road of terrors, misgivings, and regrets. To call in the police, to give up the body, to cover London with handbills describing John Dickson and Ezra Thomas, to fill the papers with paragraphs, Mysterious Occurrence in the Temple—Mr Forsyth admitted to bail, this was one course, an easy course, a safe course; but not, the more he reflected on it, not a pleasant one. For, was it not to publish abroad a number of singular facts about himself? A child ought to have seen through the story of these adventurers, and he had gaped and swallowed it. A barrister of the least self-respect should have refused to listen to clients who came before him in a manner so irregular, and he had listened. And O, if he had only listened; but he had gone upon their errand—he, a barrister, uninstructed even by the shadow of a solicitor—upon an errand fit only for a private detective; and alas!—and for the hundredth time the blood surged to his brow—he had taken their money! "No," said he, "the thing is as plain as St. Paul's. I shall be dishonoured! I have smashed my career for a five-pound note."

Between the possibility of being hanged in all innocence, and the certainty of a public and merited disgrace, no gentleman of spirit could long hesitate. After three gulps of that hot, snuffy, and muddy beverage, that passes on the streets of London for a decoction of the coffee berry, Gideon's mind was made up. He would do without the police. He must face the other side of the dilemma, and be Robert Skill in earnest. What would Robert Skill have done? How does a gentleman dispose of a dead body, honestly come by? He remembered the inimitable story of the hunchback; reviewed its course, and dismissed it for a worthless guide. It was impossible to prop a corpse on the corner of Tottenham Court Road without arousing fatal curiosity in the bosoms of the passers-by; as for lowering it down a London chimney, the physical obstacles were insurmountable. To get it on board a train and drop it out, or on the top of an omnibus and drop it off, were equally out of the question. To get it on a yacht and drop it overboard, was more conceivable; but for a man of moderate means it seemed extravagant. The hire of the yacht was in itself a consideration; the subsequent support of the whole crew (which seemed a necessary consequence) was simply not to be thought of. His uncle and the houseboat here occurred in very luminous colours to his mind. A musical composer (say, of the name of Jimson) might very well suffer, like Hogarth's musician before him, from the disturbances of London. He might very well be pressed for time to finish an opera—say the comic opera *Orange Pekoe*—*Orange Pekoe*, music by Jimson—"this young maestro, one of the most promising of our recent English school"—vigorous entrance of the drums, etc.—the whole character of Jimson and his music arose in bulk before the mind of Gideon. What more likely than Jimson's arrival with a grand piano (say, at Padwick), and his residence in a houseboat alone with the unfinished score of *Orange Pekoe*? His subsequent disappearance, leaving nothing behind but an empty piano case, it might be more difficult to account for. And yet even that was susceptible of explanation.

For, suppose Jimson had gone mad over a fugal passage, and had thereupon destroyed the accomplice of his infamy, and plunged into the welcome river? What end, on the whole, more probable for a modern musician?

"By Jove, I'll do it," cried Gideon. "Jimson is the boy!"

Chapter 11   The Maestro Jimson

Mr Edward Hugh Bloomfield having announced his intention to stay in the neighbourhood of Maidenhead, what more probable than that the Maestro Jimson should turn his mind toward Padwick? Near this pleasant riverside village he remembered to have observed an ancient, weedy houseboat lying moored beside a tuft of willows. It had stirred in him, in his careless hours, as he pulled down the river under a more familiar name, a certain sense of the romantic; and when the nice contrivance of his story was already complete in his mind, he had come near pulling it all down again, like an ungrateful clock, in order to introduce a chapter in which Richard Skill (who was always being decoyed somewhere) should be decoyed on board that lonely hulk by Lord Bellew and the American desperado Gin Sling. It was fortunate he had not done so, he reflected, since the hulk was now required for very different purposes.

Jimson, a man of inconspicuous costume, but insinuating manners, had little difficulty in finding the hireling who had charge of the houseboat, and still less in persuading him to resign his care. The rent was almost nominal, the entry immediate, the key was exchanged against a suitable advance in money, and Jimson returned to town by the afternoon train to see about dispatching his piano.

"I will be down tomorrow," he had said reassuringly. "My opera is waited for with such impatience, you know."

And, sure enough, about the hour of noon on the following day, Jimson might have been observed ascending the riverside road that goes from Padwick to Great Haverham, carrying in one hand a basket of provisions, and under the other arm a leather case containing (it is to be conjectured) the score of *Orange Pekoe*. It was October weather; the stone-grey sky was full of larks, the leaden mirror of the Thames brightened with autumnal foliage, and the fallen leaves of the chestnuts chirped under the composer's footing. There is no time of the year in England more courageous; and Jimson, though he was not without his troubles, whistled as he went.

A little above Padwick the river lies very solitary. On the opposite shore the trees of a private park enclose the view, the chimneys of the mansion just pricking forth above their clusters; on the near side the path is bordered by willows. Close among these lay the houseboat, a thing so soiled by the tears of the overhanging willows, so grown upon with parasites, so decayed, so battered, so neglected, such a haunt of rats, so advertised a storehouse of rheumatic agonies, that the heart of an intending occupant might well recoil. A plank, by way of flying drawbridge, joined it to the shore. And it was a dreary moment for Jimson when he pulled this after him and found himself alone on this unwholesome fortress. He could hear the rats scuttle and flop in the abhorred interior; the key cried among the wards like a thing in pain; the sitting-room was deep in dust, and smelt strong of bilge-water. It could not be called a cheerful spot, even for a composer absorbed in beloved toil; how much less for a young gentleman haunted by alarms and awaiting the arrival of a corpse!

He sat down, cleared away a piece of the table, and attacked the cold luncheon in his basket. In case of any subsequent inquiry into the fate of Jimson, It was desirable he should be little seen: in other words, that he should spend the day entirely in the house. To this end, and further to corroborate his fable, he had brought in the leather case not only writing materials, but a ream of large-size music paper, such as he considered suitable for an ambitious character like Jimson's.

"And now to work," said he, when he had satisfied his appetite. "We must leave traces of the wretched man's activity." And he wrote in bold characters:

ORANGE PEKOE.

Op. 17.

J. B. JIMSON.

Vocal and p. f. score.

"I suppose they never do begin like this," reflected Gideon; "but then it's quite out of the question for me to tackle a full score, and Jimson was so unconventional. A dedication would be found convincing, I believe. 'Dedicated to' (let me see) 'to William Ewart Gladstone, by his obedient servant the composer.' And now some music: I had better avoid the overture; it seems to present difficulties. Let's give an air for the tenor: key—O, something modern!—seven sharps." And he made a businesslike signature across the staves, and then paused and browsed for a while on the handle of his pen. Melody, with no better inspiration than a sheet of paper, is not usually found to spring unbidden in the mind of the amateur; nor is the key of seven sharps a place of much repose to the untried. He cast away that sheet. "It will help to build up the character of Jimson," Gideon remarked, and again waited on the muse, in various keys and on divers sheets of paper, but all with results so inconsiderable that he stood aghast. "It's very odd," thought he. "I seem to have less fancy than I thought, or this is an off-day with me; yet Jimson must leave something." And again he bent himself to the task.

Presently the penetrating chill of the houseboat began to attack the very seat of life. He desisted from his unremunerative trial, and, to the audible annoyance of the rats, walked briskly up and down the cabin. Still he was cold. "This is all nonsense," said he. "I don't care about the risk, but I will not catch a catarrh. I must get out of this den."

He stepped on deck, and passing to the bow of his embarkation, looked for the first time up the river. He started. Only a few hundred yards above another houseboat lay moored among the willows. It was very spick-and-span, an elegant canoe hung at the stern, the windows were concealed by snowy curtains, a flag floated from a staff. The more Gideon looked at it, the more there mingled with his disgust a sense of impotent surprise. It was very like his uncle's houseboat; it was exceedingly like—it was identical. But for two circumstances, he could have sworn it was the same. The first, that his uncle had gone to Maidenhead, might be explained away by that flightiness of purpose which is so common a trait among the more than usually manly. The second, however, was conclusive: it was not in the least like Mr Bloomfield to display a banner on his floating residence; and if he ever did, it would certainly be dyed in hues of emblematical propriety. Now the Squirradical, like the vast majority of the more manly, had drawn knowledge at the wells of Cambridge—he was Wooden Spoon in the year 1850; and the flag upon the houseboat streamed on the afternoon air with the colours of that seat of Toryism, that cradle of Puseyism, that home of the inexact and the effete Oxford.

Still it was strangely like, thought Gideon.

And as he thus looked and thought, the door opened, and a young lady stepped forth on deck. The barrister dropped and fled into his cabin—it was Julia Hazeltine! Through the window he watched her draw in the canoe, get on board of it, cast off, and come dropping downstream in his direction.

"Well, all is up now," said he, and he fell on a seat.

"Good afternoon, miss," said a voice on the water. Gideon knew it for the voice of his landlord.

"Good afternoon," replied Julia, "but I don't know who you are; do I? O, yes, I do though. You are the nice man that gave us leave to sketch from the old houseboat."

Gideon's heart leaped with fear.

"That's it," returned the man. "And what I wanted to say was as you couldn't do it any more. You see I've let it."

"Let it!" cried Julia.

"Let it for a month," said the man. "Seems strange, don't it? Can't see what the party wants with it?"

"It seems very romantic of him, I think," said Julia, "What sort of a person is he?"

Julia in her canoe, the landlord in his wherry, were close alongside, and holding on by the gunwale of the houseboat; so that not a word was lost on Gideon.

"He's a music-man," said the landlord, "or at least that's what he told me, miss; come down here to write an op'ra."

"Really!" cried Julia, "I never heard of anything so delightful! Why, we shall be able to slip down at night and hear him improvise! What is his name?"

"Jimson," said the man.

"Jimson?" repeated Julia, and interrogated her memory in vain. But indeed our rising school of English music boasts so many professors that we rarely hear of one till he is made a baronet. "Are you sure you have it right?"

"Made him spell it to me," replied the landlord. "J-I-M-S-O-N—Jimson; and his op'ra's called—some kind of tea."

"SOME KIND OF TEA!" cried the girl. "What a very singular name for an opera! What can it be about?" And Gideon heard her pretty laughter flow abroad. "We must try to get acquainted with this Mr Jimson; I feel sure he must be nice."

"Well, miss, I'm afraid I must be going on. I've got to be at Haverham, you see."

"O, don't let me keep you, you kind man!" said Julia. "Good afternoon."

"Good afternoon to you, miss."

Gideon sat in the cabin a prey to the most harrowing thoughts. Here he was anchored to a rotting houseboat, soon to be anchored to it still more emphatically by the presence of the corpse, and here was the country buzzing about him, and young ladies already proposing pleasure parties to surround his house at night. Well, that meant the gallows; and much he cared for that. What troubled him now was Julia's indescribable levity. That girl would scrape acquaintance with anybody; she had no reserve, none of the enamel of the lady. She was familiar with a brute like his landlord; she took an immediate interest (which she lacked even the delicacy to conceal) in a creature like Jimson! He could conceive her asking Jimson to have tea with her! And it was for a girl like this that a man like Gideon—Down, manly heart!

He was interrupted by a sound that sent him whipping behind the door in a trice. Miss Hazeltine had stepped on board the houseboat. Her sketch was promising; judging from the stillness, she supposed Jimson not yet come; and she had decided to seize occasion and complete the work of art. Down she sat therefore in the bow, produced her block and watercolours, and was soon singing over (what used to be called) the ladylike accomplishment. Now and then indeed her song was interrupted, as she searched in her memory for some of the odious little receipts by means of which the game is practised—or used to be practised in the brave days of old; they say the world, and those ornaments of the world, young ladies, are become more sophisticated now; but Julia had probably studied under Pitman, and she stood firm in the old ways.

Gideon, meanwhile, stood behind the door, afraid to move, afraid to breathe, afraid to think of what must follow, racked by confinement and borne to the ground with tedium. This particular phase, he felt with gratitude, could not last for ever; whatever impended (even the gallows, he bitterly and perhaps erroneously reflected) could not fail to be a relief. To calculate cubes occurred to him as an ingenious and even profitable refuge from distressing thoughts, and he threw his manhood into that dreary exercise.

Thus, then, were these two young persons occupied— Gideon attacking the perfect number with resolution; Julia vigorously stippling incongruous colours on her block, when Providence dispatched into these waters a steam-launch asthmatically panting up the Thames. All along the banks the water swelled and fell, and the reeds rustled. The houseboat itself, that ancient stationary creature, became suddenly imbued with life, and rolled briskly at her moorings, like a sea-going ship when she begins to smell the harbour bar. The wash had nearly died away, and the quick panting of the launch sounded already faint and far off, when Gideon was startled by a cry from Julia. Peering through the window, he beheld her staring disconsolately downstream at the fast-vanishing canoe. The barrister (whatever were his faults) displayed on this occasion a promptitude worthy of his hero, Robert Skill; with one effort of his mind he foresaw what was about to follow; with one movement of his body he dropped to the floor and crawled under the table.

Julia, on her part, was not yet alive to her position. She saw she had lost the canoe, and she looked forward with something less than avidity to her next interview with Mr Bloomfield; but she had no idea that she was imprisoned, for she knew of the plank bridge.

She made the circuit of the house, and found the door

open and the bridge withdrawn. It was plain, then, that Jimson must have come; plain, too, that he must be on board. He must be a very shy man to have suffered this invasion of his residence, and made no sign; and her courage rose higher at the thought. He must come now, she must force him from his privacy, for the plank was too heavy for her single strength; so she tapped upon the open door. Then she tapped again.

"Mr Jimson," she cried, "Mr Jimson! here, come!—You must come, you know, sooner or later, for I can't get off without you. O, don't be so exceedingly silly! O, please, come!"

Still there was no reply.

"If he is here he must be mad," she thought, with a little fear. And the next moment she remembered he had probably gone aboard like herself in a boat. In that case she might as well see the houseboat, and she pushed open the door and stepped in. Under the table, where he lay smothered with dust, Gideon's heart stood still.

There were the remains of Jimson's lunch. "He likes rather nice things to eat," she thought. "O, I am sure he is quite a delightful man. I wonder if he is as good-looking as Mr Forsyth. Mrs Jimson—I don't believe it sounds as nice as Mrs Forsyth; but then 'Gideon' is so really odious! And here is some of his music too; this is delightful. *Orange Pekoe*—O, that's what he meant by some kind of tea." And she trilled with laughter. "Adagio molto espressivo, sempre legato," she read next. (For the literary part of a composer's business Gideon was well equipped.) "How very strange to have all these directions, and only three or four notes! O, here's another with some more. Andante patetico." And she began to glance over the music. "O dear me," she thought, "he must be terribly modern! It all seems discords to me. Let's try the air. It is very strange, it seems familiar." She began to sing it, and suddenly broke off with laughter. "Why, it's *Tommy make room for your Uncle*!" she cried aloud, so that the soul of Gideon was filled with bitterness. "Andante patetico, indeed! The man must be a mere impostor."

And just at this moment there came a confused, scuffling sound from underneath the table; a strange note, like that of a barn-door fowl, ushered in a most explosive sneeze; the head of the sufferer was at the same time brought smartly in contact with the boards above; and the sneeze was followed by a hollow groan.

Julia fled to the door, and there, with the salutary instinct of the brave, turned and faced the danger. There was no pursuit. The sounds continued; below the table a crouching figure was indistinctly to be seen jostled by the throes of a sneezing-fit; and that was all.

"Surely," thought Julia, "this is most unusual behaviour. He cannot be a man of the world!"

Meanwhile the dust of years had been disturbed by the young barrister's convulsions; and the sneezing-fit was succeeded by a passionate access of coughing.

Julia began to feel a certain interest. "I am afraid you are really quite ill," she said, drawing a little nearer. "Please don't let me put you out, and do not stay under that table, Mr Jimson. Indeed it cannot be good for you."

Mr Jimson only answered by a distressing cough; and the next moment the girl was on her knees, and their faces had almost knocked together under the table.

"O, my gracious goodness!" exclaimed Miss Hazeltine, and sprang to her feet. "Mr Forsyth gone mad!"

"I am not mad," said the gentleman ruefully, extricating himself from his position. "Dearest. Miss Hazeltine, I vow to you upon my knees I am not mad!"

"You are not!" she cried, panting.

"I know," he said, "that to a superficial eye my conduct may appear unconventional."

"If you are not mad, it was no conduct at all," cried the girl, with a flash of colour, "and showed you did not care one penny for my feelings!"

"This is the very devil and all. I know—I admit that," cried Gideon, with a great effort of manly candour.

"It was abominable conduct!" said Julia, with energy.

"I know it must have shaken your esteem," said the barrister. "But, dearest Miss Hazeltine, I beg of you to hear me out; my behaviour, strange as it may seem, is not unsusceptible of explanation; and I positively cannot and will not consent to continue to try to exist without—without the esteem of one whom I admire—the moment is ill chosen, I am well aware of that; but I repeat the expression—one whom I admire."

A touch of amusement appeared on Miss Hazeltine's face. "Very well," said she, "come out of this dreadfully cold place, and let us sit down on deck." The barrister dolefully followed her. "Now," said she, making herself comfortable against the end of the house, "go on. I will hear you out." And then, seeing him stand before her with so much obvious disrelish to the task, she was suddenly overcome with laughter. Julia's laugh was a thing to ravish lovers; she rolled her mirthful descant with the freedom and the melody of a blackbird's song upon the river, and repeated by the echoes of the farther bank. It seemed a thing in its own place and a sound native to the open air. There was only one creature who heard it without joy, and that was her unfortunate admirer.

"Miss Hazeltine," he said, in a voice that tottered with annoyance, "I speak as your sincere well-wisher, but this can only be called levity."

Julia made great eyes at him.

"I can't withdraw the word," he said: "already the freedom with which I heard you hobnobbing with a boatman gave me exquisite pain. Then there was a want of reserve about Jimson—"

"But Jimson appears to be yourself," objected Julia.

"I am far from denying that," cried the barrister, "but you did not know it at the time. What could Jimson be to you? Who was Jimson? Miss Hazeltine, it cut me to the heart."

"Really this seems to me to be very silly," returned Julia, with severe decision. "You have behaved in the most extraordinary manner; you pretend you are able to explain your conduct, and instead of doing so you begin to attack me."

"I am well aware of that," replied Gideon. "I—I will make a clean breast of it. When you know all the circumstances you will be able to excuse me."

And sitting down beside her on the deck, he poured forth his miserable history.

"O, Mr Forsyth," she cried, when he had done, "I am—so—sorry! wish I hadn't laughed at you—only you know you really were so exceedingly funny. But I wish I hadn't, and I wouldn't either if I had only known." And she gave him her hand.

Gideon kept it in his own. "You do not think the worse of me for this?" he asked tenderly.

"Because you have been so silly and got into such dreadful trouble? You poor boy, no!" cried Julia; and, in the warmth of the moment, reached him her other hand; "you may count on me," she added.

"Really?" said Gideon.

"Really and really!" replied the girl.

"I do then, and I will," cried the young man. "I admit the moment is not well chosen; but I have no friends—to speak of."

"No more have I," said Julia. "But don't you think it's

perhaps time you gave me back my hands?"

"*La ci darem la mano*," said the barrister, "the merest moment more! I have so few friends," he added.

"I thought it was considered such a bad account of a young man to have no friends," observed Julia.

"O, but I have crowds of FRIENDS!" cried Gideon. "That's not what I mean. I feel the moment is ill chosen; but O, Julia, if you could only see yourself!"

"Mr Forsyth—"

"Don't call me by that beastly name!" cried the youth. "Call me Gideon!"

"O, never that," from Julia. "Besides, we have known each other such a short time."

"Not at all!" protested Gideon. "We met at Bournemouth ever so long ago. I never forgot you since. Say you never forgot me. Say you never forgot me, and call me Gideon!"

"Isn't this rather—a want of reserve about Jimson?" enquired the girl.

"O, I know I am an ass," cried the barrister, "and I don't care a halfpenny! I know I'm an ass, and you may laugh at me to your heart's delight." And as Julia's lips opened with a smile, he once more dropped into music. "There's the Land of Cherry Isle!" he sang, courting her with his eyes.

"It's like an opera," said Julia, rather faintly.

"What should it be?" said Gideon. "Am I not Jimson? It would be strange if I did not serenade my love. O, yes, I mean the word, my Julia; and I mean to win you. I am in dreadful trouble, and I have not a penny of my own, and I have cut the silliest figure; and yet I mean to win you, Julia. Look at me, if you can, and tell me no!"

She looked at him; and whatever her eyes may have told him, it is to be supposed he took a pleasure in the message, for he read it a long while.

"And Uncle Ned will give us some money to go on upon in the meanwhile," he said at last.

"Well, I call that cool!" said a cheerful voice at his elbow.

Gideon and Julia sprang apart with wonderful alacrity; the latter annoyed to observe that although they had never moved since they sat down, they were now quite close together; both presenting faces of a very heightened colour to the eyes of Mr Edward Hugh Bloomfield. That gentleman, coming up the river in his boat, had captured the truant canoe, and divining what had happened, had thought to steal a march upon Miss Hazeltine at her sketch. He had unexpectedly brought down two birds with one stone; and as he looked upon the pair of flushed and breathless culprits, the pleasant human instinct of the matchmaker softened his heart.

"Well, I call that cool," he repeated; "you seem to count very securely upon Uncle Ned. But look here, Gid, I thought I had told you to keep away?"

"To keep away from Maidenhead," replied Gid. "But how should I expect to find you here?"

"There is something in that," Mr Bloomfield admitted. "You see I thought it better that even you should be ignorant of my address; those rascals, the Finsburys, would have wormed it out of you. And just to put them off the scent I hoisted these abominable colours. But that is not all, Gid; you promised me to work, and here I find you playing the fool at Padwick."

"Please, Mr Bloomfield, you must not be hard on Mr Forsyth," said Julia. "Poor boy, he is in dreadful straits."

"What's this, Gid?" enquired the uncle. "Have you been fighting? or is it a bill?"

These, in the opinion of the Squirradical, were the two misfortunes incident to gentlemen; and indeed both were culled from his own career. He had once put his name (as a matter of form) on a friend's paper; it had cost him a cool thousand; and the friend had gone about with the fear of death upon him ever since, and never turned a corner without scouting in front of him for Mr Bloomfield and the oaken staff. As for fighting, the Squirradical was always on the brink of it; and once, when (in the character of president of a Radical club) he had cleared out the hall of his opponents, things had gone even further. Mr Holtum, the Conservative candidate, who lay so long on the bed of sickness, was prepared to swear to Mr Bloomfield. "I will swear to it in any court—it was the hand of that brute that struck me down," he was reported to have said; and when he was thought to be sinking, it was known that he had made an *ante-mortem* statement in that sense. It was a cheerful day for the

Squirradical when Holtum was restored to his brewery.

"It's much worse than that," said Gideon; "a combination of circumstances really providentially unjust—a—in fact, a syndicate of murderers seem to have perceived my latent ability to rid them of the traces of their crime. It's a legal study after all, you see!" And with these words, Gideon, for the second time that day, began to describe the adventures of the Broadwood Grand.

"I must write to *The Times*," cried Mr Bloomfield.

"Do you want to get me disbarred?" asked Gideon.

"Disbarred! Come, it can't be as bad as that," said his uncle. "It's a good, honest, Liberal Government that's in, and they would certainly move at my request. Thank God, the days of Tory jobbery are at an end."

"It wouldn't do, Uncle Ned," said Gideon.

"But you're not mad enough," cried Mr Bloomfield, "to persist in trying to dispose of it yourself?"

"There is no other path open to me," said Gideon.

"It's not common sense, and I will not hear of it," cried Mr Bloomfield. "I command you, positively, Gid, to desist from this criminal interference."

"Very well, then, I hand it over to you," said Gideon, "and you can do what you like with the dead body."

"God forbid!" ejaculated the president of the Radical Club, "I'll have nothing to do with it."

"Then you must allow me to do the best I can," returned

his nephew. "Believe me, I have a distinct talent for this sort of difficulty."

"We might forward it to that pest-house, the Conservative Club," observed Mr Bloomfield. "It might damage them in the eyes of their constituents; and it could be profitably worked up in the local journal."

"If you see any political capital in the thing," said Gideon, "you may have it for me."

"No, no, Gid—no, no, I thought you might. I will have no hand in the thing. On reflection, it's highly undesirable that either I or Miss Hazeltine should linger here. We might be observed," said the president, looking up and down the river; "and in my public position the consequences would be painful for the party. And, at any rate, it's dinner-time."

"What?" cried Gideon, plunging for his watch. "And so it is! Great heaven, the piano should have been here hours ago!"

Mr Bloomfield was clambering back into his boat; but at these words he paused.

"I saw it arrive myself at the station; I hired a carrier man; he had a round to make, but he was to be here by four at the latest," cried the barrister. "No doubt the piano is open, and the body found."

"You must fly at once," cried Mr Bloomfield, "it's the only manly step."

"But suppose it's all right?" wailed Gideon. "Suppose the piano comes, and I am not here to receive it? I shall have hanged myself by my cowardice. No, Uncle Ned, enquiries must be made in Padwick; I dare not go, of course; but you may—you could hang about the police office, don't you see?"

"No, Gid—no, my dear nephew," said Mr Bloomfield, with the voice of one on the rack. "I regard you with the most sacred affection; and I thank God I am an Englishman—and all that. But not—not the police, Gid."

"Then you desert me?" said Gideon. "Say it plainly."

"Far from it! far From it!" protested Mr Bloomfield. "I only propose caution. Common sense, Gid, should always be an Englishman's guide."

"Will you let me speak?" said Julia. "I think Gideon had better leave this dreadful houseboat, and wait among the willows over there. If the piano comes, then he could step out and take it in; and if the police come, he could slip into our houseboat, and there needn't be any more Jimson at all. He could go to bed, and we could burn his clothes (couldn't we?) in the steam-launch; and then really it seems as if it would be all right. Mr Bloomfield is so respectable, you know, and such a leading character, it would be quite impossible even to fancy that he could be mixed up with it."

"This young lady has strong common sense," said the Squirradical.

"O, I don't think I'm at all a fool," said Julia, with conviction.

"But what if neither of them come?" asked Gideon; "what

shall I do then?"

"Why then," said she, "you had better go down to the village after dark; and I can go with you, and then I am sure you could never be suspected; and even if you were, I could tell them it was altogether a mistake."

"I will not permit that—I will not suffer Miss Hazeltine to go," cried Mr Bloomfield.

"Why?" asked Julia.

Mr Bloomfield had not the least desire to tell her why, for it was simply a craven fear of being drawn himself into the imbroglio; but with the usual tactics of a man who is ashamed of himself, he took the high hand. "God forbid, my dear Miss Hazeltine, that I should dictate to a lady on the question of propriety—" he began.

"O, is that all?" interrupted Julia. "Then we must go all three."

"Caught!" thought the Squirradical.

Chapter 12   Positively the Last Appearance of the Broadwood Grand

England is supposed to be unmusical; but without dwelling on the patronage extended to the organ-grinder, without seeking to found any argument on the prevalence of the jew's trump, there is surely one instrument that may be said to be national in the fullest acceptance of the word. The herdboy in the broom, already musical in the days of Father Chaucer, startles (and perhaps pains) the lark with this exiguous pipe; and in the hands of the skilled bricklayer, "the thing becomes a trumpet, whence he blows' (as a general rule) either *The British Grenadiers* or *Cherry Ripe*. The latter air is indeed the shibboleth and diploma piece of the penny whistler; I hazard a guess it was originally composed for this instrument. It is singular enough that a man should be able to gain a livelihood, or even to tide over a period of unemployment, by the display of his proficiency upon the penny whistle; still more so, that the professional should almost invariably confine himself to *Cherry Ripe*. But indeed, singularities surround the subject, thick like blackberries. Why, for instance, should the pipe be called a penny whistle? I think no one ever bought it for a penny. Why should the alternative name be tin whistle? I am grossly deceived if it be made of tin. Lastly, in what deaf catacomb, in what earless desert, does the beginner pass the excruciating interval of his apprenticeship? We have all heard people learning the piano, the fiddle, and the cornet; but the young of the penny whistler (like that of the salmon) is occult from observation; he is never heard until proficient; and providence (perhaps alarmed by the works of Mr Mallock) defends human hearing from his first attempts upon the upper octave.

A really noteworthy thing was taking place in a green lane, not far from Padwick. On the bench of a carrier's cart there sat a tow-headed, lanky, modest-looking youth; the reins were on his lap; the whip lay behind him in the interior of the cart; the horse proceeded without guidance or encouragement; the carrier (or the carrier's man), rapt into a higher sphere than that of his daily occupations, his looks dwelling on the skies, devoted himself wholly to a brand-new D penny whistle, whence he diffidently endeavoured to elicit that pleasing melody *The Ploughboy*. To any observant person who should have chanced to saunter in that lane, the hour would have been thrilling. "Here at last," he would have said, "is the beginner."

The tow-headed youth (whose name was Harker) had just encored himself for the nineteenth time, when he was struck into the extreme of confusion by the discovery that he was not alone.

"There you have it!" cried a manly voice from the side of the road. "That's as good as I want to hear. Perhaps a leetle oilier in the run," the voice suggested, with meditative gusto. "Give it us again."

Harker glanced, from the depths of his humiliation, at the speaker. He beheld a powerful, sun-brown, clean-shaven fellow, about forty years of age, striding beside the cart with a non-commissioned military bearing, and (as he strode) spinning in the air a cane. The fellow's clothes were very bad, but he looked clean and self-reliant.

"I'm only a beginner," gasped the blushing Harker, "I didn't think anybody could hear me."

"Well, I like that!" returned the other. "You're a pretty old beginner. Come, I'll give you a lead myself. Give us a seat here beside you."

The next moment the military gentleman was perched on the cart, pipe in hand. He gave the instrument a knowing rattle on the shaft, mouthed it, appeared to commune for a moment with the muse, and dashed into *The girl I left behind me*. He was a great, rather than a fine, performer; he lacked the bird-like richness; he could scarce have extracted all the honey out of *Cherry Ripe*; he did not fear—he even ostentatiously displayed and seemed to revel in he shrillness of the instrument; but in fire, speed, precision, evenness, and fluency; in linked agility of jimmy—a technical expression, by your leave, answering to warblers on the bagpipe; and perhaps, above all, in that inspiring side-glance of the eye, with which he followed the effect and (as by a human appeal) eked out the insufficiency of his performance: in these, the fellow stood without a rival. Harker listened: *The girl I left behind me* filled him with despair; *The Soldier's Joy* carried him beyond jealousy into generous enthusiasm.

"Turn about," said the military gentleman, offering the pipe.

"O, not after you!" cried Harker; "you're a professional."

"No," said his companion; "an amatyure like yourself. That's one style of play, yours is the other, and I like it best. But I began when I was a boy, you see, before my taste was formed. When you're my age you'll play that thing like a cornet-a-piston. Give us that air again; how does it go?" and he affected to endeavour to recall *The Ploughboy*.

A timid, insane hope sprang in the breast of Harker. Was it possible? Was there something in his playing? It had, indeed, seemed to him at times as if he got a kind of a richness out of it. Was he a genius? Meantime the military gentleman stumbled over the air.

"No," said the unhappy Harker, "that's not quite it. It goes this way—just to show you."

And, taking the pipe between his lips, he sealed his doom. When he had played the air, and then a second time, and a third; when the military gentleman had tried it once more, and once more failed; when it became clear to Harker that he, the blushing debutant, was actually giving a lesson to this full-grown flutist—and the flutist under his care was not very brilliantly progressing—how am I to tell what floods of glory brightened the autumnal countryside; how, unless the reader were an amateur himself, describe the heights of idiotic vanity to which the carrier climbed? One significant fact shall paint the situation: thenceforth it was Harker who played, and the military gentleman listened and approved.

As he listened, however, he did not forget the habit of soldierly precaution, looking both behind and before. He looked behind and computed the value of the carrier's load, divining the contents of the brown-paper parcels and the portly hamper, and briefly setting down the grand piano in the brand-new piano-case as "difficult to get rid of". He looked before, and spied at the corner of the green lane a little country public-house embowered in roses. "I'll have a shy at it," concluded the military gentleman, and roundly proposed a glass.

"Well, I'm not a drinking man," said Harker.

"Look here, now," cut in the other, "I'll tell you who I am: I'm Colour-Sergeant Brand of the Blankth. That'll tell you if I'm a drinking man or not." It might and it might not, thus a Greek chorus would have intervened, and gone on to point out how very far it fell short of telling why the sergeant was tramping a country lane in tatters; or even to argue that he must have pretermitted some while ago his labours for the general defence, and (in the interval) possibly turned his attention to oakum. But there was no Greek chorus present; and the man of war went on to contend that drinking was one thing and a friendly glass another.

In the Blue Lion, which was the name of the country public-house, Colour-Sergeant Brand introduced his new friend, Mr Harker, to a number of ingenious mixtures, calculated to prevent the approaches of intoxication. These he explained to be "rekisite" in the service, so that a self-respecting officer should always appear upon parade in a condition honourable to his corps. The most efficacious of these devices was to lace a pint of mild ale with twopence-worth of London gin. I am pleased to hand in this recipe to the discerning reader, who may find it useful even in civil station; for its effect upon Mr Harker was revolutionary. He must be helped on board his own waggon, where he proceeded to display a spirit entirely given over to mirth and music, alternately hooting with laughter, to which the sergeant hastened to bear chorus, and incoherently tootling on the pipe. The man of war, meantime, unostentatiously possessed himself of the reins. It was plain he had a taste for the secluded beauties of an English landscape; for the cart, although it wandered under his guidance for some time, was never observed to issue on the dusty highway, journeying between hedge and ditch, and for the most part under overhanging boughs. It was plain, besides, he had an eye to the true interests of Mr Harker; for though the cart drew up more than once at the doors of public-houses, it was only the sergeant who set foot to ground, and, being equipped himself with a quart bottle, once more proceeded on his rural drive.

To give any idea of the complexity of the sergeant's course, a map of that part of Middlesex would be required, and my publisher is averse from the expense. Suffice it, that a little after the night had closed, the cart was brought to a standstill in a woody road; where the sergeant lifted from among the parcels, and tenderly deposited upon the wayside, the inanimate form of Harker.

"If you come to before daylight," thought the sergeant, "I shall be surprised for one."

From the various pockets of the slumbering carrier he gently collected the sum of seventeen shillings and eightpence sterling; and, getting once more into the cart, drove thoughtfully away.

"If I was exactly sure of where I was, it would be a good job," he reflected. "Anyway, here's a corner."

He turned it, and found himself upon the riverside. A little above him the lights of a houseboat shone cheerfully; and already close at hand, so close that it was impossible to avoid their notice, three persons, a lady and two gentlemen, were deliberately drawing near. The sergeant put his trust in the convenient darkness of the night, and drove on to meet them. One of the gentlemen, who was of a portly figure, walked in the midst of the fairway, and presently held up a staff by way of signal.

"My man, have you seen anything of a carrier's cart?" he cried.

Dark as it was, it seemed to the sergeant as though the slimmer of the two gentlemen had made a motion to prevent the other speaking, and (finding himself too late) had skipped aside with some alacrity. At another season, Sergeant Brand would have paid more attention to the fact; but he was then immersed in the perils of his own predicament.

"A carrier's cart?" said he, with a perceptible uncertainty of voice. "No, sir."

"Ah!" said the portly gentleman, and stood aside to let the sergeant pass. The lady appeared to bend forward and study the cart with every mark of sharpened curiosity, the slimmer gentleman still keeping in the rear.

"I wonder what the devil they would be at," thought Sergeant Brand; and, looking fearfully back, he saw the trio standing together in the midst of the way, like folk consulting. The bravest of military heroes are not always equal to themselves as to their reputation; and fear, on some singular provocation, will find a lodgment in the most unfamiliar bosom. The word "detective" might have been heard to gurgle in the sergeant's throat; and vigorously applying the whip, he fled up the riverside road to Great Haverham, at the gallop of the carrier's horse. The lights of the houseboat flashed upon the flying waggon as it passed; the beat of hoofs and the rattle of the vehicle gradually coalesced and died away; and presently, to the trio on the riverside, silence had redescended.

"It's the most extraordinary thing," cried the slimmer of the two gentlemen, "but that's the cart."

"And I know I saw a piano," said the girl.

"O, it's the cart, certainly; and the extraordinary thing is, it's not the man," added the first.

"It must be the man, Gid, it must be," said the portly one.

"Well, then, why is he running away?" asked Gideon.

"His horse bolted, I suppose," said the Squirradical.

"Nonsense! I heard the whip going like a flail," said Gideon. "It simply defies the human reason."

"I'll tell you," broke in the girl, "he came round that corner. Suppose we went and—what do you call it in books?—followed his trail? There may be a house there, or somebody who saw him, or something."

"Well, suppose we did, for the fun of the thing," said Gideon.

The fun of the thing (it would appear) consisted in the extremely close juxtaposition of himself and Miss Hazeltine. To Uncle Ned, who was excluded from these simple pleasures, the excursion appeared hopeless from the first; and when a fresh perspective of darkness opened up, dimly contained between park palings on the one side and a hedge and ditch upon the other, the whole without the smallest signal of human habitation, the Squirradical drew up.

"This is a wild-goose chase," said he.

With the cessation of the footfalls, another sound smote upon their ears.

"O, what's that?" cried Julia.

"I can't think," said Gideon.

The Squirradical had his stick presented like a sword. "Gid," he began, "Gid, I—"

"O, Mr Forsyth!" cried the girl. "O, don't go forward, you don't know what it might be—it might be something perfectly horrid."

"It may be the devil itself," said Gideon, disengaging himself, "but I am going to see it."

"Don't be rash, Gid," cried his uncle.

The barrister drew near to the sound, which was certainly of a portentous character. In quality it appeared to blend the strains of the cow, the foghorn, and the mosquito; and the startling manner of its enunciation added incalculably to its terrors. A dark object, not unlike the human form divine, appeared on the brink of the ditch.

"It's a man," said Gideon, "it's only a man; he seems to be asleep and snoring. Hullo," he added, a moment after, "there must be something wrong with him, he won't waken."

Gideon produced his vestas, struck one, and by its light recognized the tow head of Harker.

"This is the man," said he, "as drunk as Belial. I see the whole story"; and to his two companions, who had now ventured to rejoin him, he set forth a theory of the divorce between the carrier and his cart, which was not unlike the truth.

"Drunken brute!" said Uncle Ned, "let's get him to a pump and give him what he deserves."

"Not at all!" said Gideon. "It is highly undesirable he should see us together; and really, do you know, I am very much obliged to him, for this is about the luckiest thing that could have possibly occurred. It seems to me—Uncle Ned, I declare to heaven it seems to me—I'm clear of it!"

"Clear of what?" asked the Squirradical.

"The whole affair!" cried Gideon. "That man has been ass enough to steal the cart and the dead body; what he hopes to do with it I neither know nor care. My hands are free, Jimson ceases; down with Jimson. Shake hands with me, Uncle Ned—Julia, darling girl, Julia, I—"

"Gideon, Gideon!" said his uncle.

"O, it's all right, uncle, when we're going to be married so soon," said Gideon. "You know you said so yourself in the houseboat."

"Did I?" said Uncle Ned; "I am certain I said no such thing."

"Appeal to him, tell him he did, get on his soft side," cried Gideon. "He's a real brick if you get on his soft side."

"Dear Mr Bloomfield," said Julia, "I know Gideon will be such a very good boy, and he has promised me to do such a lot of law, and I will see that he does too. And you know it is so very steadying to young men, everybody admits that; though, of course, I know I have no money, Mr Bloomfield," she added.

"My dear young lady, as this rapscallion told you today on the boat, Uncle Ned has plenty," said the Squirradical, "and I can never forget that you have been shamefully defrauded. So as there's nobody looking, you had better give your Uncle Ned a kiss. There, you rogue," resumed Mr Bloomfield, when the ceremony had been daintily performed, "this very pretty young lady is yours, and a vast deal more than you deserve. But now, let us get back to the houseboat, get up steam on the launch, and away back to town."

"That's the thing!" cried Gideon; "and tomorrow there will be no houseboat, and no Jimson, and no carrier's cart, and no piano; and when Harker awakes on the ditchside, he may tell himself the whole affair has been a dream."

"Aha!" said Uncle Ned, "but there's another man who will have a different awakening. That fellow in the cart will find he has been too clever by half."

"Uncle Ned and Julia," said Gideon, "I am as happy as the King of Tartary, my heart is like a threepenny-bit, my heels are like feathers; I am out of all my troubles, Julia's hand is in mine. Is this a time for anything but handsome sentiments? Why, there's not room in me for anything that's not angelic! And when I think of that poor unhappy devil in the cart, I stand here in the night and cry with a single heart God help him!"

"Amen," said Uncle Ned.

Chapter 13 The Tribulations of Morris: Part the Second

In a really polite age of literature I would have scorned to cast my eye again on the contortions of Morris. But the study is in the spirit of the day; it presents, besides, features of a high, almost a repulsive, morality; and if it should prove the means of preventing any respectable and inexperienced gentleman from plunging light-heartedly into crime, even political crime, this work will not have been penned in vain.

He rose on the morrow of his night with Michael, rose from the leaden slumber of distress, to find his hand tremulous, his eyes closed with rheum, his throat parched, and his digestion obviously paralysed. "Lord knows it's not from eating!" Morris thought; and as he dressed he reconsidered his position under several heads. Nothing will so well depict the troubled seas in which he was now voyaging as a review of these various anxieties. I have thrown them (for the reader's convenience) into a certain order; but in the mind of one poor human equal they whirled together like the dust of hurricanes. With the same obliging preoccupation, I have put a name to each of his distresses; and it will be observed with pity that every individual item would have graced and commended the cover of a railway novel.

Anxiety the First: Where is the Body? or, The Mystery of Bent Pitman. It was now manifestly plain that Bent Pitman (as was to be looked for from his ominous appellation) belonged to the darker order of the criminal class. An honest man would not have cashed the bill; a humane man would not have accepted in silence the tragic contents of the water-butt; a man, who was not already up to the hilts in gore, would have lacked the means of secretly disposing them. This process of reasoning left a horrid image of the monster, Pitman. Doubtless he had long ago disposed of the body—dropping it through a trapdoor in his back kitchen, Morris supposed, with some hazy recollection of a picture in a penny dreadful; and doubtless the man now lived in wanton splendour on the proceeds of the bill. So far, all was peace. But with the profligate habits of a man like Bent Pitman (who was no doubt a hunchback in the bargain), eight hundred pounds could be easily melted in a week. When they were gone, what would he be likely to do next? A hell-like voice in Morris's own bosom gave the answer: "Blackmail me."

Anxiety the Second: The Fraud of the Tontine; or, Is my Uncle dead? This, on which all Morris's hopes depended, was yet a question. He had tried to bully Teena; he had tried to bribe her; and nothing came of it. He had his moral conviction still; but you cannot blackmail a sharp lawyer on a moral conviction. And besides, since his interview with Michael, the idea wore a less attractive countenance. Was Michael the man to be blackmailed? and was Morris the man to do it? Grave considerations. "It's not that I'm afraid of him," Morris so far condescended to reassure himself; "but I must be very certain of my ground, and the deuce of it is, I see no way. How unlike is life to novels! I wouldn't have even begun this business in a novel, but what I'd have met a dark, slouching fellow in the Oxford Road, who'd have become my accomplice, and known all about how to do it, and probably broken into Michael's house at night and found nothing but a waxwork image; and then blackmailed or murdered me. But here, in real life, I might walk the streets till I dropped dead, and none of the criminal classes would look near me. Though, to be sure, there is always Pitman," he added thoughtfully.

Anxiety the Third: The Cottage at Browndean; or, The Underpaid Accomplice. For he had an accomplice, and that accomplice was blooming unseen in a damp cottage in Hampshire with empty pockets. What could be done about that? He really ought to have sent him something; if it was only a post-office order for five bob, enough to prove that he was kept in mind, enough to keep him in hope, beer, and tobacco. "But what would you have?" thought Morris; and ruefully poured into his hand a half-crown, a florin, and eightpence in small change. For a man in Morris's position, at war with all society, and conducting, with the hand of inexperience, a widely ramified intrigue, the sum was already a derision. John would have to be doing; no mistake of that. "But then," asked the hell-like voice, "how long is John likely to stand it?"

Anxiety the Fourth: The Leather Business; or, The Shutters at Last, a Tale of the City. On this head Morris had no news. He had not yet dared to visit the family concern; yet he knew he must delay no longer, and if anything had been wanted to sharpen this conviction, Michael's references of the night before rang ambiguously in his ear. Well and good. To visit the city might be indispensable; but what was he to do when he was there? He had no right to sign in his own name; and, with all the will in the world, he seemed to lack the art of signing with his uncle's. Under these circumstances, Morris could do nothing to procrastinate the crash; and, when it came, when prying eyes began to be applied to every joint of his behaviour, two questions could not fail to be addressed, sooner or later, to a speechless and perspiring insolvent. Where is Mr Joseph Finsbury? and how about your visit to the bank? Questions, how easy to put!—Ye gods, how impossible to answer! The man to whom they should be addressed went certainly to gaol, and—eh! what was this?—possibly to the gallows. Morris was trying to shave when this idea struck him, and he laid the razor down. Here (in Michael's words) was the total disappearance of a valuable uncle; here was a time of inexplicable conduct on the part of a nephew who had been in bad blood with the old man any time these seven years; what a chance for a judicial blunder! "But no," thought Morris, "they cannot, they dare not, make it murder. Not that. But honestly, and speaking as a man to a man, I don't see any other crime in the calendar (except arson) that I don't seem somehow to have committed. And yet I'm a perfectly respectable man, and wished nothing but my due. Law is a pretty business."

With this conclusion firmly seated in his mind, Morris Finsbury descended to the hall of the house in John Street, still half-shaven. There was a letter in the box; he knew the handwriting: John at last!

"Well, I think I might have been spared this," he said bitterly, and tore it open.

> *Dear Morris [it ran], what the dickens do you mean by it? I'm in an awful hole down here; I have to go on tick, and the parties on the spot don't cotton to the idea; they couldn't, because it is so plain I'm in a stait of Destitution. I've got no bedclothes, think of that, I must have coins, the hole thing's a Mockry, I wont stand it, nobody would. I would have come away before, only I have no money for the railway fare. Don't be a lunatic, Morris, you don't seem to understand my dredful situation. I have to get the stamp on tick. A fact.*
>
> —*Ever your affte. Brother,*
> J. FINSBURY

"Can't even spell!" Morris reflected, as he crammed the letter in his pocket, and left the house. "What can I do for him? I have to go to the expense of a barber, I'm so shattered! How can I send anybody coins? It's hard lines, I daresay; but does he think I'm living on hot muffins? One comfort," was his grim reflection, "he can't cut and run—he's got to stay; he's as helpless as the dead." And then he broke forth again: "Complains, does he? and he's never even heard of Bent Pitman! If he had what I have on my mind, he might complain with a good grace."

But these were not honest arguments, or not wholly honest; there was a struggle in the mind of Morris; he could not disguise from himself that his brother John was miserably situated at Browndean, without news, without money, without bedclothes, without society or any entertainment; and by the time he had been shaved and picked a hasty breakfast at a coffee tavern, Morris had arrived at a compromise.

"Poor Johnny," he said to himself, "he's in an awful box! I can't send him coins, but I'll tell you what I'll do: I'll send him the *Pink Un*—it'll cheer John up; and besides, it'll do his credit good getting anything by post."

Accordingly, on his way to the leather business, whither he proceeded (according to his thrifty habit) on foot, Morris purchased and dispatched a single copy of that enlivening periodical, to which (in a sudden pang of remorse) he added at random the *Athenaeum*, the *Revivalist*, and the Penny Pictorial

Weekly. So there was John set up with literature, and Morris had laid balm upon his conscience.

As if to reward him, he was received in his place of business with good news. Orders were pouring in; there was a run on some of the back stock, and the figure had gone up. Even the manager appeared elated. As for Morris, who had almost forgotten the meaning of good news, he longed to sob like a little child; he could have caught the manager (a pallid man with startled eyebrows) to his bosom; he could have found it in his generosity to give a cheque (for a small sum) to every clerk in the counting-house. As he sat and opened his letters a chorus of airy vocalists sang in his brain, to most exquisite music, "This whole concern may be profitable yet, profitable yet, profitable yet."

To him, in this sunny moment of relief, enter a Mr Rodgerson, a creditor, but not one who was expected to be pressing, for his connection with the firm was old and regular.

"O, Finsbury," said he, not without embarrassment, "it's of course only fair to let you know—the fact is, money is a trifle tight—I have some paper out—for that matter, every one's complaining—and in short—"

"It has never been our habit, Rodgerson," said Morris, turning pale. "But give me time to turn round, and I'll see what I can do; I daresay we can let you have something to account."

"Well, that's just where is," replied Rodgerson. "I was tempted; I've let the credit out of MY hands."

"Out of your hands?" repeated Morris. "That's playing rather fast and loose with us, Mr Rodgerson."

"Well, I got cent. for cent. for it," said the other, "on the nail, in a certified cheque."

"Cent. for cent.!" cried Morris. "Why, that's something like thirty per cent. bonus; a singular thing! Who's the party?"

"Don't know the man," was the reply. "Name of Moss."

"A Jew," Morris reflected, when his visitor was gone. And what could a Jew want with a claim of—he verified the amount in the books—a claim of three five eight, nineteen, ten, against the house of Finsbury? And why should he pay cent. for cent.? The figure proved the loyalty of Rodgerson—even Morris admitted that. But it proved unfortunately something else—the eagerness of Moss. The claim must have been wanted instantly, for that day, for that morning even. Why? The mystery of Moss promised to be a fit pendant to the mystery of Pitman. "And just when all was looking well too!" cried Morris, smiting his hand upon the desk. And almost at the same moment Mr Moss was announced.

Mr Moss was a radiant Hebrew, brutally handsome, and offensively polite. He was acting, it appeared, for a third party; he understood nothing of the circumstances; his client desired to have his position regularized; but he would accept an antedated cheque—antedated by two months, if Mr Finsbury chose.

"But I don't understand this," said Morris. "What made

you pay cent. per cent. for it today?"

Mr Moss had no idea; only his orders.

"The whole thing is thoroughly irregular," said Morris. "It is not the custom of the trade to settle at this time of the year. What are your instructions if I refuse?"

"I am to see Mr Joseph Finsbury, the head of the firm," said Mr Moss. "I was directed to insist on that; it was implied you had no status here—the expressions are not mine."

"You cannot see Mr Joseph; he is unwell," said Morris.

"In that case I was to place the matter in the hands of a lawyer. Let me see," said Mr Moss, opening a pocket-book with, perhaps, suspicious care, at the right place—"Yes—of Mr Michael Finsbury. A relation, perhaps? In that case, I presume, the matter will be pleasantly arranged."

To pass into the hands of Michael was too much for Morris. He struck his colours. A cheque at two months was nothing, after all. In two months he would probably be dead, or in a gaol at any rate. He bade the manager give Mr Moss a chair and the paper. "I'm going over to get a cheque signed by Mr Finsbury," said he, "who is lying ill at John Street."

A cab there and a cab back; here were inroads on his wretched capital! He counted the cost; when he was done with Mr Moss he would be left with twelvepence-halfpenny in the world. What was even worse, he had now been forced to bring his uncle up to Bloomsbury. "No use for poor Johnny in Hampshire now," he reflected. "And how the farce is to be kept up completely passes me. At Browndean it was just possible; in Bloomsbury it seems beyond human ingenuity—though I suppose it's what Michael does. But then he has accomplices—that Scotsman and the whole gang. Ah, if I had accomplices!"

Necessity is the mother of the arts. Under a spur so immediate, Morris surprised himself by the neatness and dispatch of his new forgery, and within three-fourths of an hour had handed it to Mr Moss.

"That is very satisfactory," observed that gentleman, rising. "I was to tell you it will not be presented, but you had better take care."

The room swam round Morris. "What—what's that?" he cried, grasping the table. He was miserably conscious the next moment of his shrill tongue and ashen face. "What do you mean—it will not be presented? Why am I to take care? What is all this mummery?"

"I have no idea, Mr Finsbury," replied the smiling Hebrew. "It was a message I was to deliver. The expressions were put into my mouth."

"What is your client's name?" asked Morris.

"That is a secret for the moment," answered Mr Moss.

Morris bent toward him. "It's not the bank?" he asked hoarsely.

"I have no authority to say more, Mr Finsbury," returned Mr Moss. "I will wish you a good morning, if you please."

"Wish me a good morning!" thought Morris; and the next

moment, seizing his hat, he fled from his place of business like a madman. Three streets away he stopped and groaned. "Lord! I should have borrowed from the manager!" he cried. "But it's too late now; it would look dicky to go back; I'm penniless—simply penniless—like the unemployed."

He went home and sat in the dismantled dining-room with his head in his hands. Newton never thought harder than this victim of circumstances, and yet no clearness came. "It may be a defect in my intelligence," he cried, rising to his feet, "but I cannot see that I am fairly used. The bad luck I've had is a thing to write to *The Times* about; it's enough to breed a revolution. And the plain English of the whole thing is that I must have money at once. I'm done with all morality now; I'm long past that stage; money I must have, and the only chance I see is Bent Pitman. Bent Pitman is a criminal, and therefore his position's weak. He must have some of that eight hundred left; if he has I'll force him to go shares; and even if he hasn't, I'll tell him the tontine affair, and with a desperate man like Pitman at my back, it'll be strange if I don't succeed."

Well and good. But how to lay hands upon Bent Pitman, except by advertisement, was not so clear. And even so, in what terms to ask a meeting? on what grounds? and where? Not at John Street, for it would never do to let a man like Bent Pitman know your real address; nor yet at Pitman's house, some dreadful place in Holloway, with a trapdoor in the back kitchen; a house which you might enter in a light summer overcoat and varnished boots, to come forth again piecemeal in a market-basket. That was the drawback of a really efficient accomplice, Morris felt, not without a shudder. "I never dreamed I should come to actually covet such society," he thought. And then a brilliant idea struck him. Waterloo Station, a public place, yet at certain hours of the day a solitary; a place, besides, the very name of which must knock upon the heart of Pitman, and at once suggest a knowledge of the latest of his guilty secrets. Morris took a piece of paper and sketched his advertisement.

> WILLIAM BENT PITMAN, *if this should meet the eye of, he will hear of* SOMETHING TO HIS ADVANTAGE *on the far end of the main line departure platform, Waterloo Station, 2 to 4 P.M., Sunday next.*

Morris reperused this literary trifle with approbation. "Terse," he reflected. "Something to his advantage is not strictly true; but it's taking and original, and a man is not on oath in an advertisement. All that I require now is the ready cash for my own meals and for the advertisement, and—no, I can't lavish money upon John, but I'll give him some more papers. How to raise the wind?"

He approached his cabinet of signets, and the collector suddenly revolted in his blood. "I will not!" he cried; "nothing shall induce me to massacre my collection—rather theft!" And dashing upstairs to the drawing-room, he helped himself to a few of his uncle's curiosities: a pair of Turkish babooshes, a Smyrna fan, a water-cooler, a musket guaranteed to have been seized from an Ephesian bandit, and a pocketful of curious but incomplete seashells.

Chapter 14   William Bent Pitman Hears of Something to his Advantage

On the morning of Sunday, William Dent Pitman rose at his usual hour, although with something more than the usual reluctance. The day before (it should be explained) an addition had been made to his family in the person of a lodger. Michael Finsbury had acted sponsor in the business, and guaranteed the weekly bill; on the other hand, no doubt with a spice of his prevailing jocularity, he had drawn a depressing portrait of the lodger's character. Mr Pitman had been led to understand his guest was not good company; he had approached the gentleman with fear, and had rejoiced to find himself the entertainer of an angel. At tea he had been vastly pleased; till hard on one in the morning he had sat entranced by eloquence and progressively fortified with information in the studio; and now, as he reviewed over his toilet the harmless pleasures of the evening, the future smiled upon him with revived attractions. "Mr Finsbury is indeed an acquisition," he remarked to himself; and as he entered the little parlour, where the table was already laid for breakfast, the cordiality of his greeting would have befitted an acquaintanceship already old.

"I am delighted to see you, sir"—these were his expressions—"and I trust you have slept well."

"Accustomed as I have been for so long to a life of almost perpetual change," replied the guest, "the disturbance so often complained of by the more sedentary, as attending their first night in (what is called) a new bed, is a complaint from which I am entirely free."

"I am delighted to hear it," said the drawing-master warmly. "But I see I have interrupted you over the paper."

"The Sunday paper is one of the features of the age," said Mr Finsbury. "In America, I am told, it supersedes all other literature, the bone and sinew of the nation finding their requirements catered for; hundreds of columns will be occupied with interesting details of the world's doings, such as waterspouts, elopements, conflagrations, and public entertainments; there is a corner for politics, ladies' work, chess, religion, and even literature; and a few spicy editorials serve to direct the course of public thought. It is difficult to estimate the part played by such enormous and miscellaneous repositories in the education of the people. But this (though interesting in itself) partakes of the nature of a digression; and what I was about to ask you was this: Are you yourself a student of the daily press?"

"There is not much in the papers to interest an artist,"

returned Pitman.

"In that case," resumed Joseph, "an advertisement which has appeared the last two days in various journals, and reappears this morning, may possibly have failed to catch your eye. The name, with a trifling variation, bears a strong resemblance to your own. Ah, here it is. If you please, I will read it to you: WILIAM BENT PITMAN, if this should meet the eye of, he will hear of SOMETHING TO HIS ADVANTAGE at the far end of the main line departure platform, Waterloo Station, 2 to 4 P.M. today."

"Is that in print?" cried Pitman. "Let me see it! Bent? It must be Dent! SOMETHING TO MY ADVANTAGE? Mr Finsbury, excuse me offering a word of caution; I am aware how strangely this must sound in your ears, but there are domestic reasons why this little circumstance might perhaps be better kept between ourselves. Mrs Pitman—my dear Sir, I assure you there is nothing dishonourable in my secrecy; the reasons are domestic, merely domestic; and I may set your conscience at rest when I assure you all the circumstances are known to our common friend, your excellent nephew, Mr Michael, who has not withdrawn from me his esteem."

"A word is enough, Mr Pitman," said Joseph, with one of his Oriental reverences.

Half an hour later, the drawing-master found Michael in bed and reading a book, the picture of good-humour and repose.

"Hillo, Pitman," he said, laying down his book, "what brings you here at this inclement hour? Ought to be in church, my boy!"

"I have little thought of church today, Mr Finsbury," said the drawing-master. "I am on the brink of something new, Sir." And he presented the advertisement.

"Why, what is this?" cried Michael, sitting suddenly up. He studied it for half a minute with a frown. "Pitman, I don't care about this document a particle," said he.

"It will have to be attended to, however," said Pitman.

"I thought you'd had enough of Waterloo," returned the lawyer. "Have you started a morbid craving? You've never been yourself anyway since you lost that beard. I believe now it was where you kept your senses."

"Mr Finsbury," said the drawing-master, "I have tried to reason this matter out, and, with your permission, I should like to lay before you the results."

"Fire away," said Michael; "but please, Pitman, remember it's Sunday, and let's have no bad language."

"There are three views open to us," began Pitman. "First this may be connected with the barrel; second, it may be connected with Mr Semitopolis's statue; and third, it may be from my wife's brother, who went to Australia. In the first case, which is of course possible, I confess the matter would be best allowed to drop."

"The court is with you there, Brother Pitman," said

Michael.

"In the second," continued the other, "it is plainly my duty to leave no stone unturned for the recovery of the lost antique."

"My dear fellow, Semitopolis has come down like a trump; he has pocketed the loss and left you the profit. What more would you have?" enquired the lawyer.

"I conceive, sir, under correction, that Mr Semitopolis's generosity binds me to even greater exertion," said the drawing-master. "The whole business was unfortunate; it was—I need not disguise it from you—it was illegal from the first: the more reason that I should try to behave like a gentleman," concluded Pitman, flushing.

"I have nothing to say to that," returned the lawyer. "I have sometimes thought I should like to try to behave like a gentleman myself; only it's such a one-sided business, with the world and the legal profession as they are."

"Then, in the third," resumed the drawing-master, "if it's Uncle Tim, of course, our fortune's made."

"It's not Uncle Tim, though," said the lawyer.

"Have you observed that very remarkable expression: SOMETHING TO HIS ADVANTAGE?" enquired Pitman shrewdly.

"You innocent mutton," said Michael, "it's the seediest commonplace in the English language, and only proves the advertiser is an ass. Let me demolish your house of cards for you at once. Would Uncle Tim make that blunder in your name?—in itself, the blunder is delicious, a huge improvement on the gross reality, and I mean to adopt it in the future; but is it like Uncle Tim?"

"No, it's not like him," Pitman admitted. "But his mind may have become unhinged at Ballarat."

"If you come to that, Pitman," said Michael, "the advertiser may be Queen Victoria, fired with the desire to make a duke of you. I put it to yourself if that's probable; and yet it's not against the laws of nature. But we sit here to consider probabilities; and with your genteel permission, I eliminate her Majesty and Uncle Tim on the threshold. To proceed, we have your second idea, that this has some connection with the statue. Possible; but in that case who is the advertiser? Not Ricardi, for he knows your address; not the person who got the box, for he doesn't know your name. The vanman, I hear you suggest, in a lucid interval. He might have got your name, and got it incorrectly, at the station; and he might have failed to get your address. I grant the vanman. But a question: Do you really wish to meet the vanman?"

"Why should I not?" asked Pitman.

"If he wants to meet you," replied Michael, "observe this: it is because he has found his address-book, has been to the house that got the statue, and—mark my words!—is moving at the instigation of the murderer."

"I should be very sorry to think so," said Pitman; "but I still consider it my duty to Mr Sernitopolis..."

"Pitman," interrupted Michael, "this will not do. Don't seek to impose on your legal adviser; don't try to pass yourself off for the Duke of Wellington, for that is not your line. Come, I wager a dinner I can read your thoughts. You still believe it's Uncle Tim."

"Mr Finsbury," said the drawing-master, colouring, "you are not a man in narrow circumstances, and you have no family. Guendolen is growing up, a very promising girl—she was confirmed this year; and I think you will be able to enter into my feelings as a parent when I tell you she is quite ignorant of dancing. The boys are at the board school, which is all very well in its way; at least, I am the last man in the world to criticize the institutions of my native land. But I had fondly hoped that Harold might become a professional musician; and little Otho shows a quite remarkable vocation for the Church. I am not exactly an ambitious man..."

"Well, well," interrupted Michael. "Be explicit; you think it's Uncle Tim?"

"It might be Uncle Tim," insisted Pitman, "and if it were, and I neglected the occasion, how could I ever look my children in the face? I do not refer to Mrs Pitman..."

"No, you never do," said Michael.

"...but in the case of her own brother returning from Ballarat..." continued Pitman.

"...with his mind unhinged," put in the lawyer.

"...returning from Ballarat with a large fortune, her

impatience may be more easily imagined than described," concluded Pitman.

"All right," said Michael, "be it so. And what do you propose to do?"

"I am going to Waterloo," said Pitman, "in disguise."

"All by your little self?" enquired the lawyer. "Well, I hope you think it safe. Mind and send me word from the police cells."

"O, Mr Finsbury, I had ventured to hope—perhaps you might be induced to—to make one of us," faltered Pitman.

"Disguise myself on Sunday?" cried Michael. "How little you understand my principles!"

"Mr Finsbury, I have no means of showing you my gratitude; but let me ask you one question," said Pitman. "If I were a very rich client, would you not take the risk?"

"Diamond, Diamond, you know not what you do!" cried Michael. "Why, man, do you suppose I make a practice of cutting about London with my clients in disguise? Do you suppose money would induce me to touch this business with a stick? I give you my word of honour, it would not. But I own I have a real curiosity to see how you conduct this interview—that tempts me; it tempts me, Pitman, more than gold—it should be exquisitely rich." And suddenly Michael laughed. "Well, Pitman," said he, "have all the truck ready in the studio. I'll go."

About twenty minutes after two, on this eventful day, the vast and gloomy shed of Waterloo lay, like the temple of a dead religion, silent and deserted. Here and there at one of the platforms, a train lay becalmed; here and there a wandering footfall echoed; the cab-horses outside stamped with startling reverberations on the stones; or from the neighbouring wilderness of railway an engine snorted forth a whistle. The main-line departure platform slumbered like the rest; the booking-hutches closed; the backs of Mr Haggard's novels, with which upon a weekday the bookstall shines emblazoned, discreetly hidden behind dingy shutters; the rare officials, undisguisedly somnambulant; and the customary loiterers, even to the middle-aged woman with the ulster and the handbag, fled to more congenial scenes. As in the inmost dells of some small tropic island the throbbing of the ocean lingers, so here a faint pervading hum and trepidation told in every corner of surrounding London.

At the hour already named, persons acquainted with John Dickson, of Ballarat, and Ezra Thomas, of the United States of America, would have been cheered to behold them enter through the booking-office.

"What names are we to take?" enquired the latter, anxiously adjusting the window-glass spectacles which he had been suffered on this occasion to assume.

"There's no choice for you, my boy," returned Michael. "Bent Pitman or nothing. As for me, I think I look as if I might be called Appleby; something agreeably old-world about Appleby—breathes of Devonshire cider. Talking of which, suppose you wet your whistle? the interview is likely to be trying."

"I think I'll wait till afterwards," returned Pitman; "on the whole, I think I'll wait till the thing's over. I don't know if it strikes you as it does me; but the place seems deserted and silent, Mr Finsbury, and filled with very singular echoes."

"Kind of Jack-in-the-box feeling?" enquired Michael, "as if all these empty trains might be filled with policemen waiting for a signal? and Sir Charles Warren perched among the girders with a silver whistle to his lips? It's guilt, Pitman."

In this uneasy frame of mind they walked nearly the whole length of the departure platform, and at the western extremity became aware of a slender figure standing back against a pillar. The figure was plainly sunk into a deep abstraction; he was not aware of their approach, but gazed far abroad over the sunlit station. Michael stopped.

"Holloa!" said he, "can that be your advertiser? If so, I'm done with it." And then, on second thoughts: "Not so, either," he resumed more cheerfully. "Here, turn your back a moment. So. Give me the specs."

"But you agreed I was to have them," protested Pitman.

"Ah, but that man knows me," said Michael.

"Does he? what's his name?" cried Pitman.

"O, he took me into his confidence," returned the lawyer. "But I may say one thing: if he's your advertiser (and he may be, for he seems to have been seized with criminal lunacy) you can go ahead with a clear conscience, for I hold him in the hollow of my hand."

The change effected, and Pitman comforted with this good news, the pair drew near to Morris.

"Are you looking for Mr William Bent Pitman?" enquired the drawing-master. "I am he."

Morris raised his head. He saw before him, in the speaker, a person of almost indescribable insignificance, in white spats and a shirt cut indecently low. A little behind, a second and more burly figure offered little to criticism, except ulster, whiskers, spectacles, and deerstalker hat. Since he had decided to call up devils from the underworld of London, Morris had pondered deeply on the probabilities of their appearance. His first emotion, like that of Charoba when she beheld the sea, was one of disappointment; his second did more justice to the case. Never before had he seen a couple dressed like these; he had struck a new stratum.

"I must speak with you alone," said he.

"You need not mind Mr Appleby," returned Pitman. "He knows all."

"All? Do you know what I am here to speak of?" enquired Morris— "The barrel."

Pitman turned pale, but it was with manly indignation. "You are the man!" he cried. "You very wicked person."

"Am I to speak before him?" asked Morris, disregarding these severe expressions.

"He has been present throughout," said Pitman. "He opened the barrel; your guilty secret is already known to him, as well as to your Maker and myself."

"Well, then," said Morris, "what have you done with the money?"

"I know nothing about any money," said Pitman.

"You needn't try that on," said Morris. "I have tracked you down; you came to the station sacrilegiously disguised as a clergyman, procured my barrel, opened it, rifled the body, and cashed the bill. I have been to the bank, I tell you! I have followed you step by step, and your denials are childish and absurd."

"Come, come, Morris, keep your temper," said Mr Appleby.

"Michael!" cried Morris, "Michael here too!"

"Here too," echoed the lawyer; "here and everywhere, my good fellow; every step you take is counted; trained detectives follow you like your shadow; they report to me every three-quarters of an hour; no expense is spared."

Morris's face took on a hue of dirty grey. "Well, I don't care; I have the less reserve to keep," he cried. "That man cashed my bill; it's a theft, and I want the money back."

"Do you think I would lie to you, Morris?" asked Michael.

"I don't know," said his cousin. "I want my money."

"It was I alone who touched the body," began Michael.

"You? Michael!" cried Morris, starting back. "Then why haven't you declared the death?"

"What the devil do you mean?" asked Michael.

"Am I mad? or are you?" cried Morris.

"I think it must be Pitman," said Michael.

The three men stared at each other, wild-eyed.

"This is dreadful," said Morris, "dreadful. I do not understand one word that is addressed to me."

"I give you my word of honour, no more do I," said Michael.

"And in God's name, why whiskers?" cried Morris, pointing in a ghastly manner at his cousin. "Does my brain reel? How whiskers?"

"O, that's a matter of detail," said Michael.

There was another silence, during which Morris appeared to himself to be shot in a trapeze as high as St. Paul's, and as low as Baker Street Station.

"Let us recapitulate," said Michael, "unless it's really a dream, in which case I wish Teena would call me for breakfast. My friend Pitman, here, received a barrel which, it now appears, was meant for you. The barrel contained the body of a man. How or why you killed him..."

"I never laid a hand on him," protested Morris. "This is what I have dreaded all along. But think, Michael! I'm not that kind of man; with all my faults, I wouldn't touch a hair of anybody's head, and it was all dead loss to me. He got killed in that vile accident."

Suddenly Michael was seized by mirth so prolonged and excessive that his companions supposed beyond a doubt his reason had deserted him. Again and again he struggled to compose himself, and again and again laughter overwhelmed him like a tide. In all this maddening interview there had been no more spectral feature than this of Michael's merriment; and Pitman and Morris, drawn together by the common fear, exchanged glances of anxiety.

"Morris," gasped the lawyer, when he was at last able to articulate, "hold on, I see it all now. I can make it clear in one word. Here's the key: I NEVER GUESSED IT WAS UNCLE JOSEPH TILL THIS MOMENT."

This remark produced an instant lightening of the tension for Morris. For Pitman it quenched the last ray of hope and daylight. Uncle Joseph, whom he had left an hour ago in Norfolk Street, pasting newspaper cuttings?—it?—the dead body?—then who was he, Pitman? and was this Waterloo Station or Colney Hatch?

"To be sure!" cried Morris; "it was badly smashed, I know. How stupid not to think of that! Why, then, all's clear; and, my dear Michael, I'll tell you what—we're saved, both saved. You get the tontine—I don't grudge it you the least—and I get the leather business, which is really beginning to look up. Declare the death at once, don't mind me in the smallest, don't consider me; declare the death, and we're all right."

"Ah, but I can't declare it," said Michael.

"Why not?" cried Morris.

"I can't produce the corpus, Morris. I've lost it," said the lawyer.

"Stop a bit," ejaculated the leather merchant. "How is this? It's not possible. I lost it."

"Well, I've lost it too, my son," said Michael, with extreme serenity. "Not recognizing it, you see, and suspecting something irregular in its origin, I got rid of—what shall we say?—got rid of the proceeds at once."

"You got rid of the body? What made you do that?" wailed Morris. "But you can get it again? You know where it is?"

"I wish I did, Morris, and you may believe me there, for it would be a small sum in my pocket; but the fact is, I don't," said Michael.

"Good Lord," said Morris, addressing heaven and earth, "good Lord, I've lost the leather business!"

Michael was once more shaken with laughter.

"Why do you laugh, you fool?" cried his cousin, "you lose more than I. You've bungled it worse than even I did. If you had a spark of feeling, you would be shaking in your boots with vexation. But I'll tell you one thing—I'll have that eight hundred pound—I'll have that and go to Swan River—that's mine, anyway, and your friend must have forged to cash it. Give me the eight hundred, here, upon this platform, or I go straight to Scotland Yard and turn the whole disreputable story inside out."

"Morris," said Michael, laying his hand upon his shoulder, "hear reason. It wasn't us, it was the other man. We never even searched the body."

"The other man?" repeated Morris.

"Yes, the other man. We palmed Uncle Joseph off upon another man," said Michael.

"You what? You palmed him off? That's surely a singular expression," said Morris.

"Yes, palmed him off for a piano," said Michael with perfect simplicity. "Remarkably full, rich tone," he added.

Morris carried his hand to his brow and looked at it; it was wet with sweat. "Fever," said he.

"No, it was a Broadwood grand," said Michael. "Pitman here will tell you if it was genuine or not."

"Eh? O! O, yes, I believe it was a genuine Broadwood; I have played upon it several times myself," said Pitman. "The three-letter E was broken."

"Don't say anything more about pianos," said Morris, with a strong shudder; "I'm not the man I used to be! This—this other man—let's come to him, if I can only manage to follow. Who is he? Where can I get hold of him?"

"Ah, that's the rub," said Michael. "He's been in possession of the desired article, let me see—since Wednesday, about four o'clock, and is now, I should imagine, on his way to the isles of Javan and Gadire."

"Michael," said Morris pleadingly, "I am in a very weak state, and I beg your consideration for a kinsman. Say it slowly again, and be sure you are correct. When did he get it?"

Michael repeated his statement.

"Yes, that's the worst thing yet," said Morris, drawing in his breath.

"What is?" asked the lawyer.

"Even the dates are sheer nonsense," said the leather merchant. "The bill was cashed on Tuesday. There's not a gleam of reason in the whole transaction."

A young gentleman, who had passed the trio and suddenly started and turned back, at this moment laid a heavy hand on Michael's shoulder.

"Aha! so this is Mr Dickson?" said he.

The trump of judgement could scarce have rung with a more dreadful note in the ears of Pitman and the lawyer. To Morris this erroneous name seemed a legitimate enough continuation of the nightmare in which he had so long been wandering. And when Michael, with his brand-new bushy whiskers, broke from the grasp of the stranger and turned to run, and the weird little shaven creature in the low-necked shirt followed his example with a bird-like screech, and the stranger (finding the rest of his prey escape him) pounced with a rude grasp on Morris himself, that gentleman's frame of mind might be very nearly expressed in the colloquial phrase: "I told you so!"

"I have one of the gang," said Gideon Forsyth.

"I do not understand," said Morris dully.

"O, I will make you understand," returned Gideon grimly.

"You will be a good friend to me if you can make me understand anything," cried Morris, with a sudden energy of conviction.

"I don't know you personally, do I?" continued Gideon, examining his unresisting prisoner. "Never mind, I know your friends. They are your friends, are they not?"

"I do not understand you," said Morris.

"You had possibly something to do with a piano?" suggested Gideon.

"A piano!" cried Morris, convulsively clasping Gideon by the arm. "Then you're the other man! Where is it? Where is the body? And did you cash the draft?"

"Where is the body? This is very strange," mused Gideon. "Do you want the body?"

"Want it?" cried Morris. "My whole fortune depends upon it! I lost it. Where is it? Take me to it?

"O, you want it, do you? And the other man, Dickson—does he want it?" enquired Gideon.

"Who do you mean by Dickson? O, Michael Finsbury! Why, of course he does! He lost it too. If he had it, he'd have won the tontine tomorrow."

"Michael Finsbury! Not the solicitor?" cried Gideon.

"Yes, the solicitor," said Morris. "But where is the body?"

"Then that is why he sent the brief! What is Mr Finsbury's private address?" asked Gideon.

"233 King's Road. What brief? Where are you going? Where is the body?" cried Morris, clinging to Gideon's arm.

"I have lost it myself," returned Gideon, and ran out of the station.

Chapter 15   The Return of the Great Vance

Morris returned from Waterloo in a frame of mind that baffles description. He was a modest man; he had never conceived an overweening notion of his own powers; he knew himself unfit to write a book, turn a table napkin-ring, entertain a Christmas party with legerdemain—grapple (in short) any of those conspicuous accomplishments that are usually classed under the head of genius. He knew—he admitted—his parts to be pedestrian, but he had considered them (until quite lately) fully equal to the demands of life. And today he owned himself defeated: life had the upper hand; if there had been any means of flight or place to flee to, if the world had been so ordered that a man could leave it like a place of entertainment, Morris would have instantly resigned all further claim on its rewards and pleasures, and, with inexpressible contentment, ceased to be. As it was, one aim shone before him: he could get home. Even as the sick dog crawls under the sofa, Morris could shut the door of John Street and be alone.

The dusk was falling when he drew near this place of refuge; and the first thing that met his eyes was the figure of a man upon the step, alternately plucking at the bell-handle and pounding on the panels. The man had no hat, his clothes were hideous with filth, he had the air of a hop-picker. Yet Morris knew him; it was John.

The first impulse of flight was succeeded, in the elder brother's bosom, by the empty quiescence of despair. "What does it matter now?" he thought, and drawing forth his latchkey ascended the steps.

John turned about; his face was ghastly with weariness and dirt and fury; and as he recognized the head of his family, he drew in a long rasping breath, and his eyes glittered.

"Open that door," he said, standing back.

"I am going to," said Morris, and added mentally, "He looks like murder!"

The brothers passed into the hall, the door closed behind them; and suddenly John seized Morris by the shoulders and shook him as a terrier shakes a rat. "You mangy little cad," he said, "I'd serve you right to smash your skull!" And shook him again, so that his teeth rattled and his head smote upon the wall.

"Don't be violent, Johnny," said Morris. "It can't do any good now."

"Shut your mouth," said John, "your time's come to listen."

He strode into the dining-room, fell into the easy-chair,

and taking off one of his burst walking-shoes, nursed for a while his foot like one in agony. "I'm lame for life," he said. "What is there for dinner?"

"Nothing, Johnny," said Morris.

"Nothing? What do you mean by that?" enquired the Great Vance. "Don't set up your chat to me!"

"I mean simply nothing," said his brother. "I have nothing to eat, and nothing to buy it with. I've only had a cup of tea and a sandwich all this day myself."

"Only a sandwich?" sneered Vance. "I suppose YOU're going to complain next. But you had better take care: I've had all I mean to take; and I can tell you what it is, I mean to dine and to dine well. Take your signets and sell them."

"I can't today," objected Morris; "it's Sunday."

"I tell you I'm going to dine!" cried the younger brother.

"But if it's not possible, Johnny?" pleaded the other.

"You nincompoop!" cried Vance. "Ain't we householders? Don't they know us at that hotel where Uncle Parker used to come. Be off with you; and if you ain't back in half an hour, and if the dinner ain't good, first I'll lick you till you don't want to breathe, and then I'll go straight to the police and blow the gaff. Do you understand that, Morris Finsbury? Because if you do, you had better jump."

The idea smiled even upon the wretched Morris, who was sick with famine. He sped upon his errand, and returned to find John still nursing his foot in the armchair.

"What would you like to drink, Johnny?" he enquired soothingly.

"Fizz," said John. "Some of the poppy stuff from the end bin; a bottle of the old port that Michael liked, to follow; and see and don't shake the port. And look here, light the fire—and the gas, and draw down the blinds; it's cold and it's getting dark. And then you can lay the cloth. And, I say—here, you! bring me down some clothes."

The room looked comparatively habitable by the time the dinner came; and the dinner itself was good: strong gravy soup, fillets of sole, mutton chops and tomato sauce, roast beef done rare with roast potatoes, cabinet pudding, a piece of Chester cheese, and some early celery: a meal uncompromisingly British, but supporting.

"Thank God!" said John, his nostrils sniffing wide, surprised by joy into the unwonted formality of grace. "Now I'm going to take this chair with my back to the fire—there's been a strong frost these two last nights, and I can't get it out of my bones; the celery will be just the ticket—I'm going to sit here, and you are going to stand there, Morris Finsbury, and play butler."

"But, Johnny, I'm so hungry myself," pleaded Morris.

"You can have what I leave," said Vance. "You're just beginning to pay your score, my daisy; I owe you one-pound-ten; don't you rouse the British lion!" There was something indescribably menacing in the face and voice of the Great

Vance as he uttered these words, at which the soul of Morris withered. "There!" resumed the feaster, "give us a glass of the fizz to start with. Gravy soup! And I thought I didn't like gravy soup! Do you know how I got here?" he asked, with another explosion of wrath.

"No, Johnny; how could I?" said the obsequious Morris.

"I walked on my ten toes!" cried John; "tramped the whole way from Browndean; and begged! I would like to see you beg. It's not so easy as you might suppose. I played it on being a shipwrecked mariner from Blyth; I don't know where Blyth is, do you? but I thought it sounded natural. I begged from a little beast of a schoolboy, and he forked out a bit of twine, and asked me to make a clove hitch; I did, too, I know I did, but he said it wasn't, he said it was a granny's knot, and I was a what-d'ye-call-'em, and he would give me in charge. Then I begged from a naval officer—he never bothered me with knots, but he only gave me a tract; there's a nice account of the British navy!—and then from a widow woman that sold lollipops, and I got a hunch of bread from her. Another party I fell in with said you could generally always get bread; and the thing to do was to break a plateglass window and get into gaol; seemed rather a brilliant scheme. Pass the beef."

"Why didn't you stay at Browndean?" Morris ventured to enquire.

"Skittles!" said John. "On what? The *Pink Un* and a measly religious paper? I had to leave Browndean; I had to, I tell you. I got tick at a public, and set up to be the Great Vance; so would you, if you were leading such a beastly existence! And a card stood me a lot of ale and stuff, and we got swipey, talking about music-halls and the piles of tin I got for singing; and then they got me on to sing *Around her splendid form I weaved the magic circle*, and then he said I couldn't be Vance, and I stuck to it like grim death I was. It was rot of me to sing, of course, but I thought I could brazen it out with a set of yokels. It settled my hash at the public," said John, with a sigh. "And then the last thing was the carpenter—"

"Our landlord?" enquired Morris.

"That's the party," said John. "He came nosing about the place, and then wanted to know where the water-butt was, and the bedclothes. I told him to go to the devil; so would you too, when there was no possible thing to say! And then he said I had pawned them, and did I know it was felony? Then I made a pretty neat stroke. I remembered he was deaf, and talked a whole lot of rot, very politely, just so low he couldn't hear a word. 'I don't hear you,' says he. 'I know you don't, my buck, and I don't mean you to,' says I, smiling away like a haberdasher. 'I'm hard of hearing,' he roars. 'I'd be in a pretty hot corner if you weren't,' says I, making signs as if I was explaining everything. It was tip-top as long as it lasted. 'Well,' he said, 'I'm deaf, worse luck, but I bet the constable can hear you.' And off he started one way, and I the other. They got a spirit-lamp and the *Pink Un*, and that old religious paper, and another periodical you sent me. I think you must have been drunk—it had a name like one of those spots that Uncle Joseph used to hold forth at, and it was all full of the most awful swipes about poetry and the use of the globes. It was the kind of thing that nobody could read out of a lunatic asylum. The *Athaeneum*, that was the name! Golly, what a paper!"

"*Athenaeum*, you mean," said Morris.

"I don't care what you call it," said John, "so as I don't require to take it in! There, I feel better. Now I'm going to sit by the fire in the easy-chair; pass me the cheese, and the celery, and the bottle of port—no, a champagne glass, it holds more. And now you can pitch in; there's some of the fish left and a chop, and some fizz. Ah," sighed the refreshed pedestrian, "Michael was right about that port; there's old and vatted for you! Michael's a man I like; he's clever and reads books, and the *Athaeneum*, and all that; but he's not dreary to meet, he don't talk *Athaeneum* like the other parties; why, the most of them would throw a blight over a skittle alley! Talking of Michael, I ain't bored myself to put the question, because of course I knew it from the first. You've made a hash of it, eh?"

"Michael made a hash of it," said Morris, flushing dark.

"What have we got to do with that?" enquired John.

"He has lost the body, that's what we have to do with it," cried Morris. "He has lost the body, and the death can't be established."

"Hold on," said John. "I thought you didn't want to?"

"O, we're far past that," said his brother. "It's not the tontine now, it's the leather business, Johnny; it's the clothes upon our back."

"Stow the slow music," said John, "and tell your story from beginning to end."

Morris did as he was bid.

"Well, now, what did I tell you?" cried the Great Vance, when the other had done. "But I know one thing: I'm not going to be humbugged out of my property."

"I should like to know what you mean to do," said Morris.

"I'll tell you that," responded John with extreme decision. "I'm going to put my interests in the hands of the smartest lawyer in London; and whether you go to quod or not is a matter of indifference to me."

"Why, Johnny, we're in the same boat!" expostulated Morris.

"Are we?" cried his brother. "I bet we're not! Have I committed forgery? have I lied about Uncle Joseph? have I put idiotic advertisements in the comic papers? have I smashed other people's statues? I like your cheek, Morris Finsbury. No, I've let you run my affairs too long; now they shall go to Michael. I like Michael, anyway; and it's time I understood my situation."

At this moment the brethren were interrupted by a ring at the bell, and Morris, going timorously to the door, received from the hands of a commissionaire a letter addressed in the hand of Michael. Its contents ran as follows:

> *MORRIS FINSBURY, if this should meet the eye of, he will hear of SOMETHING TO HIS ADVANTAGE at my office, in Chancery Lane, at 10 A. M. tomorrow.*
>
> MICHAEL FINSBURY

So utter was Morris's subjection that he did not wait to be asked, but handed the note to John as soon as he had glanced at it himself.

"That's the way to write a letter," cried John. "Nobody but Michael could have written that."

And Morris did not even claim the credit of priority.

Chapter 16 Final Adjustment of the Leather Business

Finsbury brothers were ushered, at ten the next morning, into a large apartment in Michael's office; the Great Vance, somewhat restored from yesterday's exhaustion, but with one foot in a slipper; Morris, not positively damaged, but a man ten years older than he who had left Bournemouth eight days before, his face ploughed full of anxious wrinkles, his dark hair liberally grizzled at the temples.

Three persons were seated at a table to receive them: Michael in the midst, Gideon Forsyth on his right hand, on his left an ancient gentleman with spectacles and silver hair.

"By Jingo, it's Uncle Joe!" cried John.

But Morris approached his uncle with a pale countenance and glittering eyes.

"I'll tell you what you did!" he cried. "You absconded!"

"Good morning, Morris Finsbury," returned Joseph, with no less asperity; "you are looking seriously ill."

"No use making trouble now," remarked Michael. "Look the facts in the face. Your uncle, as you see, was not so much as shaken in the accident; a man of your humane disposition ought to be delighted."

"Then, if that's so," Morris broke forth, "how about the body? You don't mean to insinuate that thing I schemed and sweated for, and colported with my own hands, was the body of a total stranger?"

"O no, we can't go as far as that," said Michael soothingly; "you may have met him at the club."

Morris fell into a chair. "I would have found it out if it had come to the house," he complained. "And why didn't it? why did it go to Pitman? what right had Pitman to open it?"

"If you come to that, Morris, what have you done with the colossal Hercules?" asked Michael.

"He went through it with the meat-axe," said John. "It's all in spillikins in the back garden."

"Well, there's one thing," snapped Morris; "there's my uncle again, my fraudulent trustee. He's mine, anyway. And the tontine too. I claim the tontine; I claim it now. I believe Uncle Masterman's dead."

"I must put a stop to this nonsense," said Michael, "and that for ever. You say too near the truth. In one sense your uncle is dead, and has been so long; but not in the sense of the tontine, which it is even on the cards he may yet live to win. Uncle Joseph saw him this morning; he will tell you he still lives, but his mind is in abeyance."

"He did not know me," said Joseph; to do him justice, not without emotion.

"So you're out again there, Morris," said John. "My eye! What a fool you've made of yourself!"

"And that was why you wouldn't compromise," said Morris.

"As for the absurd position in which you and Uncle Joseph have been making yourselves an exhibition," resumed Michael, "it is more than time it came to an end. I have prepared a proper discharge in full, which you shall sign as a preliminary."

"What?" cried Morris, "and lose my seven thousand eight hundred pounds, and the leather business, and the contingent interest, and get nothing? Thank you."

"It's like you to feel gratitude, Morris," began Michael.

"O, I know it's no good appealing to you, you sneering devil!" cried Morris. "But there's a stranger present, I can't think why, and I appeal to him. I was robbed of that money when I was an orphan, a mere child, at a commercial academy. Since then, I've never had a wish but to get back my own. You may hear a lot of stuff about me; and there's no doubt at times I have been ill-advised. But it's the pathos of my situation; that's what I want to show you."

"Morris," interrupted Michael, "I do wish you would let me add one point, for I think it will affect your judgement. It's pathetic too since that's your taste in literature."

"Well, what is it?" said Morris.

"It's only the name of one of the persons who's to witness your signature, Morris," replied Michael. "His name's Moss, my dear."

There was a long silence. "I might have been sure it was you!" cried Morris.

"You'll sign, won't you?" said Michael.

"Do you know what you're doing?" cried Morris. "You're compounding a felony."

"Very well, then, we won't compound it, Morris," returned Michael. "See how little I understood the sterling integrity of your character! I thought you would prefer it so."

"Look here, Michael," said John, "this is all very fine and large; but how about me? Morris is gone up, I see that; but I'm not. And I was robbed, too, mind you; and just as much an orphan, and at the blessed same academy as himself."

"Johnny," said Michael, "don't you think you'd better leave it to me?"

"I'm your man," said John. "You wouldn't deceive a poor orphan, I'll take my oath. Morris, you sign that document, or I'll start in and astonish your weak mind."

With a sudden alacrity, Morris proffered his willingness. Clerks were brought in, the discharge was executed, and there was Joseph a free man once more.

"And now," said Michael, "hear what I propose to do. Here, John and Morris, is the leather business made over to the pair of you in partnership. I have valued it at the lowest possible figure, Pogram and Jarris's. And here is a cheque for the balance of your fortune. Now, you see, Morris, you start fresh from the commercial academy; and, as you said yourself the leather business was looking up, I suppose you'll probably marry before long. Here's your marriage present—from a Mr Moss."

Morris bounded on his cheque with a crimsoned countenance.

"I don't understand the performance," remarked John. "It seems too good to be true."

"It's simply a readjustment," Michael explained. "I take up Uncle Joseph's liabilities; and if he gets the tontine, it's to be mine; if my father gets it, it's mine anyway, you see. So that I'm rather advantageously placed."

"Morris, my unconverted friend, you've got left," was John's comment.

"And now, Mr Forsyth," resumed Michael, turning to his silent guest, "here are all the criminals before you, except Pitman. I really didn't like to interrupt his scholastic career; but you can have him arrested at the seminary—I know his hours. Here we are then; we're not pretty to look at: what do you propose to do with us?"

"Nothing in the world, Mr Finsbury," returned Gideon. "I seem to understand that this gentleman"—indicating Morris—"is the fons et origo of the trouble; and, from what I gather, he has already paid through the nose. And really, to be quite frank,

I do not see who is to gain by any scandal; not me, at least. And besides, I have to thank you for that brief."

Michael blushed. "It was the least I could do to let you have some business," he said. "But there's one thing more. I don't want you to misjudge poor Pitman, who is the most harmless being upon earth. I wish you would dine with me tonight, and see the creature on his native heath—say at Verrey's?"

"I have no engagement, Mr Finsbury," replied Gideon. "I shall be delighted. But subject to your judgement, can we do nothing for the man in the cart? I have qualms of conscience."

"Nothing but sympathize," said Michael.